UNDERGRADUATE RESEARCH AND THE ACADEMIC LIBRARIAN:
CASE STUDIES AND BEST PRACTICES

edited by
Merinda Kaye Hensley & Stephanie Davis-Kahl

Association of College and Research Libraries
A division of the American Library Association
Chicago, Illinois 2017

The paper used in this publication meets the minimum requirements of American National Standard for Information Sciences–Permanence of Paper for Printed Library Materials, ANSI Z39.48-1992. ∞

Cataloging-in-Publication data is on file with the Library of Congress.

Copyright ©2017 by the Association of College and Research Libraries.
All rights reserved except those which may be granted by Sections 107 and 108 of the Copyright Revision Act of 1976.

Printed in the United States of America.

21 20 19 18 17   5 4 3 2 1

Cover designed by Ania Bui.

Table of Contents

VII ... ACKNOWLEDGMENTS

IX .... FOREWORD. Adding Value to the Undergraduate Research Experience

XXI .. INTRODUCTION

1 ..... CHAPTER 1. Beyond Embedded Librarianship: Co-Teaching with Faculty to Integrate Digital Scholarship in Undergraduate Research
Sarah Clayton and Jeffrey M. Widener

19 ... CHAPTER 2. The Cooperation of Many Minds: Cultivating the Undergraduate Researcher in the Humanities and Social Sciences through Team-Based Curricular Design
Susette Newberry

29 ... CHAPTER 3. A Triumph, a Fail, and a Question: A Pilot Approach to Student-Faculty-Librarian Research Collaboration
Missy Roser and Sara Smith

41 ... CHAPTER 4. Framing Information Literacy as Scholarly Practice with Undergraduate Student Journals: A Grassroots Approach
Deena Yanofsky, Michael David Miller, and Urooj Nizami

53 ... CHAPTER 5. Building Relationships, Advancing Services: Piloting Open Conference Systems with the Indiana University Undergraduate Research Conference
Shayna Pekala and Jane Rogan

69 ... CHAPTER 6. Doing the Honors: Designing a Curriculum for a Year-Long Thesis Project
Amanda Piekart-Primiano, Matthew Regan, and Lily Sacharow

83 ... CHAPTER 7. Dreaming Big: Library-led Digital Scholarship for Undergraduates at a Small Institution
Janelle Wertzberger and R.C. Miessler

93 ... CHAPTER 8. Engaging in the Undergraduate Researcher Writers' Process: Creating a Thesis Writers' Bootcamp
Katie Harding and Lora Leligdon

103.. CHAPTER 9. Engaging Our Student Partners: Student Leadership in a Library-Initiated Experiential Learning Project
Michelle Reed, Philip Duncan, and Germaine Halegoua

115.. CHAPTER 10. Freshman Framework: Collaboratively Developing a Set of Required Instructional Modules for Freshman Research Scholars
Matt Upson, Tim O'Neil, and Cristina Colquhoun

129.. CHAPTER 11. From the Archives to the Institutional Repository: A Collaborative Approach to Research and Publishing for Undergraduate Creative Writers
Brandon T. Pieczko and Laura MacLeod Mulligan

147.. CHAPTER 12. Harnessing the Winds: Collaboration and the *Aeolus* Undergraduate Research Journal
Alyson Gamble, Amelia Kallaher, Neal Lacey, Alexandra Maass, Caitlyn Ralph, Tyrone Ryba, and Mai Tanaka

157.. CHAPTER 13. Image of Research: Celebrating and Sharing Undergraduate Work
Michelle Reed and Merinda Kaye Hensley

173.. CHAPTER 14. Impact Outside the Classroom: Preparing Undergraduate Researchers for Success
Lisa Becksford, Kyrille Goldbeck DeBose, and Carolyn Meier

183.. CHAPTER 15. Informal Learning Teams and the Digital Humanities: A Case Study of Faculty/Librarian Collaboration
Lora L. Smallman and Jessica DeSpain

195.. CHAPTER 16. Landscape Architecture, Embedded Librarianship, and Innovation with Special Collections: Historic Landscapes Research with Primary Sources by University of Arkansas Undergraduates
Joshua C. Youngblood

209.. CHAPTER 17. Mentoring a Peer: A Feminist Ethic for Directing Undergraduate Humanities Research
Amy Hildreth Chen and Kathryn Ross

219..CHAPTER 18. Re-imagining Furman Engaged: Transformation through a Library Partnership
Andrea M. Wright and John G. Kaup

229..CHAPTER 19 Connecting Students to the Research Lifecycle and to Each Other: Planning an Event to Support Undergraduate Journal Publishing
Heather Buchansky and Graeme Slaght

243..CHAPTER 20. Reward Research, Benefit All: The Case of the Library Undergraduate Research Award at Kennesaw State University
Ariel Turner and Aajay Murphy

253..CHAPTER 21. Sharing Student Research: Student Colloquia at University of South Florida St. Petersburg
Camielle Crampsie and Kaya van Beynen

261..CHAPTER 22. Teaching Integrity in Empirical Economics: The Pedagogy of Reproducible Science in Undergraduate Education
Norm Medeiros and Richard J. Ball

269..CHAPTER 23. The Honors Colloquium at QCC: A Decade of Excellence
Dale LaBonte, Denise Cross, Fyiane Nsilo-Swai, Matt Bejune, Susan McPherson, and Tiger Swan

281..CHAPTER 24. Transcribing Women's Diaries in the Digital World
Elizabeth A. Novara and Jessica Enoch

293..CHAPTER 25. Undergraduate Research in the Archives: A Case Study of Collaborative Teaching and Dissemination of Aerospace History
Tracy B. Grimm

305..Author Bios

DEDICATION: To the students who keep our professional lives challenging

Acknowledgments

We would like to thank George Kuh for his eloquent and powerful foreword. Professor Kuh's work in undergraduate research is unparalleled and we are so pleased he agreed to be part of this project.

We would like to extend our most grateful thanks for the amazing folks at ACRL, especially the publication staff Kathryn Deiss, Erin Nevius, and Dawn Mueller.

We would also like to extend our thanks to our supportive colleagues at the University of Illinois at Urbana-Champaign and Illinois Wesleyan University.

Many thanks to Ania Bui, an undergraduate student at Illinois Wesleyan University, for designing the front and back cover of the book.

Most important, thank you to all of the authors that support undergraduate research in so many unique and creative ways—thank you for sharing your expertise with our readers.

And finally, we thank our families, Shawn and Dahlia, Chad and Xavier. We could not have completed this book without your laughs, dinners, and willingness to do laundry.

FOREWORD
Adding Value to the Undergraduate Research Experience

Among the many things I've learned visiting several hundred colleges and universities during the past forty years is the variety of contributions librarians can make to the quality of the student experience. For the most part, librarians interact with students outside of formal classroom settings—observing, listening, and answering questions. Some of these conversations expose students' vulnerabilities along with their inadequate understanding about what is required to succeed in college. As much as any campus group, librarians tend to be well informed about what students need to do to take greater advantage of the resources schools provide for their learning and personal development. For my money, every campus committee that deals with curricular and student life matters should include among its members one or more librarians.

My appreciation for the work librarians do spiked more than two decades ago when I was directing the College Student Experiences Questionnaire (CSEQ) Research Program. Since replaced by the National Survey of Student Engagement (NSSE), the CSEQ was an ingenious instrument expertly designed in the 1970s by C. Robert Pace;[1] it had more than a dozen scales, one of which measured how much time and effort students devoted to using library resources and interacting with librarians. Librarians were interested in these kinds of data, as at the time there were few other sources of information available to gauge how students were using the library. Also, it was possible to use CSEQ results to compare students' library experiences at different institutions, which gave participating colleges and universities an idea of areas where library policies and practices could be modified to improve student learning. We presented some of these findings at a national ACRL meeting and published a paper about the quality of effort students expended using library resources and how they benefited from these interactions.[2]

Seventeen years ago—just after NSSE was introduced—some librarians expressed interest in being briefed about the conceptual and empirical underpinnings of this student engagement instrument and how NSSE findings could be used to further enhance the library's role in teaching and learning.[3] Unlike the CSEQ, NSSE does not have a scale devoted specifically to library experiences, though a module subsequently was developed in collaboration with college and university librarians to query students about the proper use of information sources; this set of questions complements items on the core NSSE survey about higher-order learning and how much writing students do.[4]

Given these experiences, I was delighted to be asked to pen the foreword to this book, which contains many campus-based examples about using undergraduate research to enhance the student experience. These efforts are salutary in their own right. And they can be even more powerful when they are linked with or incorporate the features characteristic of a set of effective educational activities now known as high-impact practices.

HIPs—The Cliff Notes Version

The phrase "high-impact practices (HIPs)" refers to the eleven intentionally designed, institutionally structured student experiences inside or outside of the classroom associated with elevated performance across multiple engagement activities and desired outcomes, such as deep learning, persistence, and satisfaction with college.[5] Endorsed by the Association of American Colleges and Universities (AAC&U), HIPs include the following:

- first-year seminars
- learning communities
- common intellectual experiences
- writing- and inquiry-intensive courses
- collaborative assignments and projects
- service- and community-based learning
- study abroad and other experiences with diversity
- undergraduate research
- internships and other types of field experiences
- culminating experiences (e.g., capstone seminar, demonstration, or project)
- ePorfolio[6]

These activities have several features in common. For example, when done well, a high-impact practice typically demands students devote substantial effort to challenging tasks over an extended period of time, presents numerous opportunities for student-faculty interaction and feedback from both instructors and peers, and puts students in situations where they have to transfer and apply what they are learning. When students are asked by faculty, staff, or internship or field supervisors to systematically reflect on and distill meaning from these experiences and connect them to other aspects of their education and life, these experiences become even more meaningful and impactful.

These features of a high-impact practice explain in large part why students who participate in, for example, a learning community or service-learning course engage more frequently and deeply in a variety of educationally purposeful behaviors, such as talking more often with their teachers and peers about substantive matters compared with their peers who do not participate in a HIP. In addition, students involved in one or more HIPS report making greater gains in general education outcomes, personal and social development, and practical competence. They also more often use deep learning behaviors, such as integrating and applying information from different courses to practical problems and making judgments about the value of information.

A fair amount of empirical evidence confirms these patterns of desired outcomes. For example, data from the California State University (CSU) system show that students who participate in one or more high-impact practices are more likely to persist and graduate;[7] they also gain more from their studies.[8] Moreover, the positive relationships between doing a HIP and desired outcomes generally hold for all students, background characteristics notwithstanding. In fact, students who are less well prepared academically (as indicated by pre-college achievement test scores such as ACT or SAT) or are from underserved backgrounds appear to benefit more than their better prepared peers,[9] which is a form of compensatory effect.[10]

These and related findings have spurred efforts at different types of colleges and universities to "scale up" the numbers of students participating in HIP-like activities. For example, the aforementioned twenty-three-campus CSU system is working with the National Association of System Heads to make a high-quality HIP available to more CSU students. The sixty-four-campus State University of New York (SUNY) system now requires every student to have at least one "applied learning experience," which is a key component of several HIPs, such as service learning, community-based projects, field work, and internships. Private colleges and universities, such as Cornell University, Elon University, Hendrix College, and Luther College, are also promoting their respective versions of such activities.

Ensuring That Educational Policies and Practices Are High Quality

An animating purpose of this book is to encourage librarians to incorporate the developmentally powerful features of HIPs in their work with students and colleagues. Among these features are the following:[11]

- **Expectations set at appropriately high levels.** Students feel challenged and assignments are constructed accordingly.
- **Significant investment of time and effort over an extended period.** Students must expend considerable effort to complete a series of assignments or a project.
- **Interactions with faculty and peers.** Students frequently participate in substantive discussions with their teachers and engage in activities with peers requiring collaboration, often outside the classroom.
- **Experiences with diversity.** Students are exposed to differing viewpoints, ways of knowing, and life circumstances.
- **Frequent and constructive feedback.** Students receive suggestions from faculty and staff about how to improve their performance and engage more effectively with learning opportunities.
- **Periodic and structured opportunities for reflection and integration.** Reflection assignments and activities are a regular part of learning experiences, which can be synthesized and documented using an electronic portfolio.
- **Relevance through real-world applications.** Students are put in situations where they must connect learning to life experiences or current social contexts.
- **Public demonstration of competence.** Students make public presentations to their peers, such as a capstone poster presentation or participation in a colloquium event.

These characteristics of HIPs are key to inducing students to engage frequently in and benefit more from the range of behaviors and activities mentioned earlier, such as interacting and collaborating with peers or applying their learning to real-life contexts.

HIPs and Librarians

What are some ways librarians can incorporate the features of HIPs in their work? Consider the following that build on and extend some of the examples presented later in this book.

Engaging students in high-quality inquiry. As many contributors to this book emphasize, embedding effective educational practices through working with students on research projects can increase their level of engagement with the inquiry process. For example, Grimm describes the archival research approach used at Purdue University that incorporates several of the characteristics of a HIP. That is, by putting students in the company of the originators of scholarly resources related to the aerospace industry, students interact directly with experts as well as their peers participating in the project. These kinds of interactions also increase the odds that students will get more feedback about their work.

The positive impact on student development from conducting research with faculty or staff members is accentuated when students are actively involved in the *entire inquiry cycle*, which typically means students must devote energy to the project over weeks if not months. While the nuances of an inquiry cycle may vary somewhat by discipline, in general the greatest benefits accrue to students who participate in determining the questions and identifying the existing literature guiding the research, collecting and analyzing the desired information, distilling the implications of the findings, and presenting the results and conclusions orally, in writing, or another demonstration form.

The collaborative approach to teaching undergraduate research courses at Amherst College described by Roser and Smith is also instructive in this regard (see also the chapters by Medeiros and Ball and Wertzberger and Miessler). The adaptable template used at Amherst provides structure and guidance for how librarians can work effectively with faculty colleagues from the respective academic department, incorporating several qualities of a HIP. Especially important is the systematic focus on reflective activities tuned to the inquiry norms of the respective discipline. The summer boot camp extends the amount of time students devote to cultivating research skills, which in turn deepens learning and gives students more practice in using archival literacy skills. Equally important, in many instances students taking the co-instructed research skills seminar are exposed to the entire inquiry cycle. When combined with flipped classroom instructional approaches, students are actively engaged in and responsible for their own learning.

Using the work experience in the library to deepen learning. Essential to insuring a learning experience is high quality is periodic, structured reflection by students about the meaning and relevance of the experience. In addition to helping students acquire inquiry skills, librarians are in a fortuitous position to extend and deepen learning by engaging students who work in the library in conversations about what they are learning from their research experience, coursework, and library job. Indeed, the potential benefits of facilitating this kind of meta-cognitive activity can have a profound influence on the value students derive from their college experience,[12] and address a common concern of employers—that too many college graduates are not prepared to function effectively in the workplace.[13] Among employer worries is that while students generally know a good deal about the subjects they studied, they are not able to readily transfer what they know to the unstructured problems and circumstances they encounter on the job. This is a major reason employers much prefer to hire college graduates who have had one or more internships or a similar kind of experience, such as a co-op. Too often overlooked is that a campus job, such as working in the library, often puts students in situations where they can apply what they are learning from their studies and other experiences, on and off the campus. This allows students to demonstrate—for better or worse—how well they interact with others to address unstructured situations.

Now imagine if the part-time hourly or work-study library job featured periodic structured, focused conversations among several peer co-workers facilitated by a librarian about what they are learning from one or more of their classes or from their research experience that they are using in their library job. And vice versa. Initial conversations of this nature can be stilted and occasionally stifled by silence; indeed, most students have difficulty saying anything substantive or making the kinds of connections that lead to a facility with deep, integrated learning. Most often, this is because students have not before thought about the prospect that *there should be links between their library employment, inquiry project, and classroom learning*. Or even that they had the ability to connect and think deeply about such matters! But over time, between and during such discussions, students begin to pay attention and bring into awareness how their work, classroom learning, and research experiences relate, making them less abstract and more practical.

Granted, not every inquiry project or class meeting will present material or discussions students can draw on to apply to their work in the library, or vice versa. But it only takes a few examples to demonstrate the relevance of the combination of these experiences to matters that students consider personally important and meaningful.[14]

These kinds of interactions also can stimulate and further the development of a capacity for thinking about one's own thinking in terms of the value of what one is learning and its concrete, real-world applications. This form of intrapersonal interrogation is a kind of metacognitive transformer through which one learns how to connect various experiences inside and outside of class with other aspects of life. And by discussing these reflections and related activities with work and research supervisors and their peers, students are able to construct and practice describing key components of their learning and what they can do with it, which will be invaluable later when interviewing for other jobs on campus and after college.

What I've briefly described is the premise that sparked the development of the University of Iowa's Guided Reflection on Work (GROW) initiative (http://vp.studentlife.uiowa.edu/initiatives/grow/) eight years ago in which librarians have participated. GROW is one of the more advanced, comprehensive efforts that can inform and be adapted to other institutions. Making the library work experience more educationally purposeful by connecting the job to classroom learning and the research process promises to benefit students, institutions, and employers.

Information and media literacy: An essential learning outcome. The interest and enthusiasm for embedding the features of HIPs into various learning settings are well founded. At the same time, these experiences cannot substitute for insuring that students acquire the proficiencies and dispositions that constitute information and media literacy (IML). Technological advances have accelerated and accentuated the relevance of IML, especially with the rapid proliferation of "fake news" and other forms of generating information that sometimes to serve questionable purposes.[15] The media component of IML is increasingly important, as we are "inundated with images, words, and sounds"[16] via Twitter, YouTube, Instagram, and so on.

The times demand an educated citizenry with well-honed critical reasoning skills to evaluate why a message is sent, by whom, and the various ways it might be interpreted. No wonder almost all (98 percent) of the Association of American Colleges and Universities (AAC&U) member schools report that critical thinking is an important learning goal along with research skills (75 percent)[17] both of which are core IML competencies.

Equally important, a twenty-first-century education also requires knowing *how* to apply what is determined to be good information to innovate and solve contextualized complex, unanticipated problems.[18] None of this is possible without being IML proficient, which is why AAC&U[19] declared information literacy as an "Essential Learning Outcome." In fact, more than three quarters (76 percent) of AAC&U member schools say that information literacy is an expected learning outcome. The AAC&U does not feature "media" in its definition of information literacy, but these various forms of communication are inferred, which is why I have taken the liberty to refer to the cluster of relevant competencies as IML.

As with the writing-across-the-curriculum movement introduced decades ago, helping students become IML proficient is everyone's duty, not just librarians. That is, to learn to write (as well as think) well, students need a good deal of practice in different courses throughout their studies (not just in the required first-year writing class) coupled with feedback about their performance. Indeed, IML requires extensive practice across the curriculum, in the context of progressively more challenging problems, projects, and standards for performance.

Several chapters in this book (e.g., Wertzberger and Miessler, Yanofsky, Miller and Nizam) illustrate educationally effective approaches for developing IML proficiency and related dispositions and skills through undergraduate research projects. In addition, other resources offer guidance about how librarians and their colleagues can collaborate to advance this important work. For example, Gilchrist and Oakleaf[20] discuss how librarians have worked at different levels of the institution to help design curricular and other experiences that assist students in cultivating IML skills and dispositions. They also provide examples of initiatives from different types of institutions as well as the development of rubrics used to evaluate IML proficiency, drawing on the AAC&U Valid Assessment of Learning in Undergraduate Education (VALUE) initiative, an effort to assess authentic student learning demonstrated through such activities such as research, writing, oral presentations, performances, demonstrations, and so forth.[21]

Last Word

Libraries and librarians have always been indispensable to collegiate quality. They can add even more value by consistently infusing the features of a high-impact educational experience into undergraduate research and other interactions with students, inside and outside the classroom.

Thanks to the editors of and contributors to this volume for illustrating how librarians can help enrich and deepen student learning through engaging undergraduates in well-designed inquiry activities. I salute them and librarians everywhere for leading us with courage and conviction into this ever-evolving brave new, information-rich world and helping us navigate it with a much-needed measure of confidence and competence.

George D. Kuh, Ph.D.
Senior Scholar, National Institute for Learning Outcomes Assessment
Chancellor's Professor of Higher Education Emeritus, Indiana University

Notes

1. C. Robert Pace, *Measuring the Quality of College Student Experiences: An Account of the Development and Use of the College Student Experiences Questionnaire* (Los Angeles: University of California Los Angeles Higher Education Research Institute, 1984).
2. George D. Kuh, "Student Engagement in Learning: Does the Library Matter?" featured presentation to the Association of College and Research Libraries, Charlotte, April 2003; George D. Kuh and Robert M. Gonyea, "The Role of the Academic Library in Promoting Student Engagement in Learning, *College and Research Libraries*, 64 (2003): 256–82.

3. George D. Kuh, Polly D. Boruff-Jones, and Amy E. Mark, "Engaging Students in the First College Year: Why Librarians Matter," in *The Role of the Library in the First College Year*, ed. L. Hardesty (Monograph No. 45) (Columbia: University of South Carolina, National Resource Center for the First-Year Experience and Students in Transition, 2007).
4. Polly D. Boruff-Jones, Carrie Donovan, and Kevin Fosnacht, "Feasible, Scalable, and Measurable: Information Literacy Assessment and the National Survey of Student Engagement," presented at the annual conference of the American Library Association, Anaheim, CA, June 2012, http://cpr.indiana.edu/uploads/ALA%202012.pdf; Kevin Fosnacht, "Information Use During the First College Year: Findings from the NSSE Experiences with Information Literacy module," presented at the annual conference of the Association of College & Research Libraries, Portland, OR, March 2015, http://nsse.indiana.edu/pdf/presentations/2015/ACRL_2015_Fosnacht_paper.pdf.
5. George D. Kuh, *High-Impact Educational Practices: What They Are, Who Has Access to Them, and Why They Matter* (Washington: Association of American Colleges and Universities, 2008).
6. George D. Kuh, "Foreword: And Now There Are Eleven," in B. Eynon and L.M. Gambino, *High Impact ePortfolio Practice: A Catalyst for Student, Faculty and Institutional Learning* (Sterling: Stylus, 2017).
7. George D. Kuh, Ken O'Donnell, and Sally Reed, *Ensuring Quality and Taking High-Impact Practices to Scale* (Washington: Association of American Colleges and Universities, 2013).
8. Ashley Finley and Tia McNair, *Assessing Underserved Students' Engagement in High-Impact Practices* (Washington: Association of American Colleges and Universities, 2013).
9. Ibid.
10. Kuh, 2008; Ernest T. Pascarella and Patrick T. Terenzini, *How College Affects Students*: Vol. 2. *A Third Decade of Research* (San Francisco: Jossey-Bass, 2005).
11. Kuh, O'Donnell, and Reed, 2013.
12. George D. Kuh, "Making Learning Meaningful: Engaging Students in Ways That Matter to Them," in *Finding the Why: Personalizing Learning in Higher Education. New Directions for Teaching and Learning*, No.145, ed. M. Watts (San Francisco: Jossey-Bass, 2016), 49–56.
13. Hart Research Associates, *Recent Trends in General Education Design, Learning Outcomes, and Teaching Approaches: Key Findings from a Survey Among Administrators At AAC&U Member Institutions* (Washington: Association of American Colleges and Universities, 2015), http://www.aacu.org/sites/default/files/files/LEAP/2015_Survey_Report2_GEtrends.pdf.
14. Kuh, 2016.
15. John Herrman, "Fixation on Fake News Overshadows Waning Trust in Real Reporting," *The New York Times*, November 18 2016, http://www.nytimes.com/2016/11/19/business/media/exposing-fake-news-eroding-trust-in-real-reporting.html?_r=0; Sapna Maheshwari, "How Fake News Goes Viral: A Case Study," *The New York Times*. November 20 2016, http://www.nytimes.com/2016/11/20/business/media/how-fake-news-spreads.html?_r=0.
16. Thomas C. Johnson, "A Call for Media Literacy," [web log comment] (December 2016), retrieved from https://www.luther.edu/ideas-creations-blog/?story_id=736086.

17. Hart Research Associates, 2015.
18. Todd J. Wiebe, "The Information Literacy Imperative in Higher Education," *Liberal Education* 101/102(4) (2016): 52–7.
19. Association of American Colleges and Universities (AAC&U). *The LEAP Challenge. Education for a World of Unscripted Problems* (Washington: Association of American Colleges and Universities, 2015).
20. Debra Gilchrist and Megan Oakleaf, "An Essential Partner: The Librarian's Role in Student Learning Assessment," *NILOA Occasional Paper No.14* (Urbana, IL: University of Illinois and Indiana University, National Institute for Learning Outcomes Assessment, April 2012), http://learningoutcomeassessment.org/occasionalpaper-fourteen.htm#Announcement.
21. Terrel Rhodes and Ashley Finley, *Using the VALUE Rubrics for Improvement of Learning and Authentic Assessment* (Washington: Association of American Colleges and Universities, 2013).

Bibliography

Association of American Colleges and Universities (AAC&U). *The LEAP Challenge. Education for a World of Unscripted Problems.* Washington: Association of American Colleges and Universities, 2015.

Boruff-Jones, Polly, Carrie Donovan, and Kevin Fosnacht. *Feasible, Scalable, and Measurable: Information Literacy Assessment and the National Survey of Student Engagement.* Presented at the annual conference of the American Library Association, Anaheim, CA, June 2012. http://cpr.indiana.edu/uploads/ALA%202012.pdf.

Finley, Ashley, and Tia McNair. *Assessing Underserved Students' Engagement in High-Impact Practices.* Washington: Association of American Colleges and Universities, 2013.

Fosnacht, Kevin. *Information Use During the First College Year: Findings from the NSSE Experiences with Information Literacy Module.* Presented at the annual conference of the Association of College & Research Libraries, Portland, OR, March 2015. http://nsse.indiana.edu/pdf/presentations/2015/ACRL_2015_Fosnacht_paper.pdf.

Gilchrist, Debra, and Megan Oakleaf. *An Essential Partner: The Librarian's Role in Student Learning Assessment* (NILOA Occasional Paper No.14). Urbana, IL: University of Illinois and Indiana University, National Institute for Learning Outcomes Assessment, April 2012. http://learningoutcomeassessment.org/occasionalpaper-fourteen.htm#Announcement

Hart Research Associates. *Recent Trends in General Education Design, Learning Outcomes, and Teaching Approaches: Key Findings from a Survey Among Administrators at AAC&U Member Institutions.* Washington: Association of American Colleges and Universities, 2016. http://www.aacu.org/sites/default/files/files/LEAP/2015_Survey_Report2_GEtrends.pdf

Herrman, John. "Fixation on Fake News Overshadows Waning Trust in Real Reporting." *The New York Times*, November 18 2016. http://www.nytimes.com/2016/11/19/business/media/exposing-fake-news-eroding-trust-in-real-reporting.html?_r=0.

Johnson, Thomas C. "A Call for Media Literacy," December 2016. [Web log comment]. Retrieved from https://www.luther.edu/ideas-creations-blog/?story_id=736086.

Kuh, George D. *Student Engagement in Learning: Does the Library Matter?* Featured presentation to the Association of College and Research Libraries, Charlotte, April 2003.

Kuh, George D. *High-Impact Educational Practices: What They Are, Who Has Access to Them, and Why They Matter.* Washington: Association of American Colleges and Universities, 2008.

Kuh, George D. "Making Learning Meaningful: Engaging Students in Ways That Matter to Them." In *Finding the Why: Personalizing Learning in Higher Education. New Directions for Teaching and Learning*, No.145, edited by M. Watts. San Francisco: Jossey-Bass, 2016.

Kuh, George D. "Foreword: And Now There Are Eleven." In B. Eynon and L.M. Gambino, *High Impact ePortfolio Practice: A Catalyst for Student, Faculty and Institutional Learning.* Sterling: Stylus, 2017.

Kuh, George D., Polly D. Boruff-Jones, and Amy E. Mark. "Engaging Students in the First College Year: Why Librarians Matter." In *The Role of the Library in the First College Year* (Monograph No. 45), edited by L. Hardesty. Columbia: University of South Carolina, National Resource Center for the First-Year Experience and Students in Transition, 2007.

Kuh, George D., and Robert M. Gonyea. (2003). "The Role of the Academic Library in Promoting Student Engagement in Learning." *College and Research Libraries* 64, (2003): 256–82.

Kuh, George D, Ken O'Donnell, and Sally Reed. *Ensuring Quality and Taking High-Impact Practices to Scale.* Washington: Association of American Colleges and Universities, 2013.

Maheshwari, Sapna. "How Fake News Goes Viral: A Case Study." *The New York Times*, November 20 2016. http://www.nytimes.com/2016/11/20/business/media/how-fake-news-spreads.html?_r=0.

Pace, C. Robert. *Measuring the Quality of College Student Experiences: An Account of the Development and Use of the College Student Experiences Questionnaire.* Los Angeles: University of California Los Angeles Higher Education Research Institute, 1984.

Pascarella, Ernest T., and Patrick T. Terenzini. *How College Affects Students*: Vol. 2. A Third Decade of Research. San Francisco: Jossey-Bass, 2005.

Rhodes, Terrel, and Ashley Finley. *Using the VALUE Rubrics for Improvement of Learning and Authentic Assessment.* Washington: Association of American Colleges and Universities, 2013.

Wiebe, Todd J. "The Information Literacy Imperative in Higher Education." *Liberal Education*, 101/102(4) (2016): 52–7.

Introduction

> "Moreover, we want students to understand that the answers to their research questions are not something they find lying inertly in their research sources, but something they make through their own critical thinking brought to bear on the sources."[1]

In the course of working on this volume, a common question we received from colleagues was, "What do you mean by undergraduate research?" Undergraduate research (UGR) is often conflated with end-of-the-semester major course papers, the standard "twenty-page research paper, with APA style bibliography and X number of sources." In fact, undergraduate research is one of several high-impact educational practices identified by George Kuh and the Association of American Colleges & Universities; it is an experience characterized by mentorship by faculty, by student agency and persistence, and by rigor. It is an academic mechanism for engaging students in the "habits of mind" of a discipline.

In our past work together (and with Sarah Shreeves at the University of Miami), we have cited various definitions of undergraduate research. The first, by the Council for Undergraduate Research: "An inquiry or investigation conducted by an undergraduate student that makes an original intellectual or creative contribution to the discipline." The second, by Professor Gerald Graff of the University of Chicago: "'Research' is best defined simply as work that enters the current conversation of a particular field in a significant way." Both definitions are effective in communicating the main tenets of the term. The University of Illinois at Urbana-Champaign, Office of Undergraduate Research goes a step further by describing undergraduate research on a continuum:

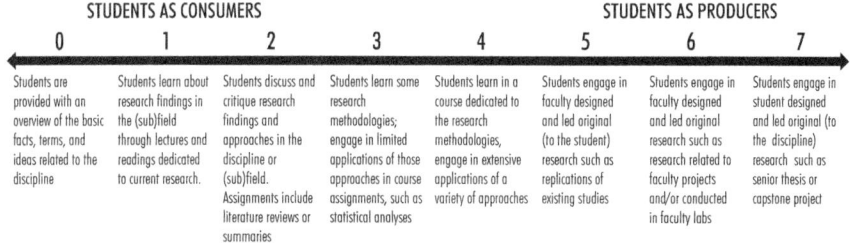

We offer this graphic as a useful and valuable summation of how a student can develop research skills across and throughout the curriculum. Even though the continuum is geared toward empirical research, one of the attractive aspects of UGR is that it is discipline-agnostic; "original intellectual or creative contributions" and "entering a conversation in a significant way" are meaningful and aspirational, no matter the discipline.

Perhaps that is why UGR (and experiences like it) is increasingly seen as a vital part of the undergraduate experience. UGR is the proving ground for deep and critical thinking, analysis, originality, and a clear indication of movement from the novice researcher voice to a growing expert researcher voice. As Bean states, "The process from moving from outsider to disciplinary insider or from novice to expert is neither simple nor linear."[2] UGR helps students connect the dots between their interests, general education courses, writing requirements, major coursework, and the habits of mind they learn in the process of becoming a "disciplinary insider."

UGR is not just for students on the road to graduate school, however. In the seminal *Reinventing Undergraduate Education: A Blueprint for America's Research Universities*, the Commission noted:

> "By the senior year, the able undergraduate should be ready for research of the same character and approximately the same complexity as the first-year graduate student; the research university needs to make that zone of transition from senior to graduate student easy to enter and easy to cross. For those who do not enter graduate school, the abilities to identify, analyze, and resolve problems will prove invaluable in professional life and in citizenship."[3]

The higher education literature is clear that UGR and similar experiences are extremely valuable, not because of the end product, but because of the *relationships* that students build and the *processes* of research that students engage in during their research. The Council on Undergraduate Research website lists the following as benefits of UGR:

- Enhances student learning through mentoring relationships with faculty
- Increases retention
- Increases enrollment in graduate education and provides effective career preparation
- Develops critical thinking, creativity, problem solving, and intellectual independence
- Develops an understanding of research methodology

- Promotes an innovation-oriented culture

The Gallup/Purdue Index Inaugural National Report sought to connect students' experiences in college to well-being and engagement in their lives and work post-graduation: "Graduates whose college experiences included forms of "experiential and deep learning—working on a long-term project, having an internship with applied learning, and being extremely involved in extracurricular activities—were also twice as likely to be engaged in their work." As higher education becomes more competitive—for dollars, for students, for grant money, for resources in general—institutions will need to increase their development of programs that provide "experiential and deep learning" like UGR. The scholarly and extracurricular *experiences* of college are, increasingly, becoming a major part of marketing college education. The college degree may not carry the same value if the opportunity to take part in high-impact educational practices are not offered and, more important, if the value of UGR to the student and their future is not clearly articulated to students and their families.

For UGR to be successful programmatically, and for students to be successful undergraduate researchers, the services that undergird UGR—like the library (but also institutional review boards, grant writing, etc.)—become part of the core infrastructure of the undergraduate experience. Academic libraries have always been engaged with undergraduate researchers but have become more strategically engaged as institutions have widened their focus due to marketing potential, establishing the quality of the undergraduate experience, highlighting faculty as mentors, etc. Libraries are, increasingly, creating services customized for UGR in a variety of areas and are collaborating with offices/services on campus to support the work of UGRs. Publishing services, such as institutional repositories, are a significant contributor, as are data services, copyright services, poster printing and design, specialized space, digital scholarship services, awards, and much more. The library is well-positioned to take on the challenge to support UGR since programs can be from any discipline, can be interdisciplinary, can be any high-impact format, and can reflect upon an institution's own history, traditions, and tensions, such as the University of Illinois' Ethnography of the University Initiative.

We do not do this work in isolation—relationships are vital. We are responding to clear and articulated needs from our faculty colleagues. UGR has high expectations of students; hence, there is a clear role for librarians to engage with faculty and students as the library is positioned to teach and mentor information literacy skills and issues, central tenets of the research process. Beyond the one-shot, beyond course-integrated instruction, UGR presents an opportunity for librarians to help students go beyond a foundation of information literacy toward advanced research and information management skills.

Along with our colleague, Sarah Shreeves, we completed two studies exploring library support services for UGR programs. In our first article, "A Survey of Library Support for Formal Undergraduate Research Programs," we found that libraries across Carnegie Classifications have been providing ongoing library support for UGR, including adapting existing services (e.g., collections, space) as well as expanding publishing services to include undergraduate work in the institutional repository, teaching workshops on poster design, hosting undergraduate research journals, expanding instructional support on scholarly communication topics, and much more. Our follow-up article, "A Survey of Campus Coordinators of Undergraduate Research Programs," examined how coordinators perceive and value library support for UGR programs, a vital partnership for reaching students across disciplines. Respondents particularly valued library instruction, including "improving search strategies, literature reviews and annotation, and preparation of research results," and acknowledged the sessions could be used as "gateways to introduce more advanced information literacy topics." Coordinators also highly valued libraries efforts to provide platforms for dissemination of original undergraduate student work. We concluded that "undergraduate researchers may increasingly have more sophisticated research needs than once understood and that their needs are beginning to more closely mirror the needs of graduate students and faculty, albeit in a novice manner."[4] Hensley delved more closely into the instructional programs libraries have designed specifically for UGR programs and found less focus on library orientation activities and more focus on scholarly communication issues, which is apt given the publication requirement for most UGR programs. All three studies provide benchmark information for libraries looking to better understand UGR and the fundamental changes happening in higher education.

Our hope is that with this collection of case studies, librarians come away with not only a better understanding of what undergraduate research entails but also with a clear vision of the potential connections and contributions they can make to support undergraduate research. George Kuh opens the volume by explaining why high-impact educational practices are increasingly foundational to the undergraduate experience. The case studies in this volume span a spectrum of themes related to UGR and provide the reader with a plethora of innovative and impressive ideas: embedded librarianship, outreach projects, publication of student work, campus partnerships, exploring the impact of the ACRL Framework on UGR, digital humanities, special collections and archives, data management, and much more.

We encourage you to do an environmental scan of undergraduate research programs on your campus, to speak with offices of undergraduate research, faculty mentors, and students to gauge their UGR needs and interests, and to envision and implement a future where the library plays a strong role in undergraduate research.

Merinda Kaye Hensley
Stephanie Davis-Kahl
Co-Editors, Undergraduate Research and The Academic Librarian: Case Studies and Best Practices

Notes

1. John C. Bean, *Engaging Ideas: The Professor's Guide to Integrating Writing, Critical Thinking, and Active Learning in the Classroom.* The Jossey-Bass Higher and Adult Education Series; Jossey-Bass Higher and Adult Education Series (San Francisco: Jossey-Bass, 1996), 236.
2. Bean, *Engaging Ideas*, 2nd ed., 228.
3. Boyer Commission on Educating Undergraduates in the Research University, *Reinventing Undergraduate Education: A Blueprint for America's Research Universities* (State University of New York: Stoney Brook, 1998), 17, http://hdl.handle.net/1951/26012.
4. Merinda Kaye Hensley, "A Survey of Instructional Support for Undergraduate Research Programs," *portal: Libraries and the Academy* 15, no. 4 (2015): 987.

Bibliography

2012-2013 Annual Report. Office of Undergraduate Research, University of Illinois, 2012-2013. Accessed January 20, 2017. https://undergradresearch.illinois.edu/assets/docs/OURAnnualReport2012-2013.pdf,

AAC&U News. "Engagement in College, Engagement in the Workplace: Findings from the Gallup-Purdue Index," June 2014. Accessed January 20, 2017. https://www.aacu.org/aacu-news/newsletter/engagement-college-engagement-workplace-findings-gallup-purdue-index,

Bean, John C. 1996. *Engaging Ideas: The Professor's Guide to Integrating Writing, Critical Thinking, and Active Learning in the Classroom.* The Jossey-Bass Higher and Adult Education Series; Jossey-Bass Higher and Adult Education Series. San Francisco: Jossey-Bass, 1996.

Boyer Commission on Educating Undergraduates in the Research University. *Reinventing Undergraduate Education: A Blueprint for America's Research Universities.* State University of New York: Stoney Brook, 1998. http://hdl.handle.net/1951/26012.

Council on Undergraduate Research. http://www.cur.org/about_cur/fact_sheet/, accessed January 20, 2017.

Ethnography of the University Initiative, University of Illinois at Urbana-Champaign. Accessed January 20, 2017. http://www.eui.illinois.edu/,

Graff, Gerald. "Confusions about Undergraduate Research," from The Reinvention Center, 2006. Accessed January 20, 2017. http://geraldgraff.com/graff_articles/On_Defining_Research.pdf.

Kuh, George D. "High-Impact Educational Practices: A Brief Overview." Accessed January 20, 2017. https://www.aacu.org/leap/hips.

Hensley, Merinda Kaye, Sarah L. Shreeves, and Stephanie Davis-Kahl. "A Survey of Library Support for Formal Undergraduate Research Programs." *College & Research Libraries* 75, no. 4 (2014): 422–41.

Hensley, Merinda Kaye, Sarah L. Shreeves, and Stephanie Davis-Kahl. "A Survey of Campus Coordinators of Undergraduate Research Programs." *College & Research Libraries* 76, no. 7 (2015): 975–95.

Hensley, Merinda Kaye. "A Survey of Instructional Support for Undergraduate Research Programs." *portal: Libraries and the Academy* 15, no. 4 (2015): 719–62.

Ray, Julie and Stephanie Kafka. "Life in College Matters for Life After College." Gallup, May 6, 2014. Accessed January 20, 2017. http://www.gallup.com/poll/168848/life-college-matters-life-college.aspx.

Rivard, Ry. "Gauging Graduates' Well-Being." *Inside Higher Ed*. May 6, 2014. Accessed January 20, 2017. https://www.insidehighered.com/news/2014/05/06/gallup-surveys-graduates-gauge-whether-and-why-college-good-well-being.

CHAPTER 1 *

Beyond Embedded Librarianship:

Co-Teaching with Faculty to Integrate Digital Scholarship in Undergraduate Research

Sarah Clayton and Jeffrey M. Widener

Introduction

In 2015, two professors at the University of Oklahoma (OU) approached the university libraries' faculty and staff with a plan to incorporate a digital humanities component in their cross-listed history and political science course on the Great Depression and New Deal. The instructors wanted fifty undergraduate students to complete original research projects on Oklahoma in the 1930s through conducting archival research, visiting local communities, collecting oral histories, constructing digital maps, and creating a multimedia website to showcase their findings. The professors, however, did not have the skills or the technological space to teach all the described techniques or design and lead a digital humanities-focused course. The projects envisioned by the professors provided a perfect opportunity for the library to engage with undergraduate researchers in a new and different way while also opening a new avenue for supporting teaching and learning with technology, specifically digital humanities tools.

---

* This work is licensed under a Creative Commons Attribution-ShareAlike 4.0 License, CC BY-SA (https://creativecommons.org/licenses/by-sa/4.0/).

In addition, OU Libraries came under new leadership in 2012. That leadership created a strategic plan that placed more emphasis on the library as a research commons for the campus community and expanded the role of the information professional in our organization. This broadening includes building a team of faculty and staff with varied specialties in digital techniques, data management, digital scholarship, and geographic information systems (GIS) to meet the needs of twenty-first century faculty and students.[1] As well, OU Libraries has created and continues to develop in-house technology-enhanced collaborative facilities, such as our Collaborative Learning Center and Digital Scholarship Laboratory.

This professional and physical expansion, concomitant to the professors' prior, positive experiences with information and archival literacy instruction, propelled them to seek assistance from librarians to complement the instruction and collaborate on the course design. This chapter will introduce how OU Libraries has grown its digital resource team to better serve instructors and students in courses that introduce digital scholarship techniques, describe how the instructors and librarians collaborated on scaling and designing the course, and provide recommendations on how librarians can go beyond subject or digital specialists to co-teachers. This work is especially relevant when considering how to best support undergraduates engaging in in-depth original research with disciplinary methodologies and archival materials.

Background

Each year, faculty at OU have an opportunity to propose a Presidential Dream Course.[2] These courses are required to couple dynamic undergraduate teaching strategies with invited guest lectures by renowned experts. When a history professor and political science professor applied and received funding in 2015 for a Dream Course entitled, "Making Modern America: Discovering the Great Depression and New Deal," they wanted to expand upon the typical dream course model.[3] Working with the library, the instructors formulated a plan to hire a Digital Scholarship Fellow, who would be co-funded by the two professors and the library. The Fellow would be fully embedded in the course, assist with designing course curriculum, and teach undergraduates how to digitally create and curate historical research projects.

While interviews for the Fellow were underway, the instructors and a team of librarians, including archivists from the Carl Albert Center and Western History Collections, the government documents librarian, the history librarian, the digital scholarship specialist, as well as the GIS librarian, began meeting to get a sense of the course's scope. The instructors had an ambitious vision for the class: they wanted students to complete three separate, original group research projects related to the Great Depression and New Deal in Oklahoma, requiring the students to not only consume but also create new knowledge through critical analysis, writing, and curating digital research projects. After conversations with administration and the partnering faculty, the group determined that librarians and would lead weekly workshops focused on research methods and technical skills hosted in the Libraries' Helmerich Collaborative Learning Center. Primarily, the newly hired Fellow would facilitate these sessions.

Because the Dream Course involved many parts, the team had to first develop a clear plan and workflow that would allow the library, our faculty partners, and the students to succeed. The instructional team examined models and recommendations via literature on incorporating digital humanities projects into the classroom and on embedded librarianship in order to create a transformative educational and research experience.

Our investigation of digital humanities models turned up significantly more examples that targeted graduate students than undergraduates. Ruth Mostern's and Elana Gainor's model of teaching spatial history to undergraduates was the example that best aligned with our situation.[4] Their course was structured how we hoped to design our course with a lab and traditional history session each week. Based on their experiences, we decided to standardize the assignments as much as possible and be prepared to allot time for extra assistance. New York University instructors, Deena Engel and Marion Thain, created a model that contained weekly technology labs, which was also similar to what our team hoped to accomplish.[5] During the lecture portion of their course, Engel and Thain addressed the theories and best practices behind the tools their students would use. Our weekly lectures, however, centered on content related to the Great Depression and New Deal. As such, our team had to work components of theory into library-led workshops. Elizabeth Macaluay-Lewis's graduate course on art history and archeology also influenced our curriculum.[6] Her focus was to re-conceptualize more traditional assignments from both disciplines, including term papers, site reports (Archeology), and object reports (Art History), and re-imagine them as digital projects. She also incorporated writing for the web and the general public into her assignments. She suggested that these skills were becoming increasingly important for developing professionals and scholars and yet were largely missing from her students' educational experience. After reading her work, our team decided to incorporate these concepts into our lessons on integrating research with digital technologies.

Within the literature on embedded librarianship, we found examples and advice for both research and classroom settings. Jake Carlson and Ruth Kneale offered helpful recommendations on building relationships, working collaboratively, gaining administrative support, and taking risks.[7] Jeffrey

Knapp and his colleagues at Penn State University[8] provided a useful discussion about being realistic in setting and communicating time commitments for an embedded librarian, which was extremely valuable not only for the fully embedded Fellow but also for all the library partners. Ultimately, based on these models and our collaborative conversations, our team scaled back the vision of the course, sequenced the workshops in a logical order, and developed an outline of the materials needed for the course. Moreover, our team went beyond the traditional sense of embedded librarianship to becoming co-teachers in a college course.

Partnerships

Having amicable faculty to work with was fruitful to developing an effective course. First, the instructors set aside half of their class sessions for librarian-led, interactive workshops. Equally important, they were willing to defer to experts in the library and work with them to design the course. The syllabus, schedule, assignments, and digital tool selection were the result of close collaboration, originating with the learning objectives for the course. In addition to a basic understanding of the subject matter, the Great Depression and New Deal, these goals included

- making learning history engaging instead of passive;
- teaching students the art of historical research so that they may reap the rewards; and
- providing students with transferable skills—not only analytical and critical thinking—but also the value of teamwork, digital techniques, and communication that will help them be competitive players in a tightening global economy.

Preparing for the course required extensive collaboration between the library and course instructors. Between July 15 and August 24, all the librarians worked together to get the resources ready. Several librarians, for instance, created research guides[9] featuring resources from the library and the local community, especially the Oklahoma Historical Society. The Carl Albert Center and the Western History Collections archivists searched their holdings and contributed their related materials to the guides. Additionally, the Western History Collections scanned images in preparation for a workshop activity focused on contextualizing historical photographs, repeat photography, and creating a geographic database. The digital scholarship specialist, the GIS librarian, and the Fellow created guides and modules on how to create maps, conduct oral histories, practice fieldwork, and populate an Omeka website.[10] See Appendix 1A: Excerpt from the Omeka Guide. While creating these resources required a tremendous amount of time and effort, each librarian developed material that could be reused in similar courses or independent instructional sessions. For example, while the Omeka guide was created to be used for developing digital content over a semester-long course, our team has adapted it for stand-alone workshops.

We also developed a workflow and timeline for the library supporting similar collaborative efforts in the future. Interested faculty need to begin conversations with one of our digital scholarship specialists at least two semesters before the course. After getting a sense of the project, specialists will bring in the appropriate subject librarian(s). The specialist will recommend tools that support the learning objectives and work with the full team to develop a curriculum and accompanying assignments. As our team's expertise and instructional materials develop, we anticipate that each course will require a lesser time commitment, but we still recognize that we need to set reasonable restraints on what we can support. Currently, our team aims to support one course per year. The success of the initial effort has led to interested faculty for the next two years.

Reflection

The students were the wildcard going into the course since there were no pre-requisites and we did not know students' comfort levels with technology or historical research. Throughout the semester, the instructional team was repeatedly impressed by students' willingness to try new techniques and their overall engagement with their research topics. They went beyond our expectations and the minimum requirements for the projects. For example, one student worked with a construction company to discover the original blueprints for a building on campus built with funding from the Public Works Administration. Another discovered historical maps and overlaid them with a modern map to show the geographic changes in eastern Oklahoma over time. Another student was even able to arrange a behind-the-scenes tour of the Oklahoma City Zoo to understand how it functioned during the 1930s. However, despite these successes, we did encounter some unanticipated challenges.

One of the biggest surprises was the students' lack of digital and information literacy skills. The workshops had to move at a slower pace than we planned because we needed to explain basic concepts, including information bias, proper attribution, working with different file formats, and searching databases and the library catalog. The structure of the course did not allow us to get a sense of what prior knowledge students had and, looking back, we should have sequenced our workshops so they progressed from the basics of conducting research to using digital tools instead of beginning with research and digital tool integration.

Even with two faculty members and at least one librarian in every workshop, we did not always have enough resources to help every student as quickly as we, and they, would have liked. This made technical workshops especially challenging. Going forward, our team recommends a course of this size be divided into smaller groups for the library workshops. Even though this means the librarians would have to teach twice as many sessions, the students would receive more personalized attention, leading to a teaching pace allowing for flexibility and responsiveness among students. During sessions with individual groups during office hours, the Fellow observed that the smaller instructor to student ratio reduced frustration among the students, which supports our conclusions about the benefits of smaller workshops.

Assessment

At the beginning of the course, students participated in an initial survey so the instructors could ascertain students' comfort level with various research methods and digital tools they would use during the semester. See Appendix 1B: Quantitative Survey Questions. The majority of students had little to no prior experience with conducting archival research, oral histories, GIS, or content management systems. The team gave students a nearly identical survey at the end of the course. Their responses suggested students did, in fact, gain an increased comfort level and familiarity with research techniques and digital tools. On average, the ranking for each tool and research method increased 33 percent. Comfort with Content Management Systems saw the largest increase of 42 percent. Students also expressed interest in continuing to explore GIS and archival research after the course.[11]

The students also shared informal feedback throughout the semester. Several students reported that completed research projects enriched their educational experience. One student commented, "I really liked the group projects because they made you feel like a part of something far bigger than a regular history course. We helped create actual history by making these projects a reality." Some students asked when the course would be offered again, and three students opted to continue their research projects as independent studies with the course instructors the following semester. Additionally, two education students created a K-12 lesson plan to accompany their research project. Their lesson plan received one of the 2016 Western History Association Redd Center Teaching Western History Award.[12]

The major critique from students was the class was somewhat disorganized. In particular, many students suggested creating more descriptive guidelines for the projects. As well, most students expressed they needed more time to finish their projects. And finally, students noted they would have preferred to work on one research project rather than divide their time between two projects.

The faculty members were pleased with the results in terms of student projects and achieving the learning objectives. The students' work also impressed the larger community. One group, who researched the University of Oklahoma, received the inaugural Dan Hobbs Prize for undergraduate research on Oklahoma History from the Oklahoma Board of Higher Education Heritage Society. The professors recognized that this course could not have succeed without the library partnership and want to repeat the course in future semesters with the library's support. Like the students, the faculty recognized this course required an increased workload and time commitment. After receiving students' feedback, the faculty and Fellow met and determined future iterations of this course should start with small, controlled research assignments to gain skills and confidence and subsequently progress to one original research project.

The students' group presentations at the end of the course were probably the clearest indication of the course's effectiveness. While the final products were impressive, the team was particularly struck by the students' level of enthusiasm. One student, for example, was passionate about an archival resource they discovered. Another student showed a time lapse video she had made of her group traveling down Route 66. And another student was excited about using maps to make a connection between history and environment. Overall, the students were proud of what they had been able to discover. Through sharing their projects on our Omeka site, they felt they were contributing to historical knowledge. As educators and information professionals, we could not have asked for anything better than our students finding exhilaration in the pursuit of lifelong learning.

Recommendations/Best Practices

From the initial planning stages to our reflection after the course, we learned valuable lessons from both our successes and our shortcomings. We have categorized these lessons into four major recommendations for other engaged in these kinds of partnerships:

Recommendation One: Communicate early, often, and efficiently. Our initiative involved seven librarians and archivists and two faculty members. In order to have a successful project, we needed to start planning and coordinating the moving parts as early as possible. The input of all the parties was invaluable for a successful initiative but it was not practical to have all of the interested parties at every meeting. The Fellow served as the connection between everyone involved in the course. The Fellow and a new staff member found it invaluable to meet one-on-one with each member of the team to learn about their perspective and priorities. Developing this understanding and maintaining communication among all the partners was critical to the success of this project.

Recommendation Two: Create reasonable expectations. A major component of the conversations involved scaling back the course's scope. The team wanted the students to be challenged, but we also wanted them to be able to succeed. The librarians were excited by our faculty partners' vision and wanted to support it in a realistic manner. Working closely with the faculty, we reduced the initial three projects down to two to make the workload more reasonable. However, based on the students' and faculty feedback, it would have been helpful to scale the scope down even further.

Selecting what to remove of the project's scope was challenging. The archivists and special collections librarians were crucial to the process. They were able to give the rest of the team a sense of what was in their collections so the instructors could create practical and achievable research topics. In the end, our decision came down to what resources were readily available in the archives and special collections, the geographic focus of the projects, and the importance of the topic to our faculty partners.

Recommendation Three: Prioritize students' learning and adjust curriculum as needed, starting with the learning objectives and selecting appropriate methodologies and/or tools that will further these goals. Our faculty partners, for example, wanted students to gain a basic understanding of what GIS was and how it could be applied to historical research. Not every student had to become an expert, but they needed to receive exposure and a foundation to continue learning. Because of time constraints, it would have been unrealistic to expect students to navigate a program like ArcGIS based on one workshop. Instead, the team opted to use the Omeka Neatline plugin because it is more intuitive to use and because it gave the students some exposure to an online mapping application.

Recommendation Four: Be adaptable and prepared to take on expanded roles. In the planning stages, the librarians and faculty recognized this initiative would require expanding the role of librarians in the classroom and even created the Fellow position to support the course. Even with this preparation, the Fellow's role had to expand during the class to accommodate the needs of the students and faculty. For instance, weekly workshops were supposed to comprise the bulk of training on research methods and digital humanities tools. In practice, however, this proved to be insufficient. Many of the students required ongoing training, which required the Fellow to establish extra office hours to help groups and individuals.

We found having these different levels of support helped students feel comfortable approaching the library team. We also learned that having the Fellow present in all components of the course was extremely important. She received the most questions and requests for appointments outside of the instruction sessions and set office hours. These requests were often made in person at other course events, including field trips, movie screenings, and lectures.

Conclusion

Through the library's efforts in this course, we have established a framework to support research and digital scholarship in the undergraduate classroom. Although the team recognizes it cannot support every course with a full-time librarian, it has developed a curriculum and approach to library-faculty collaboration that should enable less time-intensive support in the future. OU Libraries has also continued to expand its digital resource team as a result of this project. The Fellow was converted to a permanent digital scholarship specialist position. This means that OU Libraries can offer more workshops, consultations, and support interdisciplinary courses and research projects. The library's Digital Scholarship Lab, as a result, has seen a significant increase in requests for assistance since participating in the Presidential Dream Course.

Because of our increased staff, visibility, and the success of the course, the library has been invited to participate in undergraduate research courses in other disciplines. For example, in spring 2017, a digital scholarship specialist and the science librarian will be teaching undergraduate students data literacy and curation through active engagement in a Microbial Ecology lab course. Although the subject matter is very different than the Dream Course project, the core tenants of the faculty-librarian partnership remain the same. Without a doubt, the Dream Course mobilized OU Libraries digital resource team in figuring out how to create curriculum that would engage students with digital scholarship tools, like GIS and Omeka, and historical artifacts, which has prepared us to be designers and co-instructors in other undergraduate and graduate research courses.

The success of this project has rejuvenated the value of librarians on our campus as more than information providers. Librarians at OU are now involved in the planning and design of multiple courses that use not only our team's expertise but also our archival resources in new ways made possible by the rapid changes in technology. Since libraries and librarians are often imagined as the neutral commons on many campuses, it makes sense that instructors will turn to us for up-to-date information and the latest in technological and digital evolution. Undoubtedly, librarians will continue to be integrated into courses as instructors re-design and invigorate their curriculum with new tools and literacies. Indeed, our role will continue to evolve from being an embedded librarian to an established co-teacher, who collaboratively infuse digital scholarship approaches into interdisciplinary courses.

Appendix 1A: Excerpt from the Omeka Guide

GUIDE TO OMEKA

This guide was created for students in Making of Modern America: The Great Depression and the New Deal in the Fall of 2015 at the University of Oklahoma. If you see any unfamiliar terms, check the glossary. If you notice any errors, need clarification, or have suggestions for future versions of this guide, please contact me.

TABLE OF CONTENTS

What is Omeka?	2
Omeka Workflow	2
Logging in and Navigating the Dashboard	2
Items	3
Adding an Item	4
Dublin Core	*4*
Item Type Metadata	*13*
Files	*15*
Tags	*15*
Editing an Item	16
Collections	16
Exhibits	17
Exhibit Metadata	17
Pages	17
Text	*17*
File with Text	*17*
Gallery	*18*
Neatline	*18*

WHAT IS OMEKA?

Now, we are ready to start develop the platform for sharing your research. We are using an open-source tool called Omeka to manage and display your research. Omeka is a very versatile content management system (CMS) developed by the Roy Rosenzweig Center for History and New Media at George Mason University.

Omeka has been used by libraries, archives, and academics to manage and display collections. Take a moment to check out some of the projects created using this tool at the Omeka Showcase.

Much of the material in this guide is adapted from Omeka's documentation. Feel free to explore this material as an additional resource. Omeka forums are also a rich source of information.

Note: The best way to become comfortable with Omeka is to use it! You don't have to follow this guide step by step. This is a just to be used as a resource if you get confused or feel overwhelmed. Explore and play with the platform. You will quickly discover how the tool works best for you. Remember that we are hear to help. If you have any questions, don't hesitate to email me.

OMEKA WORKFLOW

Here are the basic steps and tasks you will do in Omeka. The remainder of the guide will go into each step in-depth.

1. Log in to Omeka
2. Add your items and and metadata into Omeka
3. Add items to appropriate collections
4. Create an Omeka Exhibit.

LOGGING IN AND NAVIGATING THE DASHBOARD

Each group will share one set of login credentials. One group member should have received an activation email. If you have not already, activate your account and select a group password.

Now that you account is activated, login into the system.

After logging in you will see your dashboard. This is your base of operations for controlling the content of the website. Take some time to familiarize yourself with the interface. There are two main ways of navigating the site. The main navigation bar is on the left side of the screen. You can also navigate to some of the sections of the dashboard by clicking the numbers on the top center of the page. The numbers are

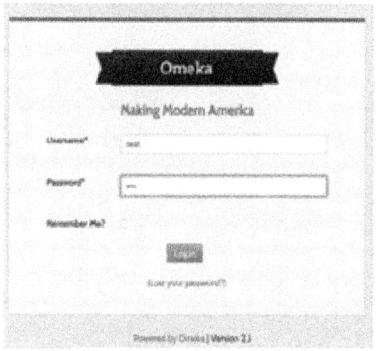

FIGURE 1: LOG IN SCREEN

Using Omeka, Version 1.0
Created by Sarah Clayton
Updated 09.28.2105

12 CHAPTER 1

reflective of all of the content on the Omeka site including other groups' additions.

The homepage will also show you the items and collections that have been edited most recently. These may be items that have other groups have added. You can view other Group's work but will not be able edit it.

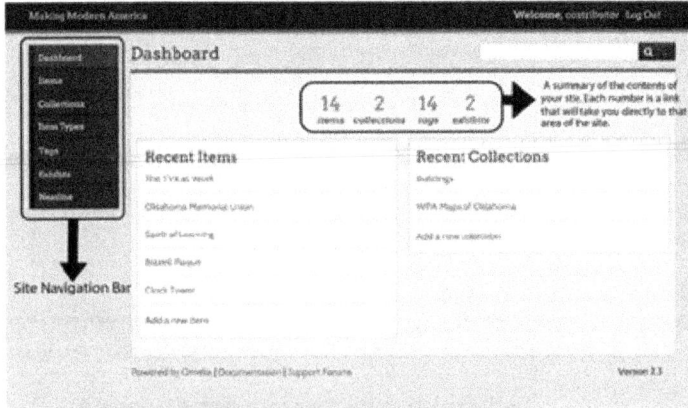

FIGURE 2: NAVIGATING THE DASHBOARD

ITEMS

ITEMS are the building blocks of your Omeka site. An item is any sort of resource you add to Omeka. Items can include images of archival documents, photographs, audio recordings, and videos. You will create collections and exhibits using your items.

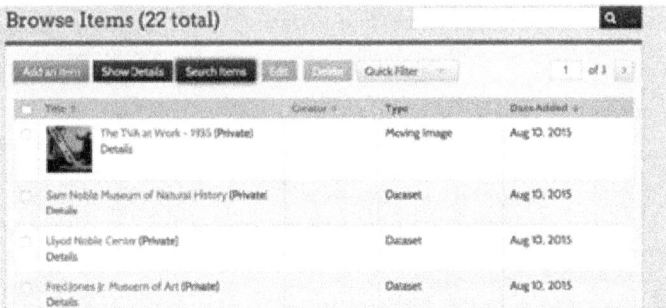

FIGURE 3: ITEMS PAGE

Beyond Embedded Librarianship   13

Click Items on the navigation bar to go to the main items page. Here you will see a list of items have already been added to the site. You will have options to "Add an Item," "Show Details," and "Search Items." The buttons are grayed out until you select an item or group of items (See Figure 3).

Let's begin by adding an item.

ADDING AN ITEM

First, click on the green "Add an Item Button."

This will take you to a screen with four tabs across the top: Dublin Core, Item Type Metadata, Files, and Tags. We will go through each of these tabs one at a time. Three out of four of the tabs relate to metadata or "data about data." Metadata is information about the file. You need this information to make sure that the item you upload is discoverable and identifiable.

For this purpose of this guide, we will add a poster from the Library of Congress's WPA poster collection. We chose this item because the LOC has provided most of the metadata we need and the work is in the public domain. Refer to the LOC page for this poster to see where the information is originating. Feel free to search through their holdings for other resources as well. We will go through the tabs and what information you will need to add an item.

FIGURE 4: WPA POSTER FROM LOC COLLECTIONS

Please note that although there is a lot of text describing how the add an item it is a fairly straight forward process once you understand the meaning behind all of the fields. If you need to stop in the middle of adding an item, you can also click the green Add Item button on the left side of the screen. You can then go back to finish creating the item records using the edit feature, which will be covered below.

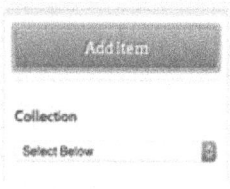

Also below the Add Item button you can select a collection for the item. We will cover collections extensively in the Collections section. You can also go back and add items to collections later so do not worry about it yet unless you already have an appropriate collection created.

FIGURE 5:ADD ITEM BUTTON

DUBLIN CORE

Our first tab is Dublin Core, which is a metadata schema. This means that it is a standardized way to gather and represent metadata. Using the same vocabulary allows different systems to work together and be interoperable. The Digital Public Library of America is a great example of what can be done using a standardized metadata.

Dublin Core was developed to be easy to use and adaptable. For our purposes, we are using Simple Dublin Core, which includes 15 elements, or categories. All 15 categories may not be relevant to your

Using Omeka, Version 1.0
Created by Sarah Clayton
Updated 09.28.2105

14 CHAPTER 1

item. See the descriptions within Omeka for more details on each field. Remember the more information you can provided, the more accessible your item will be to users.

We will now go through each of the elements and how they would apply to our WPA poster. Some of the fields will be extremely clear. Others are more ambiguous and have no clear information. Remember to use your best judgment and try to be as through as possible.

TITLE

The title field seems pretty self-explanatory and normally is so. This is where you enter the title of the resource. However, in practice some of your items may not have a clear title. If there is not an obvious title from looking at the resource, check to see how your source has titled the item. According the Library of Congress, the title for our poster is "A good lunch – one hot dish, meat, vegetables - sandwich –fruit – milk WPA school lunch." Looking at the resource, it is clear how this title was created. If the source has no title listed, you can create one. **You must include a title for every item you upload.**

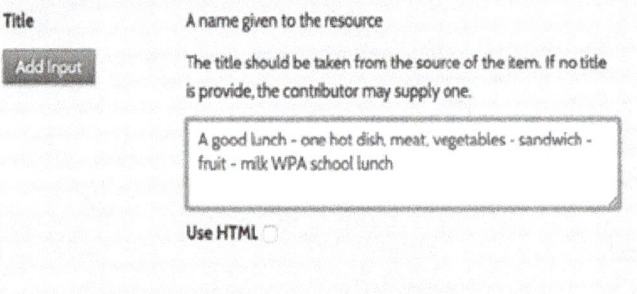

FIGURE 6: DUBLIN CORE: TITLE

SUBJECT

The Subject is the topic of your resource. They are similar to tags, which we will discuss below. **Each item may have multiple subjects.** Each individual subject will need to be input separately. To do this, simply click the green Add Input button and a new text box will appear. When you start typing, some suggestions will auto-populate. These suggestions are being pulled from the Library of Congress subject headings. For our poster, we will use the subject headings included in the LOC (Library of Congress) record. If you do not find a LOC subject term that you like. You can search for subject headings by keywords at the LOC Linked Data Service website. There are several benefits to using a controlled vocabulary. One of the most exciting is that it allows for linked data. Essentially, you can use that subject heading to quickly find related resources. If you are having trouble finding the appropriate LOC subject heading, please let Sarah know and we can determine the most appropriate thing to use.

Appendix 1B: Quantitative Survey Questions

The students were asked to rank their familiarity with the methods and tools on a scale from one to five as well as answer a few qualitative questions.

Please use the 1-5 scale to select the option that best matches your comfort level with the technology or research method.

1 = I have never heard of the technology or research method.
2 = I have heard of technology or research method but never used it.
3 = I have used the technology or research method but am not comfortable with it.
4 = I am comfortable implementing the technology or research method.
5 = I am very comfortable implementing the technology or research method.

#	Statement	1	2	3	4	5
1	Content Management Systems (CMS)	○	○	○	○	○
2	Geographic Information Systems (GIS)	○	○	○	○	○
3	Archival Research	○	○	○	○	○
4	Field Research (observation, data collection, interviews)	○	○	○	○	○
5	Oral Histories	○	○	○	○	○
6	Hyper-text markup language (HTML)	○	○	○	○	○
7	Cascading Style Sheets (CSS)	○	○	○	○	○

Notes

1. The University of Oklahoma Libraries, "The New Horizon for OU Libraries" (2012), https://lib.ou.edu/documents/OU-Libraries-Digital-PDF.pdf.
2. Jeffrey Widener and Travis J. Giledt, "Building Interdisciplinarity into Teaching: A Dream Course on Sustainability and Global Environmental Change," *Resilience: A Journal of the Environmental Humanities* 1, no. 3 (2014), https://muse.jhu.edu/article/569970/.
3. Ibid.
4. Ruth Mostern and Elana Gainor, "Traveling the Silk Road on a Virtual Globe: Pedagogy, Technology and Evaluation for Spatial History," *Digital Humanities Quarterly* 7, no. 2 (2013), http://digitalhumanities.org:8081/dhq/vol/7/2/000116/000116.html.
5. Deena Engel and Marion Thain, "Textual Artifacts and their Digital Representations: Teaching Graduate Students to Build Online Archives," *Digital Humanities Quarterly* 9, no. 1 (2015), http://digitalhumanities.org:8081/dhq/vol/9/1/000199/000199.html.

6. Elizabeth Macaulay-Lewis, "Transforming the Site and Object Reports for a Digital Age: Mentoring Students to Use Digital Technologies in Archaeology and Art History," *Journal of Interactive Technology and Pedagogy* 7 (2015), http://jitp.commons.gc.cuny.edu/transforming-the-site-and-object-reports-for-a-digital-age-mentoring-students-to-use-digital-technologies-in-archaeology-and-art-history/.
7. Jake Carlson and Ruth Kneale, "Embedded Librarians in the Research Context: Navigating New Waters," *College & Research Libraries News* 72, no. 3 (2011): 167–70.
8. Jeffrey A. Knapp, Nicholas J. Rowland, and Eric P. Charles, "Retaining Students by Embedding Librarians into Undergraduate Research Experiences," *Reference Services Review* 42, no. 1 (2014): 136.
9. These guides include Sarah Clayton, Laurie Scrivener, and Jackie Reese, "HIST 3430/PSC 3020—Making Modern America," last modified December 2015, http://guides.ou.edu/newdeal; Jeffery Wilhite, "Great Depression & New Deal Resources from the State of Oklahoma and Federal Government," last modified December 2015, http://guides.ou.edu/c.php?g=305528.
10. The students' projects are available on "Making of Modern America: Discovering the Great Depression and New Deal" (2015), http://newdeal.oucreate.com/.
11. The first survey had 100 percent participation. The final survey had approximately 25 percent participation.
12. "Charles Redd Center for Teaching Western History Award," *Western History Association*, accessed December 2, 2016, http://www.westernhistoryassociation.wildapricot.org/awards/redd.

Bibliography

Carlson, Jake and Ruth Kneale. "Embedded Librarians in the Research Context: Navigating New Waters." *College & Research Libraries News* 72, no. 3 (2011): 167–70.

"Charles Redd Center for Teaching Western History Award." *Western History Association*. Accessed December 2, 2016. http://www.westernhistoryassociation.wildapricot.org/awards/redd.

Clayton, Sarah, Laurie Scrivener, and Jackie Reese. "HIST 3430/PSC 3020—Making Modern America." Last modified December 2015. http://guides.ou.edu/newdeal.

Engel, Deena and Marion Thain. "Textual Artifacts and their Digital Representations: Teaching Graduate Students to Build Online Archives." *Digital Humanities Quarterly* 9, no. 1 (2015). http://digitalhumanities.org:8081/dhq/vol/9/1/000199/000199.html.

Knapp, Jeffrey A., Nicholas J. Rowland, and Eric P. Charles. "Retaining Students by Embedding Librarians into Undergraduate Research Experiences." *Reference Services Review* 42, no. 1 (2014): 129–47.

Macaulay-Lewis, Elizabeth. "Transforming the Site and Object Reports for a Digital Age: Mentoring Students to Use Digital Technologies in Archaeology and Art History." *Journal of Interactive Technology and Pedagogy* 7 (2015). http://jitp.commons.gc.cuny.edu/transforming-the-site-and-object-reports-for-a-digital-age-mentoring-students-to-use-digital-technologies-in-archaeology-and-art-history/.

"Making of Modern America: Discovering the Great Depression and New Deal." (2015). http://newdeal.oucreate.com/.

Mostern, Ruth and Elana Gainor. "Traveling the Silk Road on a Virtual Globe: Pedagogy, Technology and Evaluation for Spatial History." *Digital Humanities Quarterly* 7, no. 2 (2013). http://digitalhumanities.org:8081/dhq/vol/7/2/000116/000116.html.

The University of Oklahoma Libraries. "The New Horizon for OU Libraries." (2012). https://lib.ou.edu/documents/OU-Libraries-Digital-PDF.pdf.

Widener, Jeffrey and Travis J. Giledt. "Building Interdisciplinarity into Teaching: A Dream Course on Sustainability and Global Environmental Change." *Resilience: A Journal of the Environmental Humanities* 1, no. 3 (2014). https://muse.jhu.edu/article/569970/.

Wilhite, Jeffery. "Great Depression & New Deal Resources from the State of Oklahoma and Federal Government." Last modified December 2015. http://guides.ou.edu/c.php?g=305528.

CHAPTER 2 *

The Cooperation of Many Minds:
Cultivating the Undergraduate Researcher in the Humanities and Social Sciences through Team-Based Curricular Design[1]

Susette Newberry

Introduction

Cornell University's Undergraduate Research Institute harnessed the collective instructional expertise of librarians, archivists, museum curators, writing program instructors, scholarship program administrators, and faculty mentors to design a three-credit research methods course. Now an established seminar for undergraduates, it is intended for freshman or sophomores either already committed to or anticipating undertaking independent research in the humanities and social sciences. The course's central goal is to prepare students as scholars. As well-prepared researchers, students can produce substantive scholarship, contribute meaningfully to research assistantships and projects, and take advantage of locally and externally funded grant and fellowship opportunities.

---

* This work is licensed under a Creative Commons Attribution-NonCommercial 4.0 License, CC BY-NC (https://creativecommons.org/licenses/by-nc/4.0/).

This case study describes the planning and administration of a course designed to produce ambitious, independent scholars at a competitive ARL institution.

Background

Cornell University is a both a privately endowed research university and New York State's federal land-grant institution. With fourteen colleges and schools, more than 14,000 undergraduates, and more than 480 library employees, it is a large institution. Olin and Uris Libraries, two of the eighteen libraries on the Ithaca, New York, campus, are the largest humanities and social sciences libraries, and house the department of Research and Learning Services, which supports reference, instruction, collection development, and outreach to its patrons across campus and beyond, and offers the course described in this chapter.

While undergraduates in STEM disciplines have numerous opportunities to engage in research, students interested in conducting research outside of the classroom in the arts, humanities, and social sciences have fewer options. Cornell University's senior vice provost for undergraduate education and the director of undergraduate research worked with the library to recruit partners from a range of academic support services to encourage undergraduates to participate in humanities and social science-based research. Offering diverse expertise, the resulting team developed the Undergraduate Research Institute, a seminar that gives aspiring scholars the research and practical skills to undertake independent research.

The course is co-taught by two librarians and includes guest lectures and numerous opportunities for students to interact with a range of research mentors, including research librarians and faculty members.[2] As one might expect, it teaches basic and specialized research through engagement with a variety of materials and formats, such as archival photographs, images, manuscripts, social media, ethnographic studies, and statistical sources. In grooming research scholars, the course also introduces students to skills not generally taught in most curricula: how to interact and build relationships with research specialists; how to find funding; where to look for presentation opportunities on and off-campus; and how to design effective presentations, create visualizations, and control the online scholarly persona.

For the librarians who participated by designing individual class sessions and assignments, ACRL's Institute for Information Literacy had been heavily influential. In 2012, the Institute developed a special version of the Immersion Program for Cornell instruction librarians.[3] This significant experience encouraged the planning team to place greater emphasis on active- and peer-learning exercises and especially on assessing student learning.

Partnerships

The Cornell Office of Undergraduate Research encourages students to take an active role in enhancing their learning experience through research, which it specifically defines as a holistic practice that happens outside the classroom.[4] With no apparent lab space, incoming students often find it difficult to find a clear definition, let alone opportunity, for research in the humanities and social sciences. The course is designed for special programs that require independent research outside the laboratory—College Scholars, Presidential Scholars, Office of Academic Diversity Initiatives Scholars, McNair Scholars—all of which include very high-achieving, highly motivated students, and helps prepare students who aim for competitive scholarships, such as the Mellon Mays Undergraduate Fellowship Program. Many plan to attend graduate school.[5]

Realizing the extent to which this kind of instruction involves a number of skills not offered in standard curricula, the course design partnership concentrated on building a course independent from academic department boundaries. The individuals on the planning team included experts in teaching research skills and others able to expose students to the range of opportunities and collections available on a large campus, especially in connecting students with potential mentors. Special scholarship administrators were important partners in designing the course; they identified the challenges students faced in keeping up with research requirements for the programs from which the course would recruit.[6] An experienced writing instructor offered numerous ideas for assignment design, including the all-important research proposal workshop. Other team members were the director of undergraduate research, who developed a session on networking strategies and conceived the popular "speed networking" class, when small groups of students chat with faculty for a series of ten-minute bursts. The Herbert F. Johnson Museum of Art's curator of education designed an introduction to using visual primary sources, and an instruction specialist from the Division of Rare and Manuscript Collections developed a primary source investigation using artifacts, manuscripts, and archival photographs. The senior vice provost for undergraduate research, herself a distinguished professor of English Literature, took an active role in recruiting faculty mentors and underscored for them the value of encouraging young scholars.

This large team brought substantial energy and enthusiasm to the planning process in addition to an enormous number of potential directions and subjects to cover. While it was not possible to include all contributions in the syllabus, shared dedication and vision for the course made it a deeply satisfying process for team members. Indeed, writing the course outcomes (fig. 1) was an almost automatic process.

Figure 2.1
COURSE LEARNING OUTCOMES
- Develop effective search strategies and skills in order to identify and locate appropriate sources for articulating research topics.
- Assess and evaluate information sources, including unpublished primary sources, in order to determine their relevance and value for individual, targeted research needs.
- Analyze a variety of information sources, such as images, material culture, and architecture, in order to expand concepts of research materials.
- Synthesize and integrate information source material in order to demonstrate the ability to prepare clear research proposals.
- Present a plan for an independent research project in the arts, humanities, or interpretive social sciences in order to demonstrate the ability to accomplish sophisticated, well-formulated research.

Since the library is not a recognized university department, the course is offered through Cornell's Knight Institute for Writing in the Disciplines, a multi-disciplinary unit that supports writing seminars and writing-intensive courses. While it is not in fact a writing course, it is taught in the library by two librarians who manage and grade the course, are its primary instructors, and attend all class sessions. After the initial four weeks of intensive research instruction, a range of guest lecturers visit the course for sessions and workshops, or students meet individually or through field trips with curators, faculty members, writing instructors, research librarians, peer researchers, and scholarship program administrators. Each student is paired with a faculty member *and* a subject specialist librarian, which not only helps students interrogate their research content more closely, it teaches them to interact outside the classroom with members of the academic community and to position themselves as emerging scholars.

Students select their own research topics so they can pursue their passions and ideas. Topics have ranged from the development of post-traumatic stress disorder in female inmates to a comparison of Hausmannian urban modernization in Paris and Cairo. Students use their topics to explore and develop research skills, usually with the goal of continuing the work independently after the semester ends. Many are enrolled in scholarship programs that extend over several years, sometimes throughout their undergraduate experience.

Information literacy is intentionally a central part of this course, not just because it is an area of librarian expertise and a centerpiece of the Cornell University Library's strategic goals document;[7] it is also explicitly included

among the University's strategic goals.[8] The course similarly focuses on other core competencies—critical thinking, communication skills, self-directed learning, and in engaging students in the process of discovering and creating new meaning. Instruction topics are scaffolded to provide general skills first before specialized research techniques are introduced:
- The research process: conceptualizing, planning, approaching topics
- Literature review: finding, evaluating, and organizing scholarship
- Specialized research techniques (finding news, open source literature, statistical sources, archival materials, ethnographic research)
- Presenting the academic self and sharing research

The research happens outside the class—delving into archival collections, examining art or artifacts, mining print and electronic materials, and reading. Students interact with faculty members to discuss their ideas, related scholarship, the validity of developing arguments, and to consider alternative approaches. During research consultations, subject specialist librarians or archivists introduce tactics for using critical databases, subject-specific research materials, and important journals, and discuss access challenges. Each student prepares a research portfolio during the course of the semester, including an extended annotated bibliography, research proposal, and final presentation. The course culminates with a formal forum during which students share their research, not through a formal written paper but in a focused, ten-minute presentation. Attended by classmates and all the members of the community involved in designing and offering the course, the research forum is the highlight of the semester. Students propose plans for future avenues of inquiry, offering ideal scenarios that might involve travel to distant repositories, fieldwork, or complex ethnographic studies. Most of all, however, they position themselves as scholars and demonstrate their ability, based on their work throughout the semester, to enter into the scholarly argument surrounding their topics.[9]

Reflection

Among the most significant benefits of this course has been the building of strong connections with academic support units across campus and with individual faculty members. At a large, yet decentralized university, these relationships have been crucial in establishing and maintaining an academic program existing outside the traditional orbit of academic departments. One of the strongest bonds has been with the Office of Academic Diversity Initiatives (OADI), a unit that was established during the planning stages for the course. The OADI staff developed a robust Research Scholars Program (ORSP) that recruited students in the humanities and social sciences and required a for-credit research course, strongly recommending the library's course and profiling research projects from the course on its website and in its own research poster forums. Librarians have since participated in ORSP's extracurricular instruction as workshop leaders, by holding regular on-site office hours, and the course instructors serve as members of its advisory board. OSRP's chief administrator (a member of the course design team) was hired for a distinguished position at another institution, where she convinced archivists to develop a library-based course founded on similar concepts.

The administration of the course is intensive and requires a significant time commitment from the librarian instructors in addition to the time spent on planning assessments, individual units, grading, and meeting with students. Since there are so many individuals involved beyond the two main instructors, it can be a challenge to convey course objectives to and communicate with all guest lecturers and mentors so that they don't overlap course content. Similarly, monitoring student activity outside the classroom, such as appointments with faculty and progress in response to those meetings, is not always a straightforward process. A small class size (twelve or fewer) is therefore ideal for this necessarily high-touch approach.

Assessment

During its pilot semester, Cornell University Library's Department of Research and Assessment helped the course design team develop several assessment tools for the class. During the first year, they administered a survey before and after the course to determine basic skills associated with citation literacy, terminology, and bibliographic awareness, to assure that students had actually gained and retained these skills.[10]

Instructors measure student progress through assignments and in-class assessments. Students are asked to pause at the end of the semester to write a reflection of their own learning and to consider which research tools or techniques have had the greatest impact on their growth as scholars within and outside of the course's immediate requirements. They have made observations, such as, "This class opened my eyes to a whole world of possibilities." Most, however, have remarked on the confidence it gives them to move forward independently. Students also frequently note the new perspectives the course has given them on working with faculty members: "I think we are a little intimidated by professors, but being able to see that they are just regular people really helps us to not be afraid to approach them and bravely pitch our ideas." "Talking to my faculty mentor gave me a chance to get excited about my project; to have a Cornell professor approve of my topic made me confident that my project was important and something that hadn't been researched before." Individuals' progress toward their own long-range research, education, and career goals is informally tracked by members of the course design team; scholarship administrators in particular keep in close touch with students throughout their undergraduate careers.

Each year, adjustments have been made to the course content and assignment sequences based on student successes and challenges. Examples of modifications include: eliminating an assignment for an abstract and opting instead to focus more time on refining research proposals; creating a detailed annotated bibliography rubric with an associated peer review workshop; and designing a separate annotation assignment for archival, rare, and visual materials.

Recommendations/Best Practices

Although the investment of staff time in the planning process is intensive, the Undergraduate Research Institute also relies heavily on learning modules that have been used for other class sessions and in workshops, and encourages the development of transferable instruction units. It harvests knowledge, and takes advantage of a wide spectrum of experience and perspectives.

In reflecting on the process of designing and producing the course, collaboration naturally stands out as the most essential factor in assuring its success throughout its development phases. Involving course design partners in the assessment process, particularly in the final presentations and review discussions, encourages a continued interest in contributing to the curriculum and recruiting students for the course. In one particular example, a student who entered the course with vague interests and unsure of his own abilities gained substantial confidence and skills during the semester, was accepted into the Mellon Mays program, and gave a brilliant final presentation. His performance was so memorable that administrators in attendance pointed to his experience and achievements to recruit other potential students.

This course has brought faculty into a different kind of contact with library staff in which librarians are the main instructors and faculty are consultants. As expected, it has demonstrated the value of library-faculty collaboration and librarian research and teaching expertise. But the close and sustained interaction has also allowed librarians to better understand how both students and faculty approach research. It has revealed that faculty routinely presume both that students know more about the mechanics of academic publishing than they actually do and that students have acquired a disciplined approach to research before they have left high school.[11] In one instance, a faculty mentor and student emerged from their initial meeting with diverging concepts about how the student was launching into his early semester research ideas. In a follow-up discussion with the student, instructors discovered that he had misidentified a key source as a formal research study when it was in fact a working paper. Ordinarily a minor error easily corrected, the student's intelligence and original ideas convinced the faculty mentor the student knew more than he actually did, causing their discussion about the key source in question to misfire. In point of fact, students entering the class have been able to reach remarkable levels of achievement, many without having to consciously learn a process for conducting research. Although ready to accept the challenge of learning research methods, their previous successes in discovering information sources have frequently resulted in workarounds that are unsustainable, although they do not usually recognize them as such. Threshold concept theory can thus be especially powerful and intellectually compelling to challenge entrenched habits. "Open Access Publishing," for example, is a transformative lesson; when students engage with open access issues in their disciplines, they more fully understand the cycle of scholarly publishing and the significance of "closed access," licensed resources. Once students evaluate open access documents, they appreciate how publications may or may not have been subject to peer review, and gain a deeper understanding of how research literature is structured. When faculty have seen these transformative lessons, they have recognized and valued how librarians can identify omissions in research preparedness. Together, they form a strong partnership in developing information-literate scholars.

Conclusion

The Cornell Undergraduate Research Institute situates the library at the core of university-wide humanities and social sciences undergraduate research initiatives and demonstrates the library's central role in growing scholars. This course is an effective model for taking advantage of diverse expertise to produce a rich learning experience that extends well beyond the bounds of the library. It has built meaningful collaborations with faculty and academic support units through facilitating mentorships, teaches students to engage critically with research strategies, and produces well-rounded, information-literate scholars.

Notes

1. The title quotes Alexander Graham Bell: "I feel, however, a little embarrassed in taking credit myself for all the great work that has been accomplished… involving the cooperation of many minds. I may perhaps take the credit of blazing the trail for the others who have come after, but… I feel the great credit for the develop-

ments is due to others rather than to myself." Alexander Graham Bell, "Speech Accepting the Civic Forum Medal of Honor for Distinguished Public Service," (March 21, 1917), transcribed in *The Telephone Review* 8, no. 5 (May 1917): 132.
2. Librarians who have co-taught this course include the author, Susette Newberry, PhD, *head of Research and Learning Services, Olin & Uris Libraries* (2013-2016); Kaila Bussert, now *foundational experiences librarian*, Cal Poly, San Luis Obispo (2014); Gabriela Castro Gessner, PhD, *research and assessment analyst* (2015); and Michael Engle, *reference selector* (2016).
3. Three ACRL faculty (Deb Gilchrist, Lisa Hinchliffe, and Beth Woodard) developed a 3.5 day workshop, which they brought to Cornell's Ithaca campus as this course was being conceptualized.
4. "Undergraduate research is an enriching process by which you meet people, gain skills, and become an active member of the university community." Cornell University Office of Undergraduate Research, "About Research," accessed September 8, 2016, http://undergraduateresearch.cornell.edu/about-research/why-perform-research-at-cornell/.
5. The national Mellon Mays Undergraduate Fellows (MMUF) Program encourages undergraduates from underrepresented minority groups to pursue PhDs. "The fundamental objective of MMUF is to address, over time, the problem of underrepresentation in the academy at the level of college and university facultites." Mellon Mays Undergraduate Fellowship Program, *Web site home page*, accessed September 9, 2016, http://www.mmuf.org/.
6. Programs included the Office of Academic Diversity Initiatives (which was simultaneously developing a new scholarship program to encourage underrepresented students to engage more actively in the social sciences and humanities) and the Rawlings Cornell Presidential Research Scholars Program (an exclusive program that admits about fifty out of an incoming class of approximately 3,300).
7. Cornell University Library, *Toward 2015: Cornell University Library Strategic Plan, 2011-2015* (2011), https://www.library.cornell.edu/sites/default/files/CUL_Strategic_Plan_2011-2015(re-numbered)_1.pdf.
8. Cornell University has designated information literacy a core academic competency for all students. Cornell University, "Section III: The Institution and its Environment. Student Competencies in a Changing World," *The Cornell University Strategic Plan, 2010–2015*, accessed September 9, 2016, https://www.cornell.edu/strategicplan/institution.cfm.
9. For example: Students also make decisions about how they are represented as members of the academic community. One of the topics covered in the course is Open Access—how to find and identify different forms of open access documents, understanding open access issues in publishing, and abiding by copyright law. Members of one class were asked to decide for themselves whether or not to archive their research presentations in Cornell's institutional repository. The majority of the class declined, not feeling comfortable with its open access requirements. Several believed their use of images fell within the bounds of fair use, but would infringe on copyright regulations. Others simply wanted to protect their ideas for future development. Although they were encouraged to publish their work, it must be said that in envisioning the life their own work would have in the scholarly commons as well as their future intellectual products, those students demonstrated a developed self-awareness in opting to keep private the early versions of their ideas.

10. While this survey is now administered every year before the start of the course to determine baseline skills and knowledge, the course design team concluded that the assignments completed during the course adequately determine students' ability to master the skills that the test monitors. The pre- and post-assessment surveys were developed by *research and assessment analyst* Gabriela Castro Gessner, PhD, and *outreach and public services librarian* Lance Heidig, both of whom were also members of the course design team. Gabriela Castro Gessner later became one of the course co-instructors and Lance Heidig leads the rare book and archival materials interaction session in the Division of Rare and Manuscript Collections.
11. The instructors have observed that faculty generally approach published research literature with a firm foundation in print-based forms of scholarly communication, which often leads them to expect students to participate in research in ways for which students may not have been prepared. Skills once ubiquitous in U. S. high school curricula, such as note taking, simple research practices, even citation construction, are now rarely taught.

Bibliography

Bell, Alexander Graham. "Speech Accepting the Civic Forum Medal of Honor for Distinguished Public Service." (March 21, 1917), transcribed in *The Telephone Review* 8, no. 5 (May 1917): 132.

Cornell University. "Section III: The Institution and its Environment. Student Competencies in a Changing World." *The Cornell University Strategic Plan, 2010–2015.* Accessed September 9, 2016. https://www.cornell.edu/strategicplan/institution.cfm.

Cornell University Library. *Toward 2015: Cornell University Library Strategic Plan, 2011–2015,* 2011. https://www.library.cornell.edu/sites/default/files/CUL_Strategic_Plan_2011-2015(re numbered)_1.pdf.

Cornell University Office of Undergraduate Research. "About Research." Accessed September 8, 2016. http://undergraduateresearch.cornell.edu/about-research/why-perform-research-at-cornell/.

Mellon Mays Undergraduate Fellowship Program. *MMUF Web site home page.* Accessed September 9, 2016. http://www.mmuf.org/.

CHAPTER 3 *
A Triumph, a Fail, and a Question:
A Pilot Approach to Student-Faculty-Librarian Research Collaboration

Missy Roser and Sara Smith

Introduction

In 2010, Amherst College received a two-year planning grant, followed by a multiyear implementation grant, from the Andrew W. Mellon Foundation for faculty to develop a set of seminars in the humanities and social sciences. The idea was to introduce sophomores and juniors to approaches to research as a process: how to frame a researchable question, develop investigative strategies, and identify and use sources. The seminars would help students engage with topics that intersect with the scholarly interests of a faculty mentor, potentially leading to a senior thesis—a model more commonly seen in the lab sciences. The Mellon pilot eventually included the following elements:
- Four to eight research seminars each spring semester, capped at six students

---

* This work is licensed under a Creative Commons Attribution-NonCommercial-ShareAlike 4.0 License, CC BY-NC-SA (https://creativecommons.org/licenses/by-nc-sa/4.0/).

- Courses built around or directly contributing to a faculty member's own research, ideally resulting in collaborative faculty-student publication, exhibition, or presentation
- A subject librarian affiliated with each seminar, participating at varying levels, from on-call to fully embedded
- Access to other instructional staff, including project collaboration with Academic Technology Services professionals or museum curators
- A voluntary six- to eight-week summer research fellowship component for participating seminar students

Forty courses have now been offered in areas, including material culture in art history, urban planning and educational opportunity, interdisciplinary explorations of sensory systems, the world of the King James Bible, performance culture at the turn of the century, and archives of childhood. Over six years, fifteen faculty members, 229 students, and seven librarians have been involved in the seminars. Nineteen students have co-published with a faculty member in a peer-reviewed journal, seven books and ten journal articles have incorporated contributions from student researchers, and six exhibitions have been mounted in the college's library and museum.[1] Supporting this extended pilot project has encouraged librarians to stretch our ideal forms of teaching research dispositions and scaffolding undergraduate research.

Librarians working with the Mellon seminars are involved with a wide variety of activities: traditional instruction sessions on how to develop a research prospectus or using a bibliographic-management tool like Zotero, consulting on course design or digital-scholarship pedagogy, serving as interlocutors for proposal workshopping, or teaching weekly "research lab" sessions to complement course content. Our roles particularly evolved to support the initiative during the summer, when students stay on campus to continue intensive work on their projects. This opportunity came at a moment of real transition for the institution—which was in the midst of a wave of faculty retirements and hiring—and the library. A new library director had just arrived, the entire Research & Instruction department turned over during the course of the project, due to retirements and promotions, and, as a result of increasing demand for our work with undergraduate research, we were able to add two additional teaching-librarian positions that also addressed such identified needs as outreach and user experience. The shifts in our priorities and identity seem to echo the debates and direction of instruction librarians in the profession more broadly over the same period.

Background

The original grant proposed experimental seminars as a way to expand the student research program beyond thesis work and a longstanding summer-science program by developing "activities that help us (1) enhance student understanding of how research questions are developed and pursued—and how they connect to the "big questions" underlying the liberal arts, (2) better prepare students for successful thesis projects in the humanities and social sciences, and (3) foster a climate of intellectual excitement and engagement that pervades both the classroom and daily life at Amherst." Library instruction at Amherst, a selective residential liberal-arts college with 1,800 undergraduates and an open curriculum, is already very context-specific. Many departments offer research-methods courses for majors, usually with librarian support. But while 41 percent of seniors complete an honors thesis, survey data several years ago revealed that the experience could be isolating and fragmented. We saw potential in the Mellon grant to lay more explicit groundwork for non-STEM students embarking on independent work.

First, we had to articulate our role in the project. The grant had been awarded before any of the current Research & Instruction librarians were hired, and the library hadn't even been referenced in the original application. The faculty principal investigator declared in an initial meeting that he didn't want any of "that database stuff." Instead, he sought proposals and input from librarians regarding the forms that collaboration could take, urging us to think creatively to reinvent the library's relationship to faculty and curriculum. Our instincts were to build on previous course-integrated instruction and thesis consultations as well as to think about opportunities for embedding instruction, like those discussed by Dewey and by Smith & Sutton.[2]

We initially assigned the liaison librarian for the faculty member's home department to each seminar, and their involvement that first semester indicated a range of possible activity. One seminar had only informal consultation with their librarian. Another, in classics, had two sessions with the librarian to introduce research tools in that discipline. The seminar on education and history included a session on Zotero and organizing research, as well as a class covering resources very specific to their project, including government documents and newly acquired microfilm. The last seminar had the closest collaboration, with a librarian teaching five sessions that were heavily integrated with the content of the course, each breaking down a type of evidence that could be used to investigate a potential research question in law and culture. The distribution was similar across eight seminars the following year: two courses had only a session or two with their librarians to cover bibliographic management and basic research; two others, in art history and religion, had librarians teach two to three sessions focused on disciplinary approaches to research and following citations; and four of the courses had quasi–embedded librarians supporting their learning as they took on projects heavily based in archival or special collections in alternative newspapers, history of the early-modern book, nineteenth-century children's literature, or missionary papers from Turkey.

Because many seminars were interdisciplinary, we later went beyond liaison assignments to match seminars to librarians whose capabilities and interests closely aligned with a particular topic or mode of inquiry. As the program developed, skills such as data management and coding transcripts were integrated into research-team instruction, as were technology concepts like card-sorting and wireframing for web design. One other reference point in the first years was the University of Adelaide's Research Skills Development Framework, which helped us to describe a "research pedagogy" and distinguish the bounded-research approach we taught in regular instruction sessions from the kind of scaffolded to open-ended research characteristic of the Mellon seminars.[3] Librarians taught skills early on to help students practice asking researchable questions, discover and evaluate information, and synthesize findings. As they developed proposals at the end of the semester and moved into more independent research in the summer, goals shifted to supporting student-initiated inquiry and coaching teams through testing schemas and refining their own methodologies.

Partnerships

As the program continued, librarians played an increasingly connected role. Our department head attended working-group meetings, individual librarians took on key responsibilities in the seminars and in project management, and summer involvement and facilitation expanded. We explored how we could more fully partner with faculty, pairing their deep disciplinary understanding with our focus on the research process to address each seminar's subject area and intended outcomes. Faculty, realizing this, appreciated spending less time on nuts-and-bolts mechanics and more time on higher-level concepts. This model allowed for contextual application of big-picture process issues—a more nuanced version of the specificity we had been bringing to workshops and one-shot instruction sessions.

While not every seminar made use of its liaison librarian in an embedded sense, several things made for a very different experience of offering research support: early conversations with a faculty member, familiarity with an entire syllabus (including often doing all the course readings), getting an advance look at assignments, and regular check-ins with the course. In many cases, the librarian would suggest places of convergence during the semester where a hands-on instruction session might make sense with the content planned for that week, e.g., exploring the history of polling in newspapers in relation to public support for the death penalty, or tracing the underlying research for a popular account of the Silk Road by connecting examples to the book's bibliography. In several other courses, faculty came to increasingly value an "unsyllabus" at times, where the messiness and uncertainty of developing a research question or proposal focus would benefit from building flexibility into planning.

Eighty-nine students over the past four years have stayed after the completion of the semester to continue their work with faculty, and the library is now a hub of summer research activity. Most Mellon seminar teams set up camp in the library—with librarians continuing to act as on-call coaches—and Research & Instruction librarians convene weekly Research Table meetings for students to share progress, ask questions, and learn from peers. We've established a spinoff Thesis Research Table and broadened our workshop offerings and community-building events to better serve the needs of student researchers over these months while faculty are often not on campus. We've also inaugurated an annual daylong showcase of undergraduate research and creative work in the spring, in partnership with the Writing Center, Center for Community Engagement, and Academic Technology. The event is held in the library and current and past Mellon students are well represented.

Reflection

There have been ripple effects from the Mellon initiative in nearly every aspect of our work as Research and Instruction librarians. Our approach has led to a broadening of the research skills and methods we teach, a greater focus on transferable aspects of learning to do research, and improved relationships with teaching faculty. There has been increased collaboration with non-Mellon faculty as word has spread, and we have seen more student-to-student referrals as well. Student evaluations described greater understanding of how to develop researchable questions, analyze research methodologies, and evaluate the relevance of sources. Our extended engagement with the motivated students in these disciplinary seminars also led to more interaction with many of them as they subsequently became thesis writers in the same departments.

The research undertaken by students in the Mellon seminars involved a sustained project that was longer than a final course paper but shorter than an honors thesis. The highly situational orientation of the research in these seminars prepared students for thesis research in a new way, revealing the benefits of a longer timeframe for a research experience, especially for transfer or less-prepared students. For librarians, this also meant being more deliberate about the affective and metacognitive elements of research instruction, particularly using the summer to introduce often-tacit aspects of research and peer learning (and to encourage students to explore and report back on off-campus experiences, as well).[4] When asked about tangible skills they took away from summer Research Tables, students described learning how to build in time for reflection and understanding the emotional ups and downs involved. Our work with these students in particular led us to incorporate more aspects of team-based research—including an awareness of the stages of successful team formation and project management—and how to teach communication skills to support it, for students' dual roles as peer colleagues and working with a faculty lead investigator. For us, this not only applies to classroom instruction but also extends to building community, increasing librarian visibility, and connecting to other instructional staff on campus, such as the writing center and academic technology.

Some of the successes of this project have been accompanied by challenges. We continue to wrestle with practical questions that have arisen regarding fuzzy boundaries when we're not the instructor of record, as well as pedagogical questions of how best to integrate subject content with information-literacy concepts, as Bowler and Street found.[5] The sustainability and scaling of an embedded model is also a perpetual concern. Although the work has been incredibly satisfying for librarians involved, it has led to an expanded workload in summer, taken more time to be truly and effectively embedded in these courses, and meant disproportionate attention to some disciplinary research practices over others in a situation where each librarian works with multiple academic departments.

Expressly designating these seminars as experimental has helped emphasize an iterative and developmental approach to research, encouraging students to try out new ideas (a potentially vulnerable but generative space not always common to the Amherst experience). We have had success working with faculty to "unstuff" syllabi in order to create more time and space to focus on process, and we now regularly collaborate on rethinking course outcomes. There is, of course, the potential to make this program stronger. Attending every class session doesn't necessarily ensure collaboration between faculty and librarians, and we have begun to develop strategies to address this concern. In one seminar last spring, instead of having the librarian join the course four times over the semester, the faculty member asked her to hold weekly "research lab" sessions to provide more in-depth, hands-on instruction that built to the students' collaborative research proposals. While an excellent opportunity, this format needs some revision for better integration: the labs lost the symbolic value of being in the same classroom with the professor, though their worth was evident when the students needed much less time to get up to speed for summer research.

Assessment

In addition to their regular course evaluations, students generally filled out separate evaluations for their faculty about how Mellon seminars differed from other courses. While librarians didn't see most of those, we did talk with faculty individually and in the planning group about changes to larger structural issues as well as specific session topics. We spearheaded a concerted focus on building a research community in the summer, which in turn led to more awareness of the increasing number of students doing independent work and a resulting task force convened by the dean of faculty's office to better coordinate summer opportunities for students. Because of the relationships we developed with students, we got quite a bit of informal feedback. The library sponsored an information session each fall to promote the Mellon seminars to other students before course pre-registration, and these participant panels were very helpful for candid reports of how the previous seminars and summer research had gone.

Most valuable for formative assessment, though, were the weekly summer Research Tables, which were positioned at the point of need. We structured these sessions by asking teams to report on "a triumph, a fail, and a question" of the past week; besides facilitating peer learning, it allowed us to address unanticipated gaps and build essential concepts into the next version of the course. Many of these gaps involved research practices with concrete aspects—naming conventions for shared files, choosing coding software, finding CVs for scholars in a particular subfield, using the *U.S. Newspaper Directory* to identify what was missing from digitized coverage—that were situated in a larger social context of academic and research culture that we could unpack together and make more transparent for students.

What we heard overwhelmingly from students in evaluations and in person was that they became more critical readers, with much more attention given to how research is created or a claim is made—that the process was revealed and permission granted to "look under the hood" of arguments made by even senior scholars in a field. This experience also modeled pathways for how they might go about starting to research specific questions. Despite increased autonomy and self-direction in Mellon seminars, students told us that it was less intimidating than expected, that "this isn't just learning about something but doing it." While we hadn't been familiar with Indiana University's Decoding the Disciplines project at the outset of our experience, this collaborative approach to demystify how an expert would go about a disciplinary task was very consonant with our objective to make the research process more explicit.[6]

One of the original goals for the grant was to connect students to potential thesis topics earlier in their undergraduate careers, and this has indeed been the case. While not every student developed Mellon research into thesis projects, quite a few continued in related areas, and many continued to make use of librarians as their "research coaches" through graduation. Initial analysis by our Institutional Research office shows that a much higher percentage of Mellon seminar students go on to complete a thesis: 68 percent overall, with increases from 10–37 percentage points for students of color, first-generation, and low-income students compared to non-Mellon students. Self-selection for the seminars is likely one factor, but the nature of these courses means that these students have previous experience with advanced research and with working closely with faculty and librarians.

Several academic departments have embraced the summer Thesis Research Table model of sustained support for their thesis cohorts, asking liaison librarians and writing associates to lead monthly meetings for them through the academic year, often with a rotating faculty partner. Feedback from students has guided discussion topics, with an augmented focus on scholarly communication and open access to be added this year to help bridge the transition from consumer to producer of information. In addition, the college's strategic plan recommended investigating half-credit courses, possibly taught by instructional staff, which could build on this departmental model or the weekly research labs in conjunction with the semester-long seminars.

Recommendations/Best Practices

Throughout the Mellon project, we've worked with faculty to articulate how this research seminar will be different from other courses in order to design the learning experience accordingly. The project's coordinating working group—with a librarian at the table with faculty—helped surface these issues; it also was the most effective mechanism to raise awareness among faculty about ways to define and incorporate the librarian role. For the librarians, we've had to be prepared to go beyond our comfort zones in terms of discussing course content, observing and deconstructing for students the research approaches of faculty members and their larger disciplinary or interdisciplinary communities, and thinking on our feet to solve problems that emerge. We did "translation" work to scaffold and interpret research processes in the archives, the GIS lab, art museums, the Folger Shakespeare Library, and other settings through give and take with the faculty instructors, librarians, and students. This immersive alignment with faculty research process has given us a deeper understanding of methodologies and practices in particular fields, which has also been very rewarding for our own intellectual engagement in our work.

These contexts and outcomes lent themselves organically to bigger-picture thinking. As the ACRL *Framework for Information Literacy for Higher Education* drafts and final version emerged over the same period, its focus on threshold concepts, dispositions, metacognition, and affective aspects of learning to do research resonated with our experience in these intensive settings.[7] It also prompted us to think about alternative research products, such as digital-scholarship projects, archival exhibitions, Wikipedia articles, or website development. Organizationally, the Mellon project helped us as a department in this time of transition to think about how to prioritize and scale our teaching, as well as about the nature of collaboration with faculty on research and acknowledgment of librarian work. As faculty considered the question of how to credit undergrads for contributions to their scholarship in the humanities and social sciences, they also came to us with questions about how to credit embedded librarians for their role in teaching or research support at an institution where librarians don't have faculty rank or tenure. Being able to draw on this experience was also crucial for librarian involvement in strategic planning around the integration of research and teaching, as well as on the committee examining potential changes to the college's curriculum.

In reflecting on the Mellon project as a whole, we identify several important elements of the experience:

1. Bringing our teaching identities into classrooms in a much more overt way, to where faculty have asked for librarians to co-teach or have considered fully collaborating on future research projects or seminars; this in turn creates increased awareness of the need for our expertise in teaching research-specific approaches for students.
2. The need for time to think through and continually revisit pedagogy for teaching the messiness of research and all it entails, including the need to negotiate conceptual space for this work in research seminars within majors modeled on the Mellon seminars. A larger question remains for how to scale this perspective for shorter engagements.
3. The ongoing balance between creating structure (including designing instruction and planning specific sessions) and thinking on our feet, which incorporates many other aspects of our personalities and scholarly/teaching/librarian identities—particularly in working with multiple cohorts over subsequent years.

Conclusion

The Mellon pilot project gave us the incentive and space to implement new ideas for teaching the research process. We drew on the new *Framework* to further make sense of our own practice and make connections across outcomes and skills that might have seemed to fall outside library instruction previously. Most important, we were able to develop relationships with students and build trust with faculty as they took risks of their own.

Notes

1. Examples include Austin Sarat, with Katherine Blumstein '13, Aubrey Jones '13, Heather Richard '13, and Madeline Sprung-Keyser '13, *Gruesome Spectacles: Botched Executions and America's Death Penalty* (Stanford, CA: Stanford University Press, 2014); Hilary Moss, Yinan Zhang '12, and Andy Anderson, "Assessing the Impact of the Inner Belt: MIT, Highways, and Housing in Cambridge, Massachusetts," *Journal Of Urban History* 40, no. 6 (2014): 1054–078; Caitlin Britos '14, James Hall '15, Soo Kim '14, Daniel Schulwolf '14, *Karl Loewenstein and the American Occupation of Germany*, http://loewenstein.wordpress.amherst.edu; and *Unlocking Wonder: A Peek into the World of Luxury Cabinets* (art exhibition curated by Pablo Morales '16, Claire Castellano '16, Robert Croll '16, Martha Morgenthau '16, and Madeleine Sung '16, Mead Art Museum, Amherst College, Amherst, MA, October 25 2014–February 9 2015).
2. Barbara I. Dewey, "The Embedded Librarian: Strategic Campus Collaborations," *Resource Sharing & Information Networks* 17, no. 1–2 (2004): 5–17, doi:10.1300/J121v17n01_02; Susan Sharpless Smith and Lynn Sutton, "Embedded Librarians: On the Road in the Deep South," *College & Research Libraries News* 69, no. 2 (2008): 71–4, 85, http://crln.acrl.org/content/69/2/71.
3. John Willison and Kerry O'Regan, "Commonly Known, Commonly Not Known, Totally Unknown: A Framework for Students Becoming Researchers," *Higher Education Research and Development* 26, no. 4 (2007): 393–409, doi:10.1080/07294360701658609; see also http://www.adelaide.edu.au/rsd/framework.
4. Anastasia Efklides, "Metacognition, Affect, and Conceptual Difficulty," in *Overcoming Barriers to Student Understanding: Threshold Concepts and Troublesome Knowledge*, ed. Jan H. F. Meyer and Ray Land (New York: Routledge, 2006), 48–69.
5. Meagan Bowler and Kori Street, "Investigating the Efficacy of Embedment: Experiments in Information Literacy Integration," *Reference Services Review* 36, no. 4 (2008): 438–49, doi:10.1108/00907320810920397.
6. Leah Shopkow, "What Decoding the Disciplines Can Offer Threshold Concepts," in *Threshold Concepts and Transformational Learning*, ed. Jan Meyer, Ray Land, and Caroline Baillie (Boston: Sense Publishers, 2010), 317–32; see also http://decodingthedisciplines.org.
7. Association of College and Research Libraries, "Framework for Information Literacy for Higher Education," http://www.ala.org/acrl/standards/ilframework.

Bibliography

Association of College and Research Libraries. "Framework for Information Literacy for Higher Education." http://www.ala.org/acrl/standards/ilframework.

Bowler, Meagan, and Kori Street. "Investigating the Efficacy of Embedment: Experiments in Information Literacy Integration." *Reference Services Review* 36, no. 4 (2008): 438–49. doi:10.1108/00907320810920397.

Dewey, Barbara I. "The Embedded Librarian: Strategic Campus Collaborations." *Resource Sharing & Information Networks* 17, no. 1–2 (2004): 5–17. doi:10.1300/J121v17n01_02.

Efklides, Anastasia. "Metacognition, Affect, and Conceptual Difficulty." In *Overcoming Barriers to Student Understanding: Threshold Concepts and Troublesome Knowledge*, edited by Jan H. F. Meyer and Ray Land, 48–69. New York: Routledge, 2006.

Shopkow, Leah. "What Decoding the Disciplines Can Offer Threshold Concepts." In *Threshold Concepts and Transformational Learning*, edited by Jan Meyer, Ray Land, and Caroline Baillie, 317–32. Boston: Sense Publishers, 2010.

Smith, Susan Sharpless, and Lynn Sutton. "Embedded Librarians: On the Road in the Deep South." *College & Research Libraries News* 69, no. 2 (2008): 71–4, 85. http://crln.acrl.org/content/69/2/71.

Willison, John, and Kerry O'Regan. "Commonly Known, Commonly Not Known, Totally Unknown: A Framework for Students Becoming Researchers." *Higher Education Research and Development* 26, no. 4 (2007): 393–409. doi:10.1080/07294360701658609.

CHAPTER 4*

Framing Information Literacy as Scholarly Practice with Undergraduate Student Journals:
A Grassroots Approach

Deena Yanofsky, Michael David Miller, and Urooj Nizami

Introduction

Many undergraduate student associations and societies publish independent research journals, but very few studies exist to report on their development or success.[1] Often self-directed, with little to no faculty support, student-driven research publications are a prime target for outreach and education efforts around scholarly communication. This chapter presents the development of a partnership initiated between the authors and undergraduate students involved in the publication of research journals in the Faculty of Arts at McGill University. Sharing our expertise in information literacy and scholarly com-

---

* This work is licensed under a Creative Commons Attribution 4.0 License, CC BY (https://creativecommons.org/licenses/by/4.0/).

munication with undergraduate editorial boards and student associations, we developed a local, grassroots engagement approach with far-reaching outcomes. In addition to training students in scholarly communication issues and related concepts, the authors established direct and personal ties with undergraduate students committed to making a difference within the open access movement. These students eventually initiated other networks and grassroots development initiatives with the aim of adopting and promoting scholarly communication practices, developing policies to support them, and establishing these changes as an essential part of their student-led organizational structures—a critical step, the authors believe, that will lead to the institutionalization of information literacy interventions within the university research culture as a whole.

Background

The traditional model of targeted collaboration between librarians and teaching faculty to integrate information literacy programs within undergraduate education is well-established in the LIS literature and is widely viewed as the most effective route to success.[2] This model, however, often relegates the role played by librarians to "support services" rather than active contributors to the educational process. Librarians must often wait for an invitation or special request from faculty to engage students on issues related to scholarly communication and information literacy since these initiatives largely take place in the classroom. The focus on learning through coursework and within the formal curriculum also tends to overlook another key stakeholder: the students. Within the traditional librarian-faculty IL model, student information needs are, in large part, prescribed by teaching faculty with little room for direct student input. In contrast, the authors argue that working directly with undergraduate students engaged in research outside the classroom provides librarians with an opportunity to position themselves as distinct educators, with subject-specific expertise not only relevant to students' curriculum-based research needs, but also appropriate to guide and provide structure to students' research experiences as members of the scholarly community.

At McGill University Library, the partnership between undergraduate students engaged in research journals and liaison librarians, began in 2015 when the liaison for Political Science was approached by the editor of the undergraduate publication, the *McGill Journal of Political Studies*, to ask if the Library would add the most recent issue of the journal to its print collection. While the student's request seemed quite modest, it was clear that her question stemmed from a much broader array of scholarly communication issues, including publishing practices, access to information, the commodification of personal information, and intellectual property laws. The "local issue" as identified by the undergraduate student (and by extension her peers) presented an opportunity to connect student-defined, bottom-up goals—dissemination and access to student research—with the scholarly communications expertise and services offered by the library.

The initial meeting with the student editor at the reference desk led to a discussion of publishing practices, and a two-way relationship developed in which the liaison librarian and undergraduate student representative were able to engage directly and personally on issues that mattered to them both. The editor went back to the journal and shared some of the ideas and issues discussed with her peers. This conversation led to more discussions with the undergraduate council of the Political Science Student Association. Within a few weeks, the student-run Arts Undergraduate Society (AUS) that represents and governs all students enrolled in the Faculties of Arts and Arts & Sciences, approached the authors, and librarians began to hear first-hand about the interests and concerns of the undergraduate student community. This approach highlights a key characteristic of grassroots activities. Starting from the ground up and including the undergraduate student community as a stakeholder in our campaign to promote campus-wide literacy in scholarly communication issues and concepts, we experienced exceptional participant buy-in, which resulted in stronger programs and ultimately greater impact.

Another clear benefit to approaching this relationship as a grassroots initiative is that the direct relationship between students and librarians allows for a collaborative approach to IL instruction, where liaison librarians can meaningfully support undergraduates by customizing instruction based on a direct needs assessment. This dynamic approach allows librarians to be in continuous conversation with undergraduates, responding to their needs as they arise, rather than making assumptions and risking disengagement with redundant, irrelevant, or unhelpful material. A bottom-up or grassroots initiative "helps identify local problems and chalks out local innovative strategies and methods to mitigate these. This approach taps the indigenous knowledge bases and local expertise."[3] Working with students to address "local issues" as identified by the undergraduate student community enables liaison librarians to adapt and develop strategies that make use of their expertise in scholarly communications in a way that is directed and, therefore, made more meaningful for the student community. This approach provides a unique opportunity for librarians to connect information literacy skills with student empowerment at the local level.

A grassroots model for supporting undergraduate, student-driven research initiatives can have a number of significant advantages over the traditional librarian-faculty IL model.

- Students who participate in undergraduate, student-driven research journals do so of their own volition, and are already actively engaged in the research process.
- Students who are committed to carrying out and publishing research have the potential for graduate-level scholarship, where IL skills can be beneficial to the quality of their research and their personal academic goals.
- An early intervention with undergraduate students can aid in normalizing considerations of scholarly communications issues, including publishing practices, access to information, intellectual property laws, and information privilege.

Partnerships

As the liaison librarian for political science began working with the undergraduate *McGill Journal of Political Studies*, a network of grassroots initiatives began to extend to students working with other journals across campus. Student editors spoke to friends and peers, which extended to broader discussions with the Arts Undergraduate Society responsible for providing funding, support, and services for students. In turn, the liaison librarian for political science began connecting with colleagues from various subject areas to build capacity in the library for a larger, more direct program that could become institutionalized within the library and the roles and responsibilities of liaison librarians. To better illustrate the development of these partnerships, we have broken down our project into five broad objectives: (1) continue partnering with AUS to support undergraduate research; (2) assist liaison librarians to connect in new ways with undergraduate students in line with the ACRL *Framework for Information Literacy for Higher Education*;[4] (3) prepare and train liaison librarians with skills in scholarly communication; (4) promote partnerships from within the library; and (5) contribute to the general research culture of the university. Table 4.1 below details the five parts to this project.

Table 4.1
Undergraduate Student Journal Project Objectives

1	Partner with the Arts Undergraduate Society (AUS) to support undergraduate research via student journals	
1.1	Support AUS in reviewing and updating their publishing program	Reviewed student association's bylaws; provided feedback and suggestions for how to institutionalize research standards for undergraduate student journals. Our suggestions included: • Tying AUS funding to mandatory training for journal staff • Requiring journals to deposit a print copy of each issue with the library[5] • Requiring journals to register an ISSN (electronic and print)
1.2	Provide tailored workshops for journal editors and editorial staff	• Designed a two-part library workshop series to introduce undergraduate students to best practices in journal publishing; showcased Open Journal Systems as a potential hosting platform • With new bylaws, workshop attendance is now mandatory for any student association receiving funding from AUS to publish a journal
1.3	Library outreach to individual journals	• Collaborated with AUS to identify journals interested in partnering with the library • Matched journal editors with corresponding (and interested) subject liaison librarians
1.4	Write and submit proposal to digitize back issues of all AUS-funded journals	• Provided support and guidance to AUS project staff conducting an inventory of all journal titles (current or ceased) • Ensured physical or digital copies are catalogued and made available in the library • In collaboration with librarians from copyright, digital initiatives, and scholarly communications coordinated and designed documentation (author agreements, licenses, metadata schema, etc.) for students and subject liaison librarians

Table 4.1
Undergraduate Student Journal Project Objectives

2	Provide partnership opportunities for subject liaison librarians to work directly with undergraduate students	
2.1	Outreach to subject liaison librarians	• Presented project, activities, and desired outcomes to liaison librarians working with departments in the Faculty of Arts and Arts & Science • Connected liaison librarians with journal editors • Provided ongoing support and materials for librarians to liaise with student-driven journals
3	Build capacity for librarians to support best practices for student journals	
3.1	Coordinate scholarly communication training for librarians and library staff	Designed and presented ongoing workshop series with librarians from copyright, digital initiatives, and scholarly communications
3.2	Create scholarly communication LibGuides for liaison librarians	Collaborated with specialized librarians from other library units to create reference materials and online guides on peer-review, open access, creative commons, open journal systems, copyright, etc.
4	Support inter-departmental collaboration between librarians and professional staff	
4.1	Establish a community of practice at the McGill University Library	Initiated an ongoing relationship between liaison, scholarly communication, and copyright librarians to explore, collaborate, and build new initiatives that support grassroots outreach to undergraduate students
5	Integrate information literacy activities and initiatives into the broader McGill University research culture	
5.1	Present this project to different university faculties and units	• Encouraged liaison librarians currently working with student journals to present their activities at faculty departmental meetings • Invited faculty to become involved with journals as reviewers, advisors, and advocates

Reflection

Starting with a chance conversation at the reference desk in 2015, the number of student-driven journals and librarians who have joined forces to build a stronger, scholarly research culture for undergraduate student journals has grown quickly. More than fifteen journals have participated in some form of partnership with the library. Two librarians currently sit on editorial boards as academic advisors, six subject liaison librarians have begun working with individual journals to support their transition to peer-reviewed research publications, and all journal editors have attended at least one library workshop specifically designed to introduce them to publishing best practices.

These initiatives did not, however, develop without some concerns expressed by each group of stakeholders. The topmost concern put forward by liaison librarians was the perception that partnering with student-driven research journals would add to an already busy workload. Though we are sensitive to this concern (as it applies both to our colleagues and ourselves), our initiative does not take an additive approach to information literacy instruction that sees ineffective methods piled one on top of another, ultimately over-working librarians and often failing to resonate directly with students. The approach we have put forward at McGill Library is one that goes hand-in-hand with a reorientation of priorities and partnerships, relies on evaluating current information literacy initiatives, and updating less-effective practices in lieu of more direct, sustainable, and meaningful grassroots relationships with students.

Another concern raised by a few liaison librarians was that subject liaisons do not have the expertise and/or skills needed to support scholarly communications literacy and student publishing. Not every liaison librarian that we spoke to about our project was enthusiastic or supportive; several colleagues told us that it was not a subject area in which they felt comfortable, while others felt that these initiatives were outside the scope of their position responsibilities. In an effort to address these concerns, we developed several capacity-building and training opportunities for interested librarians and library staff. Working with the scholarly communications librarian, we contributed to the design and content of a subject guide for journal editors and librarians. We met with liaisons from several different subject areas and introduced a scaled version of our project, which provided different levels of participation for librarians, based on comfort and experience. Over the next year, we plan to introduce a workshop series for librarians and library staff, which will include modules taught by librarians from scholarly communications, digital initiatives, and copyright.

One of the most significant concerns that we heard came directly from student journal editors who were worried that partnering with librarians would lead to a set of undesirable standards forced upon their journals. Students from the McGill Undergraduate Geography Society, for example, were hesitant to work directly with a subject liaison librarian because they did not want a peer review system to be imposed upon their journal. Editors from the French Literature Student Society's journal, *lieu commun,* expressed interest in librarian-taught workshops on copyright and Creative Commons licensing but became apprehensive when their subject librarian began providing suggestions directed at their current editorial practices. In response to these hesitations and concerns, it was very important for us to create an open dialogue using traditional reference interview techniques, empowering students to set the tone for their own local needs. The goal is to create sustainable ties with student-driven research journals. To alienate students by imposing standards would be counterproductive to our project.

Assessment

One of the defining characteristics of our grassroots approach is our concern with understanding and responding directly to the information needs of our stakeholders, without privileging our own communication research models and practices. From the beginning of our project, it became clear (and not surprising) that the students we spoke to had spent little time thinking about scholarly communication issues and related concepts and were unfamiliar with the vocabulary librarians use to discuss them. This was not an indication, however, that undergraduate students do not care about scholarly communication issues, like open access and information privilege—quite the opposite. Once we began offering explanations in a clear manner without judgment and unnecessary jargon, rephrasing information needs, using open-ended questions, we learned that we shared a common interest in developing scholarly communication literacy across disciplines and publications.

At the same time, and despite our best intentions, we also discovered that it is not always easy for students to openly challenge some of the ideas that we put forward or to confess their misgivings. Over the past year, several student-driven research publications simply stopped communicating with their subject liaison librarian. While we do not know the specific reasons why they chose to end their participation in the project, their actions indicate that we need to integrate a more varied assessment approach into our activities. One assessment tool that we developed in response to this concern was a multiple-choice questionnaire for journal editors which lists different editorial models, practices, and policies. When we meet with journal staff for the first time, we ask students to select which practices they currently employ and how they fit within the model of scholarly publishing they think is the best fit for their publication. By providing a list of terms and practices, we empower students to talk about the issues they may not initially have the language or concepts to describe. The list also reinforces our commitment to helping students make decisions based on their own local needs, providing them with context while allowing them to choose the best options for themselves.

As our initiative has grown to include student journals from across the Faculty of Arts, it was also important for us to look at how we were communicating and supporting the other stakeholders in our project: liaison librarians. While there is general agreement within the profession that liaison roles are changing, not all librarians feel sufficiently prepared or are ready to take on new roles and responsibilities. It was important for us to meet with our colleagues, to introduce the project, and to invite them to provide feedback so that we could assess: (1) whether liaison librarians thought that they should provide instruction and support for scholarly communication literacy concepts and skills, (2) were librarians prepared to work directly with student journals, i.e., take on support roles like editorial advisors or similar, and (3) could this project grow in scope to become an established service offered through the library. By assessing the different skills and functional areas where liaison librarians wanted more or less support, we were able to build a community of practice, which involves an informal team of librarians with different areas of expertise who are willing to contribute to the overall knowledge base that is shared among librarians working directly with undergraduate student journals.

Recommendations/Best Practices

Working with multiple, distinct stakeholders across a diverse university campus presents a number of practical challenges and considerations. Students and librarians work on vastly different timelines. Not only do student priorities appear different in terms of work-life balance, students are largely absent from the campus during summer months when librarians have the most capacity for program development initiatives. The high turnover rate within student organizations can also have implications for the continuity or succession planning of a student-run journal. Based on our experiences, we recommend the following actions:

- Instead of approaching undergraduate journals individually, approach the larger, umbrella student association that represents and governs all students. Student associations can help to standardize and/or make mandatory certain publishing practices and activities, including direct relationships with the library.
- Assess and address student concerns early in the project. Students often feel that the expectations put forward by librarians are too high or fall outside of their local needs (librarians forcing their own agendas).

- Librarians can frame their approach within a structure of helping students to make decisions, and not making decisions for them.
- Partner early on with librarians in copyright, digitization, and scholarly communication to address liaison librarians' concerns about their lack of experience and/or expertise. These partnerships can help to clearly define liaison librarian versus functional expert roles in the project, inspire new and enhanced services, and contribute to a team approach that supports both students and colleagues.

Conclusion

One of the principle goals of our project is to demonstrate the impact that librarians can have on undergraduate student learning and research outside the classroom. While this initiative was borne out of a spontaneous encounter with a student journal editor, this initial meeting paved the way for a number of successful initiatives that enabled librarians to become involved in change-making, both from the bottom up and as a conversation space through which to formalize the discussion of scholarly communication concepts and issues within the undergraduate research community.

To be sure, there are many ways to engage with undergraduate students. Our grassroots approach is targeted to campus student journal publishing activities and provides individual points of engagement for students who already care or should care about specific issues in academic research, all within familiar contexts. The undergraduate student-driven research community is independent, and therefore responsible for making its own choices. By inspiring, mentoring, and collaborating with members of the undergraduate community, librarians can help ensure that these choices are based on a solid understanding of the scholarly communication concepts and issues that will shape the future of the information landscape.

Notes

1. Tabatha A. Farney and Suzanne L. Byerley, S. L. "Publishing a Student Research Journal: A Case Study, *portal: Libraries and the Academy* 10(3) (2010): 323, http://search.proquest.com/docview/753822429?accountid=12339.
2. Claire McGuinness, "What Faculty Think—Exploring the Barriers to Information Literacy Development in Undergraduate Education," *The Journal of Academic Librarianship* 32, no. 6 (2006): 573, doi:10.1016/j.acalib.2006.06.002.
3. Biswambhar Panda, "Top Down or Bottom Up? A Study of Grassroots NGOs' Approach," *Journal of Health Management* 9, no. 2 (2007): 261, doi:10.1177/097206340700900207.

4. Association of College and Research Libraries, "Framework for Information Literacy for Higher Education," Association of College and Research Libraries, February 2, 2015, http://www.ala.org/acrl/standards/ilframework.
5. The AUS by-laws require student journals to deposit a print copy of each issue with three different libraries: the McGill University Library, Library and Archives Canada, and the Bibliothèque et Archives nationales du Québec (BAnQ).
6. Anthony Stamatoplos, "The Role of Academic Libraries in Mentored Undergraduate Research: A Model of Engagement in the Academic Community," *College & Research Libraries* 70, no. 3 (2009): 236, doi:10.5860/crl.70.3.235.

Bibliography

Association of College and Research Libraries, "Framework for Information Literacy for Higher Education," *Association of College and Research Libraries*, February 12, 2015. http://www.ala.org/acrl/standards/ilframework.

Farney, Tabatha A., and Suzanne L. Byerley. "Publishing a Student Research Journal: A Case Study." *portal: Libraries and the Academy* 10, no. 3 (2010): 323–35.

Gilman, Isaac. "Scholarly communication for Credit." In *Common Ground at the Nexus of Information Literacy & Scholarly Communication*. Edited by Stephanie Davis Kahl and Merinda Kaye Hensley. Chicago: The Association of College & Research Libraries, 2013: 114–33.

McGuinness, Claire. "What Faculty Think—Exploring the Barriers to Information Literacy Development in Undergraduate Education." *The Journal of Academic Librarianship* 32(6) (2006): 573–82. http://eprints.teachingandlearning.ie/2970/1/McGuinness%202006.pdf.

Panda, Biswambhar. "Top Down or Bottom Up? A Study of Grassroots NGOs' Approach." *Journal of Health Management* 9, no. 2 (2007): 257–73.

Stamatoplos, Anthony. "The Role of Academic Libraries in Mentored Undergraduate Research: A Model of Engagement in the Academic Community." *College & Research Libraries* 70(3) (2009): 235–49. doi: 10.5860/crl.70.3.235.

CHAPTER 5 *

Building Relationships, Advancing Services:
Piloting Open Conference Systems with the Indiana University Undergraduate Research Conference

Shayna Pekala and Jane Rogan

Introduction

As the scholarly communication landscape evolves, libraries are continually extending their missions to include the dissemination and preservation of research through the development of library publishing services. While typically geared toward faculty and graduate students, these services are becoming increasingly available to undergraduate students. In service to the 38,000-plus undergraduate students at Indiana University's flagship campus, the Indiana University Bloomington (IUB) Libraries have provided ample support for undergraduate research in the area of scholarly publishing over the last several years. The Libraries' Scholarly Communication department has worked with undergraduate students, faculty, and campus units to enable and promote the publication of undergraduate research through its core

---

* This work is licensed under a Creative Commons Attribution-NonCommercial 4.0 License, CC BY-NC (https://creativecommons.org/licenses/by-nc/4.0/).

services: IUScholarWorks Repository, a DSpace-based institutional repository service, and IUScholarWorks Journals, an open access journal publishing service built on the Open Journal Systems (OJS) platform. Currently, IUScholarWorks Repository houses a number of undergraduate research projects, and IUScholarWorks Journals is used by four undergraduate-run scholarly journals.

In addition to providing services that support undergraduate publishing activities, the libraries have leveraged key partnerships to develop brand new services. This chapter details a collaborative pilot project between the IUB Libraries and the IU Office of the Vice Provost for Undergraduate Education (OVPUE) to test the viability of Open Conference Systems (OCS) for managing and publishing conference proceedings from the Indiana University Undergraduate Research Conference (IUURC), an annual conference that showcases undergraduate research and creative activity at Indiana University.[1] This effort was motivated by the libraries' desire to expand its open access publishing services, as well as IUURC's need for a free and flexible conference management system. While current literature captures a variety of case studies of library-supported undergraduate publishing activities, it fails to document the use of OCS for an undergraduate research conference. In addition to presenting the history of the pilot project, this chapter will offer practical considerations for engaging in effective partnerships and implementing similar undergraduate publishing initiatives.

Background

The IUB Libraries have a long tradition of supporting experimentation with new forms of research dissemination and enabling scholars to communicate their research through new vehicles and under new access models. Since 2007, the libraries have preserved and made freely available the digital research materials of Indiana University faculty, students, staff, and other affiliates by hosting more than 7,700 items in IUScholarWorks Repository (including datasets, dissertations, working papers, published articles, technical reports, conference proceedings, and multimedia), and publishing thirty-two open access journals in IUScholarWorks Journals (including six student-run and twenty-six faculty-run journals) across all IU campuses. In an effort to push the boundaries of scholarly publishing, the libraries' Scholarly Communication department is continually seeking ways to expand its services.

In summer 2014, the department began exploring the feasibility of implementing a new service to support the management and publication of conference proceedings in response to increasing requests from users. While the department already provided support for disseminating conference proceedings through IUScholarWorks Repository, the underlying platform (DSpace) does not provide tools for organizing conference events, managing the editorial workflow for submissions, or creating a customized conference website. The newly proposed service would take advantage of Open Conference Systems (OCS), an open source software platform developed by the Public Knowledge Project (PKP). Having successfully used PKP's OJS platform for the last six years to publish open access journals, the department felt comfortable experimenting with OCS.

In order to decide whether to bring OCS into its existing set of services, the Scholarly Communication department needed to thoroughly evaluate OCS's features through testing. OCS provides tools for managing attendee registration, scheduling, and other aspects conference organization. More importantly, it enables two primary functions of publishing conference proceedings: (1) managing the editorial workflow, including organizing submissions, managing peer review, and various stages of editing, and (2) making the proceedings available online. To test the latter function, the department installed a demo instance of OCS, created a test conference site for a previously held library conference, and uploaded the proceedings. To test the first function, however, the department needed to work with a real conference, since the tasks involved require communication among multiple users with varying roles.

Meanwhile, the department was seeking ways to extend its support for undergraduate research by further integrating the scholarly communication process into the undergraduate experience. The ACRL white paper, *Intersections of Scholarly Communication and Information Literacy: Creating Strategic Collaborations for a Changing Academic Environment*, suggests one way that librarians can facilitate conversations about scholarly communication issues is to participate in the organization of campus symposia and conferences;[2] collaborating with an undergraduate research conference for the purposes of testing OCS would provide this opportunity. Mark Caprio and Robert Hackey describe a comparable partnership between the Providence College Health Policy and Management program and the library's Digital Publishing Services staff to publish papers presented at their annual undergraduate conference, albeit using the institutional repository.[3] Adrian Ho outlines specific areas that libraries can assist with undergraduate journal publishing, including planning, organization, and content management,[4] all of which could also be applied to conferences. As the libraries had recently worked on an initiative to launch the *Indiana University Journal of Undergraduate Research (IUJUR)*, providing a similar service to support undergraduate publishing at a different stage of the research lifecycle seemed like a natural extension.

Partnerships

A previous partnership with OVPUE, a campus-level administrative unit, laid the foundation for what would become the OCS pilot project. Since 2013, the Scholarly Communication department had been collaborating with OVPUE and a group of undergraduate students to develop *IUJUR*. Scholarly Communication staff provided consultation services and technical infrastructure and support for the journal through IUScholarWorks Journals, while OVPUE provided funding and administrative oversight for the student organization that coordinates the journal. Although *IUJUR* did not officially launch until June 2015, most of the groundwork had been laid by fall 2014. The Libraries involvement in *IUJUR* resulted in numerous benefits, most notably a strengthened relationship with OVPUE.

It was a fortunate coincidence that, around the same time the Scholarly Communication department was searching for a conference partner for OCS, OVPUE was preparing to host the twentieth annual IUURC conference for the first time. IUURC is a university-wide initiative that takes place on a different IU campus each year. In 2014, OVPUE assumed responsibility for hosting the conference, which offered an opportunity for a technological overhaul, including a new web presence and switching to an app-based tool, Guidebook, in place of printed conference materials. In addition to these changes, OVPUE was also interested in finding a technical solution for managing conference registrations and submissions and communicating with presenters. In previous years, these tasks were dispersed across multiple systems and units: students submitted their abstracts through Oncourse, IU's learning management system; conference organizers communicated with presenters over email; and IU Conferences assisted with attendee registration and day-of conference check-in. At the time, IU Conferences also charged a per-participant fee for their services, making their continued use prohibitive for IUURC as the conference is free and does not generate revenue.

Hoping to find a single platform to manage all aspects of IUURC (including publishing the proceedings, which had never previously been done), OVPUE turned to the libraries for help. The Scholarly Communication department recognized the opportunity to use OCS with a real conference and proposed partnering with OVPUE on IUURC. After meeting with OVPUE staff to provide a brief demonstration of OCS, the two units decided to embark on a second joint project, using OCS to manage the registration and submission workflows for IUURC and to publish the resulting proceedings in an open access platform. The goals of the project were twofold: (1) to use OCS to facilitate the organization and management of IUURC, and (2) to determine whether OCS is a useful tool for stakeholders.

Beginning in September 2014, Scholarly Communication staff trained IUURC's student conference coordinator on the basics of using OCS and helped set up the initial conference website. IUURC has a relatively simple format featuring posters and oral presentations from students across IU's eight campuses. Because of this simplicity, just a few of the OCS utilities were used. Conference attendees registered through the conference participant registration feature. Student presenters uploaded their abstracts to a relevant conference track, either a poster or oral presentation linked to their home campus. A faculty liaison from each campus was given the role of track director for their campus and verified each student's submission with the faculty mentor before approving or denying the submission for inclusion in the conference. The student conference coordinator extracted data from OCS using built-in plugins to create a full conference schedule of oral presentation and poster abstracts in the Guidebook app.

Over the course of the fall 2014 semester, the student conference coordinator and Scholarly Communication staff worked to identify and troubleshoot ongoing bugs and usability problems with OCS. After the conference concluded in November, the proceedings were ultimately not able to be published due to copyright concerns from a number of faculty mentors in the bench science disciplines. These faculty mentors communicated to OVPUE that they did not want their student's work, which is often derivative of the faculty member's research, to be available in an open access forum for fear of being scooped and to avoid limiting both the student's and faculty member's ability to publish the findings in another venue in the future. As these are legitimate and practical disciplinary issues, OVPUE forwent the idea of publishing the proceedings. In the end, OVPUE was satisfied with OCS's registration and submission management features and elected to use it again for these purposes the following year.

Reflection

OVPUE found OCS to be a helpful tool for handling the conference planning and organization for IUURC. Using OCS to communicate with conference registrants offered simplicity and consistency. In prior years, the conference coordinator handled hundreds of emails using both personal and conference email accounts, which led to confusion for student participants. OCS also helped speed up the review process. Student submissions were quickly assigned to a conference track by the student conference coordinator, and track directors were able to swiftly verify submissions and make small typographic edits to ensure consistency with submission guidelines. Approvals took place on a rolling basis and each track director, not just the conference manager, edited and imposed conference guidelines and standards.

As a new tool for IUURC, OCS was embraced by students who found little difficulty navigating through OCS and quickly understood how to register for and submit to the conference. Staff and faculty who served as track directors or who wanted to register for the conference found the platform less intuitive. After the first year of using OCS, the IUURC conference manager and student conference coordinator created a simple guide for faculty track directors that details the steps for reviewing, editing, and accepting (or denying) submissions within the platform.[5] Moving forward, it would be helpful to create similar guides for other processes, like registering for or submitting to the conference. While PKP does provide some helpful materials, such as *OCS in an Hour*,[6] most of this documentation is intended for the conference manager, rather than for the faculty reviewer or track director.

Over the course of the project, OVPUE staff faced several technical challenges using OCS, the biggest of which involved exporting data. OCS provides standard plugins for exporting data, which return results in either XML or CSV format. The conference organizers found that specific tasks, like creating participant name tags (which include the presenter's name, home campus, and track), required data from more than one plugin. Subsequently, conference organizers resorted to copying and pasting from screen views to fill in missing data. The conference organizers also found OCS limiting due to its inherent complexity. Because OCS is designed for professional conferences, there are essential features built into the system, such as complex peer review management, conference tracks, and themes, which far exceed the needs of a modest, single-day student conference.

From the libraries' perspective, the OCS pilot project enabled the Scholarly Communication department to understand potential problems with launching and supporting a conference management service. On an administrative level, uncovering the platform's limitations helped the department realize that it would need to provide a greater amount of technical support than anticipated, calling into question the department's ability to manage the service with its current level of staffing (one FTE librarian and one FTE professional/administrative staff). Similarly, observing the ways that users struggled with certain parts of the system illustrated the need for Scholarly Communication staff to create supplemental instructional materials before rolling out the service. The project also demonstrated how certain conferences may desire a level of platform customization that cannot be fully accommodated through OCS out-of-the-box, which highlighted the importance of establishing clear policies about the libraries' role in supporting the platform, likely through a service agreement. Despite these issues, by displaying technical knowledge and providing support for an administrative unit like OVPUE, Scholarly Communication staff were able to challenge outdated and prevailing views of the role of academic libraries and librarians.

Using OCS for IUURC not only benefited OVPUE and the libraries, but also students. OCS enabled students to have a seamless conference submission experience and, more important, it provided them with a framework for understanding how academic scholarship is produced. Using a system like OCS exposes students to the review process and its role in the publication life cycle. By being able to log in and track the progress of an abstract submission through the review, editing, and publication stages, students gain insight into important editorial processes that often go unrecognized, which ultimately expands students' understanding of the scholarly communication system. From a practical standpoint, student conference participants gained experience using a conference management system to submit presentation and poster abstracts, which prepared them for the process of submitting to a future professional conference.

Assessment

The initiative was assessed informally through conversations between the Scholarly Communication department and OVPUE, which drew on additional communications with IUURC stakeholders—students, faculty, and staff—to determine whether the goals of the partnership had been achieved. As evidenced by IUURC's OCS website,[7] OVPUE was able to successfully use OCS to facilitate the organization and management of IUURC. The conference organizers found OCS to be a helpful tool in efficiently managing a complex process, as well as documenting and memorializing the research and creative activity efforts of student researchers and faculty mentors. The archived submissions offer a series of data points that demonstrate the commitment of undergraduates and their faculty mentors to research and creative activity endeavors.

There are several factors to consider when evaluating a digital tool like OCS. Stewart Varner identifies five different areas to examine: exports (what the tool allows you to do with what it creates), data storage and intellectual property (what terms and conditions govern the tool), documentation (instructions available to help users understand the tool), stability (how long a tool will be available), and usefulness (whether the tool adds a new dimension to the way the material is engaged with without being distracting).[8] The OCS pilot project was largely focused on helping the Scholarly Communication department determine the software's usefulness factor, though it ended up providing information about the exports and documentation factors as well. In the future, it would be useful to convert these five factors into a rubric with which to provide a numeric measurement to complement the informal feedback from stakeholders. Together, these two forms of assessment could provide a more complete picture of the initiative's relative success.

Recommendations/Best Practices

Interdepartmental partnerships, as demonstrated through this project, can be mutually beneficial and rewarding. The OCS pilot project provided clear benefits to both the libraries and OVPUE. The opportunity to work together on this initiative came from a prior collaboration to launch *IUJUR*. Although the two units already had a positive working relationship, they agreed upon simple definitions and expectations for the OCS initiative related to the goals, success, and timeline of the project. These guidelines helped to manage the scale and scope of the work and to understand when the partnership had come to an end.

1. Set simple and well-defined goals for the partnership, including a realistic outline of individual contributions and roles.
2. Create shared definition(s) for success and determine how these will be measured.
3. Establish a realistic time frame for the partnership.
4. Keep an open mind about how the partnership can be extended or built upon beyond the initial scope of the project.

As for the tool itself, OCS has proved to be an effective solution for managing undergraduate research conferences. Librarians wishing to implement OCS should recognize that the system's complex peer review management features may exceed the needs of an undergraduate-level conference, and, therefore, librarians should be prepared to work with conference organizers to design workflows in OCS that fit the unique needs of each conference. In addition, before implementing OCS, librarians should be advised that the future of the software is unclear. In September 2016, PKP began soliciting community feedback to decide whether or not to continue to develop OCS, which has seen few changes over the last several years aside from security updates.[9] Depending on the outcome of PKP's decision, OCS may or may not continue to be a viable option for libraries to use to support conference management.

Conclusion

The OCS pilot project strengthened and elevated the relationship between OVPUE and the libraries. Whereas OVPUE previously viewed the libraries as a *provider* of systems and services, the unit now views the libraries as a valuable *collaborator*. Furthermore, the pilot project provided a clear example of how the libraries can support the administrative function of the university in addition to its teaching and learning mission.

The newfound perception of the role of the libraries led OVPUE to continue to work with the Scholarly Communication department to develop other library programs. In fall 2015, the two units collaborated on a library workshop titled, "Research and Publishing Opportunities for Undergraduates," which presented ways for undergraduates to get involved in research and publishing at IU, including *IUJUR* and IUURC. At present, the two units are working to expand this into a three-part workshop series that covers all aspects of the publication lifecycle. The partnership also generated a new credit-bearing course in the IU College of Arts and Sciences designed for the student leaders of *IUJUR*, which focuses on issues and best practices in scholarly publishing. The course debuted in fall 2016 and is taught by the Scholarly Communication Librarian. The continued successful collaborations between OVPUE and the libraries demonstrate the importance of finding campus partners, and of nurturing positive and productive relationships across diverse campus units. These partnerships benefit the departments and personnel involved and, most important, they are essential in enhancing the experience of undergraduate students.

CHAPTER 5

Appendix 5A: IUURC20 Author Information and Abstract Review and Approval

IUURC20 Author Information and Abstract Review and Approval

Step By Step Instructions

Logging In

Login to http://scholarworks.iu.edu/conferences/index.php/iuurc/iuurc20/login using username and password sent via email on Tuesday, 11/4/14

Navigate to **USER HOME**

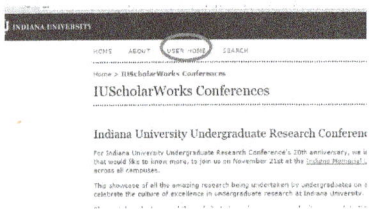

Finding Your Students' Work

Select the **In Review** link across from your **Director** role to access your students' work

In the **Assigned To**: drop-down menu, select **Me** and press Search. Click on the **TITLE** of an Abstract to open it up

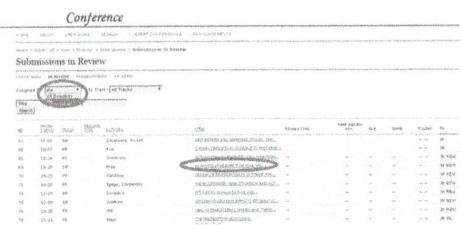

Verifying Your Students' Work

Click on **SUMMARY** and begin verifying author information, departmental and school affiliation (contained in **Submission Metadata**).

In the **Submission Metadata**, look at the **Title** and **Abstract** entries. **The Abstract must include the mentor name, departmental and campus affiliation. It will speed up the conference program process remarkably if you would all take these editing steps and ensure the mentor name, department and campus affiliation in the format given in the example below. This is a GREAT example. The student has included their faculty mentor's name, department and campus affiliation with the right formatting. Job well done!**

Correct Identifiers

Please use the correct departmental names for your campus. [E.g. in Bloomington it is the Department of Psychological and Brain Sciences, in Indianapolis it is the Department of Psychology.]

Please adhere to the IU-sanctioned campus names and not their acronyms. [Indiana University Bloomington, Indiana University Southeast, Indiana University-Purdue University Indianapolis, Indiana University-Purdue University Columbus, Indiana University East, Indiana University Kokomo, Indiana University-Purdue University Fort Wayne, Indiana University Northwest, or Indiana University South Bend].

Mentor Information is Missing

If the mentor name is missing, please look in the PDF file attached to the submission (scroll back up to the top of the **Summary** page) and click on the **Original File PDF**. If a student has not included the mentor information in the Abstract entry (in the Summary Metadata) they have most likely included the mentor's name in the PDF. Please copy and paste the mentor name, department and campus affiliations from the PDF and into the Abstract Metadata, formatting as above.

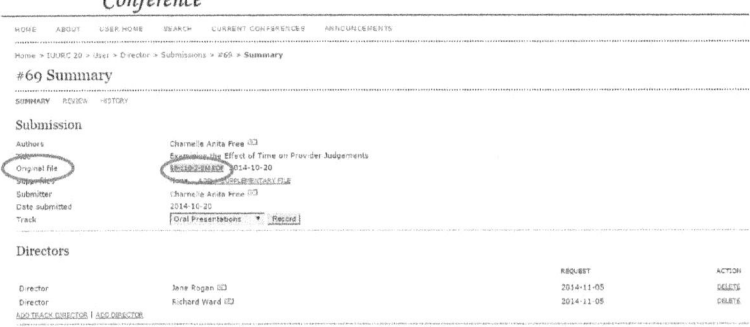

At this stage, if you've verified the metadata is correct and that the abstract isn't too long, or that the title isn't misleading, you can move ahead with the review approval.

Approving Your Students' Work

From the Summary page, click on **REVIEW**.

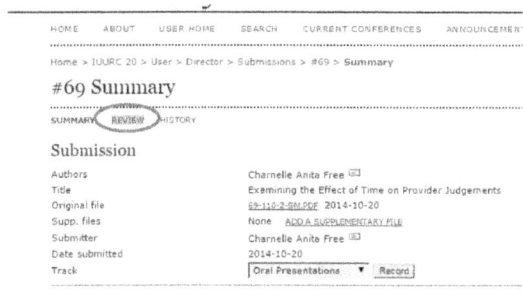

Scroll to **Director Decision** and select **Accept Submission** and click **Record Decision**. The system will ask you to verify your choice.

Revisions to Content-Specific Areas

If you feel the author needs to make some **content-specific changes**, i.e. edit the **abstract** or **title** (more than a simple typo, which you can easily correct in the "Edit Metadata" function on the SUMMARY page), you can select **Revisions Required** in the **Director's Decision**. In the same area you will notice an icon for **Notify Author**. Use this to email the author directly about content-specific changes the author needs to make. You can also add **Comments** to the system by clicking on the speech balloon icon. Comments are safeguarded for future reference.

If you have notified a student that changes need to be made to the abstract/title, please give the student a day to get the changes back to you. Once changes have been submitted by the student (probably via email) and they are to your satisfaction, you can edit the Submission Metadata (see above notes on SUMMARY page Title and Abstract Metadata). Once you've made the changes you may then change the **Director Decision** to **Accept Submission**.

In the unlikely event that ~~we have to make a water landing~~ a student fails to provide edits in a timely fashion you may need to **Decline a Submission** using the **Director Decision** drop box.

Please let me know if you have ANY questions about the system. It appears clunky at first, but it is so helpful to have a record of all the conversations between Directors and Authors within the system. And never fear, it is REALLY hard to break this system. (Please don't take that as a challenge!)

Notes

1. "Indiana University Undergraduate Research Conference," accessed September 5, 2016, https://iuurc.indiana.edu/.
2. Association of College and Research Libraries: Working Group on Intersections of Scholarly Communication and Information Literacy, *Intersections of Scholarly Communication and Information Literacy: Creating Strategic Collaborations for a Changing Academic Environment* (Chicago: Association of College and Research Libraries, 2013), 17–18.
3. Mark Caprio and Robert Hackey, "If You Built It, They Will Come; Strategies for Developing an Undergraduate Research Conference," *The Journal of Health Administration Education* 31, no. 3 (2014): 247–66.
4. Adrian K. Ho, "Library Services for Creating and Publishing Student Research Journals," in *Library Publishing Toolkit*, ed. Allison P. Brown (Geneseo: IDS Project Press, 2013): 237–42.
5. See Appendix 5A.
6. "OCS in an Hour," Public Knowledge Project, last modified September 2, 2008, https://pkp.sfu.ca/files/OCSinanHour.pdf.
7. "Indiana University Undergraduate Research Conference," accessed September 5, 2016, https://scholarworks.iu.edu/conferences/index.php/iuurc.
8. Stewart Varner, "Library Instruction for Digital Humanities Pedagogy in Undergraduate Classes," in *Laying the Foundation: Digital Humanities in Academic Libraries*, ed. John W. White and Heather Gilbert (West Lafayette: Purdue University Press, 2016), 216–18.
9. Kevin Stranack, "Upcoming PKP Software Development Plans," Public Knowledge Project, November 21, 2016, https://pkp.sfu.ca/2016/11/21/upcoming-pkp-software-development-plans/.

Bibliography

Association of College and Research Libraries: Working Group on Intersections of Scholarly Communication and Information Literacy. *Intersections of Scholarly Communication and Information Literacy: Creating Strategic Collaborations for a Changing Academic Environment*. Chicago: Association of College and Research Libraries, 2013.

Caprio, Mark and Robert Hackey. "If You Built It, They Will Come: Strategies for Developing an Undergraduate Research Conference." *The Journal of Health Administration Education* 31, no. 3 (2014): 247–66.

Ho, Adrian K. "Library Services for Creating and Publishing Student Research Journals." In *Library Publishing Toolkit*. Edited by Allison P. Brown. Geneseo: IDS Project Press, 2013: 235–50.

Varner, Stewart. "Library Instruction for Digital Humanities Pedagogy in Undergraduate Classes." In *Laying the Foundation: Digital Humanities in Academic Libraries*. Edited by John W. White and Heather Gilbert. West Lafayette: Purdue University Press, 2016: 205–22.

CHAPTER 6*

Doing the Honors:
Designing a Curriculum for a Year-Long Thesis Project

Amanda Piekart-Primiano, Matthew Regan, and Lily Sacharow

Introduction

The personal librarian approach enables a deeper level of one-on-one contact with students beyond the typical reference interaction, and is often employed for student groups who may benefit from more targeted library services, such as student athletes, developmental education students, and international students. Honors students are another such cohort. The Honors Program at Berkeley College offers students the opportunity to participate with a group of their peers who are focused on pursuing a more academically rigorous path than what is ordinarily expected of undergraduate students. Students are admitted to the program either as freshmen or as continuing upperclassmen. Three components of the Honors Program are community service, advanced honors seminars (three courses taken during an academic year), and scholarship. Librarians support the third objective, which takes the form of a scholarly research paper on a topic of each student's choice, written during the upper-level seminars and typically twenty to fifty pages in length. The aim of this chapter is to describe the development and implementation of an Honors

---

* This work is licensed under a Creative Commons Attribution-NonCommercial-ShareAlike 4.0 License, CC BY-NC-SA (https://creativecommons.org/licenses/by-nc-sa/4.0/).

Thesis Project Curriculum through which students receive intensive research and writing support.

Background

Throughout 2012 and 2013, the Honors Program director met with the library's information literacy coordinator to establish a method for librarians to support honors students writing their theses. From these discussions, the coordinator proposed a highly distilled version of the research process rooted in the four concepts of exploration, identification, development, and completion. Following ongoing conversation with support staff and faculty regarding these concepts, the director's vision evolved from a single training module to a learning community support structure that would guide students from idea formation to sharing their work. This model ensures personal guidance, one-on-one attention, ongoing development, and progress monitoring in a way that a "one-shot" video tutorial could not. These values were prioritized by the director and led to the formal adoption of the curriculum and learning community. The learning community is a cohort of honors students matriculating through a year of seminars together, assisted by support staff. Learning communities are assigned a number based on which honors cycle they are participating in (e.g., Learning Community #5, the fifth Honors Program cohort, or LC5, LC6, etc.).

The development of the Honors Thesis Project Curriculum took place over what can be described as four "phases"—exploration and planning, interim execution, implementation, and preliminary revisions—articulated in figure 6.1. This chapter is primarily concerned with the implementation phase.

During the exploration and planning phase, the information literacy coordinator was invited to collaborate with honors seminar faculty and Writing Center staff to strategize how best to reorganize the final scholarship component across the full academic year. Historically, the paper was researched and written entirely in the students' final term; the new curriculum was intended to be integrated with all honors seminar curricula so that students worked concurrently on seminar coursework and preparations for the culminating research requirement. Rather than one video module, the library planned to support with the following:

- a LibGuide organized to serve as a hub for general information and to host research training video tutorials, building progressively through the year;
- active learning elements such as worksheets and opportunities for exploration of resources beyond the college;
- digital badges awarded to students as they progressed through the modules;

- additional writing and citing training in collaboration with the Writing Center;
- a personal librarian to foster individual relationships and improve outcomes, and a personal writing consultant to provide the same.

Figure 6.1

Honors Thesis Project Curriculum Development Phases

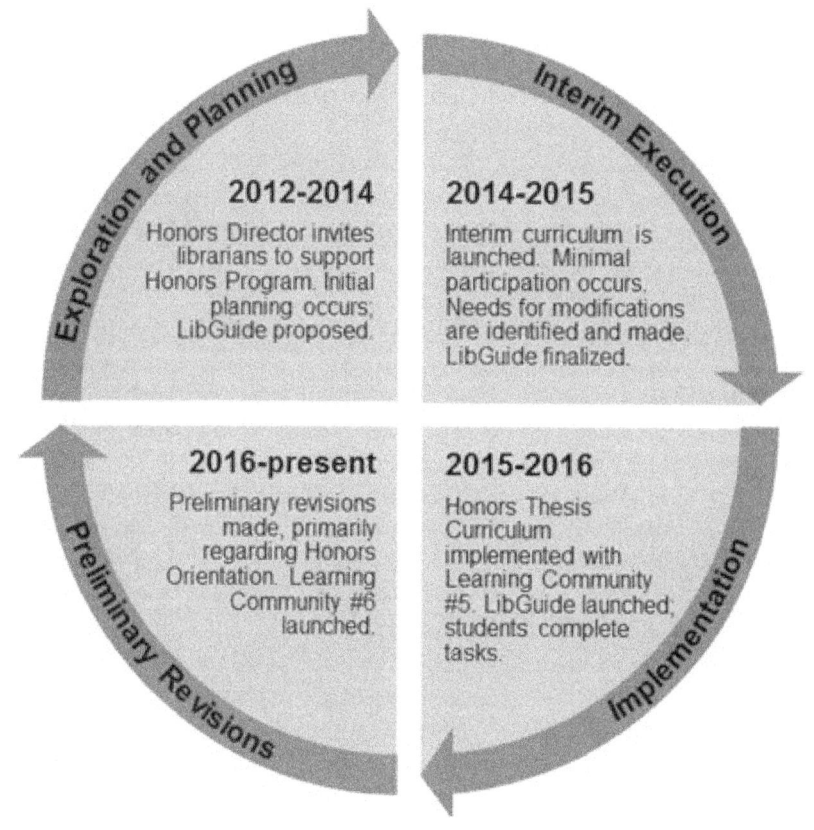

Following exploration and planning, an interim curriculum was executed beginning in late 2014. The most critical development, however, and the basis of this chapter, was the implementation of a full Honors Thesis Project Curriculum for the 2015–2016 academic year. This curriculum has served as a microcosm of the library's ideal information literacy program: well-structured, integrated within the larger curriculum, and serving to advance interdepartmental collaboration, promote student-librarian relationships, and improve student outcomes.

Librarians conducted research to explore potential directions and best practices that had not been considered for this thesis curriculum. The list of citations in Anna Marie Johnson's 2012 article, "Information Literacy Instruction for an Honors Program First-Year Orientation," was enormously helpful and served as a valuable literature review and compilation of recent sources on trends in librarian support of honors programs.[1] Additionally, a large number of library websites and LibGuides were reviewed, but no public resources were identified with the same depth of curricular support as this effort.

During the summer of 2015, the librarians finished creating the Honors Thesis Project Curriculum. The newly developed curriculum provided scaffolding for honors students to take part in the information lifecycle over the course of an academic year: the first term was dedicated to topic exploration; the second focused on introductory research and compiling initial sources; the third highlighted developing a thesis statement and creating an annotated bibliography; and the fourth targeted the writing and editing process. Students would craft the final paper and an accompanying presentation for a culminating honors symposium, which gives them an opportunity to share and showcase their scholarly work.

In preparation for the initial launch of the Honors Thesis Project Curriculum, the Writing Center, honors seminar faculty, the honors program director, and three honors librarians created multiple learning components to guide both students and faculty through the year-long thesis process, as outlined in the table on the next page.

The new Thesis Project Curriculum, its accompanying LibGuide, and the digital badge system were implemented into the Honors Program in the fall of 2015. During an introductory session, librarians and writing consultants met the incoming honors cohort, distributed the curriculum packet, and answered initial questions about the thesis process.

Honors students were assigned librarians by class section to divide the work evenly. Students were required to meet at least once with their librarian during each of the first two terms, and that librarian became responsible for providing individual feedback on two bibliography submissions.

Tracking of completed tasks began right away. As quizzes and e-form submissions were received, an internal spreadsheet was kept updated for librarians, writing consultants, and faculty, while the LibGuide-embedded badges spreadsheet was updated for students to view their progress.

For the graded components of the thesis curriculum, including the source identification (preliminary ten-source list) and annotated bibliography (full twenty-five-source list), librarians and writing consultants held a norming session to ensure consistent scoring against the rubrics. These submissions were graded by each student's assigned librarian and then factored into their seminar grade at the professor's discretion.

Learning Object	Purpose	Developed with...	Deliverable
Curriculum packet (thesis project syllabus)	Divides the thesis process into manageable stages with clear deadlines; links each task to a particular stage within the process as a whole	Microsoft Word	PDF
Learning outcomes document	Outlines the expected skills and knowledge that students acquire throughout Honors Thesis Project Curriculum	Microsoft Word	PDF
Video tutorials	Provides students with research essentials needed to gain knowledge to complete Honors Thesis Project (basic research, advanced research, and the lifecycle of information; and an APA citation tutorial provided by the Writing Center)	PowerPoint; Camtasia; Screencast.com; articulate storyline	LibGuide-embedded video tutorials
Tutorial quizzes	Ensures students have met skills mastery requirements	EmailMeForm.com	LibGuide-embedded electronic forms
Electronic submission forms	Allows librarians to track and view student submissions by time stamp, and to provide immediate messages to students outlining additional requirements; sends automatically graded quizzes directly to students and librarians	EmailMeForm.com	LibGuide-embedded electronic forms
Rubrics	Sets a standard for scoring and providing feedback on the source identification, annotated bibliography, and Final Thesis Project assignments	Excel	PDF
Digital badges	Offers visual incentive to complete each milestone on time and successfully; fosters self-accountability and competition among students, who can view everyone's badge progress on the private LibGuide	Credly.com; Google Sheets	Badge images displayed on LibGuide-embedded spreadsheet

Beginning in 2016, Berkeley College converted its academic calendar from four quarters to three semesters, which altered the distribution of goals and assignments across the terms. For the 2016–2017 honors cohort, several revisions were made to the curriculum, although the overall process remained the same. The most significant change was the addition of a standalone Thesis Project Orientation, which aimed to clarify some of the most common questions students had throughout the process, and to have them complete some preliminary tasks, including basic research skills and potential topic selection, prior to enrollment in their first honors seminar in the fall. This way, before any of the tasks are incorporated into their honors course grades, expectations and workload are revealed early, along with a sense of the bigger picture. Librarians increased efforts to include honors faculty at every stage of planning, including rubric norming sessions when scoring the annotated bibliographies, and incorporating honors tasks into the syllabi and blackboard each term.

Partnerships

Throughout all phases of the initiative, librarians, Writing Center staff, and faculty members met in collaboration with the honors program director to develop the Thesis Project Curriculum. Meetings occurred each term during exploration and planning, increasing to nearly monthly in the lead-up to the interim execution phase (see figure 6.1).

The fundamental challenges of partnership are largely predictable and can be attributed to insufficient communication and differing perceptions and expectations. Lack of clarity of vision contributed to these challenges; no one stakeholder asserted a strong unifying voice. Seeking a fully collaborative experience, librarians were reluctant to assert this sole leadership role, despite frequent empowerment from the honors program director. Seminar faculty, brought in from different departments to support the honors program, were less familiar with the process of curriculum development and at times did not prioritize thesis requirements and the need to communicate a consistent message to students. This led to miscommunication of expectations, deadlines, and assignment values, which did not go unnoticed by students: one reflected in her exit survey, "The professor, [the director], and the librarians would, at times, give different directions and different due dates. This made me stress even more, since I was never really sure who to listen to." In the future, librarians will work to establish roles and responsibilities earlier in the process to ensure clarity for faculty, support staff, and, most important, the students.

Despite these challenges, major benefits arose from the partnerships in this initiative: enhanced interdepartmental relationships, more creative liberties, and new perspectives on student learning.

Librarians' relationships with staff from other departments grew and developed through this sometimes challenging partnership. The curriculum served as a common frame of reference even to librarians and Writing Center staff who were not working firsthand with the honors students; librarians came quickly to know which of their colleagues were supporting the honors cohort, and the same was true of the Writing Center staff. Because the honors program was fairly small and intimate (approximately fifty-three students at the outset of the thesis project) and some students transferred from one campus to another, having visible and easily recognized staff helped our multi-campus library system direct students to the appropriate liaisons in a timely manner. Furthermore, automated responses were added to our chat service and Library Knowledge Base (FAQs), so all librarians could be of assistance to honors students.

Working under the auspices of a program director allowed for creative liberty. The reward of demonstrating trustworthiness is being free to make recommendations and trust that they will be taken seriously: librarians had nearly complete autonomy in determining the format and content of the curriculum, from developing logistical documents such as the curriculum packet provided to students, to the actual tutorials and assessments the students completed. When the director expressed confidence in the librarians' abilities, meeting the research needs of the program become a responsibility librarians eagerly embraced, for example, by setting project deadlines and creating rubrics before submitting to other stakeholders for approval.

Partnering with multiple departments enabled all stakeholders to view students from different perspectives and share that knowledge with each other. Students seeking support from writing consultants are in a different phase than those in the midst of research in the library. Faculty benefit from having a support team to corroborate their perspectives on student engagement and quality of work, or to counter those perspectives with additional insights as necessary.

Reflection

After the new curriculum was launched, there were several aspects of this project that improved from the interim implementation (see figure 6.1). First and foremost, the articulation of the thesis project as a year-long curriculum delivered to students (including the curriculum packet and LibGuide) was an effective tool that allowed students to map out their project. Despite occasional miscommunications, having the curriculum also helped keep students accountable: whenever there was uncertainty about a task or deadline, the support staff could point to the same document with the same deadlines.

The LibGuide, which housed all e-forms, tutorials, quizzes, and the digital badges, acted as the Curriculum Packet come to life; it was organized in a simple and consistent format that allowed students to become familiar with the layout and navigate with ease. The e-forms worked like a well-oiled machine, providing automatic grading of quizzes and instantaneous feedback to students. Using these forms reduced the workload for librarians and provided them with automated updates to ensure students were staying on task and not falling too far behind.

Assigning librarians to students for a complete year was a successful example of the personal librarian model. Students communicated with librarians in person, through email, on the phone, and over Skype, and took comfort in having the ability to go to the same person with any questions they might have. In fact, 89 percent of exit survey respondents (twenty-five out of twenty-eight) indicated that they "agreed" or "strongly agreed" that their "experience working with honors librarians was helpful." In turn, being assigned to a specific set of students allowed the librarians to provide motivational support and engage more deeply in open, honest communication.

The librarians' approach to designing this curriculum has had a strong impact on other long-term library initiatives: planning, timelining, and executing multifaceted team projects, especially those with instructional components, has been streamlined and more widely adopted.

Sharing this undertaking with librarian colleagues has increased awareness of holistic methods of curriculum design, instruction, and assessment, and has opened up a library-wide conversation about the value of undergraduate research and the need to archive student scholarship.

With the involvement of a wide variety of disciplinary faculty and support staff, librarians are able to make the case to the larger college community for the personal librarian model, and in turn have drawn attention to a wider variety of ways librarians can support courses.

The personal librarian approach has positively influenced honors librarians in their one-on-one reference support skills with all students. Because they engage in regular, mandatory meetings with honors students and see the results of those interactions, there has been a refinement to reference interview techniques and lines of questioning when working with students on any research project.

Assessment

The nature of the curriculum allows for continuous assessment of student learning and their progress through the stages of a research project. The following methods were used for evaluation:

Tracking documents. To keep track of the students' progress, a single Excel tracking document was created that included columns for all of the tasks and major graded assignments. This was used as a tool for librarians to check in with students as needed if there was an indication that they were falling behind in the completion of tasks. The document was also sent monthly to the faculty so that they could integrate thesis task grades into final grades for each honors seminar.

Completion rates of thesis project tasks. With the development of the tracking documents, analyzing completion rates was simplified. The cohort started out strong during the first seminar with an 89 percent completion rate of thesis tasks. In the next two terms, there was a decrease in students enrolled in the program as well as a decrease in task completion rates: 53 percent and 77 percent, respectively. By the final term there were only thirty-two students of the original fifty-three still in the program, and of that thirty-two only 57 percent were able to complete all of the tasks. Completion of thesis tasks was linked with overall success in the honors program. The majority of students who consistently completed tasks and received badges persisted in and successfully graduated from the program. For a full breakdown of the number of students who completed each task, refer to figure 6.2 below.

Figure 6.2
LC5 Task Completion Rates and Badges Awarded

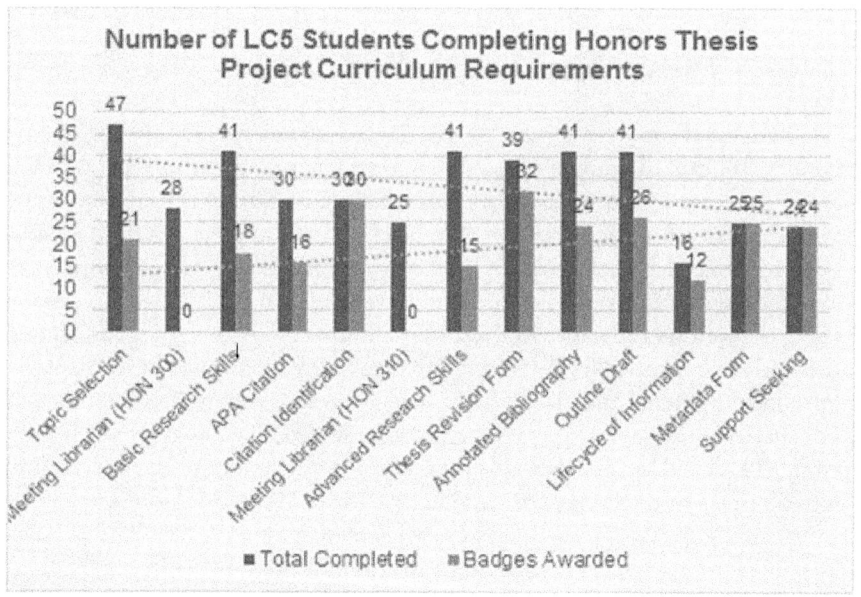

Graded assignments. The two major graded assignments were the source identification and the annotated bibliography. The source identification was used to ensure that students had exposure to introductory research skills, had settled on one topic, and had begun their research. After the submission of the source identification, it was evident that students needed additional support, and librarians provided a template and clearer instructions in preparation for the annotated bibliography. More than half of the students improved their scores from the source identification to the full annotated bibliography (an average improvement of six points on a 100-point scale). The annotated bibliography was one of the final tasks students needed to complete. Regardless of their grade, students could not register for the final honors seminar unless this was submitted.

Figure 6.3
All 12 Digital Badges Available for LC6

Badges. Honors students are typically motivated by competition, and the honors program director suggested that librarians and other support staff find a way to incentivize or gamify the student's completion of the Honors Thesis Project tasks. This need was met through the development of a digital badge system, meant to be challenging and reward only those students who truly excelled. The librarians designed and developed ten digital badges, created using the web-based platform Credly (see figure 6.3). Although students have the option to register for Credly, the badges were used internally, displayed for honors students and faculty in an Excel spreadsheet on the LibGuide, but not available to the public. Each badge represented a task students needed to complete related to their Honors Thesis Project. Throughout the curriculum, for example, students needed to view five video tutorials and complete accompanying quizzes. If a student completed each quiz on time and received 80 percent or higher, they would earn the digital badge available for that task. By achieving the badge, students were demonstrating that they retained the content needed to pass the quiz and were able to keep up with the deadlines.

The remaining badges were awarded when a student completed additional tasks on time, including the annotated bibliography, an outline, and meeting with the support staff. The badge system doubled as an assessment strategy: badges enabled support staff to see which students were completing tasks on time and with a passing score. Unfortunately, none of the students from LC5 was able to achieve all ten badges; however, 66 percent (twenty-one students) achieved more than half (six to nine) of the badges, and 34 percent (eleven students) achieved half or fewer (one to five) of the badges. This data has also allowed the support staff to reflect on the tasks, the level of expectations, and the timing of each submission.

In addition to the assessment methods above, the support staff collected feedback from various stakeholders and have already made improvements for LC6. For example:

Grading. Faculty were uncertain about how to incorporate and give weight to tasks that they did not create or grade and requested that in future iterations, more guidance be provided. In LC6, all seminars will allocate 30 percent of the final grade to Honors Thesis Project tasks.

Writing timeline. Writing consultants recommended that more time be allocated for students to draft their papers, and students from LC5 provided the same feedback in their exit survey. For LC6, students will have a full semester to revise and finalize their paper and will begin drafting the semester before.

Presentation skills. All stakeholders agreed that additional support is needed for presentation development and delivery at the Honors Symposium. Optional drop-in workshops to support these needs are under consideration.

Consistent message. Students expressed frustration that they often received different messages from seminar faculty and support staff, particularly about deadlines and grading. For LC6, faculty are including all tasks in their syllabi, and more robust collaboration between support staff and seminar faculty will occur.

Metacognitive assessment. The Teaching and Learning Commons suggested that students reflect on their experience during each seminar. This feature would allow the students an outlet to reflect on their experience during the thesis process and would allow support staff to make improvements based on common themes identified by the cohort. Support staff are exploring such platforms, publications, and procedures for LC6.

Recommendations/Best Practices

An institution wishing to implement a research curriculum for an undergraduate cohort should be mindful of the following:

Prioritize clear vision and long-term planning. In late 2013, when supporting the Honors Program was first proposed, few of the stakeholders could have imagined the direction this project would take. The value of long-term planning was critical. Librarians used a timeline in late 2014 while developing curriculum documents and throughout 2015 while reconstructing the LibGuide. All stakeholders must buy in and share the same vision in order to make long-term planning feasible.

Remain willing to collaborate. While librarians, writing consultants, and administration were all responsible for the creation of the Honors Thesis Project Curriculum, not all stakeholders were as collaborative as others, and seminar faculty members could have been brought into conversations earlier to ensure lasting and consistent support.

Assert different influence strategies. Librarians were responsible for regularly keeping, sharing, and disseminating data about the thesis project (e.g., percentages of task completion, student topics, and thesis statements) to stakeholders, and attempted to inspire support through rational persuasion. However, assuming this would rally participants was not enough. A coalition/participatory style of influence might have been more successful, appealing to stakeholders' innate commitment to a larger effort because of the benefits it derives for them individually, for the whole, and for the most important stakeholders, the students. Instead of merely reporting numbers such as scores and task completion rates, which can be overlooked if not immediately relevant, librarians could instead share student comments and anecdotes, progress in thesis writing, the development of ideas, etc., which would have inspired greater support for the research component of the honors program.

Continually consider student perspectives. An essential lesson is that students value structure and process. Many students responded positively to the division of tasks for the curriculum. Sixty-four percent of exit survey respondents (eighteen out of twenty-eight) agreed that "the Honors Thesis Project was divided into manageable stages." It is important not to assume honors students' knowledge or ability. While many may be more equipped in some ways than an average undergraduate to tackle research projects of greater magnitude, many may also need the same level of support as their non-honors peers. Students are a key stakeholder, yet they were minimally involved in the planning of this curriculum. With the development of an exit survey, student input is now being more directly incorporated.

Conclusion

The creation of the Honors Thesis Project Curriculum at Berkeley College has legitimized librarians as faculty among their peers and has given them an influential role in the development of a burgeoning program. Furthermore, they have a critical voice in authentically integrating information literacy skills and concepts in a way that demonstrates their value. Despite obstacles, honors librarians have been able to demonstrate the value of collaboration to support a robust undergraduate research program. By working with departmental stakeholders, meeting regularly, and engaging in ongoing revision, the librarians have developed a curriculum that successfully supports a new target group of students, making the research process a rewarding personal learning experience.

Notes

1. Anna Marie Johnson, "Information Literacy Instruction for an Honors Program First-Year Orientation," *Communications in Information Literacy* 6 (2012): 143

Bibliography

Johnson, Anna Marie. "Information Literacy Instruction for an Honors Program First-Year Orientation: Lessons Learned Over 15 Years of a Sustainable Partnership." *Communications in Information Literacy* 6, no. 2 (2012): 141–50.

CHAPTER 7 *
Dreaming Big:
Library-led Digital Scholarship for Undergraduates at a Small Institution

Janelle Wertzberger and R.C. Miessler

Introduction

In the summer of 2016, Gettysburg College's Musselman Library piloted a student-focused, library-led initiative designed to promote creative undergraduate research: the Digital Scholarship Summer Fellowship.[1] The fellowship is a ten-week, paid summer program for rising sophomores and juniors that introduces the student fellows to digital scholarship, exposes them to a range of digital tools, and provides space for them to converse with appropriate partners about research practices and possibilities. Unlike other research fellowship opportunities, the Digital Scholarship Summer Fellowship is programmatic, based on a curriculum designed to provide students a broad introduction to digital scholarship. Digital tools, project management, documentation, and the philosophy behind digital scholarship are equally considered. While a student-created, public-facing project is an expected outcome of the fellowship, the process of getting to that point is the primary pedagogical emphasis. Students are encouraged to use materials from Gettysburg College's Special Collections & College Archives when conceiving their projects.

---

* This work is licensed under a Creative Commons Attribution-NonCommercial-ShareAlike 4.0 License, CC BY-NC-SA (https://creativecommons.org/licenses/by-nc-sa/4.0/).

Using our historic collections as the foundation of a digital project strengthens existing connections between the library and the academic curriculum and provides additional exposure to the library's collections. The fellowship was inspired by digital scholarship initiatives at peer institutions and grew from the library's position as a campus leader in supporting creative undergraduate research. By combining the best aspects from a variety of sources, we were able to create a new learning experience that allowed our students to start small and dream big.

Background

In July 2015, two teams from Gettysburg College attended the first Institute for Liberal Arts and Digital Scholarship (ILiADS)[2] held at Hamilton College. A joint project of Hamilton's Digital Humanities Institute and the College of Wooster, ILiADS sought to bring together digital scholarship practitioners from liberal arts colleges and provide the time, space, and resources to engage in digital projects of their choosing. The teams from Gettysburg were cross-institutional, made up of representatives from the faculty, educational technology, and the library. While the opportunity to deep dive into a digital project for a week was invaluable, the teams were especially interested in the level of student involvement at ILiADS. Several teams from other institutions included student collaborators; those students continued to meet after each day's formal activities were concluded, working on their digital projects well into the night and building a community of practice that crossed institutional lines.[3] The enthusiasm of the students was infectious, and we asked the question, "How do we bring this interest in digital scholarship back with us to Gettysburg?"

We continued to discuss this question at the start of the fall 2015 semester. A Digital Scholarship Working Group formed in the library and was charged to find ways of engaging students in digital scholarship research activity. At the second Bucknell University Digital Scholarship Conference (BUDSC15) in November 2015, the idea of a library-led, student-focused digital scholarship program began to take shape. The conference featured several student-focused scholarship initiatives, two of which served as models and inspiration: Lafayette College's Digital Humanities Summer Scholars program[4] and Haverford College's Digital Scholarship Fellowship.[5] While many of the presentations at BUDSC15 included student projects, these were two examples of structured programs that demonstrated library-led, student-focused digital scholarship initiatives already in place. It was apparent from the creative, digitally-focused, undergraduate research on display at ILiADS and BUDSC15 that students were capable of developing compelling and robust digital scholarship projects when libraries provide the support structure.

While we used undergraduate digital humanities programs at other institutions to inspire our own program, we also looked to existing undergraduate research programs on our campus as models. In 2008, Gettysburg College obtained a grant from The Andrew W. Mellon Foundation to support a college-wide program of undergraduate research that is embedded within the curriculum. As part of the grant, ten to twelve students were awarded a Mellon Summer Scholarship to conduct faculty-mentored summer research each year in the humanities or social sciences. Our fellowship was modeled after the Mellon research opportunity in several ways. For instance, we planned for a ten-week experience, the same stipend amount ($3,500) was awarded to students, a common living space for the cohort was provided, and students gave a public presentation of research at the completion of the project. In other ways, we made alternative decisions regarding fellowship administration. For example, we designed a low barrier to entry for applicants and a high degree of structure throughout the ten-week fellowship period. Our fellowship complemented an existing campus research opportunity while being distinct and attractive to a different population of applicants.

Another model program which informed our planning was the Peer Research Mentor program at our library. We began hiring student Peer Research Mentors to work alongside librarians at our Research Help Desk in 2014 and experienced success in training students to mentor their peers in how to conduct research.[6] Gettysburg College has an established culture of using peer mentors in a variety of ways, and we were optimistic that the approach would support student learning in digital scholarship, as well.

We also had two "aha moments" that helped shape our Digital Scholarship Summer Fellowship. The first one emerged from a conversation about how to create a research experience that was accessible and inclusive to all students. We realized that most students who successfully earn other coveted undergraduate research opportunities on our campus do so because of pre-existing relationships with professors who encourage them to apply, offer to mentor their work, and so on. Many students are capable of doing this type of research, but the opportunity isn't accessible to them without a developed network of faculty supporters to encourage and recommend them for that work. It also tends to be an option later in a student's undergraduate career, after a student has declared a major and formed stronger relationships with faculty. We wanted our fellowship to feature a lower barrier to entry that didn't rely on a professor's availability to support a student's research during the summer and was accessible to rising sophomores and juniors.

We also designed the application process to be as transparent and inclusive as possible.[7] We knew that the concept of "digital scholarship" would be new to students and so we devoted considerable space to describing it in our call for applications. We linked to several digital projects and to a range of digital tools. To apply, we asked students to submit a statement of interest addressing what they hope to learn and accomplish during the fellowship, describing ideas for potential projects and outlining their experience with technology and digital tools. Applicants listed a faculty reference but the application process did not require a reference letter. We also offered to speak with students about their ideas before the application due date. Many applicants took advantage of this opportunity and, consequently, application materials were stronger because of it. Finally, we conducted interviews to allow students to further explain their vision in-person. These choices were designed to encourage students to apply who might have been daunted by the application processes for other undergraduate research opportunities. One of our refrains was to "dream big"—we encouraged students to approach the fellowship with a big-picture idea that we would help them refine as needed.

The second "aha" moment had to do with research materials for digital projects. While we wanted students to have the freedom to choose any type of project on any topic, we also knew some students would thrive with more guidance. Consequently, we identified some primary source collections in our Special Collections and College Archives that were already digitized and ready to be used and interpreted in digital scholarship projects. We directed students to those materials for inspiration and possible use, but did not restrict their ideas to projects involving these collections. The scope of the primary source documents in Musselman Library's Special Collections encouraged narrative digital scholarship projects that tell stories of people and places through artifacts such as photographs, letters, and scrapbooks (as opposed to the more analytical digital scholarship approaches that draw conclusions from large amounts of data).

Partnerships

The library initiated the Digital Scholarship Summer Fellowship and continues to lead student-centered digital scholarship activities on our campus. Our campus climate is like that of many small liberal arts colleges, where employees tend to play many roles. Christina Bell emphasizes the collaborative ethos of the small college and concludes that the "library is a natural place to form the type of collaborative team that can bring the methods, practices, and tools of digital scholarship to a small college."[8] That is true at Gettysburg College, and we have many partners who are vital to supporting the range of activities included under the umbrella of "digital scholarship." Seventeen individuals created and facilitated one or more workshops for our student fellows during the summer, and only seven of them are local librarians or archivists.[9] The others included three educational technologists from our Information Technology department, an education professor, a computer science professor, two administrators from our Civil War Institute, a recent graduate now working in the IT field, and representatives from digital humanities initiatives at two other liberal arts colleges.

We also had support from our Provost's Office. Specifically, we received funding for one of the three summer fellows ($4,000). More important, the Associate Provost for Academic Technology Initiatives & Faculty Development was keenly interested in this initiative. One of his roles is to promote use of digital tools in faculty scholarship or in teaching. While our goal was to directly support student use of digital tools, the associate provost was watching closely to review student accomplishments. He was impressed by what the students had learned and created over the summer and subsequently allocated funds to allow the three fellows to continue working during the following academic year to assist with digital scholarship needs in the library and in the classroom. We put a call out to faculty who are interested in DS support for their classes and have begun collaborating with them on assignment design and discussing how the DSSFs can help students succeed on the digital assignments. This work has also engaged new faculty partners who are not regular users of our information literacy instruction services.

Reflection

The 2016 Digital Scholarship Summer Fellowship taught us that it is possible for undergraduates to become novice digital scholars during an intensive, ten-week research experience. With a scaffolded approach and a healthy dose of mentoring, students can plan and execute digital projects during a short time period. Prior to the summer, we were a little worried that students would not be able to finish during the fellowship. We had many conversations and negotiations about "right sizing" their projects in order to bring them to completion by the deadline—and all three students were successful. While this approach worked for the students, it was very time-intensive for the members of the Digital Scholarship Working Group. We are still musing on how to reduce the load on library employees without reducing the quality of the student experience.

We anticipate offering the Digital Scholarship Summer Fellowship again in 2017 and have begun to think about changes in the curriculum. The 2016 syllabus worked well for new fellows, but in 2017 we hope to involve the 2016 fellows as DS mentors. The 2016 fellows are already eager to lead some of the workshops. We also need to consider how they can continue to advance their own digital skills while mentoring a new set of students.

Assessment

When designing our ten-week fellowship, we included a variety of formative assessment activities. Members of the Digital Scholarship Working Group had a lot of face time with the student fellows during the summer. In addition to several workshops per week, we had a daily check-in meeting every morning and a weekly lunch meeting. These gatherings served as informal assessments and we continuously encouraged the students to reflect on how they were progressing toward their project goals. Fellows wrote several blog posts each week, and one of those posts was a response to a reflective prompt.[10] We used writing prompts to help students assess their own understanding of digital scholarship as well as their progress toward completing a digital project.

Asking students to talk and write about their learning also helped us understand what they needed, even if the fellows didn't articulate it directly. For example, when we heard the fellows describing themselves as "not tech savvy" at the start of the summer, we initiated conversations about projecting confidence and competence. Their intent was to show how far they'd come during the summer (they started as "not tech savvy" and grew into digital scholars), but we knew not everyone would hear what they meant. It was a perfect opportunity to talk about how researchers are perceived, especially early career female researchers.

To more formally assess the program, we asked the fellows to complete written evaluations at the fellowship midpoint and again at the end of the summer. Both were presented to students as formative assessments designed to help us understand what was working or not working so that we could correct course as needed. These evaluations helped us understand the value of undergraduate networking. Our DSSFs benefited greatly from meeting with students in a similar fellowship at another liberal arts college and would have liked even more contact with them (we took a field trip to their campus and would have enjoyed a reciprocal visit). They indicated that another field trip would have been worthwhile and even suggested visiting the New York Public Library, as they had found their digital collections helpful and inspiring. Closer to home, our students requested that future DSSFs be assigned campus housing with other undergraduate researchers working in the humanities and social sciences. In order to provide additional time for the DSSFs to focus on their projects, workshops considered non-essential to the completion of these particular projects, such as advanced text encoding and data visualization, were eliminated (but could possibly be included in future iterations of the fellowship). The blogging requirements were also reduced. Finally, we asked the audience members who attended the fellows' final presentations to provide written feedback for the students.

Recommendations/Best Practices

For other libraries wanting to begin a DS fellowship for students, we advise thinking carefully about resources such as money and time. Money is important but not as important as you might think. We paid each summer fellow a $3,500 stipend plus $500 for campus summer housing. We had a small budget that covered occasional meals, a field trip, and office supplies. To the surprise of our library dean, we didn't request to buy a single piece of technology; we only invested in people and experiences. All the software students used was already licensed by Information Technology or freely available. Time is more important than money. Do not underestimate the time it takes to plan and implement a new initiative with so many moving parts. Also, if you're planning a summer experience, factor in staff vacations. Having the right mentors available can make or break a student experience.

This student fellowship changed how some members of the Digital Scholarship Working Group approach their work. For our Systems Librarian, it meant bringing his content expertise to a new audience (students) and approaching time management in new ways. In addition to sharing his knowledge with students, he had to think about communicating to other audiences beyond technologists and librarians, like faculty and representatives from the Provost's Office. For our assistant dean and director of scholarly communications, who has a background in public services and information literacy instruction, the fellowship required bringing a new content area (digital humanities/digital scholarship) to a familiar audience (students). Both librarians had complementary skills and communication styles. Our program could not have been implemented nearly as well by one person or the other.

Our DS student initiative has made it possible for our library to offer a new service beginning in the fall 2016 semester. We received funding from the Provost's Office to hire our three seasoned student fellows to support digital project work assigned by faculty. If professors want to create a new assignment (or enhance an existing one) with a digital component, the fellows are prepared to work with them to recommend the best digital platform, support the use of digital tools, and assist with training and mentoring students in the development of their projects. After announcing this service to campus, we heard from interested faculty in History, Spanish, and Environmental Studies.

The most important things we learned from the experience of developing, implementing, assessing, and reflecting on our initiative are:
- The experience of *daily* interaction with each other, with us, and with many campus partners was integral to the success of our inaugural group of Digital Scholarship Summer Fellows and to their happiness. Our fellows formed strong bonds and supported each

other through their struggles and their accomplishments. The interpersonal dynamic would not have been the same with fewer than three people. Developing a community of practice locally, as well as drawing upon the larger digital scholarship communities of practice, reinforces the collaborative nature of digital scholarship. Opening many of the workshops to the campus community allowed the fellows to engage with students, faculty, and administrators who were likewise interested in digital scholarship. A field trip to visit Lafayette College's Digital Humanities Summer Scholars also encouraged the fellows to collaborate cross-institutionally.

- Digital scholarship requires physical space. We suspected that the fellows would desire dedicated workspace and we reserved a large study room for them to use over the summer. They used it heavily (and creatively) but they also used many other spaces in and outside the library, too. We regularly spotted them working in a library computer lab, a library meeting room, study spaces on various floors of the library, Special Collections & College Archives, and the library patio. It would have been a mistake to invest heavily in one physical space; in the future, we will advocate for allocating flexible space to digital fellows.
- Like any new initiative, the development, implementation, and continuation of the program required a significant investment of time and human resources. Even if using other programs as guides, workshops and readings have to be tailored to the outcomes of the local program and adapted to fit with the skillsets of available partners.

Conclusion

The Digital Scholarship Summer Fellowship proved to be a success, with three creative, scholarly student projects developed in ten weeks, a well-received presentation of the student work, and a desire to continue the program beyond the summer.[11] The students dreamed big with their projects and brought them to fruition. The librarians at Gettysburg College likewise dreamed big about the possibilities of what creative undergraduate learning can be. Together, we developed a foundation for further digital scholarship activity led by Musselman Library to support innovative, public-facing student research.

Appendix 7A: Final Presentation Audience Feedback Form

Welcome to the Digital Scholarship Summer Fellow presentations!

Our 2016 student fellows have created public-facing scholarly projects. It is especially important for them to receive feedback from listeners in order to improve (or validate) their communication skills. Please share some comments that will help our student presenters understand how well they are conveying their research results to a general audience.

All audience feedback is anonymous and will be typed and compiled before sharing with the student presenters.

Thank you for your support of digital scholarship and student research!

Presenter name: _____

I learned:	I wish I had learned:
I was impressed:	Comments for Presenter to Ponder:

Thanks to Prof. Divonna Stebick for allowing us to use and modify her feedback form.

Notes

1. Gettysburg College has embraced the phrase Digital Scholarship rather than Digital Humanities in order to be inclusive of the breadth of the college's scholarly activity. Digital Scholarship, in the context of this fellowship, then, means using digital tools and methods to interpret, analyze, and present original research.
2. http://iliads.org.
3. Several students from the first ILiADS formed the Undergraduate Network for Research in the Humanities (UNRH, http://unrh.org) and have organized two conferences as of January 2017.
4. http://sites.lafayette.edu/dhss.
5. http://ds.haverford.edu/dsfellows/.
6. Janelle Wertzberger et al., "Peer Research Mentors at Gettysburg College," in *Peer-Assisted Learning in Academic Libraries*, ed. Erin Rinto, John Watts, and Rosan Mitola (Santa Barbara: Libraries Unlimited, 2017). Forthcoming.

7. The 2016 summer application is available at http://dssf.musselmanlibrary.org/2016/application/.
8. Christina Bell, "In Practice and Pedagogy Digital Humanities in a Small College Environment," in *Digital Humanities in the Library: Challenges and Opportunities for Subject Specialists*, ed. Arianne Hartsell-Gundy, Laura Braunstein, and Liorah Golomb (Chicago: The Association of College & Research Libraries, 2015), 104.
9. Musselman Library, "Schedule/Syllabus," Digital Scholarship Summer Fellows 2016, 2016, http://dssf.musselmanlibrary.org/2016/syllabus/.
10. Ibid. As an example, here is a blog post prompt from week six of the fellowship: "As digital humanities practitioners at a small liberal arts college, it's important to be aware of criticism of digital humanities work, as well as negative perceptions of liberal arts schools. Read 'Neoliberal Tools (and Archives): A Political History of Digital Humanities.' Given what you have learned so far about digital humanities and digital scholarship, what is your reaction to this article? Do you agree with the authors, disagree, or somewhere in between? Make sure you are acquainted with the concept of neoliberalism. The article 'The Neoliberal Arts: How College Sold Its Soul to the Market' by William Deresiewicz may provide some additional context. Once you've read the article and formulated some thoughts, check out some responses. Feel free to incorporate their arguments into yours, or refute them."
11. Musselman Library, "Projects," Digital Scholarship Summer Fellows 2016 (2016), http://dssf.musselmanlibrary.org/2016/projects/.

Bibliography

Bell, Christina. "In Practice and Pedagogy Digital Humanities in a Small College Environment." In *Digital Humanities in the Library: Challenges and Opportunities for Subject Specialists*, edited by Arianne Hartsell-Gundy, Laura Braunstein, and Liorah Golomb, Chicago: The Association of College & Research Libraries, 2015: 103–26.

Musselman Library. "Schedule/Syllabus." Digital Scholarship Summer Fellows 2016. (2016). http://dssf.musselmanlibrary.org/2016/syllabus/.

Wertzberger, Janelle, Baugess, Clinton, Jallas, Mallory, and Smith, Meggan. "Peer Research Mentors at Gettysburg College." In *Peer-Assisted Learning in Academic Libraries*, edited by Erin Rinto, John Watts, and Rosan Mitola. Santa Barbara: Libraries Unlimited, 2017. Forthcoming.

CHAPTER 8

Engaging in the Undergraduate Researcher Writers' Process:
Creating a Thesis Writers' Bootcamp

Katie Harding and Lora Leligdon

Introduction

Holistic support for independent undergraduate research needs to exist throughout the entire undergraduate research lifecycle. While many library programs support the beginning phases of the lifecycle—especially during the discovery phase—one area of opportunity for engagement is increased support during the writing phase. To support undergraduate researchers during this phase, libraries can provide programs such as writing bootcamps or retreats for students completing a senior thesis or other culminating project. Writing retreats and bootcamps can enable undergraduate researchers to build community with their peers, develop important time management strategies, avoid and overcome writer's block and procrastination, acquire ex-

---

* This work is licensed under a Creative Commons Attribution 4.0 License, CC BY (https://creativecommons.org/licenses/by/4.0/).

perience with goal setting and meeting deadlines, and practice good writing habits. They also provide students with the opportunity to meet with, ask questions of, and learn from experts in writing and research.

As experts in information creation, retrieval, and management, librarians have a natural affinity to support the writing phase of the research lifecycle. Our physical spaces and our identity as the hub of scholarly activities on campus are a natural fit to support this important aspect of the undergraduate research process. Thesis writers' bootcamps or retreats are an impactful, easy-to-implement, and low-cost way to support students during this process. While our discussion is based on our experiences in a science library, the information provided about writing retreats and bootcamps is easily transferable to other disciplines, colleges, and academic libraries.

Background

Dartmouth College is a private liberal arts college located in Hanover, New Hampshire. Dartmouth offers undergraduate and graduate degrees and has three professional schools: the Geisel School of Medicine, Thayer School of Engineering, and Tuck School of Business. In the fall of 2015, 4,307 undergraduate students and 2,043 graduate students were enrolled at Dartmouth.[1] All undergraduate students at Dartmouth College must complete a culminating experience in their major, such as a thesis or major research project.[2] To meet this requirement, many students in the sciences complete an undergraduate thesis.

At Dartmouth, the Kresge Physical Sciences Library supports the departments of Chemistry, Computer Science, Earth Sciences, Environmental Studies, Mathematics, and Physics and Astronomy. Librarians at Kresge Library offer traditional services, such as research consultations and reference services, information literacy instruction, and citation management workshops. We also provide services and programming to support science students in all phases of their culminating experience, such as a series of workshops on advanced research skills (e.g., information and data management) and support for undergraduate research symposia (poster preparation workshops, presentation practice sessions, and an award for library research). To support thesis writers, for the past several years, Kresge Library has offered a Thesis Writers' Bootcamp for the Sciences. Our bootcamp included the critical components of a writers' retreat as described by Stanford University: space, routine, peers, and experts.[3] These elements include:

- The library provides a dedicated, quiet space that is free of distractions to facilitate student writing.
- A daily schedule provides thesis writers with a routine and protected time in which to complete their writing.

- The presence of other students working on similar projects provides motivation and a sense of community, which the library can encourage through bootcamp programming.
- Experts such as librarians and writing specialists can help students through any problems they may encounter, and can help students get "unstuck."

In addition to each of these components, our thesis writers' bootcamp also offered several other value-added components, including:
- goal-setting opportunities for students to consider what they wish to accomplish over the course of the bootcamp
- examples of "exemplary" theses from various scientific departments
- peer review sessions in which students are able to learn from both giving and receiving peer feedback
- free lunch and snacks to keep energy levels high and ensure that students can focus on their writing

While the majority of the bootcamp was allocated to protected writing time, we were able to interact with students at several times throughout the day. This year, during the morning kick-off and goal setting session, we fielded questions on departmental thesis guidelines and how to find Dartmouth undergraduate theses using the library catalog. During the drop-in consultation sessions, we received questions about topics such as searching for literature in Web of Science and using LaTeX to typeset a thesis. At the end of each day, we had conversations with students in which we prompted them to reflect on the progress they had made toward their writing goals and we acknowledged their hard work and accomplishments.

Further ideas for programming can be found in a description of a senior thesis camp offered by librarians at the University of Notre Dame.[4] Their senior thesis camp in the College of Arts and Letters was held for five days during fall break and included workshops on such topics as citation management, conducting a literature review, intellectual property, student presentations, and undergraduate scholar opportunities and fellowships.[5] A thesis writing bootcamp also presents a valuable opportunity to talk to students about making their work available in the institutional repository and to encourage them to submit their thesis if policy allows.

Partnerships

Partnerships are a critical element of a successful bootcamp. The science librarians collaborated with several programs and departments on campus to implement the event.

Library

Science librarians organized the thesis writers' bootcamp. We were responsible for planning the event, including choosing an appropriate time and location, creating a bootcamp schedule, ordering lunch and snacks, creating signage, coordinating with the writing tutor and academic departments, marketing the event to students and faculty, coordinating registration, and providing evaluations (and incentives for completing them!). During the bootcamp, our role as organizers included setup, facilitating introductions at the start of the day, and encouraging students to set goals for the bootcamp. Liaison librarians also offered research help to students during the bootcamp, including guidance in creating literature searches, assistance with citations, and assistance with presenting data. The science library was responsible for the budget of the event. While a writing bootcamp is relatively inexpensive, the associated costs should be estimated carefully. When implementing a writing retreat or bootcamp, the costs of the following items were considered:

- lunch, beverages, and snacks for all participants
- costs associated with a campus-affiliated or external writing specialist
- prizes or incentives to encourage students to complete a short feedback survey
- printing of marketing materials, signage, and thesis guidelines
- any facility costs, such as extended weekend hours or additional custodian support

If existing campus support services (space, printing, tutors, etc.) are already included in an annual budget, only food and prizes add additional expense to the event.

Writing Center

Dartmouth's Institute for Writing and Rhetoric provided materials and tutors for the thesis writers' bootcamp. These materials included guidelines for peer reviewing and thesis writing tips. During the bootcamp, the writing tutor gave a short presentation to students about how to manage a major writing project and provided some effective strategies. The tutor was also available to meet with students for individual consultations in which to provide feedback on portions of student drafts or answer questions related to writing. Finally, the writing tutor organized the peer review sessions and provided guidelines to students for peer review. During peer review sessions, students were able to receive constructive peer support and recommendations on their writing from the perspective of a peer who was not already familiar with their project. Though the paired peer review students worked independently, the writing tutor was available to answer any questions.

Academic Departments in the Sciences

Each academic department in the sciences provided us with their guidelines for students writing undergraduate theses and past examples of undergraduate theses that were particularly well done. We provided these resources as part of the bootcamp in order to help students understand expectations for their thesis.

Another important role of the academic departments was to provide publicity for the thesis writers' bootcamp. Liaison librarians emailed both students and faculty in their departments to share information about the bootcamp. We found that students were especially motivated to attend the bootcamp when it was recommended by their faculty supervisor or other faculty in the department, which is consistent with student feedback received by librarians at the University of Notre Dame.[6] Feedback provided by the faculty indicated that they appreciated the student support that the bootcamp provided.

Reflection

We found that thesis writers' bootcamps are an easy-to-implement, low-cost way for libraries to support undergraduates as they write their thesis. Students benefit from having protected and supported writing time in a quiet space free of distractions, and they are always especially grateful when free food is provided.

In our experience, it is useful to provide students with resources and experts who they can consult when they are having trouble with writing or research, but in general students use bootcamp time according to their own needs, regardless of what is on the schedule. While it is important for us to be thoughtful in creating our bootcamp schedule, it is equally important for us to be flexible and willing to adapt to the needs of students during the bootcamp. We have tried to allow our thesis writers' bootcamp to be shaped by our experiences and student feedback from our library's previous bootcamps.

A writing tutor is a highly valuable resource for students at the retreat. Students may or may not feel that they are ready to meet with a writing tutor, depending on the progress that they have made on their thesis. We recommend advertising meetings with writing tutors prior to the retreat, and providing students with clear guidelines for preparing for a discussion with a writing tutor. Although we advertised the writing tutor ahead of time, we found that few students met with the writing tutor. Smith and Kayongo noted that only two students in the University of Notre Dame senior thesis camp met with a writing tutor and that both of these students asked questions but did not bring in any drafts of their writing.[7] If retreat attendance is low or if students do not feel prepared to meet with a writing tutor, it can be difficult to balance making the writing tutor available to students and ensuring that the writing tutor's time is well used. This is especially true if there is a cost associated with hosting a writing tutor. We balanced this by choosing to invite the writing tutor to attend one day of our two-day bootcamp.

Scheduling and timing are challenging when organizing a writing bootcamp or retreat. Senior undergraduates tend to be very busy, so when choosing dates we considered thesis deadlines, deadlines for other major assignments, and exam schedules. Additionally, our library supports students in a number of different disciplines and with different requirements, and we wanted to be as inclusive as possible when offering our thesis writers' bootcamp. Because the deadline for undergraduate theses varies by department, choosing dates that would be useful to students in different disciplines was difficult. We attempted to address this challenge by offering two bootcamp dates several weeks apart.

We offered our thesis writers' bootcamp on the weekend to ensure that students had a full day of uninterrupted writing time and did not have scheduling conflicts with their courses. We found that scheduling a bootcamp to start mid-morning on a Sunday meant that attendance was relatively low early in the day. Going forward, it may be worthwhile to consider a later start time or to plan for the welcome session to coincide with a meal or snack.

In developing a bootcamp schedule for our students, it was difficult to find a balance between writing time and time with experts in writing and research. We recommend that writing bootcamps emphasize writing time over instruction. It was useful for us to share some of our expertise with students and to be available when needed, but students primarily needed protected time and space to write.

Bootcamp events benefit both the students and the library. While students benefit in the ways described above, the library also gains from the event. One notable benefit of writing retreats and bootcamps is they help librarians to promote our role in research to students, faculty, and campus partners. We sometimes find it difficult to convey to faculty, students, and staff on campus the breadth of expertise and services that we can offer. A thesis writers' bootcamp helped us to demonstrate to our patrons that supporting all phases of research is a priority for libraries, and to emphasize some of the forms that support can take.

Assessment

In evaluating our thesis writers' bootcamp, we considered both our attendance and the feedback received from students in a post-bootcamp survey. Post-event surveys from 2014–2016 assessed how helpful students found the bootcamp in terms of helping them make progress on their thesis, what items or sessions were helpful, and any suggestions for improvements or changes for future events. When the writing tutor and peer-to-peer review sessions were added in 2015, we added questions on how helpful students found these sessions.

Overall, 74 percent of students rated the bootcamps as "very helpful," 26 percent found them "helpful," and no students rated the events "not particular helpful" or "'not helpful at all." When students were asked what was particularly useful at the event, frequent responses included snacks, lunch, the environment, peers, dedicated writing time, and support. Based on feedback from the 2014 survey requesting additional support, we added writing support in the form of a writing tutor and peer editing sessions for 2015 and 2016.

When we examined the results of the survey, we noticed that many students attended only one day of the bootcamp. This indicated to us that it is important to ensure that each day of thesis writers' bootcamp is self-contained. Verbal feedback from the attendees, both during and after the event, indicated that the event is very appreciated, useful, and even fun.

Informal feedback received from library administration, the writing tutor, and faculty indicated that the bootcamp is appreciated and beneficial to students. We were encouraged to continue to hold the event each year.

Recommendations/Best Practices

Thesis bootcamps or writing retreats support students in the writing phase of the research lifecycle by providing the space, routine, peers, and experts needed for students to successfully engage with their thesis. By engaging with faculty and academic departments early in the process, the materials and support needed are easy to acquire. Best practices for successful bootcamps include providing a balance of writing time and activities, carefully considering the timing and schedule of the event for maximum impact during the term, offering a variety of value-added components to let bootcampers design their own experience, and having plenty of food and drinks available.

Successful bootcamp events could also be used to transition into other new initiatives. Building off the event to offer ongoing undergraduate writers groups or stand-alone bootcamp events for graduate students and faculty writers are ways to provide new programs. At Dartmouth, we are building on the success of our thesis writers' bootcamp and planning to offer a writers' retreat for graduate students and postdoctoral fellows in the sciences.

Conclusion

Events like writing bootcamps and retreats not only help raise the library's profile as partner and an integral part of the undergraduate research process, they also demonstrate that the library provides full research workflow support, going well beyond traditional collection and instruction. We strongly recommend that other libraries implement these low-cost, easy, and well appreciated events.

Sample thesis bootcamp schedule

Time	Program	Day 1	Day 2
10:00 a.m.	Bootcamp starts		
10:10 a.m.–10:30 a.m.	Kick-off event	Set a writing goal for the day and hear tips on how to tackle a big writing project.	Set a writing goal for the day and hear about the benefits of peer to peer review.
10:30 a.m.–12:00 p.m.	Focused writing time	Individual writing time. Exemplary sample theses, departmental guidelines, and writing and style guides available for review.	
12:00 p.m.–1:15 p.m.	Lunch	Join us for a healthy group lunch on us!	
1:15 p.m.–1:30 p.m.	Campers' check-in	Goal check-in and afternoon schedule review.	
1:30 p.m.–2:30 p.m.	Focused writing time Drop-in consultations (optional)	Meet with a librarian for help with: research and literature reviews; bibliographies and reference management software (Zotero, Mendeley); Word/Excel (formatting; charts, figures, tables).	Meet with a writing tutor for help with: expert feedback on your draft; writing style and guidelines; thesis writing tips.

2:30 p.m.–3:30 p.m.	Focused writing time Peer review sessions (optional)		Give and receive feedback on your introduction, lit review, data amd analysis, or conclusion from other thesis writers.
3:30 p.m.–5:00 p.m.	Focused writing time	Individual writing time. Exemplary sample theses, departmental guidelines, and writing and style guides available for review.	
5:00 p.m.	Bootcamp ends		

Notes

1. Dartmouth College, "Enrollment," accessed June 24, 2016, https://www.dartmouth.edu/~oir/data-reporting/factbook/enrollment.html.
2. Dartmouth College, "Culminating Experience in the Major," accessed June 23, 2016, http://dartmouth.smartcatalogiq.com/en/2015/orc/Regulations/Undergraduate-Study/Requirements-for-the-Degree-of-Bachelor-of-Arts/Culminating-Experience-in-the-Major.
3. Stanford University, "Dissertation Boot Camp," accessed March 2, 2016, https://undergrad.stanford.edu/tutoring-support/hume-center/writing/graduate-students/dissertation-boot-camp.
4. Cheri Smith and Jessica Kayongo, "Senior Thesis Camp: Partnerships in Practice at the University of Notre Dame," *Journal of Academic Librarianship* 37, no. 5 (2011): 437–42, doi:10.1016/j.acalib.2011.06.008.
5. Ibid., 440.
6. Ibid., 438.
7. Ibid., 441.

Bibliography

Dartmouth College. "Culminating Experience in the Major." Accessed June 23, 2016. http://dartmouth.smartcatalogiq.com/en/2015/orc/Regulations/Undergraduate-Study/Requirements-for-the-Degree-of-Bachelor-of-Arts/Culminating-Experience-in-the-Major.

Dartmouth College. "Enrollment." Accessed June 24, 2016. https://www.dartmouth.edu/~oir/data-reporting/factbook/enrollment.html.

Smith, Cheri, and Jessica Kayongo. "Senior Thesis Camp: Partnerships in Practice at the University of Notre Dame." *Journal of Academic Librarianship* 37, no. 5 (2011): 437–42, doi:10.1016/j.acalib.2011.06.008.

Stanford University. "Dissertation Boot Camp." Accessed March 2, 2016. https://undergrad.stanford.edu/tutoring-support/hume-center/writing/graduate-students/dissertation-boot-camp.

CHAPTER 9*
Engaging Our Student Partners:
Student Leadership in a Library-Initiated Experiential Learning Project

Michelle Reed, Philip Duncan, and Germaine Halegoua

Introduction

This chapter discusses aspects of Undergraduates Speak: Our Rights and Access, a library-initiated and student-led pilot project aimed at advancing educational initiatives in the realm of scholarly communication. The project provided undergraduate students with opportunities to engage in experiential learning. Experiential learning, commonly defined as "learning by doing," emphasizes the role that experience and self-reflection play in the learning process. In recent years, universities across the country have increasingly committed to providing such opportunities for undergraduate students. One reason for this emphasis is because experiential activities have a demonstrated impact on student retention and engagement.[1] Among these high-impact practices are undergraduate research, internship, and service-learning opportunities. This chapter examines all three via Undergraduates Speak, where

---

* This work is licensed under a Creative Commons Attribution 4.0 License, CC BY (https://creativecommons.org/licenses/by/4.0/).

103

undergraduate students actively participated in exploratory research at multiple stages along the research continuum.

Background

The University of Kansas Libraries have a long history of leadership and innovation in scholarly communication and, more specifically, in Open Access (OA), a movement aimed at making peer-reviewed published scholarship available free of charge to the public and to the global scholarly community. The University of Kansas (KU) was the first public institution in the United States to adopt a faculty-led OA policy. Additionally, the KU Libraries were a signatory of the Berlin Declaration on Open Access to Knowledge in the Sciences and Humanities and a founding member of the Coalition of Open Access Policy Institutions (COAPI). Outreach and engagement with undergraduate students on these issues, however, are limited.

In 2012, KU initiated Bold Aspirations, a strategic plan for 2012–2017 that adopted enhanced experiential learning opportunities as a strategy to "strengthen recruitment, teaching, and mentoring to prepare undergraduate students for lifelong learning, leadership, and success."[2] KU Libraries likewise issued a strategic plan in 2012 that mirrored the time frame and aligned closely with the principles of Bold Aspirations, though experiential learning was not listed as an explicit outcome.[3] Relevant key goals and strategies unique to the libraries' plan included:
- collaborate with campus partners to develop online, reusable teaching modules, digital learning objects, tutorials, and assignments;
- assess campus needs for expanding scholarly communication services to KU faculty and students; and
- collaborate with campus partners to expand the libraries' scholarly communications outreach, education, and advocacy program.

The grant-funded pilot Undergraduates Speak was created to achieve the goals above through undergraduate-centered experiential learning.[4] The project was divided into two phases that spanned the fall and spring semesters of the 2015/16 academic year. The first phase actively involved undergraduate students in exploratory research about scholarly communication and OA. This was accomplished by offering an internship to an undergraduate student, whose primary responsibility was to lead focus group discussions with other undergraduates about these topics. The second phase relied on data collected during the first phase to inform the production of an open educational resource (OER) that could be integrated into KU's undergraduate curriculum as an introduction to copyright and OA. Design and production of this resource was accomplished by the libraries' participation in a service-learning course, Digital Storytelling, offered by campus partners. Undergraduates Speak thus presented an opportunity to increase the libraries' understanding of undergraduate perspectives on scholarly communication issues concerning copyright and openness, in addition to advancing other goals of building collaborative partnerships and growing the libraries' collection of sustainable learning objects.

Partnerships
Internship Partners

For the first phase of the project, KU Libraries hired two student research assistants to serve as interns. One graduate student with experience in human subjects research and qualitative methods partnered with an undergraduate student with no experience in research methodology or design. The principal investigator (PI), a librarian, adopted a challenge-and-support approach to the project's development. The student team was charged with designing and conducting exploratory research using focus group discussions and were provided the following four research questions to guide their work:

1. To what extent are undergraduate students aware of the rights and restrictions of copyright law?
2. What rights associated with copyright do undergraduate students value most, and is there a correlation between these values and students' online behaviors?
3. To what extent are undergraduate students aware of OA publishing?
4. To what extent do undergraduate students support "open" models of scholarly publishing?

The PI communicated the major objective of the pilot: to begin addressing the gap in student engagement on key issues related to scholarly communication. The PI also provided a timeline and introductory reading materials and facilitated connection with a support system for the students, consisting of subject experts, faculty mentors, and librarians.[5]

The student team took immediate ownership of the project and expanded the scope to collect survey data in addition to the focus group discussions. They created a protocol that received approval from KU's Institutional Review Board (IRB); they developed a recruitment strategy and designed recruitment flyers and social media posts; they created and implemented three surveys, a focus group discussion guide, and additional focus group activities; they drafted informed consent documents; and they managed all communication with study participants. At the conclusion of the project, the students wrote reflectively about their experiences using a prompt that asked them to describe their role in the project, discuss what they gained from the experience, and apply what they learned to future work.

The overall project design was divided between the two members of the student team based on their interests and expertise, with the onus for developing protocol and managing participant communication placed on the graduate student. Both students designed materials for use in the focus groups and actively contributed to the creation of the moderator guide. The undergraduate student, who had experience moderating debates in high school, designed participant recruitment materials and led all focus group discussions. The PI arranged two mock focus group discussions, one with library staff and another with other student employees, so that the undergraduate intern could practice before engaging with study participants. Guided by published reflections on undergraduate partnerships, the PI regularly stressed the importance of adhering to the moderator guide for consistency among groups.[6] In addition, both students were tasked with coordinating with KU's Media Production Studio to capture audio and video of the focus group discussions for review by the PI, and for potential use in the second phase of the project.[7]

The student team conducted a total of five videotaped focus group discussions involving twenty-seven participants (twenty-four female, three male), all of whom were traditional undergraduates. Each class level was represented, though the participants were overwhelmingly sophomores (n = fifteen), as were eighteen different majors from within the College of Liberal Arts and Sciences. Days prior to the focus groups, the graduate research assistant prompted each participant to complete an online survey aimed at collecting information on awareness, experience, and attitudes related to copyright and OA. The goal in this survey was to elicit responses that might illuminate both students' knowledge and behaviors, which could be explored in greater depth during the focus groups. Additionally, participants filled out a short exit survey at the close of each session, which addressed opinions regarding who should benefit from and be able to access scholarly work. It also probed student interest in further learning opportunities about copyright and OA.

Though the sample size of participants in the pilot was small, the data points to significant gaps in undergraduates' knowledge of copyright and its implications for access to information. Students' self-reported understanding of copyright was much higher than that of OA (virtually none reported familiarity with OA), yet students demonstrated little engagement with particulars about copyright. This was borne out in both the surveys and the focus groups. For example, when asked in a survey, "Are you a copyright owner?" only one respondent indicated "Yes," another "I don't know," and all others selected "No." This suggests that students are unaware that copyright automatically applies to their created works. One of the focus group activities explored the notion of copyright as a "bundle" of rights (reproduce, distribute, derive, perform, display). The team presented students with a concise definition of the rights associated with copyright and asked them to rate each in terms of importance to themselves and, separately, importance to researchers. One point of interest was that nearly all students acknowledged that they were uninformed about the bundle of rights to begin with. This is potentially surprising in light of the fact that several of our participants had received explicit instruction on copyright previously, such as through a course at KU.

Another interesting theme that consistently emerged from the focus groups pertained to the process of scholarly publishing. This again showcased crucial knowledge gaps, but here an interesting intersection between copyright and OA centered on the role of researchers and how the work they produce relates to rights and access. Nearly all participants assumed that researchers are paid for the articles they publish, much like artists might be paid for songs produced. Students were also typically unaware that authors in traditional publishing models are asked to transfer copyright to publishers prior to publication.

Although precise knowledge of copyright and OA was limited and highly variable among participants, the pilot data reveals students demonstrating a nuanced sensitivity to and robust support for core principles that underlie them. For example, students strongly associated copyright with ownership and creatorship, and they saw copyright as a means of protection against improper use.

At this phase, Undergraduates Speak achieved the objective of narrowing a gap in undergraduate engagement with scholarly communication in two ways: by providing an opportunity to engage a new student in undergraduate research as well as creating space for meaningful dialog and reflection among undergraduates.

Service-learning Partners

In the second phase of the project, KU Libraries partnered with undergraduate students in a Digital Storytelling class on the creation of an OER informed by focus group and survey data collected during phase one. Digital Storytelling is a service-learning course offered by KU's Film and Media Studies (FMS) Department. The partnership between the libraries' staff and FMS faculty originated the previous year at a university event intended to foster interdisciplinary collaboration and resulted in the libraries' integration into two consecutive Digital Storytelling classes. The course, established in spring 2015, incorporates the study and production of interactive storytelling in order to critically analyze and create stories with digital media.[8] Over the course of the semester, students produce research papers and digital stories based in the theories and histories discussed in class as well as a capstone assignment where small groups of students are paired with community partners to create digital projects addressing the partner's needs and mission. Students work collaboratively with peers, course faculty, community partners, and content experts to create a sustainable, publicly shared digital project that responds to their partner's goals. The course employs an experiential, service-learning approach to enrich students' creative practice by blending theory with the practice of producing work for a client.

In spring 2016, the libraries, represented by the PI, presented data from the pilot study to the Digital Storytelling students, along with an overview of the Undergraduates Speak project background and a brief history of open initiatives. The students assigned to the libraries' project were asked to create an OER responding to two key findings in the data: (1) undergraduate students' lack of awareness of their status as copyright owners and (2) undergraduate students' high level of interest in OA. They were provided draft learning outcomes for the resource and given access to some of the audio, video, and transcripts captured the previous semester.[9] However, the team was also encouraged to follow their own curiosities in determining the outcomes and shape of the OER. Additionally, the PI arranged for a Skype meeting between the students and Nick Shockey, Director of Programs & Engagement for SPARC (Scholarly Publishing and Academic Resources Coalition).

Students in the course assumed leadership roles in managing client communications and ownership of the narrative, themes, interactive elements, and other parameters of the project. The libraries' student team created an online resource using Moodle to educate their peers and general public about the meaning of OA, the goals of OA movements, open source resources, and alternative copyright and creative work licensing systems. Though given the option to create an original resource using audio-visual materials collected at KU during the first phase of the project, the students elected instead to reuse openly licensed materials created by other agencies, including one of the recommendations provided by Shockey.[10] The students chose to focus on a narrative about OA that encouraged others to recognize the access to information enjoyed as a college student at a major research university, the role of the libraries in securing and providing access to that information, and the boundaries of this access. All students in the course publically presented their work at a reception hosted by the libraries at the end of the semester.

Reflection and Assessment

At the conclusion of the first phase of the pilot project, both students were asked to write reflectively about their experiences working on the project. Both the formal self-reflection and informal conversations with the undergraduate intern suggest that the hands-on approach to learning was challenging though highly rewarding. Challenges of educators venturing into experiential learning include combating the student experience of feeling underprepared or inadequate and identifying a healthy balance between guiding students and allowing them to lead. Learning how to conduct research can be a difficult process for anyone, which was confounded in this situation by an accelerated timeline and the undergraduate's lack of experience or formal education in research methodology. Add to that the effect that this type of learning experience has on students, capturing their interest, bolstering their curiosity, and linking emotion and intellect in a "wholehearted affair."[11] Run-ins with concerns of failure, confusion, or disappointment are not surprising, though they can be countered effectively by developing mutual trust through authentic communication, regular feedback, flexibility, and emotional support. Ultimately, the student voiced gratitude for the experience and its practical value for her personal growth and development, a value that she expressed difficulty recognizing in her coursework—a refrain that is not uncommon among college students.

The student's reflection also demonstrated a shift in her perception of research: "Before doing this project, I didn't realize how much room for research there is in the social sciences. The image of research that I always had was people in lab coats trying to cure cancer but now I realize that research doesn't always look like that. I now appreciate that there is a lot of research, including internal projects like this one, that doesn't always get published, but it still matters." Following the undergraduate intern's involvement in Undergraduates Speak, she applied for and received an Undergraduate Research Award (UGRA) from KU's Center for Undergraduate Research for her own research project, "American Themes in Russian Rap Music: A Cultural Content Analysis." The involvement of freshmen in the UGRAs is rare; of the forty-nine students who received an award in spring 2016, she was the only freshman.

The self-reflection completed by the graduate student on the project team demonstrated positive outcomes in two exciting areas: "The knowledge that I gained about open access initiatives and open educational resources will, I believe, have a lasting effect on how I approach research and publishing, as well as teaching/mentoring undergraduates."

The second phase of the project appeared similarly rewarding for the libraries' student partners, though there seems to be a disconnect between the team's self-assessment and their actions. Completing the research, meetings, and production required for the project in Digital Storytelling changed the way students enrolled in the course understood the role of the library within the university and as a steward of information and proponent of OA to information. In final papers, students reflected on the corporatization of copyright and "copyright culture" as potential obstacles to creative production, publication, and circulation of creative and scholarly work, as well as an obstacle to accessing this work. In the spirit of service and experiential learning, the student collaborators reflected on their "hands-on" learning experience as having "real world" implications and effects on the way their peers see themselves as public citizens as well as pupils. As one student paper noted: "Students should care about open access because it could change the way we share and cultivate knowledge at a collegiate, and even universal level.... We want students to know that they are creators, that knowledge is a public good, and that they are agents of change." During their public presentation at the conclusion of the semester, the student team spoke with ease and impressive fluency on the value and importance of OA and other open initiatives.

Despite display of this deep appreciation and understanding, student production of the resource was not without hurdles. When presenting their initial idea for the OER to the PI, the student team recommended using Blackboard—proprietary (closed source) software—to host their content. The students investigated multiple alternate platforms before deciding to use Moodle, an open source course management system. However, the final product presented to their community partner was not openly licensed and therefore did not meet the criteria for an OER; it has since been removed from Moodle, restricting the libraries' ability to review, adapt, or otherwise distribute the resource. Attempts to contact the student team about removal of the resource were unsuccessful.

Recommendations/Best Practices

The student interns hired to complete phase one of the Undergraduates Speak pilot project excelled at completing the necessary tasks for the project without requiring a significant amount of oversight or intervention from the PI. This is attributed to four factors: (1) the undergraduate-graduate student combination, which allowed each student to take responsibility for project components that reflected their interests, experience, and capabilities; (2) active recruitment of high-performing students with transferable skills relevant to the project work; (3) a competitive salary to attract and retain the university's strongest talent; and (4) facilitating intentional connections with faculty and staff that will benefit the students' future work in the academy.

In spring 2016, the FMS class working on phase two of the Undergraduates Speak project was awarded a Service Learning Mini-Grant from KU's Center for Civic and Social Responsibility in order to offset student costs of creating and maintaining their service-learning projects. The Center hosted a luncheon for grant recipients and their partners to discuss course projects, which resulted in others in attendance expressing a desire to partner with the libraries. Opportunities for mutually beneficial partnerships abound in higher education, and academic libraries, which are interdisciplinary by nature, make natural partners. Catalyzing this, however, requires that librarians actively seek out the spaces where these conversations are occurring and conscientiously prepare themselves for communicating the libraries' goals and needs to potential partners with resonance and clear, complementary outcomes. The benefits of a proactive approach to developing experiential learning partnerships is well articulated in other library literature.[12]

Finally, the value of engaging with undergraduate students as the subjects of research should not be overlooked. In addition to learning about scholarly publishing during focus group activities, student participants were exposed to the principle of informed consent, confidentiality requirements, and the rights and responsibilities of researchers and their subjects. Additionally, their engagement with an undergraduate peer serving on the research team demonstrates not only that undergraduate students can be involved in research activity on campus, but also that they can serve in important leadership roles.

Conclusion

Despite efforts to involve undergraduate students in conversations about scholarly communication, as evidenced by projects led by Stephanie Davis-Kahl, Nick Shockey, and others, some of which are described in *Common Ground at the Nexus of Information Literacy and Scholarly Communication*, students frequently remain outside the scope of scholarly communication initiatives on college campuses.[13] The project discussed in this chapter demonstrates that undergraduates are interested in topics of scholarly communication and have the capacity to become conversant change agents in this area. One opportunity for engaging undergraduates in these discussions is via experiential learning. As more universities incorporate experiential learning into their strategic initiatives, service learning opportunities will continue to increase on campuses. Librarians should be aware of the roles that they can play in service learning courses and be ready to connect library needs and initiatives to university efforts in this area. Additionally, librarians are encouraged to allow undergraduate students to take ownership and play leadership roles in internal library research by providing internships. Internal research projects provide low-stakes opportunities for libraries to collaborate with students while providing students with a meaningful way to learn about the research process and about avenues for communicating research activities to other scholars.

Notes

1. George Kuh, *High-Impact Educational Practices: What They Are, Who Has Access to Them, and Why They Matter* (Washington, D.C.: Association of American Colleges and Universities, 2008).
2. *Bold Aspirations*, University of Kansas, accessed October 14, 2016, http://provost.ku.edu/strategic-plan.
3. *KU Libraries Strategic Directions 2012–2017*, University of Kansas Libraries, accessed October 21, 2016, https://lib.ku.edu/strategic-plan.
4. The project received financial support from the KU General Research Fund, the KU Libraries Research Fund, and the David Shulenburger Fund to Improve Public Access.
5. Two faculty members in KU's School of Journalism and Mass Communications volunteered to serve as mentors for the student team. They provided reading materials, met with students to discuss the project, and opened their classrooms for observation when relevant course content was presented. The undergraduate intern expressed gratitude for this opportunity to form personal relationships with faculty in her field of study.
6. Suzanne Mangrum and Kristen West, "Partnering with Undergraduate Students to Consult Library Focus Groups," *College & Undergraduate Libraries* 19 (2012): 22, doi: 10.1080/10691316.2012.652553.
7. "Media Production Studio," University of Kansas Information Technology, accessed October 14, 2016, http://technology.ku.edu/media-production-studio. The Studio "provides equipment, workspace and software for students and faculty to shoot, edit and produce digital projects."
8. KU Libraries also served as a community partner in 2015, the first year the course was offered. Information about the digital story designed by the 2015 student team is available via KU ScholarWorks at http://hdl.handle.net/1808/21508.
9. The following outcomes were provided to the student team: "After completion of this assignment, students will describe themselves as copyright owners; differentiate between rights associated with copyright ownership; identify a mechanism for articulating the freedoms/restrictions they could apply to their own work; list factors that affect how research and scholarship are or can be shared and communicated; and discuss the benefits of open movements."
10. "How Open Access Empowered a 16-Year-Old to Make Cancer Breakthrough," The Right to Research Coalition, published June 11, 2013, https://youtu.be/G55hlnSD-1Ys.
11. Janet Eyler and Dwight E. Giles, Jr., *Where's the Learning in Service-Learning?* (San Francisco: Jossey-Bass, 1999), 8.
12. Amy York, Christy Groves, and William Black, "Enriching the Academic Experience: The Library and Experiential Learning," *Collaborative Librarianship* 2, no. 4 (2010), 193–203, http://digitalcommons.du.edu/collaborativelibrarianship/vol2/iss4/4/.
13. Stephanie Davis-Kahl and Merinda Kaye Hensley, eds., *Common Ground of the Nexus of Information Literacy and Scholarly Communication* (Chicago: Association of College & Research Libraries, 2013).

Bibliography

Davis-Kahl, Stephanie, and Merinda Kaye Hensley, eds. *Common Ground of the Nexus of Information Literacy and Scholarly Communication*. Chicago: Association of College & Research Libraries, 2013.

Eyler, Janet, and Dwight E. Giles, Jr. *Where's the Learning in Service-Learning?* San Francisco: Jossey-Bass, 1999.

Kuh, George D. *High-Impact Educational Practices: What They Are, Who Has Access to Them, and Why They Matter*. Washington: Association of American Colleges and Universities, 2008.

Mangrum, Suzanne, and Kristen West. "Partnering with Undergraduate Students to Consult Library Focus Groups." *College & Undergraduate Libraries* 19 (2012): 18–32. doi: 10.1080/10691316.2012.652553.

University of Kansas Libraries. *KU Libraries Strategic Directions 2012–2017*. Accessed October 21, 2016. https://lib.ku.edu/strategic-plan.

University of Kansas Office of the Provost. *Bold Aspirations*. September 2011. http://provost.ku.edu/strategic-plan.

York, Amy, Christy Groves, and William Black. "Enriching the Academic Experience: The Library and Experiential Learning." *Collaborative Librarianship* 2, no. 4 (2010): 193–203. http://digitalcommons.du.edu/collaborativelibrarianship/vol2/iss4/4/.

CHAPTER 10*

Freshman Framework:
Collaboratively Developing a Set of Required Instructional Modules for Freshman Research Scholars

Matt Upson, Tim O'Neil, and Cristina Colquhoun

Introduction

New undergraduates often enter college assuming that they are competent in their ability to perform research for assignments but are actually overconfident and underperform when compared with the expectations of faculty.[1] Freshmen are often overwhelmed by the amount and newness of information resources available to them and find it difficult to navigate, synthesize, and revisit information as part of their research process.[2] This gap in perceived and desired abilities versus actual performance can often frustrate students and instructors, providing librarians an opportunity to offer support.

---

* This work is licensed under a Creative Commons Attribution-NonCommercial 4.0 License, CC BY-NC (https://creativecommons.org/licenses/by-nc/4.0/).

While this gap exists for many first-year students, it can be pronounced in the case of students participating in undergraduate research programs, where the level of scholarship and academic rigor is elevated when compared to the general undergraduate experience. We can expect students who participate in undergraduate research programs to be more engaged and interested in library resources and information literacy instruction; however, they "may be no more likely to go beyond superficial interrogation of resources for their research projects than they might for a short paper for a course. Though their needs can in many ways resemble those of faculty researchers, such students understandably might not always think like experienced scholars."[3]

Related to the problem of superficiality in novice research, library instruction opportunities often devolve, due to lack of time and instructor collaboration, into one-shot "bibliographic instruction" sessions that end up focusing on the simple rote mechanisms of using the library discovery service and databases, finding resources, and generating citations. While many librarians have been striving for years to break free of these instructional limitations, the Association of College and Research Libraries' (ACRL) *Framework for Information Literacy for Higher Education*[4] has provided an impetus to rethink how we approach library instruction and opens the door for more dynamic collaborative partnerships. The framework has codified a new approach to speaking with students, faculty, and partners about information, research, and how the information literacy is a crucial part of their daily lives.

The focus of this chapter is to discuss how a collaborative project between an undergraduate research office and university library attempts to use the framework to address the potential performance gap in new undergraduates. This gap may be exacerbated in cases where new students often struggle with the requirements of participating in an undergraduate research program. The Freshman Research Scholars (FRS) program at Oklahoma State University (OSU) provides an opportunity for students to engage in original research under faculty mentorship. OSU Libraries has partnered with the Office of Scholar Development and Undergraduate Research to develop required instructional modules for FRS students. These modules introduce freshman researchers to concepts highlighted by the framework, providing an initial grounding in how information is found, evaluated, used, created, and shared. The modules consist of short videos that relay concepts to students in relatable language, rather than jargon, and offer critical thinking prompts that tie into issues that FRS students would encounter as part of their formal research program. We discuss the development and assessment of these modules and their relation to the framework in this chapter.

Background

Oklahoma State University is a public doctoral university in Stillwater, Oklahoma. The university has a high undergraduate enrollment profile (approximately 21,000 undergraduates) and high research activity, which is conducive to participation in undergraduate research programs. The Research and Learning Services division of OSU Libraries connects with students, faculty, and academic support units in an effort to provide information literacy instruction, research assistance, and data management guidance. The unit consists of thirteen full-time employees; eight are academic liaison librarians who work primarily with upper-division, subject-specific courses, while four are dedicated to providing library instruction for first-year courses, partnering with various support units (e.g., diversity office, residential life, university college, undergraduate research, etc.) and initiating undergraduate outreach efforts.

This undergraduate instruction and outreach group has made a concerted effort in the recent past to increase the number and quality of instructional videos and tutorials created and maintained by the library. In the fall of 2015, the library began discussing plans for conceptual "big picture" videos, with work beginning in earnest in the spring of 2016. The plan for these videos was initially inspired by "The Big Picture" videos created by North Carolina State University Libraries, which focus on basic information literacy concepts like citation, source evaluation, and topic selection.[5] Gradually, planning efforts shifted to an emphasis on the then newly adopted framework[6] and its six frames.

The intent of the initiative was to take each of the six frames and explain the concepts in terms understandable and relevant to undergraduate students. Initially, librarians were apprehensive about the lack of a discrete audience that was more defined than the general undergraduate population. Additional context was needed to provide intentional structure and value to the planned videos. It was at this point, during the spring of 2016, a collaborative opportunity with the Office of Scholar Development and Undergraduate Research arose.

Partnerships

Scholar Development and Undergraduate Research is a divisional unit in Academic Affairs that is organized within the University College. The office reports to the associate provost/associate vice president for undergraduate education and exercises broad purview over the university's undergraduate research activities and coordinates programs for students of all classifications in all academic areas. For many years, Scholar Development's FRS program has provided an entry point into the academic life of the university for approximately sixty incoming freshmen who often take advantage of the office's student grants program and compete for prestigious scholarships.

Though the program has no formal eligibility requirements, FRS attracts a talented and ambitious pool of applicants who are selected during their senior year of high school. Students in the program represent a wide range of majors in all undergraduate colleges and typically have little-to-no experience with research. All students are required to identify a faculty member as a mentor for their research experience and present their insights in a poster session at a peer-level symposium near the end of their first year.

Some of the colleges require their cohorts to participate in a dedicated first-year seminar designed to introduce students to the fundamentals of academic inquiry, from developing a research question to writing a grant proposal, while others provide guidance more informally with small group and individual meetings. Scholar Development hosts a series of workshops throughout the year to provide support and instruction on specific topics, such as complying with university ethics policies, mentoring best practices, and delivering research presentations. Due to variations among the instructional models within the program, no comprehensive curriculum exists for all FRS to develop the information literacy required to design projects independently. Considering the goals of FRS, this video series offered the potential to provide novice researchers with the opportunity to grapple with paradigmatic shifts in their understanding of information as they explore their curiosity and learn to negotiate the academic research environment.

This partnership was not the first collaboration between the library undergraduate instruction and outreach and the undergraduate research units. Previous collaborations have included the development and management of an undergraduate library research award, the ongoing planning of a credit course on information literacy and undergraduate research skills, and the inclusion of one-shot instruction for sections of first-year orientation for freshman researchers. Thus, by the time the videos were under discussion, the two units had developed a rapport and level of trust that was conducive to creative planning.

Discussions between the library and undergraduate research offices led to the development of instructional goals that would guide the continued development of the videos and the expansion of the project. These goals included:
- contribute to bridging the gap between high school and college student research practice;
- expand student understanding of information and its role in academic research;
- assist the FRS program in determining students' research interests and pairing with associated faculty mentors;

- provide another avenue for students and faculty mentors to connect in order to build relationships and understanding; and
- engage students in metacognitive exercises regarding their own research practices, assumptions, and faculty expectations

The alignment of these goals highlights shared learning objectives among these academic units and demonstrates the critical role libraries can play in the implementation of high-impact educational practices coordinated by undergraduate research offices working across the disciplinary spectrum. Such strategic collaboration also leverages university resources to advance institutional priorities, such as retention and graduation rates.

What resulted from this collaboration was a set of modules based on the framework that include videos and sets of questions that build on the video content and connect with the FRS experience. Each video was created with the FRS student in mind and can be used with a general undergraduate audience as well. The videos were scripted by the undergraduate instruction and outreach director and the coordinator for undergraduate research. The library's instructional designer reviewed the scripts to ensure alignment to each of the framework frames. Prior to their involvement in the production of the videos, the library communications office was introduced to the framework through a reading of the frames and discussions with librarians. This was done in order to provide a context and facilitate a better understanding of the content that was to be communicated in the videos. The library communications office then edited the scripts for time and terminology concerns, then produced the videos with the assistance of undergraduate video interns and student hosts. Production of the videos was completed using components of Adobe Creative Cloud, including After Effects, Audition, Illustrator, Photoshop, and Premiere Pro. This process was handled entirely by the library communications office, which has the trained personnel to handle projects with advanced technical requirements.

The series was called Inform Your Thinking[7] and the videos were titled as follows (each title corresponds with the adjacent frame):

- *Who Do You Trust and Why?* (Authority is Constructed and Contextual)
- *How is Your Information Created?* (Information Creation as a Process)
- *Information Has Value* (Information Has Value)
- *It's All About the Questions* (Research as Inquiry)
- *Research is a Conversation* (Scholarship as Conversation)
- *Search Smarter* (Searching as Strategic Exploration)

Each video includes a set of accompanying questions that are intended to facilitate reflective thought regarding undergraduate research within the context of a particular frame. These questions are optional but encouraged, and are not intended as a "check for understanding" based on the content of the videos. The questions were structured primarily by the undergraduate research coordinator, entered into a digital form (Machform), and embedded alongside the video. Questions were designed as prompts for open-ended reflection on the specific knowledge practices and dispositions outlined in the videos' corresponding frames, and employ examples discussed in the video as a starting point for more expansive thinking. Each question invites a narrative response rather than a specific range of "correct" answers, so assessment of student engagement with the ideas addressed in the videos requires a more qualitative examination on the part of librarians and faculty that precludes the use of automated assessment. While these particular questions were written specifically for FRS students, they can easily be adapted to suit a variety of learning environments and contexts.

In the context of the FRS program, faculty leading first-year seminars were invited to embed the video series as complementary instruction within existing the existing curriculum. Based on discussions in planning meetings, the instructors' initial reception has been positive, but more detailed feedback will have to wait until the conclusion of the pilot phase. In addition to augmenting existing FRS seminars, the videos also provide an opportunity for students without a seminar to accomplish similar learning objectives. In the pilot year, all FRS students will be asked to watch and respond to each of the videos regardless of their enrollment in a program seminar. Responses will be received and reviewed by librarians, recorded for participation by the undergraduate research office, then provided to each student's faculty mentor to facilitate discussion among all parties about topics as they relate to the specifics of their research experiences.

Since the start of this project, the undergraduate research coordinator has transitioned to a similar role at a different institution and established an alternative model for implementing the video series. Where the FRS model demonstrates the ability to offer large-scale instruction to students working outside the structure of a seminar, this alternative incorporates the videos into small, themed seminars scheduled throughout the academic year. The students participating in these seminars include all classifications, but are intended to provide a similar introduction to academic inquiry as the FRS program. In these seminars, students will watch the videos in class, free-write responses to the questions individually, then discuss their responses as a group. Though the library is not currently involved in the implementation of the video series in these seminars at the new institution, discussions are underway that promise more coordinated collaboration.

Reflection

The alignment of library and undergraduate research objectives capitalizes on expertise in both areas and provides students with opportunities for both information literacy and institutional awareness. A major intention of the collaboration is to foster critical thinkers who are empowered to leverage university resources in order to accomplish academic objectives in the advancement of personal and professional aspirations. For example, these modules intend to facilitate an understanding of the nature of scholarly conversations through the process of self-reflection *and* the investigation of ongoing research at Oklahoma State University in order to experience the local and global nature of how knowledge is exchanged and built. The scalability of the online video format promises to expand inclusivity and promote diversity in undergraduate research activities by providing informal introductions to critical concepts while directing students to key university resources. With ever-increasing attention on retention rates and ever-present budgetary concerns, this project demonstrates how universities can make efficient use of resources to make progress toward some of the institution's strategic and tactical goals, which include "[providing] support for research, scholarship, and creative activities" and "identify[ing], recruit[ing], develop[ing], and mentor[ing] potential scholars."[8] Still, even though this partnership has been fruitful, the implementation of the modules has required even more buy-in and collaboration from each of the colleges on campus, due to the decentralized manner of implementing the FRS program. Thus, the effort to fully and effectively incorporate the project into the FRS program long-term will require negotiation and tailoring of content so that the programmatic goals of each college are satisfied. This effort is just beginning, but promises to offer challenges that result in better instruction.

Assessment

Planning for assessment was a vital component of project development. The concurrent reflective questions as well as feedback from instructors and faculty mentors will be used as assessment tools. The purpose of assessing the project's effectiveness is threefold: to ensure that the project goals are met, to inform a course of action with students, and to facilitate an iterative approach to the continued use and improvement of the instruction.

Student answers to the reflective questions will be reviewed by a librarian, the overall FRS coordinator, college-level FRS coordinators, and faculty mentors. Based on the responses and feedback from stakeholders, the project has already positively contributed to the instructional goals outlined previously. Feedback from students has been positive thus far and the content, activities, and reflective questions have been well received. The modules have recently been implemented in the Special Undergraduate Enrichment Programs (SUEP) Research Seminar Series at the University of Colorado Boulder, where students were queried about the content and instructional approach. One student responded that "The Inform Your Thinking Videos have been very thought-provoking in the way that they prompt the viewer to completely reevaluate what they do with new information when they receive it. The videos encourage one to think in different ways and to question their own thoughts and those of others. I really enjoy the use of animations in balance with the interview-style discussion and think they do a great job of presenting the content." Another student noted that "The videos have been helpful in changing the way I approach, read, dissect, and analyze scholarly works, and the discussion-based format has provided me with a strong foundation for research and scholarly work."

The nature of the design of the reflective questions assisted students in relating the instruction content to their personal lives and experiences, specifically their research experiences and assumptions. These questions have provided a platform to facilitate a shared understanding between students and faculty mentors concerning the nature of research and role of information in the research process. Stakeholders and students cited an increase in the shared understanding of research expectations and the students' role in academic research. Additionally, student responses were used to guide students to the proper faculty mentors and to determine if additional intervention was warranted. Faculty and instructors have also expressed the usefulness of the activities in placing the library in a more relevant context for FRS.

In an effort to continuously improve the program's effectiveness, each iteration of the program will use feedback and assessment results to shape instruction and recommended use of the videos to faculty. In the future, we envision implementing additional assessment of student research skills throughout their tenure in the FRS program to determine the long-term effectiveness of the program, as well as to provide further information concerning student understanding of information and research to their faculty mentors. Qualitative data analysis will likely be used to categorize and assign themes to student responses in order to better understand students' thought processes, as well as to guide and adjust the course of the program. Depending on the quantity of data, funding, and available staff, this process may occur through the assistance of graduate teaching assistants or the use of qualitative data analysis software such as NVivo. Additionally, the program hopes to expand use of the videos and reflective questions to cater to a variety of students outside of FRS and tailor instruction accordingly.

Recommendations/Best Practices

In general, collaboration between the library and undergraduate research office seems to be a natural fit. The library stands to gain from an explicit connection to the recruitment and retention efforts that are often built into the undergraduate research program structure. Shared goals and outcomes between the two units can ease the burden of independently handling costs and juggling staffing needs by encouraging joint projects. Additionally, combining complementary skill sets and communities of practice can increase efficiency and maximize efforts to reach students in meaningful ways. Still, it is beneficial to realize that each unit is distinct and will bring their own priorities, timetables, and relationships to the conversation. This is why constant communication and goal-setting is vital to a successful project.

Specific to this project, developing video-driven content can be a daunting endeavor, as it requires a good deal of planning and promotion, and should be relatively long-lasting in its utility and appeal in order to avoid repeating the labor-intensive process frequently, especially in instances where library instructors do not have immediate access to a multimedia production team. Accordingly, it is vital, in a collaborative effort, to obtain feedback early and often from the various stakeholders involved in the development of the project. This feedback should be iterative and involved at every stage of the process. The process of obtaining feedback should continue once the content is published. The authors intend to use instructor and student feedback to inform next steps and continue to shape the project into the future.

Recommendations include: strive to maintain relevance when creating video content; keep the videos under five minutes (shorter, when possible); use students wherever possible in the process (especially as hosts); and avoid over-explaining concepts. You do not need to attempt to cover every possible nuance of the ACRL frames. Work with your students to incorporate and articulate what seems natural and relevant to their lives and programs. This, of course, depends on your students and the culture of your institutions. Various aspects of the framework may not be as vital to your students as they would be for others. Additionally, rather than attempt to explain concepts in detail, provide opportunities for students to discover through self-questioning. The incorporation of questions into these instruction modules builds on the video content and encourages students to find their own connections and have deeper conversations concerning the material.

Conclusion

Undergraduate research offices offer the library many potentially fruitful collaborative opportunities. The project outlined in this chapter was the culmination of smaller, successful partnerships that established trust and rapport between the two entities. Thanks to this high level of comfort, the resulting modules were thoughtfully planned and implemented, with relevance to students as the highest priority. Collaborating with partners allows for the library to exist outside an instructional vacuum, connecting with students within the context of their academic experience. As undergraduate research opportunities continue to gain prominence and influence on campus as high-impact educational programs that attract and retain students, librarians should make every effort to connect to these units, not only to support their endeavors, but also to drive opportunities to inform and enable students.

Appendix 10A: Reflective Questions from *Inform Your Thinking* Modules

The following questions are from the *Who Do You Trust and Why?* module:
- How do you negotiate disagreements among experts—that is, what determines who has authority when the conclusions of experts differ?
- What can you do when confronted with information that disagrees with your own perspective?
- How do you determine the level of expertise needed to establish authority; or, when do you need to consult academic and other sources?
- What role does evidence play in determining the authority of experts; or, how do you know when to trust the evidence provided?
- What role do various types of expertise (academic/professional training, experience, etc.) have in establishing authority—that is, in what situations are different types of expertise needed?
- What is the significance of the age and location of information to its value as an authoritative source?
- What value do non-academic sources have in academic conversations?

The following questions are from the *How is Your Information Created?* module:
- How do you tend to react when you encounter inaccurate information online that has been shared as factual?
- What measures do you take to ensure that the information you create and/or share is accurate? Do these measures differ depending on the purpose of your information; for example, something shared via social media versus a research paper?
- Identify a scholarly journal in your major or area of interest. Search for the homepage of this journal and attempt to locate information on the aim and scope of the journal, article submission instructions, and information for authors. What methods are in place to ensure the publication of high-quality research?
- Do a Google search for "fake peer review" or "peer review fraud." What are some ways that peer-review has been manipulated and why might this happen? How can fraud damage the research community and the individuals involved?

The following questions are from the *Information Has Value* module:
- How do you acknowledge the value of information in your own research?

- How would your personal and academic research be affected if your access to information was restricted or limited?
- What kind of information is valuable to you in your daily life? How about in your coursework? Is there a difference in the type of information you value in different settings?
- Review recent news regarding research at Oklahoma State University. What are some examples of research at OSU that could be considered "valuable"? How is the value of this research demonstrated? See http://www.vpr.okstate.edu/ for examples.

The following questions are from the *It's All About the Questions* module:
- The decisions we face often come in the form of yes-or-no questions: "Should marijuana be legalized?" But in answering these questions, more questions arise: "How does the legalization of marijuana affect violent crime, the economy, public health, or any number of issues (or topics)?" A simple question can then lead to many complex questions like branches on a tree—that's research! What is a decision you or your community faces that requires a yes-or-no answer? What additional questions arise?
- It's easy to feel overwhelmed when you start to think about all of the questions that can come from even simple yes-or-no questions. But this is where you come in. Focusing on your own interests and experiences, how can you narrow your questions to a set of closely-related questions? Can you write a question that brings all of these together?
- You can imagine the conclusions one reaches in making a decision will depend, in part, on the questions they choose to ask. For example, someone asking questions about economics might reach a different conclusion about the legalization of marijuana than someone asking about public health. How, then, do research questions reflect personal and/or cultural values?
- Like a "reboot" of a popular movie, researchers often revisit ideas with new information, resources, technology at different times and in different cultural settings. Imagine a research question, then consider how someone at a different time or culture with access to new information might ask the same question. What variables might affect the question?

The following questions are from the *Research is a Conversation* module:
- What are some types of problems confronted in everyday conversations that might apply to scholarly conversations as well? Imagine and share some creative solutions to these issues.
- How do you decide to trust what you hear in a conversation, and how might those strategies apply to scholarly conversations?

- Conversations with new people or about unfamiliar topics can be difficult. How would you prepare for and approach a potential faculty mentor with questions about a topic on which they are an expert? How does your access to student resources work to your advantage in preparing for this situation?
- Scholarly conversations are often formal (academic journal articles), but more informal conversations are increasingly accessible through blogs, social media, and in the news. Can you identify some experts or organizations in your area of interest who are informally conversing on their topics of expertise?
- Who at your institution is participating in scholarly conversations that interest you? How did you go about finding them?

The following questions are from the *Search Smarter* module:
- Explore the research guides available through the library. Who is the subject specialist librarian for your major or area of interest? What databases and/or journals would be relevant to your own research? Research guides are available at http://www.library.okstate.edu/research-guides/subject-lists/
- Based on your own interests or class assignment, write a basic research question (example: How has climate change impacted the risk of water-related illnesses in developing countries?). For help with research questions, see our video at http://info.library.okstate.edu/informyourthinking/questions
- Use your research question above to build a set of search terms, synonyms, and related words that can be used to search for information (example: climate change, global warming, water, illness, disease, developing countries, water quality, etc.).
- Using these terms, explore one of the databases you discovered above. Try a few searches, using different combinations of terms each time. How does changing your terms alter your list of results? How does having a variety of search terms help you?
- Using the same set of search terms, compare your database search results with Google and Google Scholar results. Do you see the same articles popping up in the results? Why or why not? Are you able to access the full text of articles through Google or Google Scholar? Why or why not?

Notes

1. Meg Raven, "Bridging the Gap: Understanding the Differing Research Expectations of First-Year Students and Professors," *Evidence Based Library and Information*

Practice 7, no. 3 (2012): 18, accessed August 13, 2016, http://dx.doi.org/10.18438/B8WG79.
2. Alison J. Head, *Learning the Ropes: How Freshmen Conduct Course Research Once They Enter College* (Project Information Literacy, 2013), 3–4, accessed August 13, 2016, http://www.projectinfolit.org/uploads/2/7/5/4/27541717/pil_2013_freshmenstudy_fullreportv2.pdf.
3. Anthony Stamatoplos, "The Role of Academic Libraries in Mentored Undergraduate Research: A Model of Engagement in the Academic Community," *College & Research Libraries* 70, no. 3 (2009): 240, accessed August 13, 2016, http://dx.doi.org/10.5860/crl.70.3.235.
4. *Framework for Information Literacy for Higher Education* (Association of College & Research Libraries, 2016), accessed August 13, 2016, http://www.ala.org/acrl/standards/ilframework.
5. "Videos and Interactive Guides," *North Carolina State University Libraries,* accessed August 24, 2016, https://www.lib.ncsu.edu/tutorials/.
6. *Framework for Information Literacy for Higher Education.*
7. "Inform Your Thinking Library Tutorials," *Oklahoma State University Library*, accessed August 11, 2016, http://info.library.okstate.edu/informyourthinking.
8. "University Mission," *Oklahoma State University Institutional Accreditation*, accessed October 3, 2016, https://accreditation.okstate.edu/Mission.

Bibliography

Framework for Information Literacy for Higher Education. Association of College & Research Libraries, 2016. Accessed August 13, 2016. http://www.ala.org/acrl/standards/ilframework.

Head, Alison J. *Learning the Ropes: How Freshmen Conduct Course Research Once They Enter College*. Project Information Literacy, 2013. Accessed August 13, 2016. http://www.projectinfolit.org/uploads/2/7/5/4/27541717/pil_2013_freshmenstudy_fullreportv2.pdf.

"Inform Your Thinking Library Tutorials." *Oklahoma State University Library*. Accessed August 11, 2016. http://info.library.okstate.edu/informyourthinking.

Raven, Meg. "Bridging the Gap: Understanding the Differing Research Expectations of First-Year Students and Professors." *Evidence Based Library and Information Practice* 7, no. 3 (2012): 4–31. Accessed August 13, 2016. http://dx.doi.org/10.18438/B8WG79.

Stamatoplos, Anthony. "The Role of Academic Libraries in Mentored Undergraduate Research: A Model of Engagement in the Academic Community." *College & Research Libraries* 70, no. 3 (2009): 235–49. Accessed August 13, 2016. http://dx.doi.org/10.5860/crl.70.3.235.

"University Mission." *Oklahoma State University Institutional Accreditation*. Accessed October 3, 2016. https://accreditation.okstate.edu/Mission.

"Videos and Interactive Guides." *North Carolina State University Libraries*. Accessed August 24, 2016. https://www.lib.ncsu.edu/tutorials/.

CHAPTER 11 *
From the Archives to the Institutional Repository:
A Collaborative Approach to Research and Publishing for Undergraduate Creative Writers

Brandon T. Pieczko and Laura MacLeod Mulligan

Introduction

This chapter recounts a collaborative effort by an archivist, information services librarian, and creative writing faculty member at Ball State University to integrate information literacy and primary source literacy instruction into the curriculum for an undergraduate senior seminar course in the Department of English. The students' final project for the course, a collaborative anthology of sixteen linked, researched fiction stories, was inspired by, and ultimate-

---

* This work is licensed under a Creative Commons Attribution-NonCommercial-NoDerivatives 4.0 License, CC BY-NC-ND (https://creativecommons.org/licenses/by-nc-nd/4.0/).

ly contributed to, the long tradition of sociological and historical studies of Muncie, Indiana, known as the Middletown Studies. At the end of the course, the students published their collaborative anthology online in Ball State University's institutional repository, thereby participating in a digital scholarship and publishing opportunity that is often uncommon for undergraduate English majors. The partnership that resulted from this collaboration and the unique nature of the course should be of interest to academic librarians and archivists interested in pursuing innovative ways to support undergraduate student research, digital scholarship, and publishing.

Background

Muncie, Indiana is one of the most extensively studied communities in the United States. For nearly a century, sociologists, cultural historians, and other researchers from around the world have visited Muncie to study everyday life in a small Midwestern city that has come to be viewed as a microcosm of sorts, representative of contemporary American life from the booming industrialism of the 1920s, through the economic struggles of the Great Depression, the culture wars of the late 1970s and 1980s, and the post-industrial decline of the 1990s and early 2000s. This understanding of Muncie as America's "Middletown" began in 1929 with the publication of Robert and Helen Lynd's classic sociological study, *Middletown: A Study in American Culture*, and the research tradition it inaugurated has come to be known as the Middletown Studies.[1]

Ball State University, and in particular the university libraries, has been an active participant in and beneficiary of this long research tradition. Ball State University is a midsized Midwestern public university in Muncie, Indiana with a full-time enrollment of approximately 21,000 students, with more than 17,800 attending on campus. It offers undergraduate, master's, and doctoral degrees in a variety of sciences, social sciences, and humanities disciplines.[2] Ball State University Libraries are home to the Center for Middletown Studies—a research center dedicated to continuing the scholarship tradition inaugurated by the Lynds—and an Archives and Special Collections department that houses research data and other records from the Middletown Studies, as well as numerous other primary sources documenting the history of Muncie's people, businesses, clubs and organizations, schools, religious congregations, and social and political activities since before the city's official founding in 1865. Over the years, Ball State University students and faculty have used these resources for countless projects ranging from traditional undergraduate research papers, to projects with major social and economic implications (e.g., adaptive reuse and redevelopment plans for abandoned industrial buildings and blighted neighborhoods), and creative projects inspired by events in Muncie's history, including art installations, documentary films, musical scores, fiction, and poetry. All the while, archivists and librarians at Ball State University have been integral to these projects by providing instruction sessions tailored to the specific needs of students and faculty and by offering reference services to help support students, particularly undergraduate students, throughout the course of the research process.

The Department of English is one of the larger humanities departments at Ball State University. In fall 2015, there were 371 undergraduate English majors, 182 minors, and 79 degree-seeking graduate students enrolled in the department; in spring 2015 alone, 4,812 undergraduate students had taken a course offered by the department.[3] The English 444 senior seminar is a capstone course comprised of students from all the undergraduate concentrations within the department (creative writing, English education, English studies, literature, and rhetoric and writing), and enrolled students are required to complete "a major research-driven project." In spring 2015, Professor Cathy Day taught a seminar course, "Research and Fiction," and asked students to construct researched fictional stories rather than the traditional analytical research paper. Professor Day was the first creative writing faculty member to teach this course and decided to reinvent it as a modified version of a creative writing class she had taught previously. The emphasis on research for this particular instance of the English senior seminar was primarily born out of an impression by Professor Day prior to the course that there is something about the research process creative writing undergraduate students in the department were uncomfortable with, while students concentrating on literature and other research-focused concentrations were equally uncomfortable with the creative writing process. Julia Glassman echoes this sentiment when she writes, "most creative writing students, save those interested in historical or science fiction, probably don't think of themselves as researchers."[4] With this in mind, Professor Day wanted to develop a course students from all concentrations could benefit from while demonstrating to her students and her faculty colleagues "'a researched story' and 'a researched paper' aren't all that different."[5]

During the course, students read Sherwood Anderson's *Winesburg, Ohio*, Jennifer Egan's *A Visit from the Goon Squad*, and other books comprised of linked stories set in specific geographic locales. Professor Day also assigned the students readings from *Middletown: A Study in American Culture* and required them to watch selections from the Middletown Film Project, a series of six documentary films recorded in Muncie and broadcast on PBS in 1982.[6] The students were asked to write their own linked stories set in a semi-fictional town (based on the actual town of Muncie, Indiana) and populated with interrelated characters and plot lines. At the end of the semester, students collaborated to edit and assemble their narratives into a cohesive anthology of researched stories linked together by setting (the semi-fictional "Middletown"), characters, and major events. Inspired by original research conducted by the students and the long tradition of the Middletown Studies in Muncie and at Ball State University, the stories cover topics such as class and gender inequality, turbulent race relations in the town's past, the impact of World War II on the home front, and cultural changes of the 1960s and 1970s.[7] As "researched fiction,"[8] the students' stories were heavily influenced by secondary sources from the library's general collection, including local and national newspapers on microfilm, magazines, scholarly articles, and published memoirs, as well as primary sources from Archives and Special Collections including correspondence, diaries, yearbooks, scrapbooks, maps, oral histories, and photographs. In addition to the researched fiction stories that make up the anthology itself, the students were also required to write bibliographic reflection essays summarizing their approach to the research process and explaining types of resources that influenced their writing. The students' final creative product, an anthology of sixteen linked, researched stories, *You Are Here: Finding Yourself in Middletown (An Anthology)*, was published digitally in Ball State University's DSpace-based institutional repository (Cardinal Scholar) and via issuu, a mobile-friendly digital publishing platform used by the Department of English to provide access to the creative work of students.[9] Ultimately, the students' project was treated like other scholarly contributions to the Middletown Studies research tradition. An archival finding aid describing the research project and resulting anthology was added to the Archives and Special Collections website as part of the Middletown Studies Collection.

Partnerships

Born out of Professor Day's specific request, the type of collaboration required for this project was brand new for all involved, and there was very little local prior experience to help inform information literacy session planning. Early in the semester, the students visited the Archives and Special Collections department of the university libraries for an instructional session during which the archivist provided an introduction to discovery tools and strategies for locating and conducting research using archival collections, an overview of the history of the various Middletown Studies that have been conducted in Muncie since the 1920s, and examples of archival collections that are representative of the six aspects of everyday life covered in the original Middletown study (business and industry, home life, education, leisure, religious practice, and communities activities).[10] At the time of the first instruction session, students had not chosen precise research topics or begun writing their fictional stories. The goal of the archives instruction session was not only to teach students how to navigate the archival holdings in the library, but also to familiarize them with the long tradition of scholarly research studies conducted about the Muncie community and to encourage them to think about how their own research and creative writing projects might fit within an existing scholarly tradition.

As students' topics developed, it became clear to Professor Day that the students' "general" library research knowledge was lacking. She requested an information literacy session with the information services librarian, providing her with a list of the current story ideas, time periods, and locations in Muncie. Professor Day indicated that the students still needed help to truly "tap into the milieu of a time" and to learn to get comfortable "getting lost in the stacks."

In a way, the library is a microcosm for "the creative process" where Professor Day thinks students should spend more time intentionally getting lost and serendipitously finding interesting sources of inspiration and information. Instead of teaching students to search for keywords in electronic databases or look for specific kinds of articles (as they have become accustomed to doing in other research-based courses), the librarian led the students through physical collections of bound periodicals and microforms to showcase their vastness as well as the advantages of "browsing to discover" as opposed to "searching to find." In order to depict an accurate picture of everyday life in their chosen decade, students needed to move beyond local history and archival resources to consult additional materials contemporary with that period including periodical articles and both fiction and nonfiction books.

The partnership between the librarian and archivist in co-planning the second session helped to ensure there was little overlap between the information literacy sessions and students were learning about completely new collections and services. The librarian chose to familiarize students not only with digital collections of scholarly and popular articles, but also print and microform formats. Students were led through the library to become familiar with the locations of particular physical collections and learn to browse and navigate lesser-known formats more effectively. Students seemed fascinated to learn how to feed microform newspapers into a reader to discover the wealth of information about everyday life. Issues of *Vogue*, *Newsweek*, and other national magazines lent themselves well to a serendipitous kind of research; students could flip through the pages to get a broader view of the political, economic, and cultural climate their fictional characters would have encountered. Photographs and advertisements (not typically available in databases) proved especially useful. The librarian also included a demonstration on how to use WorldCat to search across other libraries' collections for books and other items that could be interlibrary loaned to help them round out their stories.

Several students followed up with the archivist and librarian after the research instruction sessions to schedule one-on-one and small group reference appointments. Individual attention was given to the students' specific research needs in a way that could not have taken place in the general one-shot sessions. At this point in the semester, students were able to fully describe their creative projects—their objectives as storytellers as well as researchers. Research needs among the students were extremely diverse. For instance, one student needed memoirs of female funeral directors working in the business in the 1970s. Another student sought scientific articles describing the impact on a human body after a fall from a two-story railroad bridge. Published historic maps of Muncie were used to help situate characters' movements around the city in a historically and geographically accurate way.

Near the conclusion of the semester, after consulting in advance with Professor Day about open-access publishing options for the students' creative research project, the archivist gave a short presentation to the class about the university's institutional repository, Cardinal Scholar, during which he explained how the repository was structured, how their creative project would be discoverable online, and the procedures for uploading their project to the repository. He also explained the difference between transfer of copyright and non-exclusive electronic publishing rights (all rights to the stories contained within the anthology remained with the individual student authors) and clarified that given the collaborative nature of their anthology, in order for a project to be made accessible in the institutional repository the students would need to all sign an agreement permitting the university libraries to make their content available online. The students did not voice any hesitation or concerns about sharing their work publicly in the university's institutional repository, and both they and Professor Day seemed to understand the value of their unique contribution to digital scholarship at the university. Professor Day's buy-in was integral to the publishing component of this collaborative project in that she ensured the electronic publication rights forms were distributed to all the students, signed, and returned to the archivist in a timely manner so that the anthology could be added to the institutional repository soon after the conclusion of the course.

Reflection

Reflecting on their work with Professor Day and the ENG 444 students, the authors discovered a small body of literature regarding research instruction for undergraduate creative writers. While the direction in which Professor Day took this capstone course was unique to the Department of English, and their participation in the students' information needs was less-than-common to their work at Ball State University Libraries, there is a growing body of documentation on this very line of scholarship and undergraduate research. David Pavelich asks these questions (coincidentally, the same questions the students were asking) when addressing the importance of research skills for writers of historical fiction: "How does a fiction writer create a rounded character if that character lives in the 1920s? What clothes does the character wear? What cigarette does she smoke? What buses or trains does she ride?"[11] Pavelich also specifically addresses what archives and special collections can offer for historical fiction research. In short, he believes librarians and archivists are in a unique position to provide this very necessary training:

> Creative writing programs offer special collections librarians a unique (and fun) outreach and instruction opportunity. It's commonly assumed that literature derives purely from inspiration—that novels, poems, and essays spring fully formed from their authors' heads—and because of this, creative writing students rarely receive direct outreach from libraries. The assumption, however, misses the importance of research, editing, and publication in the creation of new literature.[12]

Similarly, Jennifer Blackmer, associate provost for entrepreneurial learning and director of the Virginia B. Ball Center for Creative Inquiry at Ball State University, compares the process of creation in the performing arts to scientific research: "…the artist has an idea that she wishes to explore, and asks a question: 'How can I evoke a visceral response to the horrors of war?' or 'How can I visually represent the ethical gray spaces of genetic engineering?'"[13]

Reflecting on the partnership aspect of this project, the authors realized Professor Day's support for library research was critical to the success of these instruction sessions. The authors were thrilled to have been invited to provide classroom and one-on-one guidance to her students. Furthermore, she was an excellent co-teacher in the library classroom—asking important questions, driving home critical takeaways, and providing necessary context. Without an engaged faculty member, even the most engaging information literacy sessions can fall flat. The Association of College and Research Libraries' *Framework for Information Literacy for Higher Education* insists on faculty/librarian partnerships as critical to successful integration of information literacy concepts into the communities of practice that faculty and students inhabit.[14] Professor Day's enthusiasm and support before, during, and after the sessions made the entire experience a true partnership between creative writers/researchers and librarians, rather than a "one-shot" library instruction situation.

Looking back on this initiative to better serve undergraduate student researchers, it became clear to the authors that several aspects of the process went quite well. First, the quality of the students' research stories and self-awareness exhibited in their bibliographic reflection essays indicated the library instruction sessions, research consultations, and the format of the course in general worked in tandem to achieve Professor Day's goal of teaching students to successfully incorporate research using primary and secondary sources into their creative fiction writing. While all of the students may not have learned "to love research and collaboration,"[15] they certainly learned how to conduct analytical research more effectively and to collaborate during the editing and publishing phases of the project to produce a tangible anthology of researched fiction stories with interconnected characters and plots.

Second, the value of integrating archives and special collections resources into the course proved to be twofold: the students were able to not only gather information from primary sources in the archives to use as reference material to inform their creative writing for an assignment in a particular course, but also during the archives instruction session and subsequent research visits to the archives, the students learned skills and techniques for conducting research in archives and special collections libraries that could be used in other courses throughout their academic experience. For example, a student might have examined historic photographs from a certain decade to more accurately describe the clothing and hairstyle of a particular character in her story, or read personal letters, diaries, and yearbooks to depict the daily life and social concerns of a typical Midwestern college student in the 1930s; however, in the process of searching for and discovering those materials the student also learned important concepts unique to conducting research in the archives (e.g., how individual items relate to the archival "collection" from which they came and how the materials within a collection are systematically described in a finding aid). While various archives and special collections libraries may differ in terms of the format and subject matter of the materials they collect, the specific search tools they have implemented to facilitate discovery of those materials, or the degree to which they make their content available online through digitization, the research skills developed in one archival context are transferable and should ultimately prove to be beneficial and almost certainly applicable in another.

Third, the publication of the students' anthology in Ball State University's institutional repository was an unexpected positive outcome of the project that benefited the students and the university libraries. Convincing students, particularly undergraduate students, to contribute to the university's digital scholarship initiative by publishing their original work online in the university's open-access institutional repository can be a challenge. Undergraduate students tend to underestimate the research value of their scholarship in relation to that of their graduate student peers or faculty members and therefore can be hesitant to contribute their work. The challenge becomes even greater when the final product of an undergraduate research project has multiple authors who all must consent to adding their research to the repository. In the case of the collaborative anthology of researched stories produced by students in this course, all sixteen of the undergraduate student authors involved in the project agreed to sign an electronic publishing rights form before the anthology was uploaded to the repository. Relatively early in the course, Professor Day realized the importance of the students' contributions to undergraduate research at the university and therefore made it a priority to convince the students to sign the permission forms necessary to publish their work online.

Looking forward, there are some aspects that can be modified for future iterations of the course. First, the authors would strive for better communication, coordination, and planning between the faculty member, archivist, and librarian well in advance of the class's first instruction session in the library. While early planning and communication are crucial for any successful collaborative instruction initiative, given this was Professor Day's first time teaching the course and the authors' first time providing archives and library instruction sessions to support the course, it would have been especially useful for everyone to meet before the class began to discuss the project and, in particular, Professor Day's expectations for the students' learning outcomes for the course. Doing so would help to ensure that the instruction sessions met the specific research needs of her students.

Second, going forward, the archives instruction session could be modified to focus less on *archival intelligence* and more on *artifactual literacy* and the inspiration that can come from browsing and serendipitous discovery. Elizabeth Yakel and Deborah Torres define "archival intelligence" as "a researcher's knowledge of archival principles, practices, and institutions, such as the reasons underlying archival rules and procedures, how to develop search strategies to explore research questions, and an understanding of the relationships between primary sources and their surrogates."[16] Put more succinctly, archival intelligence is "knowledge about the environment in which the search for primary sources is being conducted."[17] A complement to archival intelligence, "artifactual literacy" is defined by Yakel and Torres as "the ability to interpret and analyze primary sources"[18] and, according to Magia Krause, incorporates observation, an understanding of historical context, evaluation, interpretation, and critical thinking.[19] Together, these two types of knowledge are referred to as "information literacy for primary sources"[20] or simply, "archival literacy,"[21] and provide the foundation for a successful research experience in the archives. The archives instruction session that was provided to the students early in the semester arguably focused too much on demonstrating how to locate resources in the archives and not enough on teaching them how to interpret the resources available and apply them in their creative writing. Rather than trying to introduce the students to as many potential resources as possible, the goal of the archives instruction session should have been to spark the students' ideas and help them "recognize their own impulses" as researchers.[22] In overemphasizing archival intelligence-based search strategies for locating archival resources and by focusing on specific resources, the instruction session also inadvertently overlooked the importance of serendipity and inspiration, in addition to facts and information, derived from primary sources. As Professor Day explained in a post-course conversation with the authors, "the creative process is about intentionally getting lost," and providing too much guidance toward pre-selected or curated content during the research process can impede that possibility.[23] One way to encourage inspiration next time might be to focus less on textual resources and more on photographs and other visual materials from the archives during the instruction session. As Glassman explains, "the importance of image resources to creative writers cannot be overemphasized. Images can be used for visual reference and accuracy checks for countless settings, characters, and historical events. They can also be used for inspiration in much the same way as subject encyclopedias."[24]

Assessment

This instruction initiative was evaluated using a combination of formal assessment and anecdotal feedback from students and Professor Day. Directly after the library instruction session, the librarian administered an anonymous survey to the ENG 444 students using the standard survey instrument that all librarians in the Information Services unit administer to students after information literacy sessions. Students were asked several general questions not specific to the course, including how many times they had visited the library for information literacy instruction, and new things they learned during the session. They were also given an opportunity to provide general feedback through comments. The students' responses ranged from "I wished I had paid more attention" to "[the librarian] took our projects that we were working on into consideration when presenting us with possible sources." When asked the very specific question, "One new thing I learned in this session was…," students overwhelmingly responded that they were surprised and excited to learn how to view newspapers on microfilm and where to find "cool" and "old" bound periodicals.

At the time that this course was offered, Archives and Special Collections had not yet implemented a formal assessment survey for instruction sessions offered by archivists in the unit and relied exclusively on anecdotal feedback from students and faculty. Krause has written about the importance of formal assessment for archival instruction sessions: "Repeated visits and use of the archives are oft-cited measures of satisfactions, as are informal discussions with instructors and students. These anecdotal impressions provide neither an accurate nor a concrete justification for the many hours of instruction archivists provide since such effort's impact on students' education is unclear."[25] Krause also emphasizes the usefulness of rubrics for formal assessment of archival instruction sessions and for collaboration with librarians and teaching faculty: "For archivists, rubrics can be useful to identify and articulate the goals of archival instruction. Rubrics can also aid collaboration with teaching faculty because they serve as tools for communicating the objectives of archival orientations and demonstrate whether or not students are acquiring specific knowledge and skills."[26] With this in mind, since this course was offered, Archives and Special Collections has successfully implemented a more formalized assessment program for archival instruction sessions that uses a survey instrument similar to the one used by instruction librarians in the Information Services unit of the university libraries.

The bibliographic reflection essays that Professor Day assigned her students also proved to be an excellent informal assessment tool for gathering feedback on the students' experiences in the library. The stated goal of the essays was to encourage students to "reflect on their education in the English department, their development as readers, writers, and critical thinkers, and to summarize and synthesize the skills they've learned as majors."[27] It was an opportunity for them to think about how the "researched" component of "researched fiction" had affected their creative experience. Students reported that handling print resources contemporary to a specific time period was a valuable exercise for experiencing the world their characters would have inhabited. One student, who adapted her ENG 444 research into an undergraduate honor's thesis, found that the "physicality of the magazines" brought her more into the world of her fictional characters, into the very real time they inhabit in her story. She believed viewing bound periodicals (especially back issues of fashion magazines) held by the library "allowed [her] to more fully inhabit the minds of [her] characters and portray them more accurately and with more nuance."[28] Another student, in his unpublished bibliographic reflection essay, examined periodicals to help him round out his understanding of music and culture during the Vietnam War. He specifically consulted issues of *Rolling Stone* from 1975 and wrote that looking into the past "gave [him] a good understanding of what it was like back in that time period—how people dressed, what music they listened to, and even what sort of ads were in magazines of that era. The strangest piece of culture shock [he] experienced while looking through these old magazines was the sheer amount of advertisements for cigarettes."²⁹ He found that the "ripple effects [of Vietnam] were felt throughout the fabric of culture,"³⁰ and it would be impossible not to address it in his story. A third student had a change of heart due to this semester's work in the library. She found using both digital and microform resources to be equally satisfying:

> This research-driven project showed me that, contrary to my former beliefs, research could be fun and interesting. Research does not always constitute sitting down in front of a laptop or toiling over dusty books. I learned how to use a microform machine, I took a field trip, and I had a great excuse to do something I love doing, looking at old photographs, even if they were on the Internet or in the microform newspapers.³¹

Finally, another student specifically mentioned seeing long-term potential for the critical thinking skills she developed during her research experience: "I feel my experience with researching and writing have prepared me to be not only a life-long learner, but a life-long questioner."³² During a follow-up meeting after the course had concluded, Professor Day reflected this sentiment when she said that she had noticed a positive paradigm shift for the students—getting literature students to think about creative writing, and creative writing students to do research and reflect on it.

Recommendations/Best Practices

After reflecting on the course and partnership with Professor Day, the authors have identified a number of take-aways that will inform future work with undergraduate students at Ball State University. First, this particular collaborative instruction initiative has increased their awareness of the unique research needs of undergraduate students from the Department of English, particularly those engaged in creative writing assignments inspired by historical people, places, and events. Prior to working with this course, in six years of combined instruction experience at Ball State University Libraries, neither of the authors had been invited to participate in an information literacy session for creative writing students. Other opportunities may exist for future collaborations with these students, or with those in other creative disciplines. As Glassman writes, "providing increased support to creative writers can spur outreach to students in other fields that traditionally lie outside the realm of academic research. How can libraries expand the services they offer to student dancers? Painters? Experimental filmmakers?"³³ This partnership has led to other collaborative initiatives in the university libraries, including additional instruction sessions with creative writing classes and a literary biography workshop developed by archivists and librarians to introduce both students and faculty members to primary and secondary resources for researching the lives and works of specific poets, novelists, and playwrights.

Second, this initiative served to reinforce the potential benefits of collaborating with interested teaching faculty to move beyond the simple "one-shot" sessions to an embedded instruction model for providing information literacy and archival instruction for undergraduate researchers. The embedded nature of the partnership with Professor Day afforded some privileges not typically possible when teaching simple "one-shot" instruction sessions. Providing multiple instruction sessions to the students, both at the beginning and toward the end of their research process, as well as engaging in one-on-one and group reference consultations throughout the research process, provided an opportunity to fill in gaps in the students' information literacy skill set that might have existed after the initial instruction session. More specifically, students whose confidence in browsing collections and knowledge of traditional periodical formats were rusty or nonexistent were given opportunities to discover the importance and ease of using these source types. Similarly, students whose topics were not chosen in the first round of information literacy instruction had more of a chance to apply their information literacy skills during and after the second round, once their research ideas had become more firmly established.

Third, Professor Day's extensive cooperation with the authors' instruction efforts both throughout and even after the course made it much easier to evaluate the effectiveness of the initiative. Not only did she grant access to the students' researched fiction stories in the anthology and reflective bibliographic essays, she also sat down with the authors in June 2016 for a debriefing conversation that helped them to recognize exactly how important the course was to the future direction of the Department of English and how influential their leadership of the research aspects of the course had been. The collaboration also turned out to be a publishing opportunity for everyone involved in the course. Not only were the students able to publish their creative anthology in Ball State University's institutional repository, but Professor Day has also written a book chapter, forthcoming in 2017, detailing the unique nature of this course within her own community of practice.[34]

For others wanting to engage in similar partnerships with creative writing faculty, and in particular to assess the effectiveness of instruction sessions for classes with research-based creative writing assignments, the authors highly recommend integrating, if possible, an analytical writing assignment similar to the bibliographic reflection essays assigned to students in this course. By reading their personal reflections about the time they spent conducting research in the library and the archives using specific types of resources, the authors learned more than they ever could have from their responses to a standard three-minute anonymous survey instrument. It was encouraging to read positive comments and know for certain that the moments of serendipitous discovery did indeed happen and ultimately provided the kind of "aha" moments that are so critical to developing their curiosity as writers, and now researchers.

Conclusion

The strategies outlined here are of particular relevance to archivists and special collections librarians interested in collaborating to introduce archival research and primary source literacy into information literacy instruction sessions. They may also prove useful for academic librarians, scholarly communication specialists, and other academic professionals looking for innovative ways to partner with faculty members to support undergraduate student research and publishing. The *Framework for Information Literacy for Higher Education* calls for greater responsibility and collaboration among all parties (students, faculty, and librarians) to "foster enhanced engagement with the core ideas about information and scholarship within their disciplines."[35] Furthermore, "[l]ibrarians have a greater responsibility in identifying core ideas within their own knowledge domain that can extend learning for students, in creating a new cohesive curriculum for information literacy, and in collaborating more extensively with faculty."[36] The authors hope that their reflection on the planning, implementation, and assessment of instruction sessions for this course inspires fellow academic librarians and archivists to partner in similar ways to support creative writing research and publishing at their own institutions in ways that engage undergraduate students and faculty in thinking critically about information literacy and archival literacy within the context of their disciplines.

Notes

1. Robert S. Lynd and Helen Merrell Lynd, *Middletown: A Study in American Culture* (New York: Harcourt, Brace and Company, 1929).
2. Ball State University, "Fact Book—Students/Enrollment," last modified July 27, 2016, http://cms.bsu.edu/about/factbook/enrollment.
3. Ball State University, "Fact Book—Students/Enrollment."
4. Julia Glassman, "Research Support for Creative Writers: Bolstering Undergraduate Fiction and Poetry through Library Instruction," *College & Research Libraries News* 75, no. 11 (December 2014): 609, http://crln.acrl.org/content/75/11/602.
5. Cathy Day, "Our Town: Teaching Creative Writing Students to Love Research and

Collaboration," *Creative Writing Innovations: Breaking Boundaries in the Classroom*, ed. Michael Dean Clark, Trent Hergenrader, and Joseph Rein (New York: Bloomsbury Academic, forthcoming), 4.
6. *Middletown*, directed by Peter Davis (1982; Brooklyn, NY: Icarus Films Home Video, 2010), DVD, 457 min.
7. Day, "Our Town: Teaching Creative Writing Students to Love Research and Collaboration," 2, 10–11.
8. Professor Day prefers the phrase "researched fiction" rather than "historical fiction" to describe her own professional writing and the creative writing style emphasized in the course. While historical fiction is an established commercial literary genre of fiction characterized by historical actors and events from the actual past, researched fiction emphasizes the historical research that is required in order to write fictionally about characters and settings from the past, some of which may have once actually existed.
9. All et al., *You Are Here: Finding Yourself in Middletown (An Anthology)* (Muncie, Ind.: Ball State University Department of English, 2015), accessed September 10, 2016, http://cardinalscholar.bsu.edu/handle/123456789/199712.
10. Lynd, *Middletown: A Study in American Culture*, 4.
11. David Pavelich, "Lighting Fires in Creative Minds: Teaching Creative Writing in Special Collections," *College & Research Libraries News* 71, no. 6 (June 2010): 295–96, http://crln.acrl.org/content/71/6/295.full.
12. Ibid., 295.
13. Jennifer Blackmer, "The Gesture of Thinking: Collaborative Models for Undergraduate Research in the Arts and Humanities—Plenary Presentation at the 2008 CUR National Conference," *Council on Undergraduate Research Quarterly* 29, no. 2 (Winter 2008): 9, http://www.cur.org/assets/1/7/winter08blackmer.pdf.
14. Association of College and Research Libraries, *Framework for Information Literacy for Higher Education*, filed February 2, 2015, accessed September 14, 2016, http://www.ala.org/acrl/sites/ala.org.acrl/files/content/issues/infolit/Framework_ILHE.pdf.
15. Day, "Our Town: Teaching Creative Writing Students to Love Research and Collaboration."
16. Elizabeth Yakel and Deborah A. Torres, "AI: Archival Intelligence and User Expertise," *The American Archivist* 66, no. 1 (Spring/Summer 2003): 52, doi:10.17723/aarc.66.1.q022h85pn51n5800.
17. Ibid.
18. Ibid.
19. Magia G. Krause, "Undergraduates in the Archives: Using an Assessment Rubric to Measure Learning," *The American Archivist* 73, no. 2 (Fall/Winter 2010): 515.
20. Yakel and Torres, "AI: Archival Intelligence and User Expertise," 61.
21. Krause, "Undergraduates in the Archives: Using an Assessment Rubric to Measure Learning," 515.
22. Cathy Day, in discussion with the authors, June 29, 2016.
23. Ibid.
24. Glassman, "Research Support for Creative Writers: Bolstering Undergraduate Fiction and Poetry through Library Instruction," 604.
25. Krause, "Undergraduates in the Archives: Using an Assessment Rubric to Measure Learning," 507.

26. Ibid, 512.
27. Cathy Day, ENG 444 Senior Seminar Syllabus, Spring 2015, 2.
28. Rachel Crawley, "New Voices from Middletown: Research in Fiction" (undergraduate senior honors thesis, Ball State University, 2015), 8.
29. Anonymous bibliographic reflection essay.
30. Ibid.
31. Ibid.
32. Ibid.
33. Glassman, "Research Support for Creative Writers: Bolstering Undergraduate Fiction and Poetry through Library Instruction," 609.
34. Day, "Our Town: Teaching Creative Writing Students to Love Research and Collaboration."
35. Association of College and Research Libraries, *Framework for Information Literacy for Higher Education*, 2.
36. Ibid.

Bibliography

All et al. *You Are Here: Finding Yourself in Middletown (An Anthology)*. Muncie, Ind.: Ball State University Department of English, 2015. Accessed September 10, 2016. http://cardinalscholar.bsu.edu/handle/123456789/199712.

Association for College and Research Libraries. *Framework for Information Literacy for Higher Education*. Filed February 2, 2015. Accessed September 14, 2016. http://www.ala.org/acrl/sites/ala.org.acrl/files/content/issues/infolit/Framework_ILHE.pdf.

Ball State University. "Fact Book—Students/Enrollment." Last modified July 27, 2016. http://cms.bsu.edu/about/factbook/enrollment.

Blackmer, Jennifer. "The Gesture of Thinking: Collaborative Models for Undergraduate Research in the Arts and Humanities—Plenary Presentation at the 2008 CUR National Conference." *Council on Undergraduate Research Quarterly* 29, no. 2 (Winter 2008): 8–12. http://www.cur.org/assets/1/7/winter08blackmer.pdf.

Crawley, Rachel. "New Voices from Middletown: Research in Fiction." Undergraduate senior honors thesis, Ball State University, 2015. Accessed November 30, 2016. http://cardinalscholar.bsu.edu/handle/123456789/199997.

Day, Cathy. ENG 444 Senior Seminar Syllabus, Spring 2015, 2.

Day, Cathy. "Our Town: Teaching Creative Writing Students to Love Research and Collaboration." In *Creative Writing Innovations: Breaking Boundaries in the Classroom*, edited by Michael Dean Clark, Trent Hergenrader, and Joseph Rein. New York: Bloomsbury Academic, forthcoming.

Glassman, Julia. "Research Support for Creative Writers: Bolstering Undergraduate Fiction and Poetry through Library Instruction." *College & Research Libraries News* 75, no. 11 (December 2014): 602–04, 609. http://crln.acrl.org/content/75/11/602.

Krause, Magia G. "Undergraduates in the Archives: Using an Assessment Rubric to Measure Learning." *The American Archivist* 73, no. 2 (Fall/Winter 2010): 507–34. http://www.jstor.org/stable/23290757.

Lynd, Robert S., and Helen Merrell Lynd. *Middletown: A Study in American Culture*. New York: Harcourt, Brace and Company, 1929.

Middletown. Directed by Peter Davis. Brooklyn, NY: Icarus Films Home Video, 2010. DVD, 457 min. Originally broadcast in 1982 on PBS.

Pavelich, David. "Lighting Fires in Creative Minds: Teaching Creative Writing in Special Collections." *College & Research Libraries News* 71, no. 6 (June 2010): 295–97, 313. http://crln.acrl.org/content/71/6/295.full.

Yakel, Elizabeth, and Deborah A. Torres. "AI: Archival Intelligence and User Expertise." *The American Archivist* 66, no. 1 (Spring/Summer 2003): 51–78. doi:10.17723/aarc.66.1.q022h85pn51n5800.

CHAPTER 12*
Harnessing the Winds:
Collaboration and the *Aeolus* Undergraduate Research Journal

Alyson Gamble, Amelia Kallaher, Neal Lacey, Alexandra Maass, Caitlyn Ralph, Tyrone Ryba, and Mai Tanaka

Introduction

This case study describes the collaborative experience of creating an undergraduate research journal, offered as a course at New College of Florida. The college, a public liberal arts institution with an undergraduate enrollment of under one thousand students, promotes self-directed learning and assesses undergraduates by written evaluations of their performance rather than by quantitative grades. New College of Florida students initiated and edited the journal, with librarians and other faculty and staff members providing support and instruction. The journal required developing cross-campus collaborations among formerly disparate groups. This chapter explores the pedagogy and partnerships of the project and offers recommendations for organizations

---

* This work is licensed under a Creative Commons Attribution 4.0 License, CC BY (https://creativecommons.org/licenses/by/4.0/).

wishing to support their undergraduates by launching a student research journal with librarians championing the initiative and providing instruction.

Background

The *Aeolus* journal began in fall 2015 when New College of Florida students wanted to highlight undergraduate research and connect a variety of collaborators.[1] The students were influenced by open access undergraduate research journals, including the *MIT Undergraduate Research Journal* (MURJ) and *Stanford Undergraduate Research Journal* (SURJ).[2] Students appreciated the journals' inclusion of primary research articles alongside feature-style pieces on academic pursuits.

Realizing they needed campus support to develop the *Aeolus* journal, and drawing on their established faculty relationships, the students engaged two science professors for guidance. Librarian participation began soon after, when one of the professors asked the science librarian to assist with the project. For a month-long group independent study program, students worked under the direction of the bioinformatics professor with assistance from the science librarian to develop foundational materials for the journal, including a management structure and submission guidelines. The science librarian, recognizing additional collaboration was necessary, reached out to library administration, the Writing Resource Center, the Office of Research Programs and Services, the New College Foundation, the Center for Engagement and Opportunity, the Alumnae/i Association, and the Office of Communications and Marketing.

During the independent study period, faculty and students decided to create a full-semester course to teach scholarly communication and provide students with academic credit for their work producing the journal. The *Aeolus* course has taken various forms since its inception in fall 2015; this chapter will focus on the spring 2016 version of the course. In spring 2016, all enrolled students in the *Aeolus* journal course were required to attend weekly instruction sessions led by the science librarian and biostatistics professor. Student editors also met outside of class to generate policy documents, article layouts, and other operational necessities. At weekly meetings, the board groups shared the materials they produced with their classmates and instructors via in-class reports, group Google Drive folders, and the *Aeolus* WordPress website.[3]

The science librarian created instructional materials by combining student goals of producing a scholarly journal with the four metaliteracy objective domains.[4] The science librarian worked both independently and with assistance from other faculty and staff members to create these resources. All instructional materials were organized into themed modules, available via the

Course Management System (CMS) Moodle. For example, the lesson "Publication Ethics & Citations" required students to complete an eLearning exercise introducing publication ethics, read an article on "bibliographic negligence," review a selection of citation style guides and instructions to authors, and apply lessons about the ethical importance of citations when creating instructions to authors and designing a citation style guide for the journal.[5]

In the "Publication Ethics & Citations" lesson, most students reached all four metaliteracy learning domains. Students achieved behavioral learning objectives by creating ethically sound publication materials, particularly citation style guides, for *Aeolus*. The cognitive learning objective was met by students comprehending the basics of publication ethics and the reasons citations are used in scholarly articles. Students achieved affective domain objectives by changing their attitudes about citations and explaining the necessity of attributing authorship through clear style guidelines, attitudes they did not express prior to completing this lesson.[6] Finally, students reached the metacognitive domain by understanding what they formerly did not know about publication ethics and identifying locations for exploring this topic. Students then applied their critical thought into the active process of creating citation style guides and instructions to authors for the *Aeolus* journal.[7]

Partnerships

Cross-campus collaboration was vital to the *Aeolus* journal and course. Divisional faculty and librarians worked closely with students to identify potential campus partners. Many offices were keen to provide support. The science librarian created course materials with assistance from the Writing Resource Center, fellow librarians, and divisional faculty. Student editors and the science librarian asked the Office of Research Programs and Services and the New College Foundation for information about funding. The student editors and science librarian worked with the Center for Engagement and Opportunity to recruit journal submissions. Student editors contacted the Alumnae/i Association for help creating a peer-review network. At the student editors' request, the Office of Communications and Marketing offered space to publish highlights from the journal in the college's monthly e-newsletter and bi-annual magazine.

Of course, collaboration is not without its challenges. Creating an academic journal is a major undertaking in itself, as is designing a course. Since some faculty were concerned about the instructional role of librarians, this was an especially rich opportunity to expand and enrich faculty understanding of librarians' strengths. The science librarian used questions about instructional duties and professional competencies as "teachable moments" to explain the role of librarians as educators.[8] The science librarian worked closely with advocates of the project to communicate the value added to undergraduate research by offering the *Aeolus* journal course as a librarian-led instructional opportunity.

Reflection

Until recently, librarians at New College of Florida mainly provided reference and instruction or technical services duties. They were not permitted to be instructors of record on courses. Building connections between groups on campus to support the *Aeolus* journal course helped gain support for librarians becoming instructors of record. Using the *Aeolus* journal course as a catalyst, the librarians worked with their colleagues to help clarify and stimulate the development of metaliteracy instruction. By doing so, the librarians learned how to be more active campus partners to support students' academic pursuits.

Granting students control over the journal gave them the ability to direct their learning, which continued to fuel their intrinsic motivation for learning about scholarly publishing.[9] Now that the journal editors have solidified journal management, *Aeolus* can be run by a smaller staff who devote more class time to editing, with a librarian providing guidance. Training for student editors will be continually assessed and improved by a librarian. Project leaders are also considering long-term preservation of journal formative documents and published articles. These may be held in the library's digital repository. In the future, student editors plan to continue to lead the *Aeolus* journal, with instruction provided by a librarian.

Assessment

Metacognition, the metaliteracy learning domain most influential for the *Framework for Information Literacy for Higher Education,* requires evaluating one's learning efforts.[10] To encourage metacognitive learning, the *Aeolus* course required in-class discussion and students' self-assessment of their work. Students directly stated they did not understand a subject or, through class discussion and work editing articles and policy documents, demonstrated they did not grasp a concept. Through formative assessment, the science librarian was able to address these issues immediately and modify lessons to concentrate on a subject until students expressed comprehension. For example, a student expressed concern about communication during group meetings and another student asked for assistance when writing to authors. These two questions were addressed in the moment and in future lessons on professional communication.

The science librarian conducted summative assessment for the *Aeolus* journal course. At the end of the semester, students created e-portfolios of their work from the *Aeolus* journal. These e-portfolios contained each student's completion of certificate from the eLearning module, examples of the student's work in the course, and a self-evaluation form. The science librarian used these e-portfolios to evaluate students' work and the achievements of the course's learning objectives. Students evidenced knowledge of scholarly communication in examples of their classwork and summaries of their learning experiences.

All students who submitted an e-portfolio expressed achievement of goals related to the broad metaliteracy objectives. The clearest indicators of success were noted in the behavioral and cognitive domains, where most students provided clear evidence of development in their project management skills and improved comprehension regarding scholarly communication. For example, one student who began the course with no understanding of scholarly publishing reflected on his expanded understanding of the process at the end of the course. Another student who demonstrated initial competency in scholarly publishing, particularly in the sciences, expanded her knowledge of academic communication while demonstrating her improved group communication skills. All students exhibited metacognitive development when stating their learning about scholarly publishing and future goals for the journal.

The students also assessed the *Aeolus* journal course and their instructors at the end of the semester through instructor evaluations and e-portfolio self-analyses. All of the students expressed that they learned a great deal from the *Aeolus* journal course but would have liked more chances to edit submissions rather than create policy documents. Since the journal was new, there were not many submissions and journal guidelines needed to be developed. The students offered a variety of solutions to address the dearth, including simplifying the submission process. Students suggested having *Aeolus* journal editors write feature articles to make academic subjects accessible to non-specialists. Students appreciated the self-direction of the course and their instructors' accessibility and support.

Plans for expanding scholarly publishing opportunities for students on campus are in development. Students are interested in starting a creative writing journal, which the library could support. To improve accessibility for the *Aeolus* journal, the project leaders will try to procure an ISSN, assign DOIs to articles, add the journal record to the library's catalog, export the catalog record to OCLC Worldcat, and register the journal with the Directory of Open Access Journals.[11] Students suggested many of these initiatives after learning about them in the *Aeolus* course.

Recommendations/Best Practices

The three most important lessons from this project are: students can choose their own research opportunities, including producing an academic journal; partnership is necessary to support this undergraduate research initiative; and metaliteracy can be developed through the experience of producing a research journal. Student agency is a powerful force for change on a college campus. Because students saw a need to share undergraduate research beyond campus, they sought out the necessary partners to achieve their vision. Campus offices were able to provide students with the resources and support necessary to make the students' journal a reality. Through their experience creating the journal, students developed an understanding of what collaboration is in a digital era and critically engaged information as a community.

Faculty supervision ensures students receive the information and guidance necessary for creating a successful research publication.[12] If librarians at another college have faculty standing, it is recommended that a librarian provide this support. Librarians' expertise in scholarly communication and information literacy are ideally suited for assisting undergraduate research journals.[13] Since undergraduates may be unfamiliar with the basics of scholarly communication, this project demonstrated that student editors can benefit from completing a course on these topics. Armed with knowledge about academic publishing, students are able to take responsibility for necessary administrative tasks surrounding the journal.

A cross-campus team is necessary to support students' initiative. Without collaboration among all of the partners involved, *Aeolus* would be impossible. Collaboration on the journal helped create new opportunities for the library to work with other departments across campus. By promoting association between formerly siloed groups, *Aeolus* created potential for integrating varied perspectives and approaches on joint projects. Witnessing multiple departments working together on *Aeolus* offered a positive model of collaboration for students.[14] Joint instruction provided faculty and the student editors with new opportunities for active learning while facilitating interdisciplinary dialogue about important issues in scholarly publishing.

As interdisciplinary departments are staffed by information professionals, libraries are fertile environments for undergraduate journals to develop. In this innovative domain, librarians can use research journals to initiate collaborations both on campus and outside of the organization to support student editors and their efforts on the journal. By collaborating with many different groups on a common project, while serving in an instructional role, librarians can act as change agents in their organizations, demonstrate their abilities to move beyond the often limited expectations of campus colleagues, and disrupt stereotyped concepts of librarian work.[15] Achieving these lofty goals requires the willingness of the college and the library to support a librarian in teaching a course and students in publishing a journal.

Conclusion

The *Aeolus* journal gave students, faculty, and staff a chance to collaborate on a scholarly initiative based on key metaliteracy concepts, with student engagement in scholarly publishing as the main goal. As a result, students at New College of Florida have an improved support system for their academic endeavors, including a place to publish their research. Supporting undergraduate research has longstanding effects not only for the students involved but also for librarians. Through involvement with the *Aeolus* journal, the library has been able to help evolve the liaison model at the organization. This has led to increased conversation with other departments about curriculum development, pedagogy, and the instructional value of librarians. Helping students publish their scholarship gives librarians a chance to highlight their professional competencies. By championing students, librarians promote our expertise, knowledge, skills, and other abilities to support scholarly initiatives on campus.

Notes

1. Students chose the name for the journal from the Greek mythological character Aeolus, a minor deity and custodian of the four winds ("Aeolus," *Encyclopedia Mythica*, last modified 25 August 1999, http://www.pantheon.org/articles/a/aeolus.html). The seal of New College of Florida is a representation of four winds ("New College Seal, Color Studies," I.M. Pei and Associates, ca. 1964, New College Digital Collections, http://ncf.sobek.ufl.edu/AA00025604/00001; "The Four Winds sculpture dedication in honor of Senator Bob Johnson," New College of Florida, 2011, http://ncf.sobek.ufl.edu/AA00025832/00001/).
2. Massachusetts Institute of Technology Undergraduate Research Journal, "MURJ—MIT Undergraduate Research Journal," last modified May 2016, http://murj.mit.edu/; SURJ, The Stanford Undergraduate Research Journal, "Journal Archives," last updated spring 2015, http://surj.stanford.edu/journal-archives-2/.
3. "Aeolus," last updated November 2016, https://ncfaeolus.wordpress.com/.
4. Metaliteracy learning has four domains (behavioral, cognitive, affective, metacognitive), each with its own goals and objectives. The behavioral domain encompasses actions, notably the development of skills and competencies. The cognitive domain involves knowledge and its comprehension, evaluation, organization, and application. The affective domain creates changes in learners' emotions or attitudes. The metacognitive domain, which was especially influential to the updated *Framework for Information Literacy for Higher Education*, is achieved by learners reflecting on their own thinking and continuing to expand their education in an evolving

information landscape. [Association of College and Research Libraries Board of Directors, "Framework for Information Literacy for Higher Education," (January 11, 2016): 2, http://www.ala.org/acrl/standards/ilframework; Thomas P. Mackey and Trudi E. Jacobson, "Reframing Information as a Metaliteracy," *College & Research Libraries* 72.1 (2011): 62, doi:10.5860/crl-76r1; Thomas P. Mackey and Trudi E. Jacobson, *Metaliteracy: Reinventing Information Literacy to Empower Learners*, (Chicago: Neal-Schuman, 2011); Donna Witek and Teresa Grettano, "Revising for Metaliteracy: Flexible Course Design to Support Social Media Pedagogy," in *Metaliteracy in Practice*, ed. Trudi E. Jacobson and Thomas P. Mackey (Chicago: Neal-Schuman, 2016), 3; "Goals and Learning Objectives," last modified September 11, 2014, https://metaliteracy.org/learning-objectives/.
5. Committee on Publication Ethics, "Introduction to Publication Ethics," http://publicationethics.org/resources/elearning/introduction-publication-ethics-0; Council of Science Editors, "Resource Library," last updated 2016, https://www.councilscienceeditors.org/resource-library/; Council on Undergraduate Research, "Undergraduate Journals," last updated 2016, http://www.cur.org/resources/students/undergraduate_journals/; Richard Gallagher, "Citation Violations," *The Scientist* 23.5 (2009): 13.
6. Metaliteracy.org, "Goal 2: Understand personal privacy, information ethics, and intellectual property issues in changing technology environments," last updated September 11, 2014, https://metaliteracy.org/learning-objectives/.
7. Sharon A. Weiner and Charles Watkinson, "What Do Students Learn from Participation In an Undergraduate Research Journal? Results of an Assessment," *Journal of Librarianship and Scholarly Communication* 2.2 (2014), eP1125.
8. Susan Avery, "When Opportunity Knocks: Opening the Door Through Teachable Moments," *The Reference Librarian* 49.2 (2008), doi:10.1080/02763870802101260.
9. Trudi E. Jacobson and Lijuan Xu, *Motivating Students in Information Literacy Classes* (New York: Neal-Schuman, 2004), 6; Weiner and Watkinson, "What Do Students Learn from Participation in an Undergraduate Research Journal? Results of an Assessment," eP1125.
10. Jennifer A. Livingston, "Metacognition: An Overview," Online paper, State University of New York at Buffalo, Graduate School of Education (1997), http://gse.buffalo.edu/fas/shuell/cep564/metacog.htm.
11. Adrian K. Ho, "Library Services for Creating and Publishing Student Research Journals," in *Library Publishing Toolkit*, ed. Allison P. Brown (Geneseo: IDS Project Press, 2013): 241, http://uknowledge.uky.edu/libraries_facpub/77.
12. Ibid.
13. Elizabeth C. Turtle and Martin P. Courtois, "Scholarly Communication: Science Librarians as Advocates for Change," *Issues in Science and Technology Librarianship* (Summer 2007), http://www.istl.org/07-summer/article2.html.
14. Judy Artz, "Library and Learning Center Collaborations: Within and Outside the Walls," in *Centers for Learning: Writing Centers and Libraries in Collaboration*, ed. James K. Emborg and Sheril Hook, (Chicago, IL: Association of College and Research Libraries, 2005), 97.
15. Annie Pho and Turner Masland, "The Revolution Will Not be Stereotyped: Changing Perceptions Through Diversity," in *The Librarian Stereotype: Deconstructing Perceptions and Presentations of Information Work*, ed. Nicole Pagowsky and Mir-

iam Rigby (Chicago: Association of College and Research Libraries, 2014), 257–82; Elizabeth C. Turtle and Martin P. Courtois, "Scholarly Communication: Science Librarians as Advocates for Change," *Issues in Science and Technology Librarianship* (Summer 2007), http://www.istl.org/07-summer/article2.html.

Bibliography

Aeolus. "Aeolus." Last modified November 2016. https://aeolus.scholasticahq.com/.
Aeolus. "Aeolus." Last modified November 2016. https://ncfaeolus.wordpress.com/.
Artz, Judy. "Library and Learning Center Collaborations: Within and Outside the Walls." In *Centers for Learning*, edited by James K. Elmborg and Sheril Hook. ACRL Publications in Librarianship no. 58. Chicago: Association of College and Research Libraries, 2005.
Association of College and Research Libraries Board of Directors. "Framework for Information Literacy for Higher Education." Last modified January 11, 2016. http://www.ala.org/acrl/standards/ilframework.
Avery, Susan. "When Opportunity Knocks: Opening the Door through Teachable Moments." *The Reference Librarian* 49.2 (2008): 109–18. doi:10.1080/02763870802101260.
Committee on Publication Ethics. "Guidelines." Last modified July 2016. http://publicationethics.org/resources/guidelines.
Committee on Publication Ethics. "Introduction to Publication Ethics." http://publicationethics.org/resources/elearning/introduction-publication-ethics-0.
Council of Science Editors. "Resource Library." https://www.councilscienceeditors.org/resource-library/.
Council on Undergraduate Research. "Undergraduate Journals." http://www.cur.org/resources/students/undergraduate_journals/.
Gallagher, Richard. "Citation Violations." *The Scientist* 23.5 (2009): 13. http://www.the-scientist.com/?articles.view/articleNo/27336/title/Citation-Violations/.
Ho, Adrian K. "Library Services for Creating and Publishing Student Research Journals." Library Faculty and Staff Publications, Paper 77. http://uknowledge.uky.edu/libraries_facpub/77. Originally published in *Library Publishing Toolkit*, edited by Allison P. Brown. Geneseo: IDS Project Press, 2013. http://opensuny.org/omp/index.php/IDSProject/catalog/book/25.
Jacobson, Trudi E., and Lijuan Xu. *Motivating Students in Information Literacy Classes*. The New Library Series, Vol. 8. New York: Neal-Schuman Publishers, 2004.
Jungck, John R., Margaret Harris, Renée Mercuri, and Joshua Tusin. "Points of View: Should Students be Encouraged to Publish their Research in Student-Run Publications?: Undergraduates: Do Research, Publish." *Cell Biology Education* 3.1 (2004): 24-26. doi:10.1187/cbe.04-01-0022.
Livingston, Jennifer A. "Metacognition: An Overview." Online paper, State University of New York at Buffalo, Graduate School of Education (1997), http://gse.buffalo.edu/fas/shuell/cep564/metacog.htm.
Mackey, Thomas P., and Trudi Jacobson. *Metaliteracy: Reinventing Information Literacy to Empower Learners*. Chicago: Neal- Schuman, 2014.
Mackey, Thomas P., and Trudi E. Jacobson. "Reframing Information Literacy as a Metaliteracy." *College & Research Libraries* 72.1 (2011): 62–78. doi:10.5860/crl-76r1.

Massachusetts Institute of Technology Undergraduate Research Journal. "MURJ—MIT Undergraduate Research Journal." Last modified May 2016. http://murj.mit.edu/.

Metaliteracy.org. Last modified September 11, 2014. https://metaliteracy.org/learning-objectives/.

Pho, Annie, and Turner Masland. "The Revolution Will Not Be Stereotyped: Changing Perceptions Through Diversity." In *The Librarian Stereotype: Deconstructing Perceptions and Presentations of Information Work*, edited by Nicole Pagowsky and Miriam Rigby, Chicago: Association of College and Research Libraries, 2014: 257–82.

SURJ, the Stanford Undergraduate Research Journal. "Journal Archives." http://surj.stanford.edu/journal-archives-2/.

Turtle, Elizabeth C., and Martin P. Courtois. "Scholarly Communication: Science Librarians as Advocates for Change." *Issues in Science and Technology Librarianship* (Summer 2007). http://www.istl.org/07-summer/article2.html.

Wallis, Lauren, and Andrew Battista. "The Politics of Information: Students as Creators in a Metaliteracy Context." In *Metaliteracy in Practice*, edited by Trudi E. Jacobson and Thomas P. Mackey. Chicago: Neal-Schuman, 2016: 23–45.

Weiner, Sharon A., and Charles Watkinson. "What Do Students Learn from Participation in an

Undergraduate Research Journal? Results of an Assessment." *Journal of Librarianship and Scholarly Communication* 2.2 (2014). doi:10.7710/2162-3309.1125.

Witek, Donna, and Teresa Grettano. "Revising for Metaliteracy: Flexible Course Design to Support Social Media Pedagogy." In *Metaliteracy in Practice*, edited by Trudi E. Jacobson and Thomas P. Mackey. Chicago: Neal-Schuman, 2016: 1–22.

CHAPTER 13 *
Image of Research:
Celebrating and Sharing Undergraduate Work

Michelle Reed and Merinda Kaye Hensley

Introduction

In 2013 and 2015 respectively, the University of Illinois at Urbana-Champaign (Illinois) and the University of Kansas (KU) implemented an Image of Research competition, a library-led initiative designed to showcase original research of undergraduate students. The Image of Research competition is a multidisciplinary competition celebrating the diversity and breadth of undergraduate student research by inviting students to submit entries consisting of an image and brief text that articulates how the image relates to their research.[1] The work of the students is shared widely and archived in the institutional repository, providing students with an easy-entry experience to "publishing" their research. Additionally, students are rewarded with monetary and category prizes.

The goals for Image of Research are threefold:
- Provide students with an opportunity to reflect on what their research means to them and how to represent that research in a visual manner
- Proactively engage with undergraduate students as creators of information
- Address educational issues around scholarly communication by designing learning opportunities that help students confront the complexities of copyright and their online presence

---

* This work is licensed under a Creative Commons Attribution 4.0 License, CC BY (https://creativecommons.org/licenses/by/4.0/).

At Illinois, project personnel were inspired by the University of Chicago Library's Image of Research competition, established in 2008 (http://grad.uic.edu/image-research-exhibit), and KU began their competition after reading about Illinois in a column for *C&RL News* outlining examples of the intersections of scholarly communication and information literacy.[2] Both libraries were looking for avenues to engage with undergraduate students participating in high-impact educational practices as part of wider information literacy and outreach goals.

Background
University of Illinois at Urbana-Champaign

The competition at the University of Illinois began in spring 2014 with both graduate and undergraduate student versions and is sponsored by the library's digital scholarship center.[3] Entrants were asked to submit images of, or reflective of, their research or research process. Broadly speaking, research is an iterative process that involves asking questions, seeking answers from multiple information sources, and remaining open to new or contradictory ideas; creating visual representations can be a challenge for researchers at any stage of their career. Because definitions of research and the research process vary from discipline to discipline, Illinois expected to receive many different representations of research in the images. Project personnel wrote the Illinois competition details and requirements to be as inclusive as possible to students from all disciplines.[4] First, undergraduate students must be registered and in good standing for the semester, and they are encouraged to seek support from a faculty mentor. To date, all of the students who entered the competition were engaged in an undergraduate research program within their discipline. Support from faculty mentors is crucial as students learn to talk about their own role in the research process and seek guidance on complex issues such as research ethics.

Second, there are a few specifics students must follow to submit an entry (e.g., file type, size, resolution). These requirements have been refined over time to make sure images submitted can be viewed clearly online and printed. All images for Illinois must include a 100–200-word narrative explaining the connection to the students' research in layman's language. Students may collaborate with a faculty mentor and may only submit images where they are the principle creator of the image. Third-party content can be used as long as it is mixed with other content to create an original work. Students using such content must either abide by fair use or have permission from the copyright owner to share the image(s). As part of the submission process, students must accept competition rules based upon language from the institutional repository guidelines that were originally vetted by campus legal counsel. The agreement the students sign as a click through is a nonexclusive license that grants the library the ability to use the submissions for archiving, promotion, and marketing purposes, while students retain all copyright. All student work is archived in the institutional repository, providing the library with a formal record of the competition and the students with a permanent URL for their résumés. Submissions are gathered through an online webform. The competition is marketed through Office of Undergraduate Research's (OUR) Advisory Board, through OUR's and the library's social media accounts, through email communication between subject liaison librarians and teaching faculty, on the digital signage in the libraries, and through an ad in the student newspaper. Information about the competition and past winners can be viewed at https://publish.illinois.edu/imageofresearch-undergrad/.

The Illinois competition is open for eight weeks at the beginning of the spring semester. The library received the most undergraduate submissions in its initial year: twenty-three submissions in 2014, eleven in 2015, sixteen in 2016, and eleven in 2017. Most of the students are identified with science disciplines, with 71 percent of the entries coming from STEM, 15 percent from fine arts, and only 14 percent from the social sciences. Juniors and seniors make up the bulk of the entries, with only a few freshmen and sophomores. This may reflect the demographic of students participating in high-impact educational practices, such as undergraduate research, which tends to recruit students who are further along in their academic careers.

Submissions are judged on three criteria: originality, visual impact, and connection among image, text, and research. These categories are meant to be broad and to allow the judging panel substantial leeway in making decisions about the awards. Judges are recruited from the library, OUR, and among the teaching faculty. The awards at Illinois are substantial ($300 for first place and $200 for second place) and funded by a generous donation from the Illinois Division of Intercollegiate Athletics.[5] Since the library is committed to recognizing as many pieces of student work as possible, one or two honorable mentions are also awarded. The winners are celebrated at the annual Undergraduate Research Symposium held during Undergraduate Research Week in April. Each submission is printed on a poster board (appropriate for framing by the students) and displayed at the entrance of the venue for the symposium. In addition, all entries are displayed on the digital monitors at the Illinois Undergraduate Library and the Main Library, shared in an Omeka.org exhibition (discontinued 2017), and shared on the library's Instagram account (as of 2017).[6]

University of Kansas

In spring 2015, after the publication of "Weaving the Threads: Scholarly Communication and Information Literacy"[7] describing the Image of Research competition at Illinois, the KU Libraries initiated its own pilot competition directed at undergraduate students.[8] KU's competition relied on Instagram as the primary platform for submission, though email submissions were also permitted. Like the Illinois competition, entrants were asked to submit images of, or reflective of, their research or research process. Entrants were also asked to include brief text in layman's language (approximately 50–100 words) accompanying the image and to tag the entry using the competition hashtag, #KUImage15. Unlike Illinois, multiple submissions were encouraged in an effort to capture the dynamic, reflective nature of the research process and the evolution of the researcher's perspective over time.

Goals of the KU pilot were to develop a brand for the competition and build a sustainable infrastructure to support submissions and their evaluation. A small project team (consisting of staff from the Center for Undergraduate Initiatives & Engagement, Office of Communications & Advancement, and Digital Initiatives & Discovery Services Division) published promotional flyers, a webpage, and a webform (See Appendix 13A: Promotional Flyer). There were a few additional differences between the Illinois and KU competitions. Guided by an NPR article on photo contests, the KU team also created an If This Then That (IFTTT) "recipe" to autopopulate a Google Sheet each time an image was added to Instagram with the competition hashtag.[9] Following submission, students were directed via Instagram Messaging to the competition webform in order to verify their eligibility, accept the contest terms, and provide the libraries a nonexclusive license to use their submissions in a variety of ways, including for research and marketing. The competition was marketed via the libraries' and its partners' social media channels, table tents, and email communication with teaching faculty, who were asked to share the promotional flyers with their students. Additionally, the project manager directly emailed Undergraduate Research Symposium presenters using a contact list provided by the university's Center for Undergraduate Research, which hosts the symposium each spring and provides financial support to undergraduate student researchers.

The competition was open for submissions for approximately two weeks in early April. The libraries received twenty-eight submissions from seventeen entrants. Eleven of the entrants were seniors, five were juniors, and one was unverified. Thirteen majors were represented, and seven of the students were enrolled in the KU University Honors Program. Entries were pre-screened by library staff, who were instructed to flag any entries that did not meet the requirements of the competition or that were verbally abusive, grossly offensive, or otherwise inappropriate. Four judges were recruited from across campus reflecting expertise in the visual arts, humanities, and sciences. This multidisciplinary panel of judges selected a grand-prize winner and additional winners in the following award categories: Originality, Visual Impact, Social

Impact, and Connection. The grand-prize winner received $100 and each category winner received $50. A poster collage of all eligible entries was framed and displayed in the Learning Studio at Anschutz Library alongside individual prints of the winning submissions.

In the competition's second year, the project team maintained the infrastructure and marketing strategies developed in the pilot but expanded the competition's web presence, which included adding a new collection for winning entries to the institutional repository, KU ScholarWorks, and developing an online form for web submissions.[10] Additionally, the libraries hosted an awards ceremony that featured lightning talks by Image of Research winners. In alignment with the strategic priority of proactively engaging with researchers to advance scholarship and improvement in scholarly communication, the libraries also developed an educational copyright series shared with students via social media and invited two speakers from KU Libraries' Shulenburger Office of Scholarly Communication & Copyright to present at the awards event about visibility and the ethos of Open Access.[11] Compensation remained the same, but award categories were expanded and adjusted to reflect knowledge practices and dispositions described in the ACRL *Framework for Information Literacy for Higher Education*.[12] A "Research Is a Process" award was added to encourage multiple entries and eligibility was restricted to entrants who submitted a minimum of three entries on the same subject. A new, sponsored award, "Open for Collaboration," was based on the theme of Open Access Week 2015. "Story of Research" and "Vision" awards emphasized the quality of submitted text and image, respectively. A "Libraries Choice" award, created to honor submissions that reflected library spaces, resources, or services, was not awarded due to a lack of submissions meeting the criteria for the category (despite an abundance of such submissions the previous year). Descriptions of each and additional information about the competition are available at www.lib.ku.edu/ior. Following a request by judges who served during the first year, a rubric was developed and provided to year-two judges to assist with prioritizing and eliminating submissions.

In its second year, the competition accepted submissions for approximately six weeks, opening near the end of the fall semester and closing a few weeks into the spring semester. The libraries received forty-five submissions from seventeen entrants, though only thirteen of the entrants accepted the contest terms (at least one was a graduate student and therefore ineligible). Of those, nine were seniors, three were juniors, and one was a sophomore. Three of the five award winners accepted the invitation to present at the awards ceremony. An invitation was also extended to and accepted by one of the award winners from the previous year. Additionally, all of the submissions were shared with KU's Center for Undergraduate Research, which selected one image for their annual Undergraduate Research Symposium program cover and marketing materials.

Partnerships

To gain the attention of students, partnerships with departments and campus organizations that work with undergraduate researchers are essential. Both institutions cultivated relations in order to reach faculty mentors and others working closely with the students on a daily basis. These groups were invited to contribute to the competition by providing feedback on competition rules and participating in the judging process. At Illinois, OUR invited the project coordinator to speak to their Advisory Board about the competition to raise awareness on campus and provided the space and resources to celebrate the winners at the annual symposium. At KU, partnerships with the University Honors Program and the Center for Undergraduate Research provided invaluable opportunities for the project coordinator to interact directly with students engaged in research. Both organizations invited the libraries to conduct outreach at their events, provided information about students' research schedules, and participated in brainstorming sessions.

Reflection

The hallmark of high-impact educational practices involves opportunities for students to share and/or present their research (e.g., posters presentations, presentations at student conferences, publication in undergraduate research journals).[13] Given that Image of Research is a mechanism for visualizing research, both institutions have gained considerable insight into running a competition and working with students on sharing their research. Since most entrants are juniors and seniors, project managers suspect this is an indication that students at lower levels are reluctant to consider themselves researchers. One goal is to reach out to freshman and sophomore students participating in undergraduate research and offer extra assistance to better prepare them for submitting an entry to the competition as well as to share their research more widely.

The nature of the competition lends itself to exploring the intersections of scholarly communication and information literacy. At Illinois, project personnel are working on developing a series of workshops geared toward the needs of undergraduate researchers including: (1) data management, (2) authors' rights issues from the perspective of students owning their copyright, and (3) research visualization in the social sciences and humanities. Illinois plans to pilot the new workshops in spring 2018.

During the second year of Image of Research at KU, the project manager developed a copyright education series that was shared on the libraries' social media channels. Goals of the series were twofold: to market the competition and to introduce students to basic copyright concepts. The libraries shared catchy images and short facts about copyright while also modeling best practices in attribution. Posts discussed the recent news story of "Happy Birthday to You" entering the public domain, how copyright is a bundle of rights as opposed to a single right, and details of Creative Commons licensing. KU aimed to share information with students in informal ways; the drawback of this approach is the inability to measure direct impact on student behavior. Additionally, KU crafted copyright language in the competition's terms and conditions, specifically to simplify language to promote student learning about such agreements. A future goal of the project manager was to develop an FAQ to replace the formal rules and guidelines, a goal shared by Illinois.

Marketing the competition is at the top of both institutions' lists for improvement. It is apparent that project personnel need to find better ways to reach students, especially in the humanities and social sciences. The project manager at Illinois has reached out to the student newspaper to publish an article on the competition in fall 2017 with the hopes that students will plan ahead for spring 2018. At KU, the project manager emailed the student newspaper prior to the awards ceremony to alert the editorial staff of the event, which resulted in a long article about the awards and presentations.[14] Additional local press opportunities could be explored prior to and during the period of open submissions to make the competition more visible to the campus and local community.

Both institutions experienced unanticipated situations. Even though students sign an agreement during the process of submitting their entry that states they agree to share their image for archiving and marketing purposes, Illinois had three students in the past four years ask to have their entries removed from the institutional repository after the competition was complete. Two cited future publication as the reason for removal; one didn't properly communicate with his or her faculty mentor prior to submission and the faculty member expressed ownership of the image. In all cases, the library immediately complied with the requests by suppressing the entries in the institutional repository and removing the entries from the Omeka and/or Instagram accounts. While all students confirmed they had read the agreement, they also confessed to misunderstanding the implications. In response, Illinois is considering re-wording the agreement in plain language to mitigate this from happening in the future.

Another complication arose in making award payments to students. At Illinois, paying student awards is complicated by student status. For example, US students can be paid through their student account with any debt on the account being paid first. However, if the student claims international status, they must provide additional paperwork to process an award. In both cases, students are responsible for any tax liability as it applies to income. The library is clear about this situation with the students ahead of time, but each year the situation must be monitored by the library Business Office to make sure all campus and federal rules are being followed carefully.

KU experienced complications from taking submissions through Instagram. Relying on social media for accepting submissions posed several challenges. First, a number of submissions were not viewable because they were tagged from private accounts. Other Instagram users temporarily adjusted their privacy settings from private to public, resulting in a reduction of final submissions tagged with the competition hashtag that are visible on social media. Second, directing students from Instagram to the web form for accepting terms and verifying eligibility was a manual process that frequently required multiple attempts. In some cases, students created public Instagram accounts solely for submission and then did not monitor the account to receive communication from the libraries. Additionally, the use of Instagram as the submission platform may have prevented students from investing more time and energy into the submission process.

Assessment

Assessment is a priority in the continual development and improvement of Image of Research. The competition at Illinois is moving into its fifth year in 2018. To date, the Illinois project team has relied mainly on quality of submissions and student feedback. Since submissions went down by almost half since its inception, Illinois is working on a plan to better reach faculty mentors and students directly through their undergraduate research programs. Informal student feedback has been positive, and several students have entered the competition in back-to-back years. However, it is evident from the entries that students who are most aware of the competition are from STEM disciplines. It is also possible that STEM students are taught through their research process about ways to visualize data that social science and fine arts students are not. Planning meetings in summer 2016 and spring 2017 have resulted in several ideas for increasing participation:

- Similar to KU, develop an in-person celebration event where entrants get to meet one another and share with their faculty mentors.
- Work with subject liaison librarians to share competition information during instructional sessions.
- Perform direct outreach to undergraduate research courses identified through OUR to promote marketing materials and offer five-minute promotional presentations during course time.
- Share past competition entries through marketing, including student newspaper and directly to faculty mentors.

- Offer drop-in library workshops on how to visualize data and include information about the competition.
- Create feedback survey for entrants asking about their experience as well as suggestions for improvement, including how to engage their peers.

To date, KU has focused on student feedback to assess the Image of Research competition. In surveys and emails, student winners expressed gratitude for the opportunity to meet other students involved in research and to share their research with others (both by presenting and by bringing their friends and family to the Image of Research display in the Learning Studio at Anschutz Library). One student comment from the awards event read, "I am blown away by the individual stories and caliber of research for undergraduates at KU. Everyone is so enthusiastic and engaged!"

The libraries also promoted the competition by tabling alongside KU's Center for Undergraduate Research during an event held near the front entrance of the libraries' Learning Studio, during which the Center offered free doughnuts. The majority of students who approached the table reported that they were aware of the competition. Some expressed reluctance due to a perceived inability to capture their research in an image. Only a small number of students who expressed interest in the competition submitted entries. However, the experience did result in the recruitment of one student who provided input on event planning and who was later designated the libraries' Image of Research "ambassador." The student was recognized as such during the awards ceremony, during which she was provided a small award, and has volunteered to lead efforts to recruit participants during the third year of the competition. Unfortunately, the competition was not conducted in the third year due to staff transitions.

During the second year of the competition, personnel from KU Libraries' Research and Learning Division developed a rubric based on the ACRL *Framework* to better understand undergraduate perceptions of research. The rubric defined six criteria that could be observed in competition submissions, each connected to one or more of the frames, with scoring metrics for high performance, low performance, and not observed. The rubric remains in draft form and has not yet been applied to submissions. See Appendix 13B: Image of Research Rubric based on the ACRL *Framework*.

Recommendations/Best Practices

1. Engage students early and often. We surmise that our marketing strategies would be more successful if we could engage past entrants to carry the message of the competition. One possibility might be to recruit an

Image of Research "ambassador." As students tend to listen to their peers, this could potentially be more effective than presenting the competition in courses ourselves.

2. Think critically about your expectations and whether submission mechanics encourage or discourage the depth of reflection you hope to see. KU found that judges were critical of submissions, hoping for longer written text with greater detail, which led us to question if there might be a disconnection between expectations and the use of social media as a submission platform. Entries submitted via KU's webform were longer and more thoughtful than those submitted via Instagram. Illinois used a traditional online form and saw well-developed narratives submitted with the images.

3. Look for as many avenues as possible to share student work and join in the celebration of their achievement. Printing student images with the narrative text on a poster board that can be framed is highly valued by the students and worth the investment. Holding an event with students and their faculty mentors, especially if students have an opportunity to publicly discuss their entry, brings an element of ongoing conversation to their research and an experience that will help in the future when discussing their work. Financial rewards are not imperative, but students appreciate the incentive. At Illinois, while we do not dictate how the money should be used, we do encourage students to consider presenting their work at future student and/or professional disciplinary conferences.

4. A component of Image of Research is professionalizing the undergraduate experience by "publishing" student work. This can be done in many ways as has been demonstrated by KU and Illinois: archiving entries in the institutional repository, sharing images and text through social media such as Instagram or Twitter, publicizing through digital signage in the library and across campus, creating an online exhibit (e.g., Omeka), reaching out to campus and local news organizations, and posting winners to the competition, library, or campus website. Students are keen on sharing their work, and libraries, with their developing publishing activities, can make this happen.

5. Use the opportunity to explore avenues to increase advanced information literacy skills through instructional efforts in partnership with offices of undergraduate research and teaching faculty. For example, visualizing research and presenting data are not easy to learn. While the library may not be best positioned to teach data visualization by the discipline, we are able to begin the conversation by offering sessions on data visualization tools and data management.

Conclusion

Overall, the Image of Research competition provides libraries with an exciting opportunity to work with students around the intersections of scholarly communication and information literacy while celebrating original student work. The competition can also complement other types of research awards often supported by libraries and has the potential to generate new or deepen existing partnerships across campus with faculty, undergraduate research offices, and others who support undergraduate researchers. The competition challenges students to think about their research in a different way, to reflect on their journeys and discoveries, and to consider how their work can be communicated visually. It weaves student perspectives and research activities into the institutional history of the university and showcases student researchers as important and worthy contributors to scholarly conversations. It provides students with public accolades that can be valuable additions to job, scholarship, or graduate school applications. With all that Image of Research has to offer those who engage in the process, it's not surprising that such competitions have been sponsored by universities and organizations across the globe.[15]

Appendix 13A: KU Promotional Flyer

Image of Research

kulibraries
University of Kansas Libraries

1. Take an original photo inspired by your research & post to Instagram
2. Include a description connecting the image to your research
3. Tag it with the hashtag #KUImage16
4. Follow and tag us on Instagram @KULibraries
5. Win up to $100!*

Entry deadline: 5 p.m. Friday, February 5, 2016
Complete rules and details at lib.ku.edu/ior

Or use online submission form
Some restrictions may apply

KU LIBRARIES
The University of Kansas

Appendix 13B: Image of Research Rubric based on the ACRL *Framework*

Image of Research Rubric				
Criteria	**Connection with Frames**	**High Performance**	**Low Performance**	**Not Observed**
Respects the original ideas of others	Information Has Value; Scholarship as Conversation; Authority is Constructed and Contextual	Submission includes textual attribution to source(s) consulted during the research process.	Text acknowledges the work of others but does not include specific attribution to a source or author.	
Seeks guidance from experts (e.g., librarians, researchers, mentors)	Searching as Strategic Exploration; Research as Inquiry	Text or image reveals consultation with a librarian, researcher, or other professional.	Text or image indicates that help from an expert is needed but does not indicate that help was sought.	
Maintains an open mind	Research as Inquiry; Authority Is Constructed and Contextual	Describes how the research and/or researcher changed over time in response to new questions/knowledge.	Describes research as a validation of the entrant's initial impression or opinion of a subject.	
Sees self as contributor to information marketplace rather than only consumer	Information Has Value; Scholarship as Conversation	Submission shows evidence of engaging in the scholarly conversation (e.g., group discussion, conference/poster presentation)	Acknowledges possible realms of scholarly conversation or identifies barriers to joining the scholarly conversation.	

Image of Research Rubric

Criteria	Connection with Frames	High Performance	Low Performance	Not Observed
Recognizes that ambiguity and disagreement can benefit research	Scholarship as Conversation; Research as Inquiry	Clearly articulates a gap, inconsistency, or unresolved problem in the knowledge or scholarly output of a discipline.	Submission acknowledges the existence of competing perspectives.	
Responds appropriately to the information need articulated in submission guidelines	Information Creation as a Process; Information Has Value	Clearly articulates connection between image and research to a lay audience.	Relies on jargon and/or fails to articulate connection between image and research.	

Notes

1. Image of Research: Overview, accessed January 4, 2017, http://publish.illinois.edu/imageofresearch/.
2. Stephanie Davis-Kahl, Terri Fishel, and Merinda Kaye Hensley, "Weaving the Threads: Scholarly Communication and Information Literacy," *C&RL News* 75, no. 8 (September 2014): 441–44, accessed May 3, 2017, http://crln.acrl.org/index.php/crlnews/article/view/9179/10146.
3. University of Illinois at Urbana-Champaign Library, "Scholarly Commons," accessed January 12, 2017, http://www.library.illinois.edu/sc/.
4. University of Illinois at Urbana-Champaign Library, "Image of Research," accessed April 2, 2017, https://publish.illinois.edu/imageofresearch-undergrad/competition-details/.
5. The Illinois Department of Intercollegiate Athletics donates money to support students' activities across campus, and in 2008, the library received funds to support the newly designed digital scholarship center.
6. The decision to move from Omeka.org to Instagram at Illinois was made in concert with the Graduate College, which manages the graduate version of Image of Research, in order to better align both contests and to reduce duplication for the location of the online "publishing" of student work. The Omeka platform was sufficient for its purposes and we would recommend its use for other institutions.
7. Davis-Kahl, Fishel, and Hensley, "Weaving the Threads: Scholarly Communication and Information Literacy," 2014.

8. University of Kansas Libraries, Image of Research, accessed May 3, 2017, https://lib.ku.edu/ior.
9. Emily Bogle and Alyson Hurt, "Managing Instagram Photo Call-Outs," *NPR Visuals Team (blog)*, May 29, 2014, accessed May 3, 2017, http://blog.apps.npr.org/2014/05/29/photo-callouts.html.
10. KU ScholarWorks Image of Research Collection, accessed May 3, 2017, https://kuscholarworks.ku.edu/handle/1808/20209.
11. University of Kansas Libraries, "Goal 2: Advance Scholarship through Proactive Engagement in Research and Scholarly Communication," *KU Libraries Strategic Directions 2012-2017*, accessed May 3, 2017, https://lib.ku.edu/strategic-plan/goal-2.
12. Association of College and Research Libraries, *Framework for Information Literacy for Higher Education*, accessed May 3, 2017, http://www.ala.org/acrl/standards/ilframework.
13. Association of American Colleges & Universities, "High-Impact Educational Practices," accessed January 28, 2017, https://www.aacu.org/leap/hips.
14. Alex Robinson, "Award-Winning Undergraduate Students Present at Second Annual Image of Research Competition," *University Daily Kansan* (Lawrence, KS), March 23, 2016, accessed May 3, 2017, http://www.kansan.com/news/award-winning-undergraduate-students-present-at-second-annual-image-of/article_fe5108c0-f131-11e5-8a03-17bc2f904584.html.
15. The University of Saskatchewan, University of Alberta, University of Leicester, University of Strathclyde, and University of Manchester are among a growing number of organizations offering an Image of Research or similarly themed competition.

Bibliography

Association of American Colleges & Universities. "High-Impact Educational Practices." Accessed January 28, 2017. https://www.aacu.org/leap/hips.

Association of College and Research Libraries. *Framework for Information Literacy for Higher Education*. Accessed May 3, 2017. http://www.ala.org/acrl/standards/ilframework.

Bogle, Emily, and Alyson Hurt, "Managing Instagram Photo Call-Outs." *NPR Visuals Team (blog)* (May 29, 2014). Accessed May 3, 2017. http://blog.apps.npr.org/2014/05/29/photo-callouts.html.

Davis-Kahl, Stephanie, Terri Fishel, and Merinda Kaye Hensley. "Weaving the Threads: Scholarly Communication and Information Literacy." *C&RL News* 75, no. 8 (September 2014): 441–44. Accessed May 3, 2017. http://crln.acrl.org/index.php/crlnews/article/view/9179/10146.

Image of Research: Overview. Accessed January 4, 2017. http://publish.illinois.edu/imageofresearch/.

KU ScholarWorks Image of Research Collection. Accessed May 3, 2017. https://kuscholarworks.ku.edu/handle/1808/20209.

Robinson, Alex. "Award-Winning Undergraduate Students Present at Second Annual Image of Research Competition." *University Daily Kansan* (Lawrence, KS) (March 23, 2016). Accessed May 3, 2017. http://www.kansan.com/news/award-winning-undergraduate-students-present-at-second-annual-image-of/article_fe5108c0-f131-11e5-8a03-17bc2f904584.html.

University of Illinois at Urbana-Champaign Library. "Image of Research." Accessed April 2, 2017, https://publish.illinois.edu/imageofresearch-undergrad/competition-details/.
University of Illinois at Urbana-Champaign Library. "Scholarly Commons." Accessed January 12, 2017. http://www.library.illinois.edu/sc/.
University of Kansas Libraries. "Goal 2: Advance Scholarship through Proactive Engagement in Research and Scholarly Communication." *KU Libraries Strategic Directions 2012-2017.* Accessed May 3, 2017. https://lib.ku.edu/strategic-plan/goal-2.

CHAPTER 14*
Impact Outside the Classroom:
Preparing Undergraduate Researchers for Success

Lisa Becksford, Kyrille Goldbeck DeBose, and Carolyn Meier

Introduction

Virginia Tech is a comprehensive, land grant, Research 1 university that provides more than 240 undergraduate and graduate degree programs to more than 31,000 students. Virginia Tech's development of undergraduate research programs continues to grow to help support its research portfolio, which has surpassed $500 million in sponsored research.[1] At Virginia Tech, students are increasingly taking part in higher-level research projects as a part of their undergraduate careers. Conventional library-based instruction focuses on developing specific information literacy skills, but after observing trends in instruction requests, librarians at Virginia Tech realized students taking part in undergraduate research needed a broader foundation. Subject librarians were asked on an individual basis to offer instruction sessions that included not only how to use the library's resources, but also citation management, ethical uses of scholarship, and scholarly publishing.[2] While the collaborations between faculty and subject librarians were well established, a conver-

---

* This work is licensed under a Creative Commons Attribution-ShareAlike 4.0 License, CC BY-SA (https://creativecommons.org/licenses/by-sa/4.0/).

sation in spring 2011 revealed that several librarians were teaching the same types of workshops to small groups of students, especially during the summer months when the university sponsored many research grant programs and projects across a range of disciplines. To prevent burnout and allow for each librarian's strength to carry through for a specific topic, it made sense for librarians to pool resources to increase efficiency. The Advanced Research Skills Certificate program, developed in partnership with Virginia Tech's Office of Undergraduate Research, was created as a way to maximize librarians' time as well as the number of students reached.

Background

Initially, the content for the Advanced Research Skills Certificate program was based on the original workshops taught by instruction librarians: data management basics, citation managers, proposals and abstracts, posters, and publishing and open access. We initially assumed students would not need additional instruction in basic library search techniques; however, student feedback after the first year indicated that this content would be beneficial. The University's learning management system was used as a repository for course materials as well as a place where students could upload reflections for each session. In the program's second year, a total of seven sessions were offered: an introduction to undergraduate research (developed in consultation with the Director of Undergraduate Research), advanced searching techniques, data basics, citation management, data ethics, research posters, and writing proposals/abstracts. As in the previous year, these sessions were taught by librarians from across the institution, with one exception: the data session was taught by the libraries' full-time data consultant. In the program's most recent incarnation in spring 2016, the same topics were repeated, but the order of the final two sessions was reversed to more closely mirror the process students would go through in presenting their work (Appendix 14A). In addition, the total number of sessions was reduced to five with the reimagining of the first two sessions as online modules using Canvas, the University's new learning management system. The development of this content into Canvas modules featuring a combination of text, videos, quizzes, and discussion boards was a way to allow students to approach the content at their own pace. The modules' inclusion also diversified the instruction of the program and encouraged students to get into the learning management system early in the program and use it much as they would the site for their regular courses.

From the beginning, the workshops primarily focused on literacies that went beyond traditional information literacy skills such as locating and evaluating information. These traditional information literacy skills were still an important foundation for the workshop series; as student feedback indicated in the first year, students expressed a need to develop these skills. However, including workshops focusing on expanded twenty-first century literacy skills, such as data literacy, communication literacy, and visual literacy,[3] recognized the complex landscape of information and research in which undergraduates are increasingly engaging. Workshop sessions were designed to build upon one another to mimic the process students go through in conducting research, from developing an initial project to presenting a poster. This systematic approach encouraged students to think of themselves as producers of information, not merely consumers.

The format of each workshop was designed to engage students both during and after each session. Because students received no course credit for attendance and participated in addition to their regular schoolwork, each session was designed to implement what students had learned through a combination of direct instruction and active learning. For instance, in the session on data literacy, direct instruction explaining types of data, its role in research, data visualization, and data management was alternated with group exercises asking students to apply what they had just learned. Students analyzed examples of data used in research, critically evaluated data visualization, and practiced file naming conventions. The follow-up reflection asked students to write about their own use of data in their current projects, applying some of the terminology and concepts covered in the workshop. Subsequent sessions followed a similar model. Because a different librarian taught each session, this similarity in format gave sessions consistency, and the attention to active pedagogies ensured maximum student learning. In addition, the follow-up reflections encouraged students to consider how the session's content was applicable to their personal research goals. The reflections served a dual purpose and proved to be a valuable resource for evaluating the program's effectiveness.

Partnerships

The partnership between the library and the Office of Undergraduate Research was the key to the development of the Advanced Research Skills Certificate program. The formation of the Office of Undergraduate Research in 2011 created the opportunity for librarians to formalize the workshop into a series, rather than workshops given upon request. The partnership with the director of undergraduate research increased the librarians' presence with undergraduate research programs across campus in summer of 2012. With assistance from the director on marketing strategies and setting up meetings with campus stakeholders, stronger relationships were formed with the College of Liberal Arts and Human Sciences' Undergraduate Research Forum, the College of Engineering, VT's National Science Foundation-Research Experiences for Undergraduates (NSF-REU), and the Summer Undergraduate Research Fellowship (SURF) programs.

Although the program was well promoted through flyers sent to the academic deans of all colleges and emails to various listservs, attendance was sporadic. However, those who attended gave positive feedback about the skills they gained. The librarians felt the program was a valuable enterprise but were concerned about to how to give students a richer and deeper experience, particularly for those not on campus during the summer months. After a consultation with the undergraduate research director, the workshops morphed into a six-week mini-course as described above. Balancing point of need and librarian availability, this program was offered once a year early in the spring semester beginning in 2014. The ultimate goal was to provide a mechanism that would attract participation yet not require a full credit course for completion. Students would be able to list the certificate on their résumés to demonstrate their abilities as they applied for positions.

Reflection

The development of the Advanced Research Skills Certificate program has taught the organizers much about student needs, successful campus partnerships, and the importance of scalability. One of the lessons learned from this program is how eager students are for additional information skills that go well beyond searching databases and evaluating sources. Students who signed up for the program came from a wide range of disciplines, and while many were involved with formal undergraduate research projects, a remarkably large number were not. One surprising conclusion was how broadly applicable the program was. While this program was designed for students who were interested in participating in undergraduate research, a surprisingly large number of students in spring 2016 participated in the program as a way to prepare themselves for graduate school. Indeed, many of the topics are highly appropriate for students pursuing graduate study, and multiple graduate students were interested in participating in the program as well. Although we will continue to offer the program only to undergraduates, future iterations of this program will be planned to ensure that students preparing for graduate study find it beneficial as well. This broader scope may mean surveying students at the beginning of the program and adjusting content as needed depending on the students' goals.

Originally, one concern was whether students would be motivated to complete a program for which they received no course credit. While the certificate of completion is not as powerful a motivator as a transcript entry, it did provide enough incentive for students not only to participate, but also to delve deeply into the content. As one student noted in the evaluation at the conclusion of the program, "I've had very little experience with research in the past, and as a physics major I felt it imperative to become more acquainted with these skills that I will eventually need to utilize." The lesson here is that students do take ownership over their learning and are motivated to fill gaps in their knowledge. Finally, while the sessions have always been open to students of all disciplines, student feedback has indicated that students want to learn more about how to conduct research in their own disciplines, so librarians are currently considering ways to differentiate some of our content broadly by discipline.

Two significant challenges in offering the program are both attrition and scalability. While the program has been growing steadily and each year a large number of students enroll in the program (106 for the 2016 series), only one-third to half of those students actually complete all the requirements for the certificate of completion. While students are allowed to miss one in-person session (the requirement is to complete the corresponding exercises associated with the session), attrition should be examined further. On the one hand, students who attend only the sessions they find valuable are still gaining some benefit from participation. On the other hand, the workshops are meant to build upon one another and assist students in developing a diverse set of research skills. While students' self-motivation has been impressive, it is still a challenge to motivate students to complete the requirements to earn the completion certificate, particularly when they need to complete coursework in the same time frame.

Despite the challenge of attrition, scalability is a challenge as well. For instance, in the 2016 offering, 241 students expressed interest in the program, and ultimately 106 students signed up to participate. This was far more than any of the library's classrooms could accommodate. While a space not primarily designed for instruction was used to host the program, incorporating an active learning environment became another challenge. To address this, the program's organizers are considering setting a limit on the number of students who are able to sign up, and they've considered opening the registration first to juniors and seniors, and to freshmen and sophomores at a later date. Keeping the series smaller would ensure that the active learning format of the in-person sessions will continue and aid in maintaining a manageable workload for the librarians who teach the sessions.

Assessment

The program has been evaluated both formally and informally. A short survey was distributed each year to determine what was most and least useful from the students' perspective. This analysis identified duplication as well as gaps in content, both of which were addressed in future renditions to support the workshop series' scaffolded approach. For example, while year two featured recordings of each workshop that students could view asynchronously, students indicated a preference for only in-person sessions, citing technology problems and the decrease in student engagement when the sessions were viewed online. In year three, the series was offered only in face-to-face sessions, with two fully online modules. The surveys also offered the chance to learn more about students' motivation for participating. Year three feedback, for instance, indicated that a smaller number of students than expected were participating in preparation for undergraduate research projects. In addition to formal assessments, the reflections or other follow-up activities that students complete after each session act as informal assessments and provide a rich source of student feedback throughout the session. These reflections can be read with an eye for whether the week's content was relevant and how students see it fitting into their own experience. For example, a common theme in students' weekly reflections was the fact that what they were learning was applicable not only to their large-scale research projects but also to other coursework. This theme was especially prominent in students' reflections following the session on citation managers.

Recommendations/Best Practices

The partnerships created and strengthened through the development of the Advanced Research Skills Certificate program were built on the strength of existing relationships between the library and campus departments. Those wanting to engage in similar partnerships should consider existing relationships, where possible, and use those as the foundation for new ventures. Within those relationships, it is important to be clear with partners about what is possible for library staff to do in order to avoid librarian burnout. These clear expectations could include issues, such as the size of the program, how sessions are scheduled, and how frequently the program is offered. Establishing clear expectations at the outset can ensure positivity within the partnerships and encourage future development. Partnerships can also help raise the library's campus profile by encouraging both faculty and students to view the library as a key partner in student learning, rather than only a repository for materials.

One unexpected benefit is that this workshop model has encouraged further collaboration between library units, particularly between the data services unit and units focused on library instruction. In addition, the program has encouraged other campus units to view the library as partners in the undergraduate research experience. For instance, the newly formed Honors College approached the library in summer 2016 about offering an honors version of the Advanced Research Skills Certificate program in spring 2017. This partnership has now expanded to include other library units, and the honors version will be offered as a full-semester course coordinated by a member of the library's Data Services unit, with librarians contributing as guest instructors.

Conclusion

One of the most important things learned was the necessity of keeping a sense of flexibility and responsiveness in mind when working with this curriculum. Having the ability to offer content not previously offered, if there is a demonstrated need, has made the course more appropriate for a larger variety of students. Additionally, thinking about different types of information literacy content helps to form connections not only with a wide variety of groups across campus but also within the library. We look forward to continuing to strengthen these partnerships and campus relationships through future iterations of the program. The success of the Advanced Research Skills Certificate program shows that thinking outside traditional information literacy and approaching goals from another angle can lead to the development of exciting new programs that provide students a chance to learn essential research skills that they may not learn anywhere else on campus. Such programs offer the opportunity for the academic library to transform undergraduate education and help students achieve their academic goals.

Appendix 14A: Spring 2016 Workshop Schedule

Advanced Research Skills Certificate Program

Online Modules:

Becoming a Researcher

Join the conversation about what it takes to be an undergraduate researcher. We will discuss research opportunities through the Office of Undergraduate Research and research support from university libraries.

Finding Scholarly Literature

Learn a variety of advanced database techniques and strategies to make your research easier. During this module, we will discuss selecting the best databases for your topic, searching for relevant literature, and managing the results of your searches.

In-person sessions:

Understanding data

This workshop will cover basic data management principle and practices and will offer strategies for and things to think about when working with research data of all shapes, sizes, and formats. Data management is an extremely important part of the research process; developing good habits early will set you up for success later in your career.

Managing and organizing information

Need a way to keep all the articles and sites for your research organized? Hate doing footnotes, endnotes, and bibliographies? Come learn about EndNote, Zotero, Mendeley, and other tools for managing and organizing your citations, research articles, and other research information.

Using data and information ethically

Discover methods of ethical data use including in-text quotations, citations, and IRB information. This workshop will help you answer questions like: When do I need to get IRB approval? What is IACUC? Is there a difference between working with animals and humans?

Writing successful conference proposals and research abstracts

In the changing landscape of scholarly publishing, most publishers and conference organizers require proposals and abstracts before publishing your research. Join us as we discuss this landscape and review different approaches for creating proposals and abstracts that will get your research noticed!

Creating effective research posters

This session will walk you through the process of designing, developing, and printing effective research posters. We will cover basic design principles in addition to strategies for successfully communicating your research.

Advanced Research Skills Certificate

Students who complete both online modules, attend all of the workshops, and complete the activity for each workshop will receive the Advanced Research Skills Certificate from university libraries. This certificate will be awarded at a ceremony and reception in March.

Notes

1. Virginia Tech, "About Virginia Tech," accessed August 19, 2016, http://www.vt.edu/about.html.
2. Rebecca K. Miller, Kyrille Goldbeck DeBose, and Carolyn Meier, "Underage Thinking: Building Tomorrow's Researchers through New Campus Collaborations," paper presented at the LOEX Annual Conference, Denver, Colorado, April 30–May 2, 2015.
3. Ron Germaine et al., "Purposeful Use of 21st Century Skills in Higher Education," *Journal of Research in Innovative Teaching* 9, no. 1 (2016): 19.

Bibliography

Germaine, Ron, et al. "Purposeful Use of 21st Century Skills in Higher Education." *Journal of Research in Innovative Teaching* 9, no. 1 (2016): 19–29.

Miller, Rebecca K., Kyrille Goldbeck DeBose, and Carolyn Meier. "Underage Thinking: Building Tomorrow's Researchers through New Campus Collaborations." Paper presented at the LOEX Annual Conference, Denver, Colorado, April 30–May 2, 2015.

Virginia Tech. "About Virginia Tech." Accessed August 19, 2016. http://www.vt.edu/about.html.

CHAPTER 15*

Informal Learning Teams and the Digital Humanities:
A Case Study of Faculty/Librarian Collaboration

Lora L. Smallman and Jessica DeSpain

Introduction

Since the 2009 founding of the Interdisciplinary Research and Informatics Scholarship Center (or IRIS), a digital humanities and social sciences center at Southern Illinois University Edwardsville, faculty, librarians, and undergraduates have been collaborating to reinvigorate humanities curriculum both within and beyond the classroom.[1] The IRIS Center has become a site where faculty and librarians work together to find solutions to budget shortfalls and changing definitions of higher education. This chapter will discuss the theory, practice, and outcomes underlying one approach to undergraduate research at Southern Illinois University Edwardsville (SIUE). This case study will include a discussion of the intersection of an undergraduate research program, a digital scholarship center, and the university library. SIUE undergraduate students function as collaborators on faculty projects and lead their own research endeavors with faculty and librarians serving as mentors.

---

* This work is licensed under a Creative Commons Attribution-NonCommercial 4.0 License, CC BY-NC (https://creativecommons.org/licenses/by-nc/4.0/).

Background

Southern Illinois University Edwardsville is a regional public university with sixty-five baccalaureate degrees located in Edwardsville, Illinois, just twenty miles northeast of St. Louis, Missouri. SIUE is the newer of two separate institutions in the Southern Illinois University System and has experienced considerable growth in recent years. According to the *2016 SIUE Fact Book*, the fall 2015 semester enrollment was the largest on record for the university, with a total student headcount of 14,265.[2] Of the students enrolled this term, 30 percent were new to the university, either as first-time freshman or as transfer students. SIUE's student population is commensurate with what one might expect at a regional university. According to Vice Chancellor for Student Affairs Jeffrey Waple, in 2015 "more than 60 percent of SIUE students are first generation students."[3]

The University consistently does well in *U.S. News and World Report* rankings among its peer institutions, with the exception of sometimes low retention rates.[4] Although the University encourages students to participate in academic life on campus, most students return home on the weekend, and are attempting to juggle the commitments of work, school, and home. There have been a multitude of studies in higher education literature on student retention rates over the last twenty years that address student financial insecurities and remedial programs, but the recent trend is to examine the environment and structure of campus life, particularly with regard to the relationship between student affairs and academics. In one comprehensive study of student retention at Hamilton College in Clinton, NY, Daniel F. Chambliss and Christopher G. Takacs discovered that close relationships with faculty beyond the classroom were among the most important factors in ensuring student success and retention.[5] Informal learning opportunities and strong mentoring relationships with faculty may be even more important at a large regional institution like SIUE, where students can become easily lost in the shuffle.

Library and Information Services (LIS) has forty employees as well as numerous student assistants and graduate student assistants. Librarians at SIUE are faculty rank and eligible for tenure. The library is home to approximately 800,000 volumes, collected to support the curricula and research interests of students and faculty. Lovejoy Library has special collections, including but not limited to the Rare Book Room, Eugene B. Redmond Learning Center, National Jazz and Ragtime Archive, and the University Archives. Many items in these collections have been reproduced as digital collections and exhibits in various online spaces, including CONTENTdm. Despite the wealth of resources that LIS provides for faculty and students, it has faced significant challenges in the last ten years. In 2008, SIUE's Lovejoy Library and Information Technology Services (ITS) were separated into two units by the Provost. This separation caused the library to relinquish various staff, funding, and electronic resources to ITS and put LIS in the same position as other university departments when asking for technological resources. The library has also been in a precarious political situation because of competing understandings of the role of the academic library in the twenty-first century at an institution of this size and type. As a result, even though there were several librarians among the founding steering committee, IRIS is not currently housed in the library and is not funded by the library budget.

When faculty from the humanities, social sciences, hard sciences, and the library met weekly to plan the IRIS Center in 2009, it became clear that they needed to rethink the R1 model of the digital scholarship center to fit the needs and strengths of the institution and to envision new approaches to faculty/librarian collaboration. The IRIS Center is located in Peck Hall at the Edwardsville Campus, and the space is equipped with a variety of computers, scanners, digital tools, and software. Despite not being housed in Lovejoy Library, the IRIS Center has found ways to collaborate with librarians and learn from their expertise in cataloging, digital preservation, and research. Through this work, both librarians and teaching faculty have learned to frame the IRIS Center as a student-centered humanities and social sciences laboratory.

In order to establish this model, the steering committee developed a relationship with undergraduate education that matched the University mission. Now IRIS has a primary goal of providing the space and opportunity for faculty and students to work closely together beyond the traditional classroom as they build technology that addresses issues and methodologies central to their disciplines.

The IRIS Center reorients how students think about their majors via experiential learning opportunities. At the 2011 Modern Language Association Convention, and later on his blog, Stephen Ramsay controversially defined the digital humanities as being about "building things." Ramsay's statement was divisive because other scholars assumed he was excluding theoretical approaches that study rather than manipulate or visualize. However, the most productive aspects of the digital humanities arise when building leads to theorization, and it is this process, unique to the scholarly production of the digital humanist, that is necessary for the undergraduate classroom. According to Tara McPherson, "hands-on engagement with digital forms re-orients scholarly imagination …because scholars come to realize that they understand their argument and their objects of study differently, even better, if they approach them through multiple modalities and emergent and interconnected forms of literacy."[6] These scholarly realizations that arise from "doing" and "building" are just as valuable for student researchers.

Yet, technological literacy can be a struggle for students. Though conventional wisdom has labeled the current student population as "digital natives," research suggests that access to technology is still largely based on socio-economic status and race. According to educational researcher Joanna Goode, students who develop a technological identity early can impact their ability to manipulate digital environments when they enter college.[7] 2009 data from the U.S. Census revealed that the lower the household income and educational level in a family, the less likely people are to have access to or use the Internet.[8] Even when students have Internet access, limited exposure and training has provided them with only basic technological skills. Katherine Mangan wrote in the *Chronicle of Higher Education* that first-generation college students encounter a host of challenges, including being "more likely to arrive academically unprepared for the rigors of college and to require remediation before they can start earning college credit."[9] As mentioned earlier, 60 percent of SIUE students are first-generation students and are no exception to these characteristics and lack of experience with technology.

Bringing faculty and students together with a curriculum and research opportunities that focus on faculty/student partnerships in which students are intimately engaged in the active building of technology is the best method for solving these problems. Students in the IRIS Center learn not just how to use technology, but how to effect technological change as they work with professors on publishable research. The IRIS Center had established a design for undergraduate research that gives students room to make mistakes, tinker, and test their knowledge. This takes time, planning, and constant mentorship, but the result is a faculty and student body who benefit from the University's teacher/scholar model.

These agreed upon pedagogical ideals have resulted in several distinct collaborative applications. Undergraduates take on the roles of project management, database design, file management, and research that traditionally belongs to graduate students. In order to offer students additional incentives for working on IRIS projects, many of the Center's affiliated faculty apply for opportunities offered through the University's Undergraduate Research and Creative Activities Program or URCA, which awards students stipends to work on faculty research. In 1990, the Undergraduate Research Academy was established to create research opportunities for SIUE students, and this program evolved into URCA in 2009. The URCA program has since organized and financially supported more than 1,600 students and involved nearly 400 faculty from forty disciplines.[10] There are two levels of this program: assistant and associate. Students are eligible to apply for the URCA associate program to lead their own projects during their senior year. Students of any grade level are welcome to apply for URCA assistant opportunities on faculty-led projects.

This helps faculty and librarians in the IRIS Center to build relationships with students as early as their freshman year. Successful faculty/student collaborations include several examples of digital community outreach, with examples including
- an NSF-funded digital atlas of endangered languages in Nepal;
- an NSF-funded project in which middle school students in East St. Louis build content-rich digital maps about the history and culture of their city;
- an internally-funded project to digitize the photographic record of the Lessie Bates Immigrant Center in East St. Louis;
- an internally-funded project to digitize early issues of the *ALESTLE*, the SIUE student newspaper;
- an internally-funded project to analyze a dataset of bibliographic information from the scholarly journal *African American Review*; and
- an internally-funded event called SIUE THATCamp 2016.

Beyond these projects, in which students play an active role alongside faculty in the design and implementation of research, this year the IRIS Center also began recruiting students for the newly minted digital humanities and social sciences minor, in which students take courses in the computer sciences as well as technology-focused courses in the humanities and social sciences prior to a culminating internship. Finally, IRIS has developed new freshman seminars, interdisciplinary studies courses, and senior assignments that contain DH/DSS content to attract new students and interject informal learning opportunities more directly into University curriculum.

Partnerships

One faculty-led project, *The Wide, Wide World Digital Edition*, led by Dr. Jessica DeSpain, associate professor of English, is a model for building partnerships between the URCA program, the IRIS Center, and the library.[11] DeSpain's teaching and research interests include transatlantic literary exchange through the form of reprinted books during the nineteenth century, textual studies, and the digital humanities. *The Wide, Wide World Digital Edition* maps transatlantic publication networks via the development of a digital edition of Susan Warner's 1851 female Bildungsroman, *The Wide, Wide World*. This project brings together, for the first time, the textual and visual variants from 141 reprints of this unstable text to demonstrate how its cultural function and significance shifted with each locale and material reproduction. DeSpain collaborates with URCA assistants who support this scholarship by digitizing materials, creating digital content, and engaging in planning and implementation. The project runs on Omeka, an open source web-publishing platform, and uses Dublin Core metadata standards to describe and organize the more than 50,000 digital objects associated with the site. Relying on the collaboration of faculty at multiple institutions, sometimes as many as thirteen student editors, University librarians, and SIUE's ITS department, the project brings together a multitude of entities.

DeSpain consults with the humanities librarian for assistance in training the URCA assistants in using the library's resources and developing their information literacy skills. The humanities librarian also contributes in planning discussions with DeSpain and the URCA assistants. The humanities librarian is the subject liaison to the Departments of Anthropology, English Language & Literature, Foreign Language & Literature, and Philosophy. Her responsibilities to these departments include outreach, reference support, library instruction, and collection development.

DeSpain's knowledge, use, and advocacy of libraries made her a natural choice to serve on the hiring committee for the humanities librarian, who began working for SIUE in August 2013. In the early weeks of the fall 2013 semester, DeSpain reached out to the humanities librarian in order to establish a working relationship and to invite her to the training session for undergraduates involved in *The Wide, Wide World Digital Edition*. This session, known as "boot camp," is a four-hour intensive training held at the beginning of every fall and spring semester to reconnect after breaks.

One of the greatest challenges to this partnership was the humanities librarian's lack of knowledge and experience in the digital humanities. This slowed collaborative initiatives as she learned more about digital humanities and gained experience with DeSpain's project and students. Another initial difficulty was defining the humanities librarian's role within the IRIS Center and the URCA program. Throughout the course of the first year, the humanities librarian attended boot camps, participated in IRIS meetings and events, and sought out professional development opportunities. One such opportunity was in November 2013, when the humanities librarian attended the Humanities and Technology Camp, a regional digital humanities unconference, also known as THATCamp St. Louis at Washington University.[12]

The success of this partnership can be attributed to the high value placed on libraries, digital humanities, and undergraduate research. DeSpain and the humanities librarian have a great deal of respect for each other as colleagues, and they also share a genuine enthusiasm and curiosity for the work they do. This temperament, coupled with their professional values and goals, results in a positive environment for undergraduates to gain professional experience and produce dynamic digital projects. This collaboration between faculty, librarians, and students resulted in the creation of a LibGuide, Nineteenth-Century Book History, which helps guide the research needed for the project.[13] Since arriving in 2013, the humanities librarian has mentored five URCA assistants involved with IRIS projects who were interested in library science careers. Overall, these types of relationships foster a sense of belonging for undergraduate students, and create experiences which positively influence their academic success.

Reflection

Digital humanities scholarship parallels that of the library science discipline: both are inherently interdisciplinary, thrive on collaboration, and require an aptitude for adopting new digital technology and tools. Academic librarians are in a unique position to understand, provide access to, and nurture the evolution of digital humanities scholarship. An unexpected role for the Humanities Librarian in this collaborative initiative was that of providing career guidance for undergraduates.

Library and information science attracts a variety of backgrounds, but English majors pursuing a graduate degree in library and information science is fairly common. Librarians in any setting have to consider their users and collaborate with each to other to classify, preserve, and manage a collection. The IRIS Center, and particularly DeSpain's project, offered invaluable opportunities to experience the work of librarians. The collaborative nature of the IRIS Center has been an important testing ground for students who want to learn what a career in modern librarianship would be like.

Students who work on the project are directly involved in the design and implementation of the site. They also interact with the faculty who collaborate on the project at SIUE, Harvard, and other institutions. In an average semester, students research publishing history, write bibliographical analyses of rare books, create their own digital exhibits for the website, consult on and implement the project's controlled vocabulary, edit portions of the novel from start to finish, and contribute to grant applications. As students become senior project members, they take on greater responsibility that involves developing original scholarly content and training other students.

In the last four years, five students involved in the IRIS Center have been admitted to library and information science programs. The humanities librarian joined *The Wide, Wide World Digital Edition* after it was already well established, but it would be wise to embed librarians in all faculty/student projects of this type from their inception going forward.

Assessment

Part of the success of *The Wide, Wide World Digital Edition* is due to those students who continue to work on the project in subsequent semesters, when they are no longer receiving financial incentives. These students are incredibly valuable and assist DeSpain in training students new to the team on the background of the project, the digital methods used, how to use software and equipment, how to handle fragile materials, rules and regulations of the IRIS Center, and project goals for the semester.

The most important outcomes to assess for *The Wide, Wide World* and projects like it in IRIS include the level of student engagement in research beyond the classroom and student success both during and beyond their college careers. Five *Wide, Wide World* students have gone on to LIS programs and another ten have gone on to graduate school in other fields. Students feel connected to their work on the project and continue to volunteer beyond the semesters they are awarded URCA funding and even after they graduate from the University.

One former student, who went on to complete an MLS program explained, "This project has taught me to take leaps and to learn with others and on my own. Coding, for example, was a process I previously avoided, but I used my newly acquired confidence to code the e-book of *The Wide, Wide World* after I graduated from SIUE, and I used these skills nearly every day in library school. In fact, I was able to apply some aspect of my work with this digital archive in every class. I knew about the hurdles involved in mass digitization, Dublin Core metadata, and how to navigate digital archive platforms before many of my classmates." Even as the research into student retention has borne out, for this student, "the most valuable thing was the community of students and faculty with which I had the opportunity to work. Having one-on-one time with a faculty member was one of the most rewarding aspects of my time on *The Wide, Wide World*. I had the opportunity to work side-by-side with Dr. DeSpain for two years; we solved major problems together and shared in frustrations and triumphs. I've felt an immense sense of responsibility to this project. It was the first time that the work I was doing and the decisions I was making would affect not only the project that Dr. DeSpain had envisioned, but also how the project would look five years in the future to researchers. This project shaped who I was as a student, and it gave me the courage I needed to add my voice in collaborations. I will continue to apply these skills as I move into my first professional position and beyond."

In addition to these substantial student outcomes, the model in which faculty and librarians work together with a team of students has had lasting reverberations for both institutions trying to navigate the limitations of a state institution with few resources. The IRIS Center has drawn significantly on the skills and expertise of Lovejoy Library's librarians. In return, the IRIS Center has trained students in the skills critical to projects taking place in the library at a time when the library cannot afford to hire experts trained in those fields.

Recommendations/Best Practices

Academic librarians who collaborate with teaching faculty and undergraduates on research projects stand to gain meaningful relationships, insight into the research needs of undergraduates and faculty, and opportunities to innovate library resources and services. In this case study, the humanities librarian stepped into a new role that involved guiding undergraduates through library resources as well as potential library science career paths. While the stakes for these informal learning environments are much different and possibly higher than they are in a classroom setting, the rewards are often richer. Collaboration, student ownership, an awareness of audience, and a dynamic that rewards student contribution are essential to a successful project design. As previously mentioned, one example of this student ownership was creating, updating, and using a LibGuide. Undergraduates worked with the humanities librarian to create a tool to make researching book history more efficient.

One of the most innovative aspects of *The Wide, Wide World Digital Edition* is that it demands collaboration among students and faculty. Developing a strategy for recruiting team members that will both complement one another and work well together is paramount for the collaborative spirit of the group to succeed. Faculty should recruit students in their classes that demonstrate an interest in the material, and it is also helpful for student editors to approach classmates that they respect. If the students like who they are working with, they'll be more likely to participate meaningfully in the project.

Likewise, in order to make sure that the group dynamic works successfully, it is important to help students establish ownership over the project while simultaneously encouraging them to relinquish a degree of control as their independent investments merge with the project's objectives. Students should be involved in both the methodological and theoretical underpinnings of the project. Weekly meetings establish consistency and a place to share recent work. At these meetings, students should train one another on aspects of the project and even develop the mechanisms for training. Graduates should also return to share the effects of their earlier work on their careers. For example, a recent NEH Humanities in the Public Square application envisions teams of two students (one from the Honors program and one from the University's program for first-generation college students) working collaboratively with professors to design community outreach curricula. The IRIS Center has found that undergraduates thrive when given the opportunity to teach other students and to take on leadership roles in project decision making.

For many students, an informal research group will be the first time their work will be shared and critiqued by an audience beyond their professors; it presents them with an opportunity to become part of a scholarly community.

The team should have frequent discussions about who the audience is for the project, and students should be expected to share their research with other students, with the broader University community, and in conference forums, so they can see directly see the impact of their work.

It is also important to reward students for their contribution using whatever means possible. They should be given attribution on all projects and paid when the project allows for it. Students have indicated that the one-on-one mentorship and sense of community that occur as a result of the project has become one of its most rewarding aspects, which bears out the results of recent research indicating that relationships with faculty mentors beyond the classroom are among the most important factors in students' retention and success on campus.

Conclusion

Since its creation, the IRIS Center has been a collaborative space that offers students unique opportunities to develop their technological, leadership, research, and critical thinking skills. Collaborating with the library builds bridges between the departments and results in an enhanced experience for undergraduates involved in faculty-led projects. The humanities librarian and DeSpain work together to train students on library research skills and digital humanities methodologies to better engage with digital projects like the *Wide, Wide, World Digital Edition*. This partnership has inspired a new wave of courses and pedagogical approaches at SIUE that employ undergraduate research in innovative ways, and these are quickly leading to a cohort of undergraduate students that are comfortable taking risks, applying new skills, and collaborating with their peers and professors. These students are proof of the value of the work, the community, and the collaboration in spaces like the IRIS Center, and the students themselves offer a compelling reason to develop and support both the digital humanities and digital scholarship centers.

Notes

1. Interdisciplinary Research and Informatics Scholarship Center, accessed September 23, 2016, https://siueiris.com/.
2. *FactBook: Institutional Research and Studies*, Southern Illinois University Edwardsville, Edwardsville, IL: Office of Institutional Research and Studies, SIUE (2016), accessed October 21, 2016, http://www.siue.edu/inrs/factbook/.
3. Logan Cameron, "New Vice Chancellor for Student Affairs Named," *The Edwardsville Intelligencer* (October 23, 2015), sec. Segue.
4. In 2016–2017, the University tied for #13 in the ranking of best public schools in the Midwest; see the full profile, at "Southern Illinois University Edwardsville," *U.S.*

New and World Report (2016), accessed September 23, 2016, http://colleges.usnews.rankingsandreviews.com/best-colleges/southern-illinois-edwardsville-1759.
5. Daniel F. Chambliss and Christopher G. Takacs, *How College Works* (Cambridge: Harvard University Press, 2014), 4; Biren A. Nagda et al., "Undergraduate Student-Faculty Research Partnerships Affect Student Retention," *Inside Higher Education* 22, no. 1 (1998): 55–72; Vincent Tinto, "Colleges as Communities: Taking Research on Student Persistence Seriously," *The Review of Higher Education* 21, no. 2 (1997): 167–77; Glenda Crosling et al., *Improving Student Retention in Higher Education: The Role of Teaching and Learning* (New York: Routledge, 2008).
6. Tara McPherson, "Introduction: Media Studies and the Digital Humanities," *Cinema Journal* 48, no. 2 (2009): 119–23.
7. Joanna Goode, "The Digital Identity Divide: How Technology Knowledge Impacts College Students," *New Media & Society* 12, no. 3 (2010): 497–513.
8. "Computer and Internet Use in the United States: Population Characteristics," May 2013. https://www.census.gov/prod/2013pubs/p20-569.pdf.
9. Katherine Mangan, "The Challenge of the First-Generation Student," *Chronicle of Higher Education* 61, no. 36 (2015): 1–9.
10. Laura Pawlow and William Retzlaff, "Undergraduate Researchers Become Change Agents for Sustainability," *Council on Undergraduate Research Quarterly* 33, no. 1 (Fall 2012): 28–32.
11. Jessica DeSpain, Jennifer Brady, Melissa White, and Jill Anderson, *Wide, Wide World Digital Edition*, accessed September 23, 2016, https://widewideworlddigitaledition.siue.edu/.
12. "THATCamp St. Louis 2013," *Washington University Libraries*, accessed September 23, 2016, http://stl2013.thatcamp.org/.
13. Lora Smallman and Jessica DeSpain, "Nineteenth-Century Book History," *Southern Illinois University Library and Information Services*, accessed September 23, 2016, http://libguides.siue.edu/bookhistory19.

Bibliography

Cameron, Logan. "New Vice Chancellor for Student Affairs Named." *The Edwardsville Intelligencer* (October 23, 2015): sec. Segue.
Chambliss, Daniel F., and Christopher G. Takacs. *How College Works*. Cambridge: Harvard University Press, 2014.
Computer and Internet Use in the United States: Population Characteristics. U. S. Census Bureau, 2013.
Crosling, Glenda, et al. *Improving Student Retention in Higher Education: The Role of Teaching and Learning*. New York: Routledge, 2008.
DeSpain, Jessica, Jennifer Brady, Melissa White, and Jill Anderson. "Wide, Wide World Digital Edition." Accessed September 23, 2016. https://widewideworlddigitaledition.siue.edu/.
Goode, Joanna. "The Digital Identity Divide: How Technology Knowledge Impacts College Students." *New Media & Society* 12, no. 3 (2010): 497–513.
Interdisciplinary Research and Informatics Scholarship Center. Accessed September 23, 2016. https://siueiris.com/.

Mangan, Katherine. "The Challenge of the First-Generation Student." *Chronicle of Higher Education* 61, no. 36 (May 22, 2015): 1–9.

McPherson, Tara. "Introduction: Media Studies and the Digital Humanities." *Cinema Journal* 48, no. 2 (2009): 119–23.

Nagda, Biren A., et al. "Undergraduate Student-Faculty Research Partnerships Affect Student Retention." *Inside Higher Education* 22, no. 1 (1998): 55–72.

Pawlow, Laura, and William Retzlaff. "Undergraduate Researchers Become Change Agents for Sustainability." *Council on Undergraduate Research Quarterly* 33, no. 1 (Fall 2012): 28–32.

Smallman, Lora, and Jessica DeSpain. "Nineteenth-Century Book History." *Southern Illinois University Library and Information Services.* Accessed September 23, 2016. http://libguides.siue.edu/bookhistory19.

"Southern Illinois University Edwardsville, Best Colleges Rankings and Lists." *U. S. News & World Report* (2016-2017). *Southern Illinois University Edwardsville FactBook: Institutional Research and Studies.* Edwardsville, IL: Office of Institutional Research and Studies, SIUE, 2016. Accessed October 21, 2016. http://www.siue.edu/inrs/factbook/.

"THATCamp St. Louis 2013." *Washington University Libraries.* Accessed September 23, 2016. http://stl2013.thatcamp.org/.

Tinto, Vincent. "Colleges as Communities: Taking Research on Student Persistence Seriously." *The Review of Higher Education* 21, no. 2 (1997): 167–77.

CHAPTER 16*

Landscape Architecture, Embedded Librarianship, and Innovation with Special Collections:
Historic Landscapes Research with Primary Sources by University of Arkansas Undergraduates

Joshua C. Youngblood

Introduction

The areas and directions—or landscapes—available for undergraduate students to explore in their research are unlimited. Special collections and archives can facilitate student use of primary sources available in the university library collections to research topics that extend far beyond institutional walls. Students in the University of Arkansas's historical landscape classes

---

* This work is licensed under a Creative Commons Attribution-NonCommercial-ShareAlike 4.0 License, CC BY-NC-SA (https://creativecommons.org/licenses/by-nc-sa/4.0/).

have shown that the resources they've learned to navigate can help illustrate the complex stories from the state's past that reside where physical and archival landscapes converge.[1]

Over the course of four years, the research services librarian for the University of Arkansas Libraries Special Collections has collaborated with a member of the teaching faculty in the Department of Landscape Architecture to assist students in semester-long research projects as part of their credit-earning coursework. Among the projects the students work on as part of the historical landscape courses are professional products, such as Historic Architectural Landscape Surveys (HALS), some of which have been submitted by the professor and students to the United States Department of Interior and the Library of Congress.[2] Students' collaborative research projects have focused on features of Arkansas's historical landscape, such as Japanese American Internment Camps, New Deal-era Resettlement Administration facilities, and abandoned mining towns. Consequently, the Special Collections of the University of Arkansas Libraries has had the opportunity to share a variety of relevant and often unique resources for the research projects, ranging from scholarly research records, activist organizational archives, and government records to tourist ephemera, historic maps, and photographs.[3]

Detailed project planning between the landscape architecture faculty and the research services librarian, one-on-one consultations with the students, special accommodations for access, and assistance with duplication and digitization all demonstrate the ability of academic librarians to facilitate original undergraduate research, as well as innovative and challenging instruction models for campus teaching faculty. This case study will show how a teaching collaboration emerged, built on using primary resources and unique holdings.[4] The case study will further illustrate how embedded librarianship enabled the services offered by university libraries' special collections to develop from initial outreach and discussion of class research project possibilities to formal instruction sessions, class visits, and, eventually, planning for subsequent semesters. Those services allowed undergraduate students unfamiliar with research in special collections to develop confidence with using primary sources as they followed their professor's lead and independently pursued new research avenues and contributed substantial work to professionally relevant projects.

Background

In their introduction to *Embedded Librarians,* Kvenlid and Calkins succinctly describe the practice as working "closely over extended periods of time with non-librarian groups, whether by joining a semester-long course, maintaining an ongoing presence in online courses, or joining the staffs of academic departments, clinical settings, or performing groups."[5] How the concept is applied varies widely, and special collections librarians and research services archivists often face different challenges than other academic librarians in making primary sources accessible, and particularly in regard to aiding the use of rare and unique, non-circulating materials.[6] Certain core concepts of embedded librarianship are integral to this case study, including a willingness to take risks, approaching research assistance as partnerships where the librarian helps to translate library science to other disciplines, and embracing opportunities to take learning and expertise outside of the normal contexts of library instruction and reference assistance.[7]

The collaboration began after a landscape architecture faculty member contacted Special Collections in 2012 for access to materials related to the cemetery at the Rohwer Japanese American Internment Site in Arkansas. They had become aware of holdings in Special Collections related to internment camps through conventional means: an article written by the special collections librarian published in the department's semi-annual newsletter.[8] The department also holds archives from War Relation Authority administrators and teachers at both of the camps located in Arkansas, as well as rare volumes published by the camps and the actual internees, obscure professional collections assembled by government officials and consultants, and personal accounts, including diaries and memoirs created by students and Arkansas residents associated with the camps.[9] An initial meeting to discuss the class assignment, access policies, and possible instruction sessions resulted in multiple class visits to the department, numerous student consultations regarding issues such as copyright and publishing permissions, and subsequent collaboration on digitization and research outside of the department's holdings.

Partnerships

Since 2012, the partnership has evolved to include four different projects. The first project entailed a semester-long, detailed class project to create a Historic Architectural Landscape Surveys (HALS) study for the cemetery still present among the scant remains of the Rohwer Japanese-American Internment Camp located in Desha County, Arkansas, during World War II. The course resulted from an innovative teaching approach the landscape architecture professor had implemented that combined student fieldwork and landscape surveys with deep historical research. Relevant primary sources would often only be available in Arkansas archival and rare books repositories, including their university libraries' special collections.[10] That initial project led to the incorporation of Special Collections into a large-scale, grant-funded digital project coordinated by the Center for Advanced Spatial Technologies (CAST), another program at the University of Arkansas.

Inspired in part by the successful HALS project created by the Landscape Architecture faculty member and his students, CAST reached out to Special Collections to take part in "Rohwer Reconstructed." That ambitious digital humanities initiative was funded by a large grant from the Japanese American Confinement Site (JACS) program administered by the National Park Service.[11] This resulted in a second collaboration with the landscape architecture students. The JACS project incorporated landscape studies and historical research produced by students with archival objects to create three-dimensional representations of portions of the Rohwer site, along with a database of archival documents. Through the JACS grant funding, a second group of enrolled undergraduate landscape architecture students, as well as a graduate assistant, completed more detailed site research at the Rohwer internment site. Under the guidance of the faculty instructor and the Special Collections librarian, undergraduate students combed through internment camp publications, correspondence, government publications, photographs, and personal and professional archives. Students recommended items for digitization, used the information they uncovered to pursue sources in other institutions, and incorporated the data gleaned from the primary research to create detailed site maps for the three-dimensional rendering. Students then conducted numerous follow up visits to Special Collections over three months as they finalized source material to be incorporated in the digital archives and 3-D rendering.

The success of the Rohwer internment camp project laid the groundwork for more collaboration. 2014 saw a third opportunity to work together, as the Landscape Architecture professor began investigating areas of Arkansas that had hosted large-scale social engineering projects during the Great Depression as part of scholarly research and for a possible class project. Given the rapport developed with Special Collections, the professor mentioned during a visit that he was looking into sites established by the federal Resettlement Administration, a New Deal program later incorporated into the Farm Security Administration (FSA), and the librarian was able to point toward unique materials that students would be soon begin using for original research. The FSA is best remembered today for the photographers that documented dust bowl migrants, farm workers, and Works Progress Administration (WPA) workers across the country.[12]

The Special Collections librarian provided access to an obscure and largely unused part of an archives related to the WPA held in the department for an instruction session, follow up research, and eventually digitization. The students soon discovered that the FSA impacted Arkansas's historical landscape far beyond the photographs of Dorothea Lange, Arthur Rothstein, and others. Six students from three different departments—landscape architecture, architecture, and history—undertook an interdisciplinary, independent study course in order to create an entry for the 2014 HALS Challenge.[13] The students used Special Collections to compile documentation for three FSA farming communities in Arkansas: Clover Bend, Lake View, and Chicot Farms. Among other sources, the students were able to incorporate scrapbooks, news clippings, and hidden caches of unpublished historical photographs from the WPA, which documented many of the New Deal projects across Arkansas in a collection that had been rarely if ever used by previous researchers.

The latest class project coordinated with Special Collections took place during the spring and summer semesters of 2016. This time, students researched the historical landscapes of the Buffalo National River. The class project was specifically focused on the historical mining boomtown of Rush, Arkansas, which companies and residents abandoned decades ago. Historical structures remain as features of the national park. Eight students visited the department multiple times after the librarian hosted a formal instruction session, where he introduced selected resources related to various aspects of the history, culture, and visual record of Rush. Again, the advice and consultation the students received in Special Collections proved useful before they conducted research in other institutions. For this course, students accessed National Park Service records held by the Buffalo National River after they received a research methods session from the Special Collections librarian. That project received attention from regional news sources and was publicized by the University of Arkansas public relations.[14]

Reflection

The collaborations with landscape architecture classes achieved several goals the Special Collections and library have with regard to information literacy and promotions of rare and unique holdings. Undergraduate students have successfully engaged a broad array of media held by special collections—historic maps, aerial maps, local and regional publications, organizational and professional archives, government publications, photographic archives—to conduct primary source-based research. The Special Collections librarian was also able to facilitate that learning through tailored instructional tools embedded librarians frequently employ, such as class-specific library guides.[15] The collaboration with a faculty member in the School of Architecture provided the opportunity for students to develop research skills with many media formats beyond site plans and building schematics. In addition to familiarity with types of primary sources, students from the landscape architecture program, some of whom have now worked on multiple projects in the Special Collections department, have developed literacy on the use of finding aids, federated catalogs, library OPACs, and internal research guides.

The four years of classes has introduced a variety of research skills to students who could very possibly have completed their program of studies without ever interacting with the libraries' special collections.[16] While students collaboratively developed bibliographies of the archival and published sources for the group projects, they also learned how to more effectively navigate the variety of materials held in a research library, and how to use sources such as microfilm, government documents collections, and newspaper databases to augment the data gleaned from archival records groups, scrapbooks, aerial maps, and rare publications. Conversely, student's discovered that the gaps they found in large research collections, for instance the microfilmed, yet incomplete government records of the War Relocation Authority, could be addressed with additional digging in the archives.

In addition to the "landscapes" scholars in the landscape architecture discipline study more often—the structures and physical environment created by society—historical research requires navigating the informational landscape. Through special collections research, students learned how their field work and creation of graphic illustrations related to archives, historical texts, microfilm, and other two-dimensional records—a different set of structures created by people and society. Sometimes students could address the gaps and the need for further documentation with the resources in Special Collections, while other times they learned, just as professional researchers would, that large-scale, primary resource-based research often requires ferreting out archival and rare material at a variety of institutions.

The student work in Special Collections has helped strengthen the bridge between the library and the School of Architecture, fulfilling essential outreach needs to undergraduates in the program. Although Special Collections has a close partnership as an archival collection institution with School of Architecture working professionals and scholars, its undergraduate students rarely engage in historical research in the collections. That is in part because of the professional practice orientation of the program. Work with the archives and historical records in Special Collections opens other fields of inquiry to undergraduates, such as cultural studies, social history, and the evolving roles of the design professions in the development of American society. Ongoing responsive and enthusiastic support for all students in the School of Architecture sends a positive message to faculty and administration about the library's contribution to their academic mission.

Assessment

One of the strongest indicators of the success of the collaboration between the Special Collections Department and Landscape Architecture since 2012 is the comfort Landscape Architecture students now have working in the reading room.[17] Instruction included guided searching with the library catalog to identify ancillary resources that would be useful for a contextual research strategy for local history. Students also received instruction on locating and using maps housed in special collections, which could be found in historic maps collections, USGS and state government publications, in archives, or in published monographs and theses and dissertations. The librarian used hypothetical research questions to demonstrate how to broaden possible search material and identify pertinent data that could inform the use of other sources, from regional newspapers to obscure serials and other often hidden resources.[18] With more experience in Special Collections, students refined their research questions and increasingly identified and began analyzing resources independently.

The work with the classes allowed Special Collections to establish personal relationships with the students and their professor, while also instilling in them a familiarity with the research environment and all personnel in the department. For those who do not spend a lot of time in the cloistered, quiet space of a special collections or archives reading room, special collections can seem remote or subject to special privileges not available to "regular" students, especially undergraduates. The approach of the University of Arkansas Special Collections in every instruction session is to, first, make it clear to students that they are welcome and that the department's staff is willing and enthusiastic about helping them. After the instruction sessions, group research consultations and brainstorming sessions, and one-on-one follow-up visits, students who have worked on the historic landscape projects often return at their own leisure outside of scheduled class times to conduct research, return to work on other projects, and are quick to drop in on the librarian or reference desk to talk about topics such as how to find materials at other repositories, how to craft citations (even for things they didn't find in the department), and how to best format digital images. However, the coursework itself has resulted in significant scholarly accomplishments for the students and their professor, including the published 2012 HALS study available from the Library of Congress.[19]

The undergraduate research completed in the summer of 2016 has generated a robust and highly detailed website, "If Walls Could Talk: The Story of the Hicks Site in Rush, Arkansas." That project, which included travel to the Rush site and digital reconstruction of the Hicks hotel, was also supported by a National Park Service grant and produced another HALS project submitted by the faculty member and his students to the Library of Congress in July 2016. The website will be published in early 2017 and will be hosted by the University's Center for Advanced Spatial Technologies.[20] Students combined recently collected documentation and surveys of the historic landscape around the ghost town of Rush including 360-degree video photographs, site drawings, and digital rendering, with the historical primary sources gathered at the University of Arkansas Libraries. The HALS research has provided students with the opportunity to present research papers that emerged from their group projects at professional conferences. Two students that participated in the Rush research project presented to historical societies in the Buffalo River region and to the non-profit support organization, the Buffalo National River Partners. Since 2012, two of the landscape architecture students have pursued Masters of Historic preservation degrees and another has already begun professional preservation work for the National Park Service.

Recommendations/Best Practices

Although the successive classes taught with the historic landscapes professor provided Special Collections a model for future collaborations, the department did not embark on the projects with the intention of establishing a recurring, embedded teaching approach. The success of the collaboration was born from enthusiastically responding to the opportunity presented by a faculty member outside of the library that was pursuing innovative approaches to undergraduate learning. When ideas like hosting a class in the department for the multiple site visits and making oneself available for all of their future research needs, the librarian did not first consider how will it impact their time and resources, such as the ability to take on other commitments or if it would place a strain on the facility and staff. Those are important questions, of course. But the first response was, what can the department do to help the course and the students succeed?

That positive and accommodating first response was made possible by setting strategic goals for instruction and outreach and having the flexibility to embrace the opportunities that will help achieve those goals. The department had decided to pursue teaching opportunities with departments outside of those most often served, history and political science. So the landscape architecture course was immediately perceived as a chance to add a new campus department to the roster of those served by Special Collections. The assumption of being able to host additional classes was predicated upon the department's previous experience in hosting sessions in the reading room alongside regular patron activity. The University of Arkansas Libraries does not have a dedicated classroom or secure public space suitable for groups accessing archives or rare books outside of the reading room. The success of the embedded librarian approach with rare materials, however, has informed recommendations for facility development, including future plans for a dedicated Special Collections instruction space.[21]

Lessons learned from the collaboration also include opportunities not taken when working with the classes while they are all together for scheduled instruction sessions. While discussion of the subject-specific material and how to access rare and fragile resources was essential, class projects destined for professional publication or public distribution of student work would benefit from more library instruction directed to topics such as copyright and citation earlier in the process.

Conclusion

Undergraduate students increasingly have access to state-of-the art-technology and unlimited digital information, and with that they have greater opportunities to conduct original and exciting research. Special collections and archival research is still integral to many of those possible research projects, and academic librarians can join in collaborative, cross-campus teaching approaches allowing undergraduate students to produce scholarship and useful professional studies even before they graduate. The Special Collections of the University of Arkansas Libraries learned over the course of four years of working with the historic landscape architecture class projects that some of the most valuable information the students could receive is still rooted in information literacy and research methodology: how to find primary sources and strategically research with rare and archival materials, even those not necessarily held in the department. The librarian's expertise with archival and databases research, and willingness to work with the students, were the impetus for most of the follow-up consultations, as well as the continuing outreach of successive class projects. The opportunity to make the resources that are held in the department available to those that don't know about them, and to make the breadth of print and archival collections available for innovative research and instruction, remains a strong benefit of the work with landscape architecture classes.

Notes

1. Emma Marya Coonan, "Navigating the Information Landscape," *Serials Librarian* 61, no. 3–4 (October 2011): 323-333; Library Literature & Information Science Full Text (H. W. Wilson), EBSCOhost, accessed December 9, 2016.
2. "Preparing a HALS History," National Park Service, https://www.nps.gov/hdp/

standards/HALS/HALSHistoryBrochure.pdf, accessed September 8, 2016; "Professional Practice: Documented Historic Landscapes," American Society of Landscape Architects, accessed September 8, 2016, https://www.asla.org/ContentDetail.aspx?id=37489.
3. University library special collections, as well as local historical societies and museums, often hold rich collections on local history that can prove invaluable to students engaged in locally focused research projects, as well as great outreach opportunities for the institutions. For one recent discussion, see Mary Alice Anderson, "From Tiny Museums to the Library of Congress Discovering Local History Resources in the Digital Age," *Internet@Schools* 18 (5): 24–26, http://0-search.proquest.com.library.uark.edu/docview/904159716?accountid=8361.
4. For a discussion of one example of how valuable landscape archives can be for researchers, see Audra Bellmore, Claire-Lise Bénaud, and Sever Bordeianu, "J. B. Jackson, Cultural Geographer: Evolution of an Archive," *Collection Building*, Vol. 31 Iss: 3 (2012): 115–19, accessed September 7, 2016.
5. Researchers have devoted a great deal of scholarly interest on embedded librarianship in the last several years since published studies of the topic first appeared in the early 2000s and after Barbara Dewey put a name to the emerging methodology.
6. Cassandra Kvenild and Kaijsa Calkins, *Embedded Librarians: Moving Beyond One-Shot Instruction* (Chicago: Association of College and Research Libraries, 2011), vii. The 2011 edited volume by Kvenild and Calkins brings synthesize the first decade of work on "embedded librarian. Select early publications on embedded librarianship include Victoria Matthew and Ann Schroeder, "The Embedded Librarian Program: Faculty and Librarians Partner to Embed Personalized Library Assistance into Online Courses," *EDUCAUSE Quarterly* 29, no. 4 (2006): 61–65; Karen M. Ramsay and Jim Kinnie, "The Embedded Librarian: Getting Out There Via Technology to Help Students Where They Learn," *Library Journal* 131, no. 6 (2006): 34–35; Lynne Marie Rudasill, "Beyond Subject Specialization: The Creation of Embedded Librarians," *Public Services Quarterly* 6, no. 2/3: 83–91; Library & Information Science Source, EBSCOhost, accessed September 9, 2016. For conceptual framework for the development of embedded librarianship approaches, also see Alexius Smith Macklin, "Theory into Practice: Applying David Jonassen's Work in Instructional Design to Instruction Program in Academic Libraries," *College & Research Libraries* vol. 64 no. 6; Anderson, "From Tiny Museums to the Library of Congress Discovering Local History Resources in the Digital Age: 494–500.
7. Jake Carlson and Ruth Kneale, "Embedded Librarianship in the Research Context: Navigating New Waters," *College & Research Libraries News*, Association of College and Research Libraries (2011), accessed September 7, 2016, http://m.crln.acrl.org/content/72/3/167.full.
8. Joshua Youngblood, "Arkansas and Captivity During World War II," *The Arkansian: The Newsletter of the University of Arkansas Libraries Special Collections Department* v. 5 no. 2 (Fall 2011): 4–5. Upon joining the faculty of the University of Arkansas Libraries as the Research and Outreach Services Librarian in Special Collections, the librarian began to orient himself to the strengths of the collections and which collecting areas would lend themselves to new outreach initiatives. He found that the Special Collections archival and published materials related to Japanese American internment were both substantial and surprisingly varied. There are re-

search collections copied from the National Archives and well-known publications. The newsletter article explored the variety of materials related to World War II-era confinement in Arkansas (prisoners of war and Japanese Americans), with special attention given to highlights from the collections related to the Jerome and Rohwer internment camps.

9. See the University of Arkansas Libraries Special Collections topic guide, "Japanese Americans Interned in Arkansas," http://libinfo.uark.edu/specialcollections/research/guides/japaneseamericans.asp, accessed September 7, 2016.
10. For discussion of collaborative responses to innovative faculty teaching approaches, see Lisa Coats and Bojana Beric, "More Than a One-Shot: Innovative Faculty-Librarian Collaboration," in *Embedded Librarians: Moving Beyond One-Shot Instruction*, ed. Casandra Kvenlid and Kaijsa Calkins (Chicago: Association of College and Research Libraries, 2011), 165–84.
11. "Rohwer Reconstructed: Interpreting Place through Experience," http://risingabove.cast.uark.edu/.
12. Of the ninety-nine experimental farms established by the FSA, federal authorities placed seven in Arkansas in order to offer a place that landless or impoverished farmers could move with their families. Perhaps the most famous example in Arkansas was the Dyess Colony, where a very young Johnny Cash moved with his family. Other sites less well known today include the Lake View all-African American farm in the Delta land of Phillips County and the Clover Bend cooperative farm in Lawrence County.
13. The HALS Challenge is annual contest sponsored by the National Park Service encouraging citizens to document historical landscapes: https://www.nps.gov/hdp/competitions/HALS_Challenge.html.
14. Bill Bowden, "Project Offers View into History of Hotel in Arkansas Ghost, Town," *Arkansas Democrat-Gazette*, July 17, 2016, accessed through Arkansas Online September 10, 2016, http://www.arkansasonline.com/news/2016/jul/17/project-offers-view-into-hotel-s-histor/?print.
15. See the LibGuide, "LARC History of Land Preservation: Rohwer Cemetery," accessed September 7, 2016, http://uark.libguides.com/c.php?g=79021.
16. For a discussion of the importance of sustaining effective teaching partnerships, see Macklin, "Theory into Practice: Applying David Jonassen's Work in Instructional Design to Instruction Program in Academic Libraries," 498.
17. Nancy O'Hanlon, "Information Literacy in the University Curriculum: Challenges for Outcomes Assessment," *portal: Libraries and the Academy* 7, no. 2 (2007): 169–89, accessed September 9, 2016, https://0-muse.jhu.edu.library.uark.edu/, 171–72.
18. Lindsay Blake, Darra Ballance, Kathy Davies, Julie K. Gaines, Kim Mears, Peter Shipman, Maryska Connolly-Brown, and Vicki Burchfield, "Patron Perception and Utilization of an Embedded Librarian Program," *Journal of the Medical Library Association* 104, no. 3 (July 2016): 226–30, accessed September 9, 2016, CINAHL Complete, EBSCOhost.
19. HALS Study completed in 2012, Rohwer Relocation Center Memorial Cemetery, Arkansas Highway #1, Rohwer, Desha County, AR, http://www.loc.gov/pictures/item/ar1148/.
20. Hicks Site, Rush Historic District, Buffalo National River, Arkansas: "If Walls

Could Talk: The Story of the Hicks Site in Rush, Arkansas," Kimball Erdman, Principal Investigator of web-based interpretive project with Center for Advanced Spatial Technologies, 2017.
21. The Special Collections Department had experience navigating multiple and simultaneous uses of the reading room space—for instance, having students on one side of the room, separating them from visiting researchers, maintaining security and preservation protocols, while librarians and outside faculty discussed the materials, and combining introductions to archival research methods with subject-based class work.

Bibliography

Anderson, Mary Alice. "From Tiny Museums to the Library of Congress Discovering Local History Resources in the Digital Age." *Internet@Schools* 18 (5) (2011): 24–26. http://0-search.proquest.com.library.uark.edu/docview/904159716?accountid=8361.

Bellmore, Audra, Claire-Lise Bénaud, and Sever Bordeianu, "J. B. Jackson, Cultural Geographer: Evolution of an Archive." *Collection Building*, Vol. 31 Iss: 3 (2012): 115–19.

Blake, Lindsay, et al. "Patron Perception and Utilization of an Embedded Librarian Program." *Journal of the Medical Library Association* 104, no. 3 (July 2016): 226–30. Accessed September 9, 2016. CINAHL Complete, EBSCOhost.

Carlson, Jake, and Ruth Kneale. "Embedded Librarianship in the Research Context: Navigating New Waters." *College & Research Libraries News*. Association of College and Research Libraries (2011). Accessed September 7, 2016. http://m.crln.acrl.org/content/72/3/167.full.

Carlson, Jake, Megan Sapp Nelson, Lisa R. Johnston, and Amy Koshoffer. "Developing Data Literacy Programs: Working with Faculty, Graduate Students and Undergraduates." *Bulletin of the American Society for Information Science and Technology (online)*, 41(6) (2015):14–17. http://0-search.proquest.com.library.uark.edu/docview/1812272351?accountid=8361.

Coonan, Emma Marya. "Navigating the Information Landscape." *Serials Librarian* 61, no. 3–4 (October 2011): 323–33. Library Literature & Information Science Full Text (H. W. Wilson). Accessed December 9, 2016. EBSCOhost.

Cox, Richard J., and David A. Wallace. *Archives and the Public Good: Accountability and Records in Modern Society*. Westport: Quorum Books, 2002.

Duff, Wendy M., Elizabeth Yakel, and Helen Tibbo. "Archival Reference Knowledge." *American Archivist* 76, no. 1 (2013): 68–94. Library Literature & Information Science Full Text (H. W. Wilson). Accessed September 9, 2015. EBSCOhost.

Fitzgerald, Kathryn, Laura Anderson, and Helen Kula. "Embedded Librarians Promote an Innovation Agenda: University of Toronto Libraries and the MaRS Discovery District." *Journal of Business & Finance Librarianship* 15, no. 3–4 (July 2010): 188–96. Business Source Complete. Accessed September 9, 2016. EBSCOhost.

Harris, Valerie A., and Ann C. Weller. "Use of Special Collections as an Opportunity for Outreach in the Academic Library." *Journal of Library Administration* 52, no. 3–4 (2012): 294–303. Library & Information Science Source. Accessed September 9, 2015. EBSCOhost.

Jimerson, Randall C. "Archives 101 in a 2.0 World: The Continuing Need for Parallel Systems." In *A Different Kind of Web: New Connections Between Archives and Our Users*, edited by Kate Theimer, 304–33. Chicago: Society of American Archivists, 2011.

Kolowich, Steve. "Embedded Librarians." *Inside Higher Ed* (June 9, 2010). Accessed September 7, 2016. www.insidehighered.com/news/2010/06/09/hopkins.

Lawrimore, Erin. "Mission Critical: Effective Internal Advocacy for Your Archives." *Journal for the Society of North Carolina Archivists* 11, no. 1: 2-18 (2014). Library & Information Science Source. Accessed September 9, 2015. EBSCOhost.

Macklin, Alexius Smith. "Theory into Practice: Applying David Jonassen's Work in Instructional Design to Instruction Program in Academic Libraries." *College & Research Libraries*, vol. 64 no. 6 (November 2003): 494–500.

Matthew, Victoria, and Ann Schroeder. "The Embedded Librarian Program: Faculty and Librarians Partner to Embed Personalized Library Assistance into Online Courses." *EDUCAUSE Quarterly* 29, no. 4 (2006): 61–65.

O'Hanlon, Nancy. "Information Literacy in the University Curriculum: Challenges for Outcomes Assessment." *portal: Libraries and the Academy* 7, no. 2 (2007): 169–89. Accessed September 9, 2016. https://0-muse.jhu.edu.library.uark.edu/.

Ramsay, Karen M., and Jim Kinnie, "The Embedded Librarian: Getting out There Via Technology to Help Students Where They Learn," *Library Journal 131, no. 6 (2006):* 34–35.

Rudasill, Lynne Marie. "Beyond Subject Specialization: The Creation of Embedded Librarians." *Public Services Quarterly* 6, no. 2–3: 83–91. Library & Information Science Source. Accessed September 9, 2016. EBSCOhost.

Shumaker, David. "Embedded Librarians in Special Libraries." *Information Today* (July 2012): 1–34. http://0-search.proquest.com.library.uark.edu/docview/1024444592?accountid=8361.

Shumaker, David, and Mary Talley. "Models of Embedded Librarianship: A Research Summary." *Information Outlook* 14, no. 1 (2010): 27–35.

White, Kelvin L., and Anne J. Gilliland. "Promoting Reflexivity and Inclusivity in Archival Education Research, and Practice." *Library Quarterly* 80, no. 3 (2010): 231–48. Library & Information Science Source. Accessed September 9, 2015. EBSCOhost.

CHAPTER 17*

Mentoring a Peer:
A Feminist Ethic for Directing Undergraduate Humanities Research

Amy Hildreth Chen and Kathryn Ross

Introduction

During the academic year of 2015–2016, Special Collections instruction librarian Dr. Amy Hildreth Chen served as Kathryn (Katie) Ross's mentor through the Iowa Center for Research by Undergraduates (ICRU) at the University of Iowa in order to direct Katie's scholarship on the overlooked role of women editors in science fiction. Specifically, Katie examined how women editors of science fiction fanzines shaped the genre throughout the twentieth century as well as contributed to the development of fan culture.

While our time together began as an official affiliation mediated by university bureaucracy, we quickly realized that we did not fit into the binary roles prescribed within higher education. For example, classifications like faculty/student, faculty/librarian, and librarian/researcher did not describe our relationship. Many ICRU fellowships grow out of connections made between faculty and students in traditional classroom settings, but Amy is not a faculty member, so Katie was never her student. Amy oversaw Katie's research as an academic librarian who holds a PhD, not an MLIS. As a result, Amy simultaneously inhabited the role of a faculty member

---

* This work is licensed under a Creative Commons Attribution-NonCommercial 4.0 License, CC BY-NC (https://creativecommons.org/licenses/by-nc/4.0/).

and a librarian. Yet Katie's research took priority; when Katie pursued her work in special collections, Amy provided support. But the hierarchical binaries in higher education that are the most telling—and the most difficult to circumvent—are based on age, race, gender, and class. In this, we mostly avoided fitting into stereotypical roles. We are peers in race and gender as well as in age. Notably, one marker of identity—class—was a point of difference. Katie is a first-generation and nontraditional college student, while Amy was neither.

Our unconventional partnership gave Amy an opportunity to practice her feminist pedagogy. Feminist pedagogy emphasizes egalitarian relationships, mutual learning, and a student's active and equal role in academic inquiry. As a result, Katie and Amy developed a friendship, Katie pursued her research in a field outside Amy's expertise to an advanced level, and we expanded ICRU's focus on partnership to include the perspectives of a variety of other professionals throughout the university. Academic librarians, whose roles automatically place them outside traditional professor-student dyads, have the unique opportunity to employ feminist pedagogical principles of relationship, empowerment, and community to benefit their students as well as themselves.[1] Our experience shows that a feminist approach to teaching undergraduate research allows librarians to embrace the opportunities provided by their alternative route to academic mentorship.

Background

The Iowa Center for Research by Undergraduates (ICRU) is a year-long honors program that provides funding and academic mentoring to students from all disciplines who engage in scholarly or creative work. ICRU matches students to faculty members and professional staff who agree to support their project. Beyond the contribution of a poster to the undergraduate research symposia in April, ICRU has no formal requirements.

Examples of ICRU projects range widely, depending on the discipline. In September 2016, postings for ICRU students included research positions in internal medicine, anatomy and cell biology, archeology, and German literature.[2] The University of Iowa Libraries did not list any postings in September 2016. However, during Katie's fellowship with Amy in Special Collections over the 2015–2016 academic year, the university libraries also supported three other ICRU students in the Digital Scholarship and Publishing Studio (DSPS), Research and Library Instruction (RLI) division, and Conservation and Preservation.

Partnerships

While ICRU allows students to work with professional staff members, rather than only faculty, ICRU emphasizes the faculty option. This focus is notable on the center's website. For example, "What Students Say," a section of the site, only gives students the option to learn the benefits of "working with faculty mentors" alongside other choices such as "presenting at research festivals" and "the impact on career goals."[3] As can be expected, student reviews of the ICRU experience focus on connections with faculty only. For example, one student remarked, "My research experience gave me greater perspective on what a professor's job really is and the many things they do to help their students. It helped me define the attributes I should be looking for in a mentor and teacher."[4] As Katie elected for an ICRU fellowship in Special Collections, rather than in her major of English or Education, it was her decision to be paired with professional staff rather than a member of the faculty. As a result, Katie opted to learn about alternative employment opportunities while pursuing an unconventional ICRU mentor.

It is important that Katie herself chose to pursue an ICRU fellowship and then a non-traditional ICRU partnership because, while feminist pedagogy outlines a variety of theoretical approaches and applied practices to avoid the "teaching of dominance," feminist pedagogy often still assumes students have limited agency.[5] After all, most university education unfolds when students enroll in a required course administered by an instructor whose authority is prescribed through formal mechanisms, such as the use of syllabus and assignments, and learned behaviors, like a teacher's more formal dress or role as discussion leader. In contrast, Katie elected to participate in ICRU—research fellowships are not required to graduate at Iowa—and then picked a project administered by the university libraries.

Katie's specific research interest for the ICRU fellowship examined fan-produced little magazines, colloquially referred to as "fanzines," edited by women in early science fiction communities. Her paper examined three exemplary fanzines edited by women who resisted patriarchal publishing communities by producing their own works, demonstrating a feminist approach to their craft. Katie specifically examined four pioneering fanzine editors: Myrtle Douglas, Lee Hoffman, and Janice Bogstad with Jeanne Gomoll. Katie identified how each fanzine demonstrated an ethos of inclusivity, refuted patriarchal practices, and established feminist heritage within fan communities. Katie interpreted the aesthetic of each fanzine by incorporating a paratextual reading of the material objects.

Amy supported Katie's work over the course of the year by creating meetings that privileged Katie's thought process, status, and interests. First, Amy oriented herself as an interested peer seeking to enrich and expand Katie's work rather than oversee it. Second, meetings occurred at a variety of locations, such as a corner of the library where whiteboards are set up or in a coffee shop. However, Amy never suggested meetings in Special Collections' reading room or at her office, as both spaces would reiterate Katie's identity as a student, rather than Amy's peer. Third, Amy did not frame herself as Katie's only mentor. Instead, Amy introduced Katie to other librarians who had their own one-on-one meetings with Katie. This way, Katie developed a community around herself and her work that grew from Amy's support but did not require mediation.

Katie's achievements exceeded the boundaries of the ICRU Fellowship and Amy's own experience: Katie presented at a science fiction convention as well as an international academic conference during summer 2016, will co-teach a graduate class on science fiction at Iowa in fall 2016, and was nominated as a Fulbright fellow following her graduation in 2017. Amy, who also attended the University of Iowa for her bachelor's degree, did not begin presenting at conferences until after her first year in her doctoral program, enrolled in but did not teach graduate classes as an undergraduate, and was never nominated to be a Fulbright scholar!

Katie's Reflection

My success, however, should not indicate that the project was without its challenges. My difficulties varied from working with unprocessed collections, addressing a hostile graduate student at an academic conference, and coping with a fan at a science fiction convention who interrupted my presentation. Any researcher, seasoned or novice, finds unprocessed collections more difficult as they require more time to examine and may present unexpected contents. Fanzines are an excellent demonstration of investigating these unexpected contents, as they often have multiple authors (that are both established writers, "fans," and variations of these two) and contain very subjective narratives. I benefited from using collections at my university, rather than traveling as many researchers must do. Proximity, however, only made it more convenient to spend more time in Special Collections. My research took longer to complete than it would have otherwise because the collections were continuing to be processed. Then, when it came time to present my research, I faced confrontations from both my academic and public audiences. A graduate student questioned my research as she felt my status as an undergraduate de-legitimized her work. While the graduate student was likely surprised and threatened that I was an undergraduate, I needed to tactfully assert that the rigor of my work spoke for itself. When a fan talked over me during my convention presentation, overshadowing my words and taking my limited time on stage, I addressed the fan concisely, regaining my power to control my space.

I used the community and partnerships that I developed to address the challenges that arose during my ICRU fellowship. In order to better understand the unprocessed collections, I met with several librarians: Laura Hampton, digital project librarian; Lisa Gardinier, Spanish and Iberian studies librarian; and Sara Riggs, library assistant III. Pete Balestrieri, curator of science fiction and popular culture, warned me of the negative feedback I might receive from academic and popular audiences, while providing beneficial suggestions for how to react to these challenges. When I attended my academic conference during summer 2016, Amy cheered me on, provided moral support, and enjoyed my photographs of England.

It is impossible to fully articulate the immense benefits of working with a mentor whose personal philosophy aligns with that of their student, in both ideology and practice. The opportunities that Amy provided expanded my worldview and academic goals, giving me a sense of self and purpose. Amy demonstrated how a successful professional collaborates with faculty in Special Collections, and her positive presence and rigorous academic standards profoundly shaped my academic success.

Amy's Reflection

While I enjoy my role as an instruction librarian, my identity as an alternative-academic (alt-ac) occasionally makes me feel uncomfortable. I bring a different perspective to the table than my colleagues in the library and in the wider university. I often wish other librarians were more interested in my research. Likewise, when I collaborate with faculty members, they often see only my ability to serve them rather than perceive me as a fellow academic, albeit with a different job title and description. I feel like I, too, am an academic, as I perform research, teaching, and service in my role as a librarian. When I worked with Katie, I felt that my identity helped rather than hindered our relationship. As a librarian, I could provide Katie with access to collections and encourage her to consult with a variety of information professionals. As an academic, I could ensure that Katie learned how to situate her work within current disciplinary fields. Within our partnership, I benefited from both sides of my alt-ac identity without having to act solely within one role or the other. I deeply appreciated my time with Katie as a way to find the positives in my dual identity.

Additionally, over my time with Katie, I began to admire her ability to use research as an opportunity to seek support from administrators, department heads, tenured professors, curators, and specialized staff. I saw how Katie's bold approach to research meant that she practiced discussing her area of interest with different constituents, in the process learning how to adapt her message to suit her audience while gathering new insights from their feedback. As a result, Katie's research grew more sophisticated as she integrated different perspectives into her writing. In contrast, I did not learn how to use professional networking to deepen my scholarship until after I completed my PhD. Now, I use Katie as a model for how I can engage with academics as well as practitioners when I conduct my own research. Katie's approach to research reminded me of the value of community, a core principle of feminist theory.

Assessment

ICRU does not require any assessment for mentors to better understand their students' experience during the fellowship. Instead, assessment only occurs by ICRU judges during students' year-end poster presentation at the Undergraduate Research Festival. While Amy did not formally assess Katie's research, she did provide feedback throughout by holding conversations to reflect on Katie's progress through the collections she used, referring Katie to knowledgeable experts when needed and providing comments on her drafts.

If Amy wished to evaluate Katie's research formally, she could have drawn from a wide variety of literature on feminist assessment. For example, Maria T. Accardi's *Feminist Pedagogy in Library Instruction* suggests feminist teachers adopt Classroom Assessment Techniques (CAT) in class activities.[6] The CAT Amy found most useful to adapt to a non-classroom environment like the ICRU fellowship is the "muddiest point" prompt, which requires the student to write a short response to the question, "What is the muddiest point in your research?"[7] This question would function as a meeting conversation starter that would help Amy facilitate Katie's work while upholding her feminist pedagogy principles.

Similarly, Amy could have used assessment to help improve Katie's poster presentation. Four judges ranked Katie on the impact of her visual content, narrative, and presentation quality. On a 1 to 12 scale, Katie received an average of 8.75 on her visual content, 7.5 on her narrative impact, and a 9.25 on her presentation quality. Amy believes ICRU's assessment of Katie would have been higher if Amy herself had been better situated to support this style of scholarly communication. As an English PhD, Amy had not created a poster for her own research until June 2016,[8] which was after Katie presented hers in April 2016. Nevertheless, Amy should have helped Katie refine her research question(s) and polish her presentation by taking more initiative to learn the qualities Katie would be assessed on prior to the presentation. In the future, Amy will use her experience observing ICRU judges and designing her own poster to better support future mentees.

Recommendations/Best Practices

Academic librarians are well-positioned to benefit from applying feminist pedagogy to their support of undergraduate research. Our example shows that feminist pedagogical practices ideally begin even before a partnership is arranged. Students who freely decide to be mentored by academic librarians may be more likely to benefit from unconventional support. However, allowing students to opt-in to librarian mentors may not always be possible on every campus. Furthermore, providing such a choice may unintentionally affirm faculty's central role in mentoring students rather than acknowledging the diverse skillsets found among all university personnel.

Fostering egalitarian relationships between teachers and students may come more easily when considering how to approach partnerships involving non-traditional students who may be the same age, or older, than their teachers. But while working with non-traditional students may seem as though it is an opportunity to help underprivileged students from "at risk" populations, this attitude does not reflect a feminist mindset. Rather, academic librarians mentoring non-traditional students should seek to include their partner's knowledge into conversations and avoid suggestions that their expertise places them at an advantage at all times. One way to avoid reaffirming hierarchy is to schedule meetings in locations that are not affiliated with the librarian's position within the university in order to favor places where both student and librarian can talk as equals. This egalitarian approach does not mean that librarians should shy away from assessment. While assessment places the student below the teacher, academic rigor requires feedback. Frame assignments to be assessed as opportunities for peer review rather than a time for the student to be evaluated on their subject mastery. Assessment should foster conversation, rather than criticism. One way librarians can position themselves for assessment conversations is to explain to the student that you want to prepare them to be judged by their field's requirements. You want to help ensure their success as their guide on the side.

Warm connections between two people often come from a conscious or unconscious understanding of shared identities and goals. Feminist pedagogy reiterates that diversity is valuable. Students may not have similar academic interests, career objectives, or personalities to their mentors. To become a better feminist mentor, recognize how similarity fosters comfort and therefore connection. Push to expand to expand the limits of what makes you comfortable and avoid opportunities to guide students to better emulate you. Allow students to shape the relationship by valuing how their learning unfolds and how they prefer to interact. This approach may mean that some of your connections may not be as warm as the relationship we depicted here; that is fine. Appreciate the opportunity instead to contribute where and how you can rather than hold an ideal in your mind. Furthermore, welcome the possibility that students may teach you or exceed your own achievements.

The feminist pedagogy resources we appreciate the most are those that are interested in how to ensure equitable relations between mentor and mentee. For example, Paulo Freire's *Pedagogy of the Oppressed* emphasizes developing non-binary partnerships where teacher and student take turns playing each other's role.[9] Freire argues that this type of role shifting allows for more authentic and collaborative experiences to emerge. We think that academic librarians may find it even easier to practice Freire's pedagogy than professors would because our identities are exterior to traditional teacher-student roles. More recent scholarship on feminist pedagogy like John D. Rich, Rameeka Manning, and Brionne Cage's "Feminist Pedagogy in the Classroom" emphasizes how equitable relationships between educators and students can be constructed through the development of course content and the classroom environment. However, librarians who wish to learn more about feminist pedagogy should not just turn to scholarship; they also should reach out their colleagues. Many librarians probably practice their own version of feminist mentorship and can share their experiences. Combining published approaches and practical first-hand knowledge will allow you to create unique relationships that suit both your personality and skills and your students' needs.

Conclusion

Through the Iowa Center for Undergraduate Research (ICRU), Katie, a non-traditional undergraduate, chose to work with Amy, a non-traditional librarian. Our unconventional partnership, which resisted traditional hierarchical binaries so often found in academia, allowed Amy to practice her feminist pedagogy, which emphasizes empowerment, community, and relationships. The result was not only that Katie developed a successful research program and ties to professionals throughout the university libraries, but also a close friendship to Amy. Our case study shows that academic librarians who embrace their position as unorthodox mentors to undergraduates and seek to appreciate the mutual advantages that arise from these arrangements can impart as well as partake of the learning opportunities these connections provide.

Notes

1. "What is Feminist Pedagogy?" TeAchnology (blog), http://www.teach-nology.com/teachers/methods/feminist_pedagogy/.
2. "Current Research/Creative Postings for Undergraduates," Iowa Center for Research by Undergraduates (September 15, 2016), https://uiowa.edu/icru/article/current-research-postings.

3. "What Students Say," Iowa Center for Research by Undergraduates, September 15, 2016, https://uiowa.edu/icru/what-students-say.
4. "What Students Say about Working with Faculty Mentors," Iowa Center for Research by Undergraduates (September 15, 2016), https://uiowa.edu/icru/article/what-students-say-about-working-faculty-mentors.
5. Dr. John D. Rich, Rameeka Manning, and Brionne Cage, "Feminist Pedagogy in the Classroom," PsychEd (blog), *Psychology Today* (February 10, 2015), https://www.psychologytoday.com/blog/psyched/201502/feminist-pedagogy-in-the-classroom.
6. Maria T. Accardi, "Feminist Assessment," Feminist Pedagogy in Library Instruction (Sacramento: Library Juice Press): 2013, 71–87.
7. "Classroom Assessment Techniques (CATs)," Center for Teaching, Vanderbilt University, https://cft.vanderbilt.edu/guides-sub-pages/cats/.
8. Amy Chen, "Twentieth Century Literary Collection Acquisition Patterns," Poster Presented at the Society of American Archivists, Atlanta, GA, August 2016.
9. Paulo Freire, *Pedagogy of the Oppressed* (New York: Herder and Herder, 1972).

Bibliography

Accardi, Maria T. "Feminist Assessment." *Feminist Pedagogy in Library Instruction* (Sacramento: Library Juice Press): 2013, 71–87.

Chen, Amy. "Twentieth Century Literary Collection Acquisition Patterns." Poster presented at the Society of American Archivists, Atlanta, GA, August 2016.

"Classroom Assessment Techniques (CATs)." Center for Teaching, Vanderbilt University. https://cft.vanderbilt.edu/guides-sub-pages/cats/.

"Current Research/Creative Postings for Undergraduates." Iowa Center for Research by Undergraduates (September 15, 2016). https://uiowa.edu/icru/article/current-research-postings.

Freire, Paulo. *Pedagogy of the Oppressed*. New York: Herder and Herder, 1972.

Rich, John D., Rameeka Manning, and Brionne Cage. "Feminist Pedagogy in the Classroom." PsychEd (blog). *Psychology Today* (February 10, 2015). https://www.psychologytoday.com/blog/psyched/201502/feminist-pedagogy-in-the-classroom.

Shrewbury, C. M. "What is Feminist Pedagogy?" *Women's Studies Quarterly*, 3–4 (1987): 6–14.

"What Students Say." Iowa Center for Research by Undergraduates (September 15, 2016). https://uiowa.edu/icru/what-students-say.

"What Students Say About Working with Faculty Mentors." Iowa Center for Research by Undergraduates (September 15, 2016). https://uiowa.edu/icru/article/what-students-say-about-working-faculty-mentors.

"What is Feminist Pedagogy?" *TeAchnology* (blog). http://www.teach-nology.com/teachers/methods/feminist_pedagogy/.

CHAPTER 18 *
Re-imagining Furman Engaged:
Transformation through a Library Partnership

Andrea M. Wright and John G. Kaup

Introduction

In 2014, the Furman University Libraries approached the Office of Integrative Research in the Sciences to bring the annual celebration of undergraduate scholarship, Furman Engaged!, online through our new institutional repository. This project became a true partnership, as both offices worked together to re-imagine the established event as a broader sharing of student research with new opportunities to archive and disseminate some of the products of the university's award-winning research programs. Over the past two years, there has been notable progress, a few missteps, and tremendous learning. This chapter will discuss important considerations including workflow, permissions, and best practices. Our experiences can provide a framework for other institutional repositories that want to partner with existing undergraduate research programs.

---

* This work is licensed under a Creative Commons Attribution 4.0 License, CC BY (https://creativecommons.org/licenses/by/4.0/).

Background

In his 1995 inaugural address espousing the importance and impact of engaged undergraduate learning, David E. Shi, past president of Furman University, stated, "Liberal learning is not simply a spectator sport."[1] Perhaps nowhere is engaged learning better evidenced than in Furman Engaged![2] Catalyzed by an Undergraduate Science Education award from the Howard Hughes Medical Institute in 2008, Furman Engaged! was launched by the Furman University Office of Undergraduate Research and Internships. Now delivered by Furman's coordinator of science education and run out of the Office of Integrative Research in the Sciences (OIRS), it is a daylong celebration of the distinguished research, scholarship, and creative endeavors of undergraduate students at Furman University. In lieu of classes, students from all academic disciplines attend and/or present their scholarly work. The day is filled with students' presentations: more than fifty oral sessions with three or more students presenting in each session; more than 200 posters, which are on display throughout the day with students sharing their individual poster during ninety-minute intervals; and several musical and theatrical performances. With nearly 600 students participating, 20 percent of the student body is actively involved in this program.

In June 2014, the Furman University Libraries acquired bepress's Digital Commons platform to host an institutional repository. The system was locally branded as the Furman University Scholar Exchange (FUSE), and is co-administered by the assistant director of Discovery Services and the Science Outreach Librarian & University Copyright officer. FUSE is an open access collection of scholarly, research, and creative works produced by faculty, students, staff, and other members of the Furman community. It is administered by the Furman University Libraries in cooperation with individual departments and academic units of the university.

FUSE was first introduced to the university at the Faculty Retreat in August 2014 and officially launched October 15, 2014. FUSE administrators actively marketed and recruited collaborators through workshops, advertising, word-of-mouth, and numerous meetings with potential partners on campus throughout the fall semester. While some of this marketing was a general awareness campaign, there was also targeted outreach to specific faculty and programs. One of the first programs specifically targeted by the FUSE administrators was Furman Engaged!

Partnerships

Throughout the first seven years delivering the Furman Engaged! event, OIRS worked with Furman's Marketing & Public Relations Department in the development of a printed program. The extent of the partnership was solely the delivery of material and the proofing of a final document. In 2013, OIRS shifted toward a website presence with a more searchable program, though it was still a fairly limited delivery of information. When the libraries initially approached OIRS about establishing a Furman Engaged! presence in FUSE, example events from other bepress institutions[3] played an important role in highlighting both the more comprehensive search and browse capabilities for the current year event, as well as the archival potential. The ability to retain past event information and the potential to publish full-text documents would expand the opportunities for students, departments, and the entire university to highlight tremendous scholarly output of students long after the end of the event.

The current partnership between OIRS and the FUSE administrators was initiated eight months prior to the 2015 Furman Engaged! event. As part of this early planning process, the partners addressed the following questions strategically:

- How is metadata collected (e.g., poster titles, oral presentation titles, session headings, and performances)?
- What new metadata would be required to increase usability in FUSE?
- How will the system construct an online program for the day's event, including focusing on mobile friendly access?
- Can the metadata be re-purposed to construct a print program?
- What is the current and future archival nature of this work?
- What is the utility of the Furman Engaged! website to promote student and faculty dissemination of their research?

Multiple meetings during the fall 2014 semester between the partners enabled a broad exploration of existing needs as well as brainstorming of new options. Templates and examples were researched, goals for Furman Engaged! and the archival capabilities of the platform were discussed, and future directions were considered. This was the first time a broad, open reconsideration of Furman Engaged! occurred. This process transformed not only how Furman Engaged! was produced and delivered, but the internal conception of the event's potential. While initially providing a "best of" showcase for Furman's undergraduate excellence in an on-campus, live event, Furman Engaged! now also provides the opportunity to archive, disseminate, and reach out to broader communities beyond campus.

An important consideration for transitioning Furman Engaged! to the FUSE platform was capturing all the information needed for the online functionality without drastically changing the submission process for campus stakeholders. Unlike professional conferences where individual presenters are submitting their presentation proposals, most of the Furman Engaged! data is compiled at a campus department level and submitted by a single department representative. In the past, Microsoft Excel worksheets had been developed for this task. Importing large amounts of data into FUSE is easiest with Excel spreadsheets, but over time the system-generated spreadsheets from the Digital Commons software proved cumbersome and unintuitive. OIRS and the libraries worked together to modify the existing department spreadsheets to better gather data required by the FUSE system, without a wholesale redesign.

In 2015, a new submission approach was developed within the FUSE platform in which individual students or departmental representatives could input programmatic details directly into FUSE (e.g., presenters, titles, event categories, and affiliated department). Initially, it was believed this would provide a streamlined approach from a workflow perspective, and transfer the onus of submitting presentation information from the department to the student presenter. However, in practice, this caused complications within the system's approval workflow and generated resistance with departments. As described below, this workflow was ultimately changed to improve outcomes.

Some of the best evidence for collaborative nature of this project comes from the implemented workflow. This was not simply OIRS gathering metadata for the libraries to blindly post to the repository. Instead, both groups actively planned together, reviewed together, and communicated regularly to ensure the success of Furman Engaged! This collaborative effort allowed OIRS to leverage expertise in the planning of Furman Engaged!, to assign time and locations, categorize events, and communicate with participants. The libraries were then able to review content with an eye toward platform optimization and metadata completion. This required heavy communication electronically and in-person, as well as regular file sharing, particularly during the weeks immediately preceding the Furman Engaged! conference. The libraries would generate FUSE compatible worksheets that OIRS would complete with information provided by the department spreadsheets. These worksheets were then sent back to the libraries for review and ingestion into FUSE. This cycle continued with additions and corrections up to the actual day of Furman Engaged!, thus allowing a fully updated listing of the day's events.

Reflection

Undergraduate research that is integrated into the liberal arts curriculum is a hallmark of the Furman Experience. In October of 2016, the Council on Undergraduate Research recognized Furman with its Award for Undergraduate Research Accomplishment, highlighting our integrative research program that actively incorporates students into the research agenda and publishing endeavors of the faculty.[4] While Furman Engaged! is a student-centered event, many of the posters and presentations are derived from faculty-led research. This provides a valuable learning experience for students, but a complicated ethical position for sharing the work online in FUSE. From a showcase and archival perspective, we would like to provide full-text access to all the Furman Engaged! works. However, faculty members may not feel that the research, as presented during Furman Engaged!, is appropriate for dissemination or harbor concerns of their research being published prematurely. On the flip side, departments may want to highlight all of their student work, but copyright and FERPA limitations require permission from the students. This is not an uncommon situation for libraries working to showcase undergraduate student work in the institutional repository. To balance these concerns, the libraries took a conservative, dual-permission approach to full-text posting of Furman Engaged! events. After Furman Engaged!, students were emailed and asked to provide the following: the full-text document of their presentation/poster; their permission to post the full-text document online; and identification of any faculty mentors or collaborators with whom they worked. Departments were also contacted to solicit full-text documents and corresponding faculty permission. All presentations where faculty mentors could be identified required both student and faculty permission for posting full-text to FUSE. While cumbersome, this process has served to alleviate faculty concerns while still enabling full-text sharing when appropriate.

In terms of the delivery of the actual Furman Engaged! event, little has changed. The main impact has come from the use of FUSE as a means of archiving student work, linking to faculty research, and providing an externally accessible platform to share the best that Furman has to offer in terms of student research and creative endeavors. The outward-facing nature of the platform has also raised new considerations in terms of scholarship. For example, one goal was for students and faculty to freely share their research and class projects with a broader audience. This was not necessarily an initial consideration or goal when Furman Engaged! was conceived in 2009. For Furman Engaged! 2016, more than eighty artifacts (posters, presentations, etc.) were uploaded online. While this number is impressive, it represents less than 20 percent of the total presentations given at the 2016 event. To increase full-text availability for Furman Engaged! 2017, the libraries and OIRS hope to secure permission for full-text from faculty and students on the front end rather than asking after the event. It is the hope that this approach will increase full-text participation. OIRS and the libraries can use fall and early spring meetings and communications used previously to simply introduce the Furman Engaged! presence in FUSE to push for full-text inclusion. This would also offer more time and venues to explain the implications of broad, open-access distribution of scholarship. There are many benefits to Open

Access publishing for students and faculty, though the collaborative nature of the underlying research and the impact of publication in FUSE on future research plans are nuances that should be carefully considered. By proposing publication at the beginning of the process, faculty and students will have more time to balance these concerns. Since there are some past Furman Engaged! presentations available full-text in FUSE, we have several authentic examples to show faculty and students what the interface would look like, how it integrates with discovery tools like Google Scholar, and what readership metrics are available.

In addition, the successful partnership created by integrating Furman Engaged! into FUSE has opened additional collaboration opportunities. Using the knowledge gained from linking this platform with the Furman Engaged! event, the team explored the opportunity to use a similar platform to enhance the delivery of the South Carolina Junior Academy of Science (SCJAS) Annual Meeting. John Kaup became the executive director of SCJAS in 2014 and discussions on the transition of Furman Engaged! created a natural model for SCJAS. The expansion of the collaborative work to this additional endeavor has provided an enhanced experience for nearly 500 South Carolina high school students that attend and present their research at the SCJAS Annual Meeting. The unique nature of the conference required an additional series of meetings to strategize and brainstorm the best approach for SCJAS. Much like Furman Engaged!, the SCJAS project expands the benefits of student research into an institutional repository presence. In the case of SCJAS, however, the archival nature and full-text possibilities go beyond Furman to reach high school students and teachers throughout the state of South Carolina.

The integration of Furman Engaged! into FUSE has also gained notice from University administrators. There is interest across campus on capturing student work and empowering students to reflect upon these experiences. The ability to retain, refine, and share learning objects throughout a student's education could serve a dual role of providing a strong accreditation program for the university as well as providing tools for the students to demonstrate competencies for graduate school, job applications, and other post-graduation opportunities. The expansion of Furman Engaged! has offered one model for achieving this goal and has started conversations between the university libraries and university administrators on how the libraries could play a larger role in meeting a key institutional goal to enable students to demonstrate and document their educational transformation throughout their Furman experience.

Assessment

Acquiring feedback from faculty and departments on the integration of Furman Engaged! into FUSE has informed future workflows. Although Furman Engaged! is a student-focused event in which undergraduate students present their research and creative endeavors, it is largely driven by campus departments. An initial desire to shift the submissions from the departments to the students (a potentially large advantage in workflow) was unsuccessful for two reasons. First, the submissions were coming from two different sources: the submission form in FUSE was submitted by students and the spreadsheets were submitted by departments. These two sources caused conflicts and, in some cases, duplication in the system itself, resulting in a convoluted and ineffective approval and publishing workflow in FUSE. Second, the departments have historically served as the main driver in Furman Engaged! participation, and they were resistant to change the submission workflow.

Another departure from previous practice that has created friction related to how FUSE displays the Furman Engaged! presentations. As indicated above, Furman Engaged! includes more than fifty oral sessions held throughout the day. These sessions typically focus on a specific department or course, and within each session are multiple fifteen-minute presentations with three or more student presenters. Historically, the Furman Engaged! website simply listed the names and times of the entire oral sessions. However, FUSE allows for greater granularity and provides a listing at the presentation level. This is a departure from how students and faculty have traditionally looked for these events on the website. While OIRS and the libraries can force some groupings of events, this middle category of department/class event does not fit well within the platform. It has been challenging to maintain the prominence of the session title within the FUSE platform and evidences one of the potential challenges of fitting an existing event into a new, preformatted online system. Since 2012, a smaller format print program has been used that depicts the oral session titles and location and depicts the names of all student presenters without any individual student presentation titles. Continuing with the abbreviated print program has helped bridge this concern.

One of the most important lessons of the collaboration between the libraries and OIRS has been the realization that FUSE is a true partnership tool, not just expanded infrastructure. To maximize the benefit of its services to the entire campus, the libraries must provide a higher level of expertise and time than initially expected. It became evident after the first year that to continue the successful partnership with Furman Engaged! and grow other areas of the repository would require additional, dedicated personnel. A temporary staff position in the libraries was restructured as a permanent Digital Projects Specialist with a significant portion of the position dedicated to supporting

FUSE projects. This additional support within the libraries will allow us to continue to expand our partnership with OIRS and other FUSE participants, providing a high level of service and final products that meet or exceed expectations.

Recommendations/Best Practices

Reach out directly and regularly to potential partners. Highlight the potential benefits of working with the library and demonstrate examples from similar programs. Sometimes the message just needs to be heard at the right time or in the right venue to spur a response.

Take the amount of time and personnel you plan to commit and double it. Partnering, rather than simply supporting, requires devoted work from the libraries and it will take longer than you expect.

Prepare your partner for pushback. There has always been resistance to change, even when it is for the better. If the libraries and their partner(s) are prepared for pushback, their united front helps move projects forward more easily.

Don't force an existing program to fit within your repository. While there are modifications that you can make to complement the structure of the program within your system, some elements may never fit. It's okay to combine legacy practices with new online options.

Conclusion

By proactively marketing the various services of the institutional repository and reaching out to existing programs on campus, we were able to connect with OIRS to expand access to an important undergraduate research program while linking the program to ongoing institutional efforts to document/share student success. There isn't a secret approach that created this new venture; it was simply a willingness from the libraries to reach out with an offer. This opened up a channel of communication, exploration, and collaboration that has benefited the students, the department, and the Furman Engaged! event.

While the Furman Engaged! event itself has not changed significantly, our partnership with OIRS has breathed new life into the organization, delivery, and future dissemination of student work presented within this venue. The true transformation has been forging a strong partnership between central support units like OIRS and the libraries. Both offices have gained a connection that improves their provision of services, enhances the campus experience for Furman Engaged!, and opens doors to continue serving students, faculty, and administrators across the university.

Notes

1. David E. Shi, *The Bell Tower and Beyond: Reflections on Learning and Living* (Columbia: University of South Carolina Press, 2002), 6.
2. "Furman Engaged!" http://scholarexchange.furman.edu/furmanengaged/.
3. Florida State University, "Showcase of Undergraduate Research Excellence," http://diginole.lib.fsu.edu/islandora/search/?type=edismax&collection=fsu%3Ashowcase_of_undergraduate_research_excellence; Clemson University, "Graduate Research and Discovery Symposium (GRADS)," http://tigerprints.clemson.edu/grads_symposium/; Cleveland State University, "Octavofest," http://engagedscholarship.csuohio.edu/octavofest/.
4. "CUR Recognizes Campuses with Characteristics of Excellence in Undergraduate Research," *Council on Undergraduate Research*, accessed October 17, 2016, http://www.cur.org/cur_recognizes_campuses_with_characteristics_of_excellence_in_undergraduate_research/.

Bibliography

"CUR Recognizes Campuses with Characteristics of Excellence in Undergraduate Research." *Council on Undergraduate Research*. Accessed October 17, 2016. http://www.cur.org/cur_recognizes_campuses_with_characteristics_of_excellence_in_undergraduate_research/.

"Frequently Asked Questions." *Council on Undergraduate Research*. Accessed October 17, 2016. http://www.cur.org/about_cur/frequently_asked_questions_/.

Shi, David E. *The Bell Tower and Beyond: Reflections on Learning and Living*. Columbia: University of South Carolina Press, 2002.

CHAPTER 19*

Connecting Students to the Research Lifecycle and to Each Other:
Planning an Event to Support Undergraduate Journal Publishing

Heather Buchansky and Graeme Slaght

Introduction

All too often, undergraduate student journals are temporary, producing one or two issues over a couple of years, and then disappearing. Some student journals have managed to publish consistently for years, proving that these publications can be sustainable. Are there ways the library can support growing or already established undergraduate publications? Are there ways the library can facilitate a conversation among student journal editors in order to learn from the successes of their peers in the area of student journal publishing?

---

* This work is licensed under a Creative Commons Attribution 4.0 License, CC BY (https://creativecommons.org/licenses/by/4.0/).

This chapter outlines the planning and implementation of library support for student-run journals at the University of Toronto, a large research university with a full-time enrollment of approximately 69,700 undergraduate students[1] across three affiliated campuses: Downtown (St. George), the University of Toronto Mississauga, and the University of Toronto Scarborough. The focus will be on the planning goals and objectives of the University of Toronto Libraries' Student Journal Forum, held in October 2015, to support undergraduate student-run journals across disciplines, as well as continued journal support after the event.

Background

The idea for formal undergraduate journal support began with a phone call from an undergraduate student journal editor in spring 2014 wondering if and how the publication she edited could be included in the library's collection and made available in the catalogue. The conversation spurred an internal discussion regarding the types of publishing support already present in the libraries and not available elsewhere on campus that could aid in student journal production. For example, University of Toronto Libraries' Scholarly Communications and Copyright Office has expertise in the use of copyright images and Creative Commons licenses. In addition, the library's Information and Technology Services department hosts an open access journal management and publishing system, Open Journal System (OJS), that may be of interest to student journal editors looking to ensure their content is stable and searchable online. University of Toronto Archives and Records Management Services, which seeks to collect various records of the university, is also interested in preserving any print runs of student journals in their collection.

The current publishing support provided by the library includes librarians and archivists whose roles as functional specialists may not have established student connections across campus. The library wanted to bring the publishing resources and services together to make them more visible and promote them directly to undergraduate student journal editors. Our initial step, however, was to do an environmental scan of the student journals across the university campus: how many active (published an issue within the last two years) student journals exist at the University of Toronto? Were liaison librarians already involved in supporting student journals in their subject area? And, if so, could that support be formalized and scaled up?

Surveying the student journal publishing landscape at University of Toronto was a tedious task; there was no existing centralized list. The most straightforward way to determine the range of publications was to search departmental and student union websites and ask subject liaison librarians if they were aware of student journals in their discipline area. We found that while a small number of liaison librarians supported student publications by assisting with OJS support, there was no formal or informal support for student journals offered by any library unit or other divisions at the University of Toronto.

Over the course of 2015, the planning group discovered additional library-sponsored student research events. For example, speed research networking sessions were held to bring together like-minded graduate and undergraduate researchers in specific disciplines. Also, the Student Journal Fair, held at John M. Kelly Library at the University of St. Michael's College in the University of Toronto, was organized in fall 2014 to bring student journal editors together for faculty talks and to learn more about the editorial process. Elements from both of these models served as the impetus of the Student Journal Forum, planned as a day-long event to bring together student editors working on both recent and well-established student publications to present and connect with one another. One key to the Student Journal Forum would be to showcase already existing library resources and services to students, how the library supports the research lifecycle, and, alternatively, to provide the librarians with a more nuanced understanding of students' research needs. The planning group hoped that after attending the event, future and current student journal editors would be connected to new ideas as well as resources within the library to help develop or sustain their publications. In particular, attendees would gain a richer understanding of scholarly communications and copyright issues and best practices that even some professional journal editors find perplexing (e.g., author's rights management, fair use/fair dealing, and Creative Commons licensing). The planning group also hoped that attendance would encourage student journal editors to learn more about being active and sophisticated producers, instead of consumers, in the knowledge and research process.[2]

Partnerships

A Student Journal Forum planning group was formed that included functional specialists with expertise in online repositories, copyright, and outreach. The team consisted of a student engagement librarian, copyright librarian, institutional repositories librarian, and an instruction librarian from a federated college library at the university, and home to a large number of student journals. The planning group used the list of known journals compiled to contact current student journal editors at the university with a "save the date" email for the upcoming event. The form included a survey to solicit session topics (Appendix 19A). Through the invitation, the planning group received an unexpected surprise—experienced student editors volunteered to deliver presentations to their peers.

In the planning and partnering phases of the initiative, the group felt it was important students be at the front and center of the forum. The event format was designed with two main ideas in mind: to encourage increased interaction among student journal editors across the university and to elicit peer-to-peer learning by inviting student journal editors to showcase their expertise around various aspects of the student journal publishing process. Student presentation topics included best practices for successful and sustainable journals, delivered by student journal editors from a well-established publication (circa 1923!), as well as journal production and design from a cinema studies journal (Appendix 19B). In addition, librarians provided short presentations to facilitate some discussion around several essential issues, including peer review, copyright, author's rights, and the technicalities of journal production software. A faculty member was invited to speak about his experience as a writer and editor for well-established literary and scholarly publications. During the last session of the forum, student journal editors gathered informally to talk about their publications in a "show-and-tell" style. This established a community of practice, facilitating reflective discussions among student journal editors about their own experiences, including successes and issues they have encountered that would be of interest to other editors.

Reflection

The Student Journal Forum was an inaugural effort to combine a student outreach program with information literacy education in scholarly communication topics such as copyright, author's rights management and licensing, as well as in practical issues in journal publishing and production. As with most first attempts at something new, there were many lessons learned. The event involved the creation of a new ad hoc partnership among librarian functional specialists in student engagement, information technology services, and scholarly communications and copyright. This group was formed to plan and execute the event and will re-assemble in the planning of similar events in the future.

Another challenge facing the group has been to find the means and time to continue to work together even without the impetus of an upcoming event. One way that the planning group could make its partnership more tangible is to make it an explicit infrastructure or service within the library with articulated long-term and multi-year goals, allowing the group to engage in service planning or strategy more frequently. The group's first priority following the event has been to target student groups and associations involved in journal publishing in order to expand the reach of library programming beyond the audience of the forum.

Collaboration with students to showcase their already successful and sustainable journals at the University of Toronto was the most rewarding part of the planning team's work. Part of what the group of librarians learned in working with students was a sense of humility in the face of the many longstanding undergraduate research activities taking place across the University of Toronto community. For example, one of the forum's participants, the University of Toronto Medical Journal (UTMJ), has been publishing regularly since 1923. In considering how the libraries could develop a program that would support both longstanding *institutions*, such as the UTMJ as well as newer or prospective journals. Combining structured sessions taught by the librarians with peer-to-peer instruction fit productively with the diversity of attendees from across the university and, indeed, it was the peer-to-peer learning opportunities that seemed to be the most successful. While the librarian-led sessions were given high marks in our follow-up survey, it was clear the most engaging and productive sessions were those facilitated by the student editors. The student-led sessions tended to elicit more questions and address practical topics important to students. The informal show-and-tell session allowed for networking and information exchange regarding the varied practices and funding models supporting student publishing initiatives across the university. Other ways to support undergraduate researchers that we had learned about in the existing literature, such as supporting the creation of a new publication to disseminate undergraduate research,[3] or embedding scholarly communication information literacy focused on publishing into academic liaison work, seemed unnecessarily remedial given the overall maturity of the undergraduate publishing community at the university.

The planning group learned that in light of the diversity of the existing community, as well of the absence of already existing formalized programs (whether library-led or not) to support student publishing, one of the most impactful steps librarians could take was simply to engage in the accounting for and bringing together of existing publishing activities on the three campuses. The lesson here is by acting as a convenor and provider of meeting time and space, a library can have a significant impact on the student publishing community. One reason for the lack of a pre-existing central infrastructure for the support of student publishing at the university is its relatively decentralized structure compared to North American schools of its size. Many specialized programs (especially in the humanities) that might support student publications are based at federated colleges. These colleges have their own independent libraries and specialized student outreach programs, which may or may not offer services or involvement in supporting student publishing.

Within such a context, information gathering about student journals became a time-consuming and time-sensitive task. In the lead up to our event, the planning group discovered that one federated college, the University of St. Michael's College in the University of Toronto, had planned a similar event, the Scholarly Communications Retreat, scheduled only two weeks prior.[4] The Student Journal Forum planning group included a librarian involved from another federated college (Victoria University), where many undergraduate student publications are based or had longstanding affiliation with student groups or faculty members. Given these challenges, as the group worked to build the attendee list for the event, it realized that the libraries could play a meaningful role by performing an information gathering function. In the end, the planning group's work of locating and verifying the existence of a student publications for the purposes of outreach allowed us to build the most comprehensive list of ongoing student publishing activity at the university that has yet existed.

Positioning the library as a hub at the center of student publishing affords a number of benefits for student journal editors. First, it demonstrates the investment the library is willing to contribute to the success of student publishing and research at the university and introduces students to the library's role in publishing. Second, it promotes the sharing of the librarian's expertise on valuable topics in scholarly communication, journal production, and journal sustainability and stewardship. Positioning the library in this central, convening role aims to build the resources for a permanent infrastructure to underpin a community of practice at the university, one focused on collegial discussion and literacy in issues in scholarly communication and publishing. The persistence of such an infrastructure is of particular value given the constantly changing population of student journal editors.

On a practical note, planning a full-day event in the middle of the term made it difficult for students to attend every session. Also, there will be an ongoing challenge of maintaining a connection with the student journal editors in order to continue to keep the cohort informed. One solution was to create a dedicated Student Journal Publishing LibGuide[5] that would keep current student journals editors updated on any future events.

Assessment

After the event, the planning group sent out a ten-question survey via email to registered participants, six of whom responded (Appendix 19C). Attendance at the event varied throughout the day, which the planning group had anticipated would make the distribution of a hard copy survey challenging. As with most free events, registration exceeded actual attendance, but in this case, not significantly (forty-six attendees, fifty registrants). It may be worthwhile to send out the surveys more than once next time as timestamps on the received responses were all marked immediately following the time the emailed survey prompt was sent. It is likely that a reminder or two would have collected more feedback. While the survey sample was small, the feedback data has nonetheless been instructive to the planning group's approach to reviewing the event, to the decision to hold it again, and to the process for instituting changes in advance of its next iteration. All students were satisfied with the event, with half saying that they were "very satisfied." The timing of the event (early in the academic year) was rated positively, possibly because many student editors were in the planning and orientation stages of their editorial roles. Each session was listed at least once under "most informative," suggesting to us that the content presented at the event was appropriate and informative.

The planning group also examined usage data collected through our Student Publishing LibGuide, which was launched immediately after the event. This examination has shown that the "Journal Directory" has consistently ranked as the most-viewed asset within the site (other than the homepage), suggesting that the result of the information gathering process discussed above continues to be of value to members of and units within the University of Toronto community, as well as others outside the institution who might be interested in a snapshot of student journal publishing activity. Another aspect of measuring the event's success has been the tracking of follow-up questions and consultations in order to measure whether the event increased student engagement with relevant library services. The group has found that is has, particularly surrounding issues of copyright, Creative Commons licensing, and the use of institutional repositories and applications for the hosting of student journals. In total, the event produced nine meaningful engagements, including six with students interested in using our Journal Production Services (JPS) for the online publishing of journals. As a result of these inquiries, three new journals were set up, two new and one a re-activation of a journal previously on a long hiatus. In one case, one of the members of the planning group was invited to give a talk about issues in scholarly publishing for a graduate student professional development workshop, and advised on a publication they were planning to launch. Two more consultations resulted regarding the possible use of Creative Commons licenses for student publications and one more regarding copyright issues involved in the photographing of University of Toronto facilities and publishing the photographs in a student publication. Finally, ongoing assessment related to planning the next version of the event has included the identification of potential collaborators across the university, including outreach to active student groups, to other library units, and to the University of Toronto Division of Student Life.

Recommendations/Best Practices

After the first iteration of the Student Journal Forum, the planning group identified key takeaways to apply to future events, as well as evidence of ideas that worked well based on the feedback. Best practices learned from the event include:

- Work in a cross-departmental team across the library who have a vested interest surrounding student scholarly contributions is important and will leverage knowledge and experience. The events provided a rare opportunity for scholarly communications librarians, in particular, to engage directly with undergraduates.
- Look beyond the library for potential campus partners (e.g., literary clubs) with expertise, interest, and established connections with student publishing groups.
- Solicit student feedback before and after the event to help inform the structure and topics: What are students expecting? What types of scholarly communication issues are students interested in learning? What will be most interesting to them?
- Remember the importance of peer-to-peer learning and allot sufficient time for this type of activity, including time for students to talk to one another and share their publishing experiences.

Conclusion

University of Toronto Libraries will continue to support student journal publications, either by way of in-person events, such as another iteration of a Student Journal Forum, and by expanding the online resources student journal editors are interested in and making these available through the dedicated LibGuide.

While listening to the presentations and the questions received from students in the audience, it was clear student journal editors had a firm understanding of certain areas related to the scholarly communication process more than others. Peer review and the editorial process were widely understood; however, issues pertaining to copyright, Creative Commons licensing, and permissions issues were areas that novice student journal editors had neither heard of nor considered. In planning future events or support around student journal production, librarians will continue to provide instruction on these complex issues, as well as include experienced student journal editors in the conversation.

Appendix 19A: Initial E-mail to Student Journal Editors

Hello,

University of Toronto Libraries is currently planning a Student Journal Forum, to be held on Thursday, October 22, 2015 at Robarts Library. Based on last year's Student Journal Fair at Kelly Library, this year's event will include short talks throughout the day on various topics related to the undergraduate journal process.

We are currently planning a list of topics that will hopefully be of interest to your journal team, including:
- open access and copyright issues (including use of visuals and graphics)
- journal design (for online and in print)
- best practices of successful student journals (and how to maintain your journal)
- peer-review process

If there is any other topic you may be interested in, please email your suggestions to heather.buchansky@utoronto.ca

We appreciate your ideas and feedback and will be sending out more information related to the event in the following weeks.

Thank you,

U of T Libraries Student Journal Forum Committee

Appendix 19B: Student Journal Forum Program

Time	Session	Speaker
10:00–10:10	Opening Remarks	
10:10–10:40	Peer-Review Process	Richard Carter, Reference Librarian, Kelly Library
10:40–10:50	Break	
10:50–11:20	Best Practices for Successful and Sustainable Journals	University of Toronto Medical Journal
11:25–11:55	Copyright and Open Access	Graeme Slaght, Copyright Outreach Librarian
11:55–1:00	Lunch	
1:00–1:35	Faculty insights on the Editorial Process	Professor Mark Kingwell
1:40–2:10	Electronic Publishing with Open Journal System	Mariya Maistrovskaya, Institutional Repositories Librarian
2:15–2:45	Journal Production and Design	Camera Stylo
2:45–3:00	Break	
3:00–4:30	Journal Clinic and Networking Show-and-tell of participating student journals with time to get feedback on your publications. Please bring copies of your journals if you want to participate.	Various student journals

Appendix 19C: Survey Questionnaire

Student Journal Forum Feedback

Thank you for attending the Student Journal Forum, hosted by the University of Toronto Libraries. We are interested in your feedback on this event. Please take a moment and let us know your thoughts. Note: All responses are anonymous.

The following statements pertain to your involvement with the Student Journal Forum.

	Not at all	**Somewhat**	**Moderately**	**Mostly**	**A great deal**	**No opinion**
The forum introduced me to knowledge and skills I can apply in my journal publishing.						
The forum made me want to get more involved in journal publishing process.						
I enjoyed learning from other student journals during the show-and-tell networking session.						

How would you rate your overall experience at the Student Journal Forum?
- Very satisfied
- Satisfied
- Neither satisfied nor dissatisfied
- Dissatisfied
- Very dissatisfied

Which session(s) did you find most informative?
[text box]

Is there any content or information you would like to see presented in future events? Please explain.

Based on your experience at the Student Journal Forum, would you attend a similar event in the future?
- Yes
- No
- Unsure

When would be a convenient time of year to attend a similar event such as the Student Journal Forum? [text box]

What is your current involvement with student journals?
- I am on an existing editorial board
- I am interested in reviving a journal that has not published for 2+ years
- I am looking to start a new student journal
- I am a faculty advisor
- Other [text box]

How did you first hear about the Student Journal Forum? (check one)
- E-mail
- E-newsletter
- From peers / other journal editors
- Social media
- Posters
- Other [text box]

Notes

1. University of Toronto, *Quick Facts*, https://www.utoronto.ca/about-u-of-t/quick-facts.
2. Alan Jenkins, "The Role of Research in University Teaching, the Potential of Undergraduate Research for Student Learning, and the Importance of Students Publishing Their Research," in *How to Start an Undergraduate Research Journal*, ed. Alexis Hart (Washington: Council on Undergraduate Research, 2012), 1–18.
3. Sharon Weiner and Charles Watkinson, "What Do Students Learn from Participation in an Undergraduate Research Journal? Results of an Assessment," *Journal of Librarianship and Scholarly Communication* 2, no. 2 (2014), accessed September 3, 2016, doi: 10.7710/2162-3309.1125
4. St. Michael's College in the University of Toronto, *Scholarly Communications Retreat*, https://stmikes.utoronto.ca/event/register-for-the-scholarly-communications-retreat-on-october-6-2015/.
5. University of Toronto Libraries, *Student Journal Publishing*, http://guides.library.utoronto.ca/student_journals.

Bibliography

Jenkins, Alan. "The Role of Research in University Teaching, the Potential of Undergraduate Research for Student Learning, and the Importance of Students Publishing Their Research." In *How to Start an Undergraduate Research Journal*, edited by Alexis Hart, 1–18. Washington: Council on Undergraduate Research, 2012.

Weiner, Sharon, and Charles Watkinson, "What Do Students Learn from Participation in an Undergraduate Research Journal? Results of an Assessment." *Journal of Librarianship and Scholarly Communication* 2, no. 2 (2014). Accessed September 3, 2016. doi: 10.7710/2162-3309.1125.

CHAPTER 20*

Reward Research, Benefit All:
The Case of the Library Undergraduate Research Award at Kennesaw State University

Ariel Turner and Aajay Murphy

Introduction

In the fall of 2015, the Kennesaw State University (KSU) Library System implemented an Undergraduate Research Award (URA). For this project, the library partnered with an existing journal, the *Kennesaw Journal of Undergraduate Research (KJUR)*. The KSU Library System's URA comprised of two submission requirements: an undergraduate research article submitted to the *Kennesaw Journal of Undergraduate Research* and an essay documenting the research process and use of library resources. Both the article and the essay were read and reviewed by a team of judges consisting of students, faculty, and library faculty and staff. The first winning essayist, as determined by the team of judges, received a $500 prize and was guaranteed publication within

---

* This work is licensed under a Creative Commons Attribution-NonCommercial-ShareAlike 4.0 License, CC BY-NC-SA (https://creativecommons.org/licenses/by-nc-sa/4.0/).

the *Kennesaw Journal of Undergraduate Research*. The winner was also celebrated at the Symposium of Student Scholars and Undergraduate Research Reception, which is an annual event celebrating student scholarship. Financial support from the university's Office of Vice President for Operations & Chief Information Officer/Chief Business Officer was vital in the establishment of this award.

The benefits of establishing such an award are twofold: it not only highlights the research achievements of students but is also useful for improving the research experience, as it provides important qualitative data on students' research habits. This sort of data can help to inform the library's future research instruction practices. Students who submit their research and essays also receive individual, constructive feedback. Additionally, the essays provided by students featuring the library contribute potentially powerful leverage for funding and additional support from library stakeholders. While essays painting the library in a positive light can serve as effective marketing, essays decrying a lack of resources can also be useful in soliciting additional funding.

This chapter documents the process of KSU's URA implementation, from idea to practice. The authors, who coordinated the award, discuss the details of creating the award, methods, and timing of marketing the award to the KSU community, partnerships, and collaborations with other campus entities, the methodology behind a rubric used to assess award essays, and the process of and technicalities of identifying and communicating with judges. Following the first year of this award, the authors also explore lessons learned, best practices for future undergraduate research awards, and potential for expanding the URA.

Background

Kennesaw State University is Georgia's third largest university, with a student population of approximately 33,000, encompassing undergraduates, graduates, and doctoral students.[1] The KSU Library System serves the entire student population, with just over thirty librarians and twenty paraprofessionals. In 2012, the library instituted a liaison program, assigning each librarian to one or more undergraduate programs, typically dependent on the librarian's educational background or other strengths. KSU's liaison program has served as an essential part of the library's increasing involvement with undergraduate research, as it requires librarians to foster relationships that form the basis of the library's campus outreach, and pairs students with the librarian best suited to assist them with their research needs. This focus on improving the educational and research success of KSU's undergraduate students served as an important foundation for the URA.

Inspiration for this award came from speaking with colleagues at the 2015 Association of College and Research Libraries (ACRL) Conference and from researching similar pre-existing programs at other institutions. The concept of an undergraduate research award was pioneered by the University of California, Berkeley Library in 2002.[2] Other institutions with similar award programs include the University of Michigan and the University of Washington, to name just a few. The concept of such an award is simple: reward undergraduate researchers while highlighting the importance of the library in undergraduate research. Inspired by these programs, the authors began planning in the summer of 2015 by investigating potential campus partnerships, coordinating marketing of the award, and procuring funding for the award.

Undergraduate students from any point in their academic career were encouraged to submit for the award, so long as they were either still enrolled or had graduated within the year. No limitations were put on their submissions, as the content was to speak for itself. Reviewers were set to task to filter out works based on the requirements and purpose of *KJUR*, as one of the central prizes was publication in the journal. Because of this, papers for courses, independent research projects, or works created directly out of research programs were accepted.

Partnerships

Collaboration was key to the success of this initiative. With a student population as large as KSU's, the project's success depended on many different groups of people to develop, promote, review, sponsor, and execute the award. Through this project, the library developed and built on relationships extending beyond the award and repositioned the library as a focal point in undergraduate research. Specifically, the library worked closely with the organizations and people who were already championing undergraduate research on campus, and reached out to others for support and involvement, which ranged from contributing to marketing efforts to donating prizes.

A central component of the inaugural award was collaboration with the *Kennesaw Journal of Undergraduate Research*. The *KJUR*, an open access, peer-reviewed journal that aims to promote undergraduate research, is hosted on the university's digital institutional repository, the Digital Commons. The journal also served as the home for the award. *KJUR* provided not only the platform for publishing the research papers and supplemental essays but also the back-end infrastructure for submission and review of the entries.

A major contributor to the project was Dr. Amy Buddie, director of undergraduate research in the Center for Excellence in Teaching and Learning

(CETL) at Kennesaw State. As the editor and manager of *KJUR* since 2011, she was an essential early partner and champion of the award. Through Dr. Buddie and her role within CETL, the award coordinators were able to connect with the Undergraduate Research Club and the Faculty Council of Undergraduate Research, from which they recruited reviewers for the award submissions. Without Dr. Buddie's partnership, it would have been much more difficult to secure funding for the award, and the award would have lacked its publishing component.

One potential bottleneck for the project, as can often be the case for peer-reviewed journals, is the review process. The award coordinators solicited interested reviewers from library faculty and staff, and, because of the strategic partnership with Dr. Buddie, the Undergraduate Research Club and the Faculty Council of Undergraduate Research. From the pool of volunteers, the award coordinators selected reviewers with backgrounds from diverse disciplines. Reviewers were given a rubric to aid their reviews of the submissions, which the award coordinators created prior to accepting submissions (Table 20.1).

To create the rubric, the coordinators reviewed criteria and rubrics for other undergraduate research awards, which are typically posted on each respective library's website. The coordinators also consulted and incorporated the publication expectations and guidelines of the *KJUR*. The rubric used four categories to assess the submissions: research strategies, topic development, depth of sources used, and quality of writing. The intention of the rubric was to provide the reviewers with an unbiased means to assess both the article submitted to the *KJUR and* the supporting essay. For the inaugural year, the rubric was intentionally broad and followed a points-based system to allow for flexibility in assessing an unknown quantity with regard to the submissions. Three of the four categories of the rubric focus on research, but because one part of the award itself is peer-reviewed publication, a writing quality assessment was also deemed important. With Dr. Buddie's permission, the award coordinators integrated the award criteria into *KJUR*'s publishing schedule. The inaugural award winner was published in the fall 2016 issue of *KJUR*.

Table 20.1
Undergraduate Research Award Rubric

Research Strategies	Topic Development	Depth of Sources Used	Quality of Writing
1—No research performed	1—Topic unclear	1—No sources consulted	1—Writing is confusing and inarticulate, with many spelling and punctuation errors
2—Applicant performed only a very basic search on topic, using an aggregate search tool such as Google	2—Topic either somewhat limited or broad	2—Use of disreputable source such as Wikipedia, or a single source	2—Writing is somewhat unclear, with spelling, grammar, and punctuation errors
3—Applicant demonstrates some ability to expound on initial topic keywords and has executed more thorough searching	3—Applicant makes some salient points on topic, but topic could use more refining or expounding	3—Use of 2-3 authoritative sources, or wide range of sources including some disreputable sources	3—Good basic writing with some minor errors in punctuation, spelling, or citation
4—Applicant has mastered advanced search options and appropriate keyword searching for the topic	4—Topic clearly defined with appropriate depth and important points addressed	4—No disreputable sources included, but potential for more research evident	4—Excellent writing with a few minor typos or citation errors

Table 20.1
Undergraduate Research Award Rubric

Research Strategies	Topic Development	Depth of Sources Used	Quality of Writing
5—Extensive researched performed: applicant has consulted multiple sources and/or worked with a librarian, and has established strong keyword searches appropriate to the topic	5—Thoroughly developed topic: advanced, complex topic	5—Excellent sources: applicant demonstrates a depth and variety of sources consulted and demonstrates ability to evaluate sources	5—Excellent writing: applicant is articulate and demonstrates a carefully crafted thesis. Lack of typos and spelling errors throughout

Source: Ariel Turner and Aajay Murphy, 2015.

Library staff involved with the award attended meetings of the Undergraduate Research Club and worked with the liaison program coordinator within the library to help promote the award through liaison outreach and library instruction sessions. Some librarians also served as reviewers for the award. The liaison program coordinator, a key partner in the project, was later offered a position as the co-editor of *KJUR* with Dr. Buddie as a result of her involvement in the award process.

Reflection

One aspect of the award's inaugural year that worked particularly well was the involvement of CETL and the opportunity to present the award at the symposium. Featuring the award at the symposium served as great marketing to an audience of potential future award winners, while also underscoring the importance of the library throughout the research process. The president and provost of the university were in attendance and both gave remarks about the award. Additionally, there is great potential to leverage the positive publicity received by the library at such a high-profile campus event and secure future award benefactors. The award coordinators are optimistic about the potential to expand the award, with the possibility of offering a scholarship as a grand prize in the future.

The coordinators learned several important lessons over the course of the inaugural year of the KSU Undergraduate Research Award. Marketing for the award centered around the $500 prize, so the coordinators waited to market the award at all until funding had been secured, which was not until November of 2015. Because the award would be presented at KSU's Symposium of Student Scholars and Undergraduate Research Reception in April, this left only five months to solicit submissions, review submissions, receive feedback from the panel of judges, select a winner, and iron out the details of presenting the award. One of the essential takeaways from the first iteration of this initiative was that the project required a longer timeline. Additionally, a number of details lacked sufficient planning at the end of the award process, e.g., securing a presenter for the award, ensuring that the award money was physically available to present, and securing a photographer for the event.

Beyond learning how to better organize the award process, there were other important takeaways from the process. A beneficial consequence of the award was an increased understanding on the library's role in supporting undergraduate students as they pursue a research project. The essays allow the library to gain perspective for how the students are using library resources and, therefore, how the library might be able to adjust its research instruction, reference services, collections, and marketing thereof in order to better serve undergraduate researchers. In the future, a larger submission pool would help the library by furthering the library's understanding of how students across disciplines perform research, so better marketing of the award in the future is essential.

The collaboration between the library and CETL was vital to the success and continuation of the program as a whole. Prior to the URA initiative, the only direct involvement between the two organizations was the hosting of *KJUR*, CETL's project, on the library's Digital Commons platform. Incorporating publication in the *KJUR* as a prize gave the initiative a crucial, innovative element thanks to the collaboration with *KJUR*, and in return the library was invited to participate in reviewing articles for the 2016 issue. Without CETL and its positive reputation and relationships across campus, the award would not have earned the level of support and prestige it needed to move forward and succeed.

Assessment

Feedback from the panel of judges served as a valuable evaluation tool in the first year of this project. This feedback included suggestions for two separate rubrics to assess the research article and the essay independently. Judges also expressed some confusion about where to upload the final review and rubric. To address this in the future, the coordinators plan to create a one-page document for judges that will clearly state their responsibilities and provide directions for uploading. Additionally, the small number of submissions received compared to KSU's sizeable undergraduate population served as its own feedback that the award needs to be marketed more effectively. This is hopefully something that will be improved upon with marketing strategies over a longer period of time. The publicity the award received at the symposium should also increase the number of submissions in the future.

An additional consideration going forward is to stress the mentioning of the library, librarians, and library resources in the research essays. One would hope that, given the library's importance to research, it would play a central role in the research process for students, but the essays submitted did not consistently reflect that. Potentially, for future awards, the library could require that those submitting an essay meet with a librarian for a research consultation, which would also presumably serve to improve the quality of research.

The additional short essay on library use provides an opportunity for students to clearly highlight the ways in which they use library services and resources. The inaugural winner, Angelica E. Perez states, "The library system and research databases at KSU gave me the tools I needed not only to learn more about the subject matter I was choosing to write about, but also to help bolster my respective arguments."[3] It is the hope that year after year of hosting this research award will result in a bank of similar assessments of the library's services and resources that could be used to leverage increased institutional support both for undergraduate research on campus and for the library.

Recommendations/Best Practices

A fundamental aspect of the award's success was building partnerships across campus. Collaborating with groups on campus, including research centers, departments, student groups, and publications, is highly recommended. This has the dual benefit of increasing visibility and support of undergraduate research as well as improving the library's role in undergraduate research. The success of the initiative rests on impactful outreach strategies. As the program coordinator, it is essential to be prepared to do most of the organizational work, to communicate effectively with potential collaborators, and follow through successfully. Approaching a possible campus partner with a solid plan, enthusiasm, and willingness to do the work makes it much easier to achieve buy-in.

The award has also significantly impacted the library. As a direct result of the URA and collaboration with other campus groups, the library has a renewed and increased focus on undergraduate research. Since the conclusion of the first award, a KSU librarian has become co-editor of the *Kennesaw Journal of Undergraduate Research*. She has used this connection to encourage liaison librarians to review submissions within their disciplines, significantly increasing the efficiency and activity of the journal, and expanding the role librarians play as undergraduate liaisons. The library also expects this to translate to an increase in participation and attendance at the annual KSU Library System Author's Reception, now that the inaugural URA winner has been invited as a published author. Additionally, the experience has made KSU's Digital Commons editor more aware of the desire for undergraduate journals, and the Digital Commons has started initial steps in creating more undergraduate journals this year with departments, colleges, and individual faculty across campus.

There are three crucial lessons the authors learned from this process. The first is that increasing the dialogue regarding undergraduate research and expanding its visibility on campus is extremely important. Shortly after developing the award program, KSU was granted the opportunity to host the 2019 National Conference of Undergraduate Research. Additionally, the library was able to establish a leading role in KSU's new focus on undergraduate research, which established credibility and future possibilities. The second lesson learned is that there are always new ways to involve the library more closely in undergraduate research. For example, the library could be the home for the monthly meetings of the Undergraduate Research Club; or, if the space is available, the library could host a research symposium. The opportunities are endless. The library on any campus should take a strong role in the entire undergraduate research cycle, not just as a place to conduct the research. The third and final lesson is that successful undergraduate research requires support from everyone including the institution, professors, students, and libraries. Research at the undergraduate level benefits every partner within the academic environment in different, yet profound, ways which are equally as impactful to academic pursuit as providing space for students and participating in academic publishing process.

Conclusion

At any institution, librarians should be the first resource that any researchers, from undergraduate students to faculty, should consult when starting, working through, or finishing a research project. Unfortunately, that is not often the case. Through small initiatives such as this research award project, libraries can foster and help to develop the skill sets required for students to successfully navigate the increasingly complicated research cycle from conception to publication.

Appendix 20A: Undergraduate Research Award Guidelines

Guidelines and information for the award are hosted here: http://digitalcommons.kennesaw.edu/ura.html. This webpage details the process, winnings, requirements, the rubric, and essay examples from other universities. The submissions process requires the undergraduate researchers to create a profile within the Digital Commons, digitally sign an article submission agreement, supply metadata for the research article, and upload both the article and essay.

The essay guidelines and requirements for the inaugural year were as follows:

- The essay must accompany the research project submitted to the *KJUR* for publication consideration.
- The essay must range between 500–750 words.
- The essay must describe the research process: selecting and narrowing a topic, keyword searching, finding and evaluating sources, and the results.
- Applicants must be currently enrolled or recently graduated undergraduate students at KSU.
- By applying, applicants allow *KJUR* to publish/share the essay, as well as the research paper, if successful.

Notes

1. "About," Kennesaw State University, accessed September 9, 2016, http://www.kennesaw.edu/about.php.
2. Jennifer L. Bonnet, Sigrid Anderson Cordell, Jeffrey Cordell, Gabriel J. Duque, et al., "The Apprentice Researcher: Using Undergraduate Researchers' Personal Essays to Shape Instruction and Services," *Libraries and the Academy* 13, no. 1 (2013): 37–59, https://muse.jhu.edu/.
3. Angelica Perez, "Library Research Essay 2016 KJUR," *Kennesaw Journal of Undergraduate Research* 4, Iss. 1, Article 4 (2016), http://digitalcommons.kennesaw.edu/kjur/vol4/iss1/4.

Bibliography

"About." *Kennesaw State University*. Accessed September 9, 2016. http://www.kennesaw.edu/about.php.

Bonnet, Jennifer L., Sigrid Anderson Cordell, Jeffrey Cordell, Gabriel J. Duque, et al. "The Apprentice Researcher: Using Undergraduate Researchers' Personal Essays to Shape Instruction and Services." *portal: Libraries and the Academy* 13, no. 1 (2013): 37–59. Accessed September 8, 2016. https://muse.jhu.edu/.

Perez, Angelica. "Library Research Essay 2016 KJUR," *Kennesaw Journal of Undergraduate Research* 4, Iss. 1, Article 4 (2016). Accessed November 4, 2016. http://digitalcommons.kennesaw.edu/kjur/vol4/iss1/4.

CHAPTER 21 *
Sharing Student Research:
Student Colloquia at University of South Florida St. Petersburg

Camielle Crampsie and Kaya van Beynen

Introduction

University of South Florida St. Petersburg (USFSP) has experienced substantial growth, evolving from a regional campus largely under the management of the University of South Florida (USF), to an autonomous and separately accredited institution within the USF system. During the 2015/16 academic year, USF St. Petersburg served nearly 5,000 students enrolled in twenty-four undergraduate and seventeen graduate degree programs. In 2014, USF St. Petersburg developed a new strategic mission across all academic units that emphasized undergraduate research and experiential learning. To complement this new strategic direction, the Nelson Poynter Memorial Library (NPML) reasserted its role as an active partner in teaching, research, and learning for the students, faculty, and staff while identifying new avenues to contribute to the strategic goals of student research and fostering experiential learning. This chapter describes the inception and development of a successful student colloquia at USFSP's Poynter Library by placing this series within the broad-

---

* This work is licensed under a Creative Commons Attribution-NonCommercial-ShareAlike 4.0 License, CC BY-NC-SA (https://creativecommons.org/licenses/by-nc-sa/4.0/).

er context of how library professionals can nurture, sustain, and strengthen relationships between students and their professors, position the library in the center of scholarly life at the institution, connect student research activities with successful presentation techniques, build bridges between town and gown, and provide students with a platform to share their experiences.

Background

USFSP celebrates "Research Month" each April with a series of events ranging from panel discussions, faculty research lightning talks, and an undergraduate student poster symposium. The poster symposium seemed to focus more on secondary research rather than original primary research that USFSP undergraduate and graduate students have conducted with greater frequency in recent years. The library was not part of the poster symposium but identified an opportunity to develop a student presentation series designed to 1) offer a campus-based initiative to highlight original student research and 2) provide students with the experience of giving a professional presentation to a friendly audience. To fill this gap, the NPML launched a student research colloquium series.

The NPML Student Colloquium was organized as a monthly event during the fall and spring semesters, expanding beyond "Research Month." Each session featured two to four students presenting their research in conference-style PowerPoint presentations. Individual presentations are approximately ten to fifteen minutes in length followed by a question-and-answer session. The librarians recruit student presenters, organize the colloquium, publicize the events internally and externally, and create a warm and welcoming experience for students, their peers, faculty, and the general public.

Originally, only student researchers were asked to participate. The majority of participants were undergraduate students engaged in original research or fieldwork, mostly from the Psychology, Anthropology, Environmental Science, and Florida Studies programs. However, the colloquium quickly expanded to highlight additional types of student work. Representative examples of this expansion include artwork created by an English/graphic design student, a reading of a play written by an English student, and an African news website created by a journalism student.

When librarians heard informally that students were increasingly participating in internships, civic engagement activities, and other forms of experiential learning, the student colloquium seemed like an ideal place for the students to talk about those experiences. For example, one colloquium featured student participants in a popular "Road to White House" course that required students to travel to New Hampshire to volunteer for the presidential primary candidates in the New Hampshire primary. Five students representing five different presidential campaigns spoke about their experiences. Other student colloquiums focusing on experiential learning gave students an opportunity to discuss their fieldwork experiences, such as the students who presented on their archaeological work in Belize and Ethiopia.

As the nature of original student work changes or expands with new programs and strategic focus, likewise the NPML student colloquium has continued to evolve. By presenting their research, fieldwork, or creative products, students share their knowledge and activities while the library continues to affirm its support of students and its place as the core of research and learning at the institution.

Partnerships

The library both hosts and coordinates the student colloquium. The colloquium is always held in the library presentation space and the library staff manages the setup and technology. Additionally, the library faculty work closely with colleagues across the colleges at USFSP to recruit participants so partnerships with student groups, individual faculty, Student Services/Student Affairs, and University Advancement are critical.

With Student groups

To develop the programs, librarians connect with students by using student-run social media portals, and connecting with disciplinary organizations, such as the anthropology and psychology student clubs. Students receive support from library liaisons and faculty mentors in developing their programs, locating resources to strengthen their presentations, and learning skills related to the academic enterprise that many students at larger institutions may not experience until entering graduate programs.

With Teaching and Research Faculty

After the first year of hosting the student colloquium, the librarians realized how important conversations with the teaching and research faculty were in discovering possible presenters for the colloquium. Networking is a crucial part to the success of this program. Near the end of the semester, faculty came to the library and asked if their students could present in the upcoming student research colloquia. Some of the faculty members had been approached earlier in the semester about their students presenting, but did not feel their students were ready yet. Other faculty had just heard about the colloquium and thought it would be a great opportunity for their students. This made organizing presentations at the end of the semester, when students were finishing up projects, much easier for both the librarians and the students. This networking opportunity also gives the library and the teaching and research faculty the opportunity to be aware of our shared commitment to the academic experience. These conversations created awareness of areas in the library collection that required additional resources as well as providing for new opportunities for the library to increase services that are offered to benefit certain types of research and learning experiences. As the library already hosted a university digital archive that contained student work, creating a new collection based on the pictures and presentations from the student colloquium provided an opportunity for institutional preservation as well as an opportunity for students to be able to get their work out and share their accomplishments.

With the University Study Abroad Program:

The coordinator for the University Study Abroad program approached the librarians looking for a way to promote student exchanges and class trips abroad. This partnership benefited both sides: the library learned about a group of students that were happy to share the stories of their trips to France, Italy, Germany, and Vietnam while the colloquia helped the Study Abroad program spread the word about the opportunities to travel and learn about other cultures. Students discussed topics of food, wine, and German business strategies, and one student presented a film he made of his semester in France.

With University Advancement and Marketing Department:

Dissemination of student presentations occurs through a variety of forums to preserve student scholarship and as a public relations tool. When possible and appropriate, portions of the presentations become part of Digital USF-SP, an institutional repository that allows them to share research with others throughout the world. Only presentations where the student has full copyright are included, whereas presentations that include unpublished research, frequently in collaboration with faculty supervisors, do not get included in the archive. University Advancement uses the colloquia as a source for uplifting stories on student achievements; thus, the library's role in supporting student research is publicly celebrated in the local media and assists in the university's broader capital campaign. Additionally, this partnership has spilled over to library events beyond the student colloquium, as the university's public relations staff vigorously promote other library events and activities.

Reflection

Part of the intent of the student research colloquium is to showcase the wide range of research and projects being done by the USFSP community. After the first year of student presentations, librarians noticed an obvious gap in student presenters from the College of Business (COB). To better understand why, one of the librarians spoke to several COB faculty to try and identify possible students engaged with original research. The conversations with COB faculty led to a clearer understanding of the needs of the students, the resources they use in their research, and how the colloquia could benefit the COB. Instead of conducting qualitative or quantitative research, many of the COB students worked with community organizations on applied research, such as developing marketing plans, branding campaigns, gap analysis, etc. Not wanting to neglect the students' product from an entire college, the librarians expanded the colloquium focus to include these presentations. A marketing campaign developed by a student for a nearby farmer's market became the first COB student presentation resulting from this expanded effort. Highlighting presentations of community engagement work also helped to align the colloquium with the university's strategic goal of partnerships and the university's commitment to the local community.

Florida Studies is an interdisciplinary program of distinction at USFSP, and many of the students frequently work with librarians on locating unique archival and historical materials. In the process of visiting the library's Special Collections and University Archives, some of the students have learned about the colloquia experience and have shared their research on topics such as the history of stock car racing in Florida and the narrative descriptions of early Spanish conquistadors.

As the library is the center of all of the programs at the university, we strive to recruit presenters representing a broad spectrum of programs. It is always very special when we have presenters from very disparate programs present within the same colloquium, especially when the presenters and audience engage with each other, find commonality as students and scholars, and have fun learning about something new. Within just one program, it is evident just how diverse the interests and research areas are at USFSP.

Student and faculty collaborative research is an initiative the university seeks to institutionalize and the student research colloquium serves as an outlet to spread the word about the work the faculty members and the students do together. As such, the NPML colloquia helps to bring to light that undergraduate students have an important role in faculty scholarship, aiding in data collection, analysis, and other elements of research.

The student research colloquium has also helped to build a strong sense of community at USFSP. Learning about the undergraduate research experiences has inspired new students to get involved in research. When students lack awareness of research opportunities, they may not know that such opportunities exist for their interests. The colloquium helps fill a void and meet the undergraduate research and experiential learning goals of the university while also preparing undergraduates for graduate programs. As some graduate programs require undergraduate research experience as a requirement for entry, participation in the colloquium gives students another way of demonstrating participation in undergraduate research other than publishing.

The NPML colloquia has also given students a platform for sharing their stories and experiences. Providing this opportunity boosts student self-confidence as well as rewards and acknowledges the work they have accomplished. It shows that students are making connections in their community and gaining new experiences, and in some cases, building international relationships. The presentations demonstrate the array of opportunities available for students to experience in and beyond the classroom and hearing student stories can act as testimonials to the reach and impact of USFSP.

Assessment

Throughout, the librarians involved in the NPML Student Colloquium have assembled a growing array of metrics to document participation and impact. Similar to all events, the marketing librarian tracked number of student presenters and colloquium attendance. Based on these metrics, the team was not sure whether efforts to find student presenters and organize the colloquium were worth the event attendance, so it was unclear whether the library would continue the program. However, despite being a pilot program, the student colloquium had received extremely positive attention from the university administration.

The next year, the librarians involved decided to continue the student colloquium, but to track additional benefits to the library and university. These additional benefits included positive media mention of the library. University Advancement came to rely on the colloquium as an easy way to find up-lifting stories about USFSP student achievements. As such, the library received great publicity on the university website, the student newspaper, and in the university e-newsletters. In addition, students, particularly from the anthropology, English, and biology programs, started to use the colloquium as a place to practice before presenting their research at a local, state, and even one international conference. Thus, the students could present their work in a less stressful forum, receive feedback, and improve their presentation before communicating at a more professional conference.

One unexpected but tangible benefit of the NPML Student Colloquium was connecting students to university donors. Thus far, two university donors have visited the colloquium to see the student research that they either already funded or that they intended to sponsor. The first donor sponsored a student trip to Spain for the student to spend the summer doing research at the Archivo General de Indias in Seville. The colloquium provided a forum for the donor to see the outcome of her donation and provided University Advancement with a photograph and news story of the student thanking the donor. The second connection came after a group of students had conducted research measuring the university's solar energy use. The faculty supervisor identified a potential donor, but needed a forum to persuade the donor to fund the students' travel to a conference in Paris, France. The NPML Student Colloquium provided this forum, and at the end of the students' presentation, the donor agreed to fund the conference travel. Both opportunities are examples of reasons why getting the word out about the colloquium, particularly to University Advancement, is so important. Because the library has the ability to bring students, faculty, university advancement, and community members together in a congenial forum, we send the message to the university administration and the community that we are an essential partner in supporting undergraduate research.

Recommendations/Best Practices

Through trial and error, we have come up with a list of best practices that guide our implementation and management of the Student Colloquia. Use these suggested recommendations to guide your own student research presentation series:

- Document presentation guidelines. Have a form that clearly outlines the presentation format and the hardware and software capacity of the presentation space.
- Regularly touch base with faculty. Key faculty frequently have undergraduate students doing original research; however, these faculty might not have the library and the student colloquium at the front of their minds. Informal conversations are a great way for the librarians to stay abreast of new student projects and remind faculty of the student colloquium.
- Keep a long-term vision on when students are willing and able to present. At the start of the research cycle, a student usually needs to do a thorough literature review—a phase where many students approach a librarian for research help. In contrast, students only want to present when they have nearly completed their analysis and writing. A long-term vision should keep in mind that that today's help-seeking students might become tomorrow's presenters.
- Be flexible with dates and times. Originally, the student colloquium took place on the second Wednesday of the month at noon, but after the first year of low attendance, the colloquium adapted for more

flexible scheduling. This made it easier to secure presenters, increase audience attendance, and attract nontraditional and commuter students. Additionally, the Doodle Polls scheduling tool helped coordinate the availability of multiple presenters.

- Timing is everything. The end of the semester is easier to get presenters because research projects are nearing completion and students feel more prepared to present.
- Partnership goes both ways. Take good quality photos of the presenters, their supervisors, and the audience. Share these photos with the partnering departments and with university advancement so that they too can claim credit while enabling other areas of the university to tell the library's story.
- Archive evidence of the student colloquium. Items to archive may include student PowerPoint slides, marketing flyers, other documents provided, and photographs from the event. Provide release forms or secure permissions from presenters before publicizing or placing content in the institutional repository. This collection tells the story of the library's effort into the future. Additionally, opportunities may arise when evidence of the library's activities to support student work will be needed to promote the library or the university in the future.

Conclusion

While the monthly Student Colloquiums usually only feature two presenters with an average of twenty people in the audience, these examples document the program's positive impact on the growth of the students' understanding, publicity for the library, and university fundraising efforts. Working in partnership with people and departments across the university, the Nelson Poynter Memorial library is able to successfully recruit student speakers eager to share their stories of research, field work, study abroad, and experiential learning. By providing a conduit for students to share their original research and experiential learning activities, the library truly becomes the center of scholarly life at the University of South Florida St. Petersburg.

Acknowledgments

We would like to acknowledge and thank James Schnur for his contribution to helping us prepare the proposal for this chapter and his in-depth institutional knowledge. He was a founding member of the team that started the USFSP Student Colloquium Series and his connections helped make it successful.

CHAPTER 22*

Teaching Integrity in Empirical Economics:
The Pedagogy of Reproducible Science in Undergraduate Education

Norm Medeiros and Richard J. Ball

Introduction

Professors and librarians choose careers at liberal arts colleges to forge meaningful relationships with students. A frequent and positive byproduct of this student-centered engagement is collaboration between professors and librarians on the provision of research services. Such collaboration is often a function of the library liaison model, a common organizational structure in college libraries that assigns a librarian to each academic department. Our collaboration began in this modest way, with associate librarian of the college providing guidance on acquiring data and appropriate literature for students in the associate professor of economics' introductory statistics course. Our collaboration has since grown into a curriculum development and outreach initiative that promotes the integration of transparency and reproducibility in the research training of students in the social sciences.

---

* This work is licensed under a Creative Commons Attribution-NonCommercial 4.0 License, CC BY-NC (https://creativecommons.org/licenses/by-nc/4.0/).

Background

This collaboration, which we now call Project TIER (Teaching Integrity in Empirical Research), grew out of two initiatives that were underway at Haverford College in the early 2000s. Although these activities began independently of one another, combining them in a novel and productive way became the basis for Project TIER.

The thesis repository. One of these initiatives was the creation of an online archive of senior theses written by Haverford undergraduates. Haverford is distinctive in that every student writes an independent senior thesis, and in 2002 the college libraries established an online repository to preserve and make public all of these projects.[1] It has become a firmly established institution, and uploading PDFs of the theses of all graduating students is now a standard part of the yearly workflow of the libraries. The librarian has been the primary developer and administrator of the repository since its inception.

Guidelines for documenting student research. At the same time, another initiative was developing the economics introductory statistics course. Students in the course are required to write research papers involving original analysis of data obtained from public sources, and the librarian works closely with them to provide assistance finding previous research on their chosen topics as well as reliable sources of data. When this research paper requirement was introduced in 2000, the results were not entirely satisfactory. In most cases, the students' descriptions of the original data they had started the project with, the steps they had taken to process the data to prepare them for analysis, and the analytical procedures they had performed on them were opaque or completely garbled. Follow-up conversations indicated that the problem was not just a matter of poor exposition or writing style but that students' own understanding of the data they had worked with and what they had done with it was often shaky.

To address this problem, we developed a set of guidelines intended to help students better understand the statistical work they do for their projects, and thereby enable them to describe and interpret their research more clearly in their papers. The focus of these guidelines is on implementing the data processing and analysis for a project by writing and iteratively revising editable command files, rather than by using drop-down menus or interactively executing one command at a time. The guidelines also give specifications for a set of electronic documents—including the original data used in the study, the command files they write, and supplementary information that serve as comprehensive replication documentation that an independent investigator could use to reproduce all their reported results. When students turn in their final papers, they are also required to submit the electronic documentation. It took some trial-and-error to develop a workable set of guidelines, but after several years we had arrived at a formulation that students were able to implement with little difficulty and a high rate of success. And as a result, the clarity of exposition and quality of argument in the papers students write in the introductory statistics class have improved as we had hoped. We have also introduced these research documentation guidelines to our senior thesis students in the economics department. Every year, several of our advisees follow the guidelines while they conduct research and then submit the prescribed replication documentation with their final theses.

Student documentation meets the thesis repository. The potential synergy between the online thesis repository and the new guidelines for the documentation of student research might have gone unnoticed had it not been for the fact that the librarian was closely involved in both initiatives. Inspired by Lynch's proposition that librarians need to think of digital objects as a distinct class of resources that present curators with novel opportunities and challenges rather than just as electronic manifestations of printed documents, he recognized that the practice of simply posting PDFs in the thesis repository could be enriched.[2] And the replication documentation we had begun teaching students to prepare for their theses (including data in multiple formats, computer code in several languages, etc.) presented an opportunity for doing so. The data and code for a research paper are certainly not just digitized versions of static print documents; they are of value only if users are able to interact with them creatively—to download, run, edit, and experiment with them. So, beginning in 2010, we put Lynch's idea into action by posting the replication documentation for selected economics theses along with the PDFs in the DSpace repository. In that first year, we posted replication documentation with three of the theses added to the repository, and the number grows each year.[3]

A tale of two platforms. DSpace has proved to be an excellent choice of platform for the Haverford College senior thesis repository. Several features, such as its robust metadata capabilities and the ability of search engines to discover materials posted there, make it an ideal platform for archiving completed projects. Through our experience advising students, however, we discovered the need for a more nimble and interactive tool for managing and sharing files throughout the process of conducting a research study. DSpace was designed specifically to support digital archives and lacks several features we deemed necessary for regular student engagement, such as an easy-to-use graphical interface for moving files, a means of authorizing individual and groups of students to have read/write access to their projects without having the same access level to other students' projects, version control, and the means of creating a directory structure to support students' visualization of the protocol. What's more, we sought an open repository that could be used by other instructors as a way of fostering a community around Project TIER.

After experimenting with several platforms, we found that the Open Science Framework (OSF), a tool developed by the Center for Open Science (COS), is ideally suited for our purposes. On the OSF website (www.osf.io), users can create accounts instantly and for free, and then are able to create "projects" for particular research topics or studies they are working on. Each project is represented by a page where files can be uploaded and downloaded, and multi-level hierarchies of folders can be created and modified easily to create whatever directory structure is most convenient for the user. The OSF provides greater functionality and structure than common tools like DropBox and Google Drive, but students who don't have a background in programming find OSF much easier to use than platforms like GitHub that are popular among computer and data scientists. We also found OSF attractive because it can be synchronized with Zotero, a bibliographic management application promoted and supported by the Haverford College Libraries.

Reflection

Given all these advantages, we now routinely direct our students to create projects on OSF for the research papers they write in our introductory statistics class as well as for their senior theses. They begin by cloning a template project we have built on OSF, consisting of a set of empty folders organized according to the workflow and documentation guidelines we teach them (see Figure 1). Students gradually populate these folders with the documents they assemble and revise as they conduct their research. The structure provided by this template enhances students' conceptual understanding of what they are doing with their data, and the fact that everything is stored in the cloud facilitates collaboration among students working on group projects. Moreover, when students come to us for help with their research, being able to download their files to our own computers and explore them in detail dramatically enhances our ability to offer constructive guidance. By the time they finish their papers, some minor cleaning up of the documents they have accumulated on OSF is all students need to do to produce the accompanying replication documentation.

For Project TIER, OSF supports the workflow of students' research while in progress, whereas DSpace is used to preserve and deliver the finished products of this research at an institutional level. Project TIER is also using Dataverse, a repository developed and supported by Harvard's Institute for Quantitative Social Science, to provide an environment in which to showcase examples of reproducible student projects across the Project TIER network of institutions. Used together, these platforms support the many aspects of students' scholarly communication needs throughout the entirety of their research projects.

Figure 22.1
The TIER Protocol template in OSF

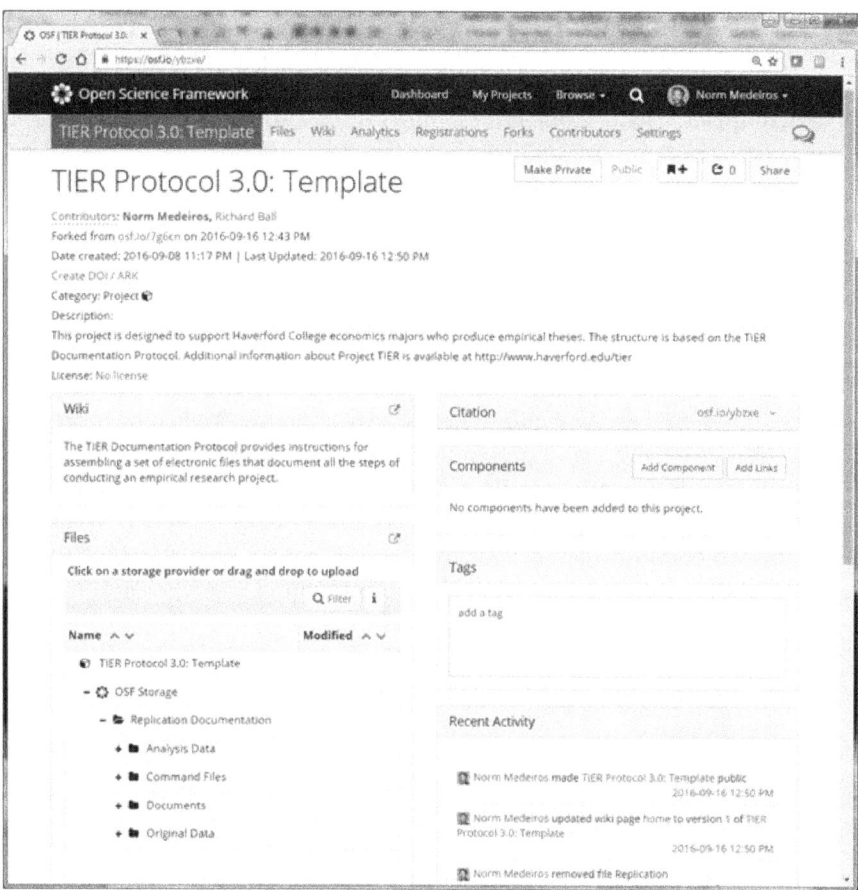

Project TIER

These positive developments led us to begin some efforts at outreach to other faculty and librarians who might be interested in teaching research methods that emphasize transparency and reproducibility, data curation, and the intersection of those two areas. We began by writing a paper about our experiences and received a start-up grant from ICPSR and the Alfred P. Sloan Foundation that allowed us to host two Faculty Development Workshops in 2013–14.[4] It was at that point that (borrowing from the title of our 2012 paper) we began calling this initiative Project TIER.

Thanks to further grant support, notably from the Sloan Foundation, we have been able to continue and expand the work of Project TIER. We continue to offer two Faculty Development Workshops per year, and in 2016 extended our outreach by visiting five graduate programs in several fields of social science to conduct workshops for doctoral students.[5] Through a program of annual TIER Faculty Fellowships, we are collaborating with leaders in research transparency and statistical education. These fellows are creating new curriculum that will be integrated into TIER's outreach efforts, organizing paper sessions at professional conferences, and working with us to evaluate the effectiveness of the pedagogical methods we are developing. More information about these and other activities are available on the Project TIER website (www.projecttier.org).

Project TIER is one of a surprisingly large number of initiatives for promoting research transparency that have emerged in just the last three to five years. Among the most prominent of these are the Berkeley Initiative for Transparency in the Social Sciences (BITSS) and the Center for Open Science (COS), but there are many others, all of whom interact and collaborate with each other extensively and productively. The niche we see for Project TIER is our focus on education and reaching students early in their professional development. We strongly subscribe to Thomas Carsey's view that "The best way to have an enduring impact on how research is conducted in the future is to affect how researchers are trained in the present."[6]

Assessment

The leading assessment measure for Project TIER is adoption rate. Our goal is to foster a network of instructors committed to using the protocol in whole or part to promote reproducible and transparent research methods in their classes. Our faculty workshops and other outreach efforts are geared toward maximizing the curricular impact of Project TIER. Our Faculty Fellows program, now in its second year, is a means of more forcibly promoting the mission and principles of our initiative. Fellows take a leadership role in Project TIER's outreach and curriculum development efforts, while at the same time adding their experience and expertise to strengthen and extend the protocol's application.[7]

Recommendations/Best Practices

Having instructed several dozen faculty and a small number of librarians on teaching reproducible research methods, we can attest that some of the most successful instances of classroom application have been when an instructor and librarian partner on provision of services. As we've seen firsthand, support for the data management aspects of TIER enables faculty to focus on the pedagogical benefits of teaching transparent research practices. Librarians can bring expertise to the creation of repositories, projects, and metadata that are the building blocks of open science. Our experience suggests that these partnerships can make all the difference when it comes to incorporating robust reproducible research methods into quantitative social science courses.

Open science initiatives at the scholarly and curricular level are increasing in quantity and scope. Subject liaisons and repository managers need to stay abreast of these initiatives and communicate directly with faculty and institutional grant offices to offer meaningful assistance. There's real opportunity in helping faculty colleagues consider open data repositories that comply with journal and funding agency mandates. To the degree faculty believe teaching transparent research practices will advance their students' understanding and application of ethical research conduct, librarians can take a leading role in describing dimensions of replicable research and guiding student and faculty use of tools and repositories that promote open science.

Conclusion

Our work in teaching computational reproducibility to instructors and students has helped us see the new opportunities in which data librarians should be involved. The traditional view of research data management as an activity that occurs after the completion of a research project neglects the opportunities we see in lifecycle data management; that is, teaching students that carefully managing data, computational code, and metadata should be inherent parts of the research process. Teaching undergraduates these skills provides benefits beyond just good organization; adherence to the protocol enhances students' understanding of their statistical analysis, as they are asked to describe the variables they are using and the exact steps they took to conduct their analysis. We believe taking a broader view of research data management, as we do with Project TIER, will provide numerous opportunities for data librarians to apply their expertise meaningfully.

Along the same lines, librarians need to make efforts to increase face-to-face interactions with the faculty and students they serve. For the past several years, the librarian has held weekly office hours in the economics suite as a means of gaining additional time with faculty and students. By being situated in the physical location of the economics department at Haverford, rather than waiting for faculty and students to come to the library, collaboration with faculty and consultation with students have both increased. This proactive approach to providing services is very much in keeping with the role data librarians need to assert in seeking out ways of supporting research data management activities.

Acknowledgments

We gratefully acknowledge support provided to Project TIER by the Alfred P. Sloan Foundation.

Notes

1. Subject to students' signing a release. This archive, which is built on the DSpace platform, can be accessed at http://thesis.haverford.edu.
2. Clifford Lynch, "Institutional Repositories: Essential Infrastructure for Scholarship in the Digital Age," *portal: Libraries and the Academy* 3, no. 2 (2003): 327–36.
3. See http://hdl.handle.net/10066/4899, http://hdl.handle.net/10066/6078, and http://hdl.handle.net/10066/4820 as early examples of senior theses built on the TIER protocol.
4. Richard Ball and Norm Medeiros, "Teaching Integrity in Empirical Research: A Protocol for Documenting Data Management and Analysis," *The Journal of Economic Education* 43, no. 2 (2012): 182–89.
5. These workshops were conducted for the economics departments of Duke University and Clark University, the University of Pennsylvania Department of Sociology, the University of Colorado School of Education, and the University of Colorado Institute for Behavioral Sciences.
6. Thomas M. Carsey, "Making DA-RT a Reality," *PS: Political Science & Politics* 47, no. 1 (2014): 72–77.
7. Selected comments from students about their experiences learning to conduct reproducible research in the classes of some past TIER Fellows can be found at http://www.projecttier.org/tier-classroom/student-testimonials/; a complete list of past TIER events, including conference presentations and paper sessions, is available at http://www.projecttier.org/events/.

Bibliography

Ball, Richard J., and Norm Medeiros. "Teaching Integrity in Empirical Research: A Protocol for Documenting Data Management and Analysis." *The Journal of Economic Education* 43, no. 2 (2012): 182–89.

Carsey, Thomas M. "Making DA-RT a Reality." *PS: Political Science & Politics* 47, no. 1 (2014): 72–77.

Lynch, Clifford. "Institutional Repositories: Essential Infrastructure for Scholarship in the Digital Age." *portal: Libraries and the Academy* 3, no. 2 (2003): 327–36.

CHAPTER 23 *
The Honors Colloquium at QCC:
A Decade of Excellence

Dale LaBonte, Denise Cross, Fyiane Nsilo-Swai, Matt Bejune, Susan McPherson, and Tiger Swan

Introduction

For a decade, the reference and instruction librarians at Quinsigamond Community College (QCC) have served as mentors to students in the Honors Colloquium, a semester-long research project. This interdisciplinary course (IDS200) is an undergraduate research seminar and serves as the capstone course for the Commonwealth Honors Program at the college. What grew out of a concern that students did not have the confidence or skills to persevere with sustained research developed into a collaboration between reference and instruction librarians and the instructors team-teaching the course. The collaboration established a formal mentoring program to match students with librarian mentors who work with them throughout the course. The desired outcome was student work that created new knowledge, demonstrated self-awareness in selecting appropriate approaches to research, and shared results to the campus community. Enthusiastic student and faculty feedback has contributed to the success of the project.

---

* This work is licensed under a Creative Commons Attribution-NonCommercial-ShareAlike 4.0 License, CC BY-NC-SA (https://creativecommons.org/licenses/by-nc-sa/4.0/).

Background

Quinsigamond is a community college centrally located in New England's second largest city, Worcester, Massachusetts. QCC enrolls a diverse student body with many nontraditional students, a number of whom participate in the Honors Colloquium. Students come to the Honors Colloquium from homeschooling, as high school students with dual enrollment, as military veterans, as refugees and immigrants, as foreign students, and from backgrounds of addiction, homelessness, and mid-life career changers. The one thing they have in common is their commitment to succeed in their studies.

The topic of the capstone course varies according to the material selected by the pair of faculty members team-teaching the course. One of the instructors has always been drawn from the English faculty, while the other teaches in a science or social science discipline. In the past, disciplines such as sociology, psychology, biology, and human services have been represented. Semester course titles range from "Eat the View" (about food, agriculture, and the environment) to "Re-writing Ourselves: An Exploration of Emerging Paradigms" (which considers advances in science, like epigenetics or transhumanism, as well as the intersection of science and culture, like the biology of belief). Having advance notice of course topics and key readings allows the librarians to note scholarly "stars" and identify top journals students should be sure to consult.

Like other community colleges, Quinsigamond has a significant interest in initiatives to mentor first-generation, low-income, or at-risk students for college success generally. Such a program had existed at Quinsigamond, according to Christine Clark's 1995 description.[1] This grant-funded project showed higher protégé satisfaction and retention, and an improvement of 30 percent in student academic performance, which a follow-up study found was sustained after completion and transfer. (Unfortunately, by a decade later we found no institutional memory of this initiative). As early as 1990, writing in the *Journal of Academic Librarianship*, Marina Snow advocated that librarians serve among the ranks of mentors for student success.[2]

As we looked for other mentoring programs, we found that many undergraduate programs existed for tutoring through peer mentoring. A few mentoring projects matched faculty with student researchers and, in the case of a University of New Hampshire study by Sharyn Potter and others, these faculty were working with students in a context similar to that of the IDS 200 course.[3] Many more examples of mentoring existed within various professions. Doreen Harwood and Charlene McCormack's (2008) internship model for attracting business students to the library profession offered an example of this approach.[4]

Hampshire College started a program to offer access to librarian mentors from students' first semester, with an eye to building relationships early in advance of the upper level, extended research required for the "Division III" thesis.[5] Hampshire later discontinued the practice because it demanded large time commitments, yet did not connect with a significant number of students.

The structure of our program was unique at its inception. Students select their own project, based on their personal interests or major, within topic choices designed to suit the course goals. Their work is guided by a course timeline that helps students pace the work on their investigations. During the second week of the semester, students attend an instruction session in the library classroom. The syllabus calls for an early draft of their thesis statement, a concept map to brainstorm the basic shape of the project, followed by a more formal outline and initial draft pages. At the end of the semester, students submit a formal paper and also present posters to share their findings with a campus-wide audience. Many of the students have also participated in an annual statewide conference open to undergraduates in the Commonwealth Honors Programs at the public colleges and universities in Massachusetts.

The faculty welcomed the librarians' expertise with information literacy and their willingness to guide the students' research. The co-instructors found the demands on their time to be significant. Helping students to master the course content and guiding the development of their papers, posters, or presentations precluded more individualized support for each project.

The faculty and librarians jointly establish a schedule of mentoring sessions intended to align with the semester timeline. Matching of students and mentors is based on mutual availability rather than the librarian's subject expertise. While this approach is arbitrary, team members have found that they can usually handle any topic students at this second-year (sophomore) level undertake. When the material is unfamiliar, the mentors relish the chance to explore the topic together with our students. Prior to the session, students sign up for open meeting times through an online poll. The initial one-on-one meeting is used to explore potential topics and to establish how prepared the students are to pursue their interests. The second meeting looks at the extent of the student's background investigation and leads to the development of a concept map to outline the topic. By the third meeting, the student's research should be well underway, with initial drafting of the research paper. Each of the student-librarian meetings is reviewed afterward, with each member of the pair sending feedback independently to the faculty.

Partnerships

Part of what makes our program unique is the collaboration between librarians and Honors Program faculty, which began as a set of conversations between the library reference and instruction team leader and a psychology instructor. The pair had worked for a year on embedding a librarian in an honors-level abnormal psychology course. As a result of the experience, they decided to expand the process and introduce it into the next colloquium. This early collaboration set the model for succeeding years.

The topic for the first seminar was "Human Rights," which students found challenging, compelling and, at times, overwhelming. They tackled difficult topics such as human trafficking, genocide in Sudan and Rwanda, child labor, religious persecution, and sweatshops. This first mentoring experience revealed to the librarians how demanding and satisfying it would be to work with students who relied on them for both research and emotional support. The librarians enjoyed the reaction of students who persevered with their projects and surprised themselves with the quality of their efforts. At the end of the semester, the students attended Quinsigamond's Liberal Arts Distinguished Lecture presented by Dr. Amii Omara-Otunnu, UNESCO chair in comparative human rights. He had been aware of the students' projects and, after the lecture, invited the students to discuss their findings with him.

The collaboration enjoyed the support of the library dean and, through her, of the Academic Affairs division, which also supplied institutional support for the Honors Program at the college. The project benefited from the ongoing involvement of Professor Susan McPherson, who chaired the program at Quinsigamond and now serves also as chair of the statewide Commonwealth Honors Program. Not only has she frequently acted as the English faculty member for the IDS course, but she has also regularly asked the librarians for their ideas on improving the course. This level of college backing assured the success of the mentoring partnership.

Both the Honors Colloquium faculty and the college librarians could see the need to support undergraduates pursuing original research. The early poster sessions were clear indicators that many students struggled to understand or embrace the challenge of undergraduate research. Bibliographies relied entirely on websites of questionable authority, and visual elements were often amateurish. Students could not articulate their project or the research process. For those projects using experiments, the work might be left unfinished, and for those based on field observations, the recording and reporting would fail to meet instructor expectations. During one of the early semesters, a co-instructor who at the time served as the English Department Chair, commented on the 2009 cohort in an email message. "…[T]he scholarly activity of locating and documenting materials demanded more time and effort than was evinced in their final papers. The kinds of sources were adequate, but I believe [the students] could have made an effort to reach deeper into more peer reviewed literature and/or discipline specific research."

Joint meetings between librarian and student set out to address weaknesses like these by inquiring about the students' needs for research help. Students have often told their mentors this was the first course for which they had written a research paper, used disciplinary sources, crafted an outline, drawn a concept map, or sustained an investigation. In general, students lacked the background to understand what was being asked of them and benefited from the guidance experienced researchers provided.

Reflection

The process between the students and the librarians evolved organically over time. As mentors, the librarians have three main opportunities for intervention: during the first meeting, the librarians conduct a thorough reference interview; at the second meeting, discussion revolves around selection of methodologies; and by the third meeting, mentors propose outreach to people with expertise in the area being studied.

Initially, the mentors engage in an extended reference interview.[6] This standard librarian tool is used to draw out the student's interest and intention. At the first meeting, students usually only have a vague understanding of what is being asked of them, either in terms of course material or the research process. The questions a mentor asks fit a pattern: What do you already know about the topic and what kinds of sources do you think would help you pursue it? Quite often, the students are unaware of how much they don't know and need the direction a mentor provides in suggesting how to proceed. Honors students are used to performing well in their studies, but beginning an investigation like this makes them feel uncertain and vulnerable. Through this discussion, a mentor works with each student to begin a search for background sources to focus the scope of the project.

A participant in the spring 2016 colloquium said when he looked through the list of topics suggested for emerging paradigms, he could not find anything on business and decided to settle for "cognitive computing." But then he found it daunting, not knowing how to proceed in a field with new information coming out daily. Ultimately, his mentor helped him to focus his research on the way businesses mine social media. Without the confidence-building guidance, a student like this might fall back on random websites rather than use a systematic search to find scholarly sources, government documents, or other reputable information.

The community college students we work with often plan to produce a timeline, a compare-and-contrast essay, or a description akin to an encyclopedia entry. Mentors also supported close reading of texts and analysis through disciplinary lenses. To narrow the focus and encourage independent thinking, the second meeting is often the point when mentors suggest methodologies. For the student who replaced a fast-food diet with home-cooked meals for "Eat the View," maintaining a diary was appropriate. Several students have reported on their participation in afterschool programs for children, documenting observations in these field settings. The student who wanted to refute a law of physics used mathematical equations to make his point. One student designed a community garden for the campus; another produced a video of interviews with farmers.

Mentors promote personal contact with researchers and authors, usually during the third mentoring session. One student studying folkways of the Hmong received invaluable assistance when a physician from a California hospital responded to her questions with information about the work done there welcoming non-"mainstream" healers. These interactions reveal scholarship is a conversation and demonstrate where budding researchers can contribute.

Often the most exciting projects are those with unexpected results. A student who wanted to advocate for the Falun Gong in China when she began her project had completely refuted her original thesis by the time she was ready to present her poster. Librarian mentors provide the support and encouragement for students to shift their focus as needed, even if that means the student realizes she has managed to disprove a hypothesis and needs to open new avenues of investigation.

In the early years, the project attempts were more hands-on and experiential, while in recent years the project has been reoriented toward a literature review incorporated into a fifteen-page paper. This re-thinking of the appropriate product for the course was based on the faculty's belief that the honors students needed the experience of writing a research paper to be ready for transfer to a four-year program. Recently, one of the seminars replaced the poster session with a formal panel-style presentation of ten-minute reports on the topic, often incorporating visuals. The librarians are comfortable with the traditional research paper, but enjoy supporting efforts like the original projects, involving experiments, participant observation, reasoned essays, or multimedia creations.

The most challenging aspect of the mentor role remains the effort to encourage students to deepen their investigations and analyses. Community college students bring varied interests, investigating everything from sports to brain activity; however, few have the academic background to delve into original research studies or evaluate experimental findings. The mentors embrace the opportunity to help these students find, interpret, and incorporate the literature relevant to their interests.

Assessment

Qualitative assessment of the program is built into the process. Before the semester starts, faculty meet with librarians to share their course objectives. After the semester ends, a follow-up meeting is held to discuss what worked and what didn't. These brief but important check-ins have reinforced to faculty the value of challenging students to produce high quality work. During the semester a sort of 360-degree evaluation occurs spontaneously: students often tell the librarians how delighted and inspired they are by the material they encounter in their course meetings, and the faculty often share their appreciation that the librarians have helped students persevere with difficult topics.

During the Honors Showcase poster session, held in the final weeks of the course, the campus community is invited to view the student work. This is an opportunity for the IDS faculty to hold conversations with their colleagues, sharing course goals and celebrating achievement. It also allows deans and the college president to speak directly with students as they tour posters. In the early days, this raised the profile of the library, with mentor guidance evident in the quality of the references students listed in their bibliographies. As the partnership continues, the showcase reminds faculty, staff, and administrators of this model of collaboration and demonstrates that students can contribute to scholarly conversations.

Formal external evaluation of our mentoring project occurred in the process of accrediting the honors program. The team was rewarded when a member of the accrediting team (2010) expressed his wish that something similar existed at all the colleges in the state's Commonwealth Honors Program. The report noted:

> Because the colloquia have been designed and are taught in close collaboration with the college's library staff, they provide students with a notably rich foundation in academic research. ***The research element of the IDS classes has potential as a model for undergraduate education in all CHP colleges.*** The college should be commended for the support of team teaching that promotes this high quality. The IDS classes certainly speak to an emphasis on library scholarship[7] [emphasis in original memo].

To date there has been no initiative to create a librarian mentorship support system for the honors research projects on every campus, although campus librarians are always ready to offer reference assistance—sometimes extensive—whenever students ask.

The one-on-one meetings are valuable but impose a cost: the librarians' time. At a minimum, a mentor spends 1.5 hours with each student over the course of three meetings. In reality, meetings are rarely less than forty-five minutes and may expand beyond the required three sessions to four or more. It is not unusual for extensive email exchanges to occur as well. Because of the library administration support, the time devoted to this has been incorporated into each librarian's workload. All the same, it would be difficult to expand this project significantly with current staffing levels. In semesters when the four librarians had six students each, the weeks when sessions occurred were often hectic and other meetings had to be postponed.

While the librarians have never held formal norming sessions to establish consistency in the mentoring activity, weekly team meetings have allowed airing of approaches and techniques.

The librarians post reports to the faculty after each meeting with students, helping the faculty to know when a student may be falling behind on research progress. Faculty could use the reports, along with those the students themselves provide, to evaluate mentor performance and offer feedback. To date, this has only happened in a very general and approving way in the post-semester wrap-up.

All the librarians are able to view the same mentor/mentee meeting reports they send to the faculty. This lets the team members comment when they have an observation about a project, recommending scholars to contact news or journal articles to pursue. Depending on the colloquium topic, it might be important to know as mundane a concept as the appropriate Library of Congress subject heading. Awareness of student progress also means one librarian can fill in for another when a student has a family crisis or health emergency and consequently asks for help outside the normal sequence.

To date, the team has been small and consensus-oriented, which has promoted consistency. If the program were to expand, or staff turnover increased, a more structured approach might be called for.

Recommendations/Best Practices

Regular feedback smooths the way. The pre-semester check-in between the librarians and the instructors helps to convey expectations about the course content. During the semester, librarian assessments of the mentoring sessions' progress let the faculty know students are on track. Student responses to the faculty signal comfort with their projects. After the semester, a final review with the faculty identifies any lingering concerns. Close collaboration among the librarian mentors also promotes professional growth as they share suggestions informally for ways to assist students with more challenging projects.

Evaluation criteria are essential. The Quinsigamond process evolved not so much from a prescribed form of evaluation as through a set of mutual understandings. These revolve around open communication channels, encouraging academic rigor and helping adult learners to engage with challenging material. Yet while seminar faculty can assess the mentorship advantage through coursework, and students regularly talk about its benefits, there has been no systematic external study. The campus outcomes assessment process could, through capture of the project artifacts or citation lists, provide evidence to support the claim that the mentoring relationship promotes scholarship. The campus office of institutional research might analyze student data or convene focus groups to study whether the seminar, with its mentoring component, fostered success later in students' academic careers and in their vocations.

Cross-disciplinary collaboration promotes esteem for library services. Most faculty members who have taught IDS 200 were already supporters of library services and proponents of information literacy instruction. As faculty from other disciplines with honors sections were informally exposed to the mentoring process, the librarians' social capital rose. These faculty and deans follow the success of students in their courses, attending the Honors Showcase where the student posters are presented. This visibility sustains and reinforces the value of the research projects and the mentorship component.

Conclusion

The library team members at Quinsigamond have been enthusiastic partners in the mentoring initiative, and the library as a whole has benefited from the involvement in the Honors program. Our scholarly horizons have expanded as we assisted students with their projects. We have learned about new fields, like epigenetics. We have found that what is old is new again, as in mindfulness meditation where ancient practices are reinterpreted through contemporary science. The library collections benefited as specialized seminar topics or individual projects prompted selections on slow food, ancient Olympians, and scientific paradigms. When projects had more experiential aspects, like food diaries or a video-recorded interviews with organic farmers, we investigated rubrics capable of assessing them and recommended these to the co-instructors. Perhaps most important, faculty members are regularly sharing their passionate interests with us, deepening the collaboration and fostering greater collegiality.

The collaboration between librarians and faculty and librarians and students over the last decade has raised the scholarship of capstone projects in the Honors Colloquium at Quinsigamond Community College. The instructors adopted librarian suggestions for assignment design and for course pacing to keep research progress on track. They welcomed the information literacy instruction librarians deliver first in a group session and then through mentoring, aware that this helps students to interpret course material and pursue high quality information. At the annual Honors Showcase, the campus takes note of the student poster sessions. Faculty, staff, and administrators applaud the quality of the projects undertaken as well as the supporting evidence the students present.

Students gained confidence in their ability to conduct quality research through mentoring by a librarian. The attitudes students adopt and the skills they develop in the research process are carried with them to future projects. The mutual fostering of the student's learning by faculty and librarian is a key component of the mentoring program's success. QCC librarians look forward to working with this cohort of researchers and making improvements to processes and measurements.

Acknowledgments

The authors would like to acknowledge the collaboration of Professor Melissa Tamas in the launch of the mentoring project with Fyiane Nsilo-Swai. Anne Pound, assistant dean of library services, provided unwavering institutional support and personal encouragement. As English faculty and department chair, Kathy Frederickson helped to establish the mentoring collaboration.

Notes

1. Christine Clark, "Innovations in the Mentoring Process," *Equity & Excellence in Education* 28, no. 2 (September 1995): 65–68.
2. Marina Snow, "Librarians as Mentor," *Journal of Academic Librarianship*, 16, no.3 (July 1990): 163–65.
3. Sharyn J. Potter, Eleanor Abrams, and Lisa Townson, "Mentoring Undergraduate Researchers: Faculty Mentors' Perceptions of the Challenges and Benefits of the Research Relationship," *Journal of College Teaching & Learning* 6, no. 6 (October 2009): 17–30.
4. Doreen Harwood and Charlene McCormack. "Growing Our Own: Mentoring Undergraduate Students." *Journal of Business & Finance Librarianship* 13, no.3 (2008): 201–15.
5. Bonnie Vigeland and Stephanie Willen Brown. "An Innovative First-Year Instruction Program at Hampshire College," *College and Research Libraries News* (Jul/Aug 2001): 717–19.
6. Stephanie Willen Brown. "The Reference Interview: Theories and Practice," *Library Philosophy and Practice* (2008).
7. Robert Darst, Susan Edgerton, Matthew Silliman, and David Winsper. *CHP Site Visit at Quinsigamond Community College, February 25, 2010* (Memorandum), (March 13, 2010).

Bibliography

Brown, Stephanie Willen. "The Reference Interview: Theories and Practice," *Library Philosophy and Practice,* (2008). Accessed April 30, 2012. http://www.webpages.uidaho.edu/~mbolin/willenbrown.htm.

Clark, Christine. "Innovations in the Mentoring Process." *Equity & Excellence in Education* 28, no. 2 (September 1995): 65–68.

Darst, Robert, Susan Edgerton, Matthew Silliman, and David Winsper. "CHP Site Visit at Quinsigamond Community College, February 25, 2010." Memorandum. March 13, 2010.

Harwood, Doreen and Charlene McCormack. "Growing Our Own: Mentoring Undergraduate Students. *Journal of Business & Finance Librarianship*," 13, no.3 (2008): 201–15.

Potter, Sharyn J., Eleanor Abrams, Eleanor and Lisa Townson. "Mentoring Undergraduate Researchers: Faculty Mentors' Perceptions of the Challenges and Benefits of the Research Relationship." *Journal of College Teaching & Learning*, v6 n6 (October 2009): 17–30. Accessed June 22, 2016. http://cluteinstitute.com/ojs/index.php/TLC/article/view/1131/1115.

Snow, Marina. "Librarians as Mentor." *Journal of Academic Librarianship*, 16, no.3 (July 1990): 163–65.

Vigeland, Bonnie, and Stephanie Willen Brown. "An Innovative First-Year Instruction Program at Hampshire College," *College and Research Libraries News* (July/August 2001): 717–19.

CHAPTER 24*

Transcribing Women's Diaries in the Digital World

Elizabeth A. Novara and Jessica Enoch

Introduction

A digital primary source transcription project is an important initiative both in supporting undergraduate learning and research, and in facilitating academic library collaborations and outreach on campus and beyond. The University of Maryland, College Park (UMD), currently enrolls more than 38,000 students, about 30,000 of whom are undergraduates. The University Libraries focus heavily on teaching information literacy skills and research methods to undergraduate students in a variety of disciplines. In the spring of 2016, a manuscripts curator from the libraries and an associate professor of English collaborated on a significant digital primary source transcription component for a course titled, "Women and Public Memory in Material and Digital Worlds." Undergraduate students in the course transcribed pages from a woman's Civil War-era diary, wrote reflection papers, and presented their projects to the university as at an Undergraduate Research Day poster session. Students also provided feedback on the newly released transcription site, "Transcribe Maryland," which was created by the libraries for classroom instruction and for use by the general public. This chapter highlights a useful and interesting way that special and digital collections can be better integrated into the undergradu-

---

* This work is licensed under a Creative Commons Attribution-NonCommercial-NoDerivatives 4.0 License, CC BY-NC-ND (https://creativecommons.org/licenses/by-nc-nd/4.0/).

ate classroom and addresses innovative practices to teach information literacy skills. This chapter should be of particular interest to academic librarians as well as teaching faculty in the arts and humanities and beyond.

Background

During fall 2015 and in preparation for the spring 2016 semester, the manuscripts curator, the English professor, and a systems librarian collaborated to compose the digital transcription site, "Transcribe Maryland." The systems librarian, as part of the UMD Libraries Digital Systems and Stewardship (DSS) Division, developed the technical aspects of the website, while the manuscripts curator selected primary source materials and provided the content. Several manuscript collections are available to transcribe on the site; however, the collaborators chose the Madge Preston diaries as the ideal collection for a digital transcription project for two main reasons. First, the diaries had already been partially transcribed and scholarship existed about the context of Preston's everyday life, and second, Preston lived outside of Baltimore, Maryland—a point of geographic similarity to many of the students at their institution that would likely interest them.[1] By having this contextual information at their fingertips, the professor and the curator believed the students would have a foundational base of general knowledge about Preston that would aid them in their transcriptions.

The following prompt guided students' work in the assignment, "Digitizing Women's Diaries":

> For this project, you will do the work of a public historian and make women's experiences public. Your task is two-fold. First, you will use a digital transcription tool made available through the UMD Libraries to transcribe and digitize Madge Preston's diary. Preston, a nineteenth-century Maryland woman, composed her diary while living through the American Civil War. Your work will be to transcribe five pages of her written diary into a digital format that will eventually be available to public audiences. Second, you will compose a four-page reflection on the transcription considering questions such as these: What was your response to the transcription process? What are your thoughts on making Preston's private writings public, especially within a digital context? How is it different to encounter her text as transcription and online rather than in original form in an archive? As you think through these questions (and others) you will also

consult the scholarship we read in this section of the course to guide and invigorate your thinking and writing.

Thus, the assignment itself was two-part: students were asked to transcribe specific pages of the diary and reflect on the transcription process. In addition to the assignment, students were also tasked with presenting their reflective work at the university's Undergraduate Research Day. For the event, students created posters explaining the complexities of digital transcription to attendees, including students and faculty in the STEM disciplines.

To begin, students visited the special collections library and where the manuscripts curator introduced Madge Preston's physical diaries and gave instruction on the proper handling of archival material. Both the English professor and the manuscripts curator believed that for students to gain a deep understanding of digital transcription, they should experience the materiality of archival work. That is, students would need to handle and read from the diaries as physical artifacts before transcribing them in a digital context. The initial experience was especially impactful for students, as many had never experienced a physical archive, did not know what archival holdings were, or ever handled a nineteenth-century document. Reading the physical diaries in the space of the archive and comparing them to the versions transcribed online became an important part of the learning process. For example, in subsequent class sessions and in reflective writing, students noted surprise at how small the physical diaries were compared to reading the enlarged pages on a monitor and expressed how they felt an emotional connection to holding the diary that Preston had held in her own hands over 150 years ago—an experience not possible when using the transcription site. These experiences led students to question how archival sources are represented in an online environment and how digital surrogates of sources may not fully represent a document, diary, or other object or evoke an emotional response. This questioning of online representations is an important information literacy skill.

On the day students visited the archive, after encouraging them to handle and read from the diaries, the manuscripts curator introduced and explained how to use the "Transcribe Maryland" document transcription site. Students spent the next class sessions transcribing both collaboratively and individually their five assigned pages, discussing and reflecting on their transcription work and problem-solving emergent issues. For example, reading nineteenth-century handwriting was particularly difficult for students who had grown up in a world where penmanship was not taught in early years of schooling. Students found that collaborating with others to decipher difficult words or passages was especially useful (and fun). In class sessions, there were a number of "aha moments" in which students figured out letters, words, and relationships among diary "characters," enabling them to make sense of whole passages and pages. Cultivating such careful reading of the diary prompted students to slow down to the pace of the diary writer and to begin to understand the rhythms and contextual elements of Madge Preston's world. This "slowing down" in order to read handwriting allowed students to break, if ever so briefly, from the fast-paced information-rich world of the twenty-first century and to understand the implications of how the pace of information was different in the nineteenth century. Students also placed their experiences in conversation with scholarly readings on the diary writer Madge Preston, digital transcription and crowdsourcing, as well as women's diary writing.[2] By creating this opportunity, students were able to see how their experiences with transcription extended a range of scholarly conversations. Additionally, students were able to consider how their experiences spoke to the concerns of *real* historians and addressed pressing and relevant historiographic questions, building their information literacy skills.

Students' in-class discussions, reflective writing, and Undergraduate Research Day posters centered on a number of compelling topics. Students compared the embodied physical experience of archival work with the digital experience of transcription, weighing their embodied interaction with the diaries within the library's special collections room against the accessibility and ease of use in terms of time and location within the digital context. Students voiced concern over accuracy and reliability within digital transcription and crowdsourcing, but they also identified the benefits of how digital texts could be shared, commented on, and transformed by group input.[3] Demonstrating their understanding of the need to critically evaluate information, students especially focused on the fact that transcription is a subjective process as each reader may interpret handwriting and meaning differently. Students also raised points about ethical issues of making private diaries publically available through digital transcription and noted trepidation over reading deeply personal passages within the Preston diary—many of which related to spousal abuse. The practice of diary writing was of interest to many students, as they explored how the genre served the needs and interests of Preston during her time period and compared this kind of writing to similar (yet different) twenty-first century practices such as blogging. Students pinpointed recurring topics in Preston's diary that were both mundane (the weather, Preston's backgammon playing) and extraordinary (spousal abuse, the Civil War) and considered the kinds of insights this type of writing revealed about women's experiences in the nineteenth century. Placing Preston's writing and their own transcriptions in conversation with scholarship on women's diaries, students also investigated diurnal writing as a kind of literary style.[4]

Another important point of focus for the course was student feedback regarding how to improve the transcription site. Since the site was in its infancy and students were piloting the site's functionality and content, students spent one class session discussing user experience and proposed changes to the site in a reflective writing and posters. Taking on the roles of expert users and advisors to the library staff, students suggested revisions, such as a better and faster image viewer, improved graphic design, more information and tips as to how to do the work of transcription, and a way to attribute credit to the transcriber of a particular page or document. Given their difficulty in reading Preston's handwriting, students suggested ways to make the reading experience easier for other users through creating handwriting keys that would aid in translating hard-to-decipher letters or words. This was another moment in which students moved into the position of expert and could see how historiography and especially digital transcription are dependent on user experience and how feedback would be helpful to those continuing the work of transcribing Preston's diaries in the future.

Partnerships

For three years previous to teaching this course, the English professor had been developing a course that focused students' attention on women's writing practices and the historiographic and methodological complexities that attend the work of researching women writers. In semesters before the spring 2016 term, students examined and conducted research on archival materials, explored digital archives, and investigated digital transcription sites such as the University of Iowa's DIY History site, "Iowa Women's Lives: Letters and Diaries," Villanova University's "Memorable Days: The Emilie Davis Diaries," and Harvard and George Mason Universities' "Martha Ballard's Diary Online." Students were deeply interested and excited by this latter investigation, and due to interest, the professor and the manuscripts curator collaborated to consider how they might create a similar historical resource through the university libraries at their institution. They had already worked together briefly on a previous research class and knew of each other's research interests.

Within the UMD Libraries, the special collections department had already begun investigations and developing plans to create a transcription website for primary source materials. The professor's new course provided much of the impetus to move this transcription project forward. Both the professor and the curator believed that by creating a digital transcription site and crafting an assignment for students that asked them to engage the site, students would be in a position to take on the real work of the twenty-first century historian, for here they would not only assist in deciphering textual historical material (transcription) but also gain a rich and deep understanding of the intellectual issues that surround historiographic recovery.

Reflection

Beyond garnering students' assessment of the transcription tool, the collaborators also reflected on and assessed the project and the transcription experience themselves. They found that providing background information and context for the diaries was an important step in the teaching process for this particular course. They intentionally selected diaries that were already partially transcribed in a published documentary edition and for which there was readily available historical background information.[5] The availability of this contextual information made teaching the historical context easier, but it also averted students from facing some of the difficulties relating to context that an historian might face during the transcription process. Future courses incorporating transcription projects may benefit from taking an alternate approach. One of the goals of many crowdsourced transcription websites is to transcribe materials that have never been transcribed or read closely before. Real-world historians are often the first to perform a close reading of particular documents in an archive. Having little or no context to begin with may be more difficult for undergraduate students, but it also better simulates the authentic work of an historian visiting the archives and painstakingly piecing together information gleaned from handwritten sources.

Furthermore, the manuscripts curator thought having one class session dedicated to teaching students about special collections, context, and the introduction of the transcription site worked well, but more class time may be needed to also discuss how crowdsourced transcription compares to scholarly documentary editing projects and how scholarly research within the archives could benefit from such transcriptions.[6] Students submitted questions to the curator before the class so she could see how to shape the instruction session, with student questions focusing on understanding the ways archives and special collections function, including how to acquire such materials and how to make the materials accessible to researchers.

After semester's end, the English professor and the curator met with the libraries' technical staff to discuss the project and consider ways the group might collaboratively improve the pedagogical and technical experience for students. The English professor found the project to be one of the most rewarding she had offered students. She saw deep student engagement and interest and felt the opportunity for students to work both with physical archival materials and digital transcription was unmatched. The curator found that the collaboration with the DSS Division presented some challenges, as the division viewed the project as one of many they needed to work on, and due to programmer vacancies and competing priorities, they could not devote current resources to support further development of the project. The result was that the transcription site, although functional, still needs improvements that will hopefully be made in the future.

Assessment

Assessment was a major concern for the professor and the curator as students moved through this project, since the project was a test of both the usability of the transcription site and the usefulness of using the site within the classroom setting. Certainly, students' posters and reflective writing revealed the efficacy of the assignment, for students explained how the assignment enabled them to engage in a unique learning experience in which they took on the difficult work of historiography. For example, one student comments in a reflective essay, "After finishing my transcription, I did not want the project to end…. If I had more free time, I would love to transcribe diaries in the future, particularly one of a person with whom I can strongly relate or fascinates me."[7] Another praised the project, writing, "I found transcribing straight onto the website to be exciting because others would be able to view my work…. I feel that I was able to digitally make my mark on a piece of history and that I am now a part of Madge's narrative." Another student explains that the project was a "valuable learning practice that let me read and interpret in a way I might not otherwise have done. I find it hard to describe the feeling which drove me to uncover, piece by piece, Madge's words and meanings…. Though it was difficult, slow, and, at times, incredibly frustrating, I'm ultimately (though perhaps somewhat incredulously) glad I had the experience." Throughout the project, students had successfully learned information literacy skills along the way, including questioning how information is presented in an online environment, interpreting and evaluating new information successfully, and understanding how to present information historical information in a scholarly way to their peers in other disciplines.

The feedback students offered regarding their transcription experience during the dedicated class time was an especially useful form of assessment, as the collaborators continue to think through how the site and the project could be improved for student learning and for general public usage. As another way to garner student responses and recommendations, the manuscripts curator created an online survey regarding the transcription site, with nineteen of the twenty-six students completing it. Results showed a majority of responding students (twelve out of nineteen) noted that the "Transcribe Maryland" site was either "extremely useful" or "very useful" for the goals of the class. Some students had never heard of either transcription or editing historical documents and had no idea how many digital resources were available via the university libraries' website. One student remarked, "Transcribing and editing original content… is not typically implemented in our humanities curriculum." The majority of students agreed that transcribing historical documents was important and appreciated collaborating on challenging pieces of the transcription process.

Recommendations/Best Practices

The main goal and success of the transcription project was for students to do the *real* work of a historian and to take part in a project that asserted women's historical presence in the digital landscape. There were a number of features of the project that were especially effective:

1. The two collaborators found value in creating and using the transcription site at their institution and in asking students to transcribe material that was specific to the local geographic location (Maryland). Incorporating local history sources is desirable, as student familiarity with local geographic references resulted in a deeper engagement with historical documents. Librarians and curators can provide research and contextual instruction related to local primary sources at the institution and facilitate visits to nearby archival repositories, if necessary. However, while it was certainly helpful to have the transcription site and archival materials "on location," it is not necessary. Students and faculty can use digital sites such as Iowa's DIY History, "Iowa Women's Lives: Letters and Diaries," Villanova University's "Memorable Days: The Emilie Davis Diaries," Harvard and George Mason Universities' "Martha Ballard's Diary Online," or even "Transcribe Maryland." Librarians and curators can assist instructional faculty members in identifying appropriate transcription websites and related local special collections.[8]
2. Engaging students in *both* the physical and digital world is key to students' understanding and learning as they enact the work of digital transcription. Students consistently compared the physical experience with the artifact with their digital transcription experience. Even if the materials are not the exact same materials available on the transcription website, it is enormously important for students to handle similar primary source materials from the same time period and of similar subject matter. This physical experience assists in students understanding of the difference in representation of a historical document online and handling the original document in the archival setting.
3. Complementing students' transcription work with scholarship helped students see that their work was of intellectual and historical value. Students gained a sense of agency and authority to engage with scholarship, since they could leverage their experiences with digital transcription to

consider and engage the arguments of others and fine-tune their own perspectives given the work they accomplished in the class.
4. Identifying a venue for students to present their work publicly held real value as students considered the ways their transcription work would be of interest to audiences beyond the class and to identify ways to speak to others about the importance of the work. "Going public" through presenting at Undergraduate Research Day was, therefore, an important part of the class. Students learned how to successfully present information about their projects in a way that was relevant to historians and to engage with other disciplines.
5. Collaboration between instructional faculty and librarian faculty was a major part of the success for this project. Each contributed her own expertise for the project, and they were in close conversation throughout the course of the unit. Additionally, it was especially effective to have similar research interests between the instructional faculty and an academic librarian. The collaborators on this project chose to focus on women's history and rhetoric; a transcription project can be applied, though, across a wide array of subject disciplines.

Conclusion

The transcription project has demonstrated the potential of an academic librarian and instructional faculty collaboration and the hope is that similar collaborations using the transcription tool will occur with other faculty in the English department as well as departments across campus. In addition, the vision is for the "Transcribe Maryland" site to become a larger general outreach initiative for the libraries' special collections. Shared interests and goals between library and teaching faculty need to be identified and developed into other successful initiatives, especially those that focus on information literacy skills. The valuable information literacy skills students developed in the digital transcription project should not be overlooked and could be more broadly applied to evaluating other digital texts, understanding digital representations of primary sources, interrogating online digital content, and understanding how to present information to various audiences.

Notes

1. Virginia Walcott Beauchamp, *A Private War: Letters and Diaries of Madge Preston, 1862–1867* (New Brunswick: Rutgers UP, 1987).
2. Scholarship included: Moya Z. Bailey, "All the Digital Humanists Are White, All the Nerds Are Men, but Some of Us Are Brave," *Journal of Digital Humanities* 1,

no..1 (Winter 2011), accessed December 15, 2016, http://journalofdigitalhumanities.org/1-1/all-the-digital-humanists-are-white-all-the-nerds-are-men-but-some-of-us-are-brave-by-moya-z-bailey/; Beauchamp, *A Private War, 1987*; Lynn Bloom, "'I Write for Myself and Strangers': Private Diaries as Public Documents," in *Inscribing the Daily: Critical Essays on Women's Diaries*, ed. Suzanne L. Bunkers and Cynthia Huff (Amherst: University of Massachusetts Press, 1996), 23–37; Jessica Enoch and Jean Bessette, "Meaningful Engagements: Feminist Historiography and the Digital Humanities," *College Composition and Communication* 64, no. 4 (2013): 634–59; May Friedman, "On Mommyblogging: Notes to a Future Historian," *Journal of Women's History* 22, no. 4 (2010): 197–208; Jennifer Redmond, "Thoughts on Feminism, Digital Humanities, and Women's History," Educating Women: Blog of The Albert M. Greenfield Digital Center for the History of Women's Education at Bryn Mawr College, accessed December 15, 2016, http://greenfield.Discussion Boards.brynmawr.edu/2013/05/20/thoughts-on-feminism-digital-humanities-and-womens-history/; Mia Ridge, "From Tagging to Theorizing: Deepening Engagement with Cultural Heritage Crowdsourcing," *The Museum Journal* 56, no. 4 (2013): 435–50; Carolyn Steedman, "The Space of Memory: In an Archive," in *Dust: The Archive and Cultural History* (New Brunswick: Rutgers University Press, 2002), 66–88.

3. For more information on crowdsourcing by libraries and other cultural institutions, see Mia Ridge, ed. *Crowdsourcing Our Cultural Heritage* (Burlington, VT: Ashgate Publishing, 2014).

4. Jennifer Sinor, "Reading the Ordinary Diary," *Rhetoric Review* 21, no. 2 (2002): 123–49.

5. Virginia Walcott Beauchamp's "Introduction" to *A Private War: Letters and Diaries of Madge Preston, 1862–1867* (New Brunswick: Rugters University Press, 1987), and the online finding aid for the Preston Family Papers at the University of Maryland Libraries (http://hdl.handle.net/1903.1/1278) provided the main sources for contextual information.

6. There are numerous guides to documentary editing that could be incorporated as part of the discussion, including Mary-Jo Kline and Susan Holbrook Perdue, *A Guide to Documentary Editing* (Charlottesville: University of Virginia Press, 2008), available online at http://gde.upress.virginia.edu/index.html. As staffing becomes more tenuous, traditional documentary editing projects are beginning to harness the potential of crowdsourced digital transcription as a first pass through the manuscript materials. See Tim Gove, "History Bytes: Citizen History Projects," *History News* 66, no. 4 (Autumn 2011): 5–6. For more on the complexities of digital editing, see Amy E. Earhart, "The Digital Edition and the Digital Humanities," *Textual Cultures* 7, no. 1 (Spring 2012): 18–28.

7. Keith Wise, "Transcriptional Inspiration," Unpublished Student Paper, March 13, 2016: 5, quoted with permission.

8. For another example of a collaborative undergraduate project that combined local history collections and digital projects, see: Kathryn Shively Meier and Kristen Yarmey, "An Authentic Archival Experience for the College Classroom in the Digital Age," *The Pennsylvania Magazine of History and Biography* 139, no. 1, A Special Collaborative Issue: Teaching Pennsylvania History (January 2015): 65–81.

Bibliography

Bailey, Moya. "All the Digital Humanists Are White, All the Nerds Are Men, but Some of Us Are Brave." *Journal of Digital Humanities* 1, no.1 (Winter 2011). Accessed December 15, 2016. http://journalofdigitalhumanities.org/1-1/all-the-digital-humanists-are-white-all-thenerds-are-men-but-some-of-us-are-brave-by-moya-z-bailey/.

Beauchamp, Virginia Walcott. *A Private War: Letters and Diaries of Madge Preston, 1862–1867.* New Brunswick: Rutgers University Press, 1987.

Bloom, Lynn. "'I Write for Myself and Strangers': Private Diaries as Public Documents." In *Inscribing the Daily: Critical Essays on Women's Diaries,* edited by Suzanne L. Bunkers and Cynthia Huff, 23–37. Amherst: University of Massachusetts Press, 1996.

Earhart, Amy E. "The Digital Edition and the Digital Humanities," *Textual Cultures* 7, no. 1 (Spring 2012): 18–28.

Enoch, Jessica, and Jean Bessette. "Meaningful Engagements: Feminist Historiography and the Digital Humanities." *College Composition and Communication* 64, no. 4 (2013): 634–59.

Friedman, May. "On Mommyblogging: Notes to a Future Historian." *Journal of Women's History* 22, no. 4 (2010): 197–208.

Grove, Tim. "History Bytes: Citizen History Projects." *History News* 66, no. 4 (Autumn 2011): 5–6.

Kline, Mary-Jo., and Susan Holbrook Perdue. *A Guide to Documentary Editing.* Charlottesville: University of Virginia Press, 2008.

McGovern, Sean. "Literariness and Affect in the Transcription of Madge Preston's Diary." Unpublished Student Paper, March 9, 2016.

Meier, Kathryn Shively, and Kristen Yarmey, "An Authentic Archival Experience for the College Classroom in the Digital Age." *The Pennsylvania Magazine of History and Biography* 139, no. 1, A Special Collaborative Issue: Teaching Pennsylvania History (January 2015): 65–81.

Redmond, Jennifer. "Thoughts on Feminism, Digital Humanities, and Women's History." Educating Women: Blog of The Albert M. Greenfield Digital Center for the History of Women's Education at Bryn Mawr College, May 20, 2013. Accessed December 15, 2016. http://greenfield.Discussion Boards.brynmawr.edu/2013/05/20/thoughts-on-feminism-digital-humanities-and-womens-history/.

Ridge, Mia, ed. *Crowdsourcing Our Cultural Heritage.* Burlington, VT: Ashgate Publishing, 2014.

Ridge, Mia. "From Tagging to Theorizing: Deepening Engagement with Cultural Heritage Crowdsourcing." *The Museum Journal* 56, no. 4 (2013): 435–50.

Rohan, Liz. "I Remember Momma: Material Rhetoric, Mnemonic Activity, and One Woman's Turn-of-the-Century Quilt." *Rhetoric Review* 23, no. 4 (2004): 368–87.

Sinor, Jennifer. "Reading the Ordinary Diary." *Rhetoric Review* 21, no. 2 (2002): 123–49.

Steedman, Carolyn. *Dust: The Archive and Cultural History.* New Brunswick: Rutgers University Press, 2002.

Wise, Keith. "Transcriptional Inspiration." Unpublished Student Paper, March 13 2016.

CHAPTER 25*

Undergraduate Research in the Archives:
A Case Study of Collaborative Teaching and Dissemination of Aerospace History

Tracy B. Grimm

Introduction

History matters. But our connection to the past is inherently mediated, requiring documentary and artifactual evidence. As such, archives and special collections repositories are, and have been, natural learning laboratories for archivists, librarians, and educators to introduce historical thinking to K-12 students and to facilitate high-impact educational practices, such as undergraduate research and experiential learning for college and university students. Observing elementary grade students holding, examining, questioning, and enthusiastically discussing archival documents is illustrative of how even the very young relate to and naturally engage with artifacts of our collective past. At the college and university level, we ask students to become

---

* This work is licensed under a Creative Commons Attribution-NonCommercial-ShareAlike 4.0 License, CC BY-NC-SA (https://creativecommons.org/licenses/by-nc-sa/4.0/).

critical thinkers and to engage with this artifactual evidence of the past, but also to consider it in the context of existing scholarship and clearly express their own conclusions. Elizabeth Yakel and Doris Malkmus point out in their chapter in *Teaching with Primary Sources*—the most recent and comprehensive publication on primary source and archival literacy instruction—the modern movement to introduce primary sources and historical thinking into the classroom coalesced in the 1990s. In the past ten years, college and university archivists and special collections librarians have embraced practicing roles in undergraduate instruction and have become proponents both in writing and on campuses for undergraduate research in the archives.

The idea to initiate a history seminar for students to produce original research using the Purdue University Flight Archives was the result of a gradual working relationship developed between Barron Hilton Archivist for Flight and Space Exploration Archivist Tracy Grimm and Purdue University History professor Michael G. Smith. More broadly, this collaboration was possible due to Purdue Libraries' active commitment to an institutional culture that is learner- and researcher-focused. The Grimm–Smith undergraduate research partnership was not the first to be based in the Purdue Archives and special collections. The archives, a division of Purdue Libraries, shares the libraries' strategic plan goal of contributing to "student success and lifelong learning through innovative educational practices" and, thus, archivists at Purdue are expected to be involved in instruction partnerships with faculty in addition to their traditional responsibilities to acquire, preserve, and make archival materials accessible.[1] The archives facility was renovated in 2008 to include the addition of classroom space designed for primary source instruction with active learning in mind. In 2011, an endowment established the position of flight archivist and included a mandate for outreach to students and faculty to promote use of the Flight Archive collections.[2] Today, Purdue employs seven archivists, most of whom participate in instruction. Over the past decade, Purdue Libraries has established a physical space infrastructure, personnel resources, and strategic collections to support robust archive-based instruction programs and partnerships with faculty.

Background
The Course

Since 2014, Smith and Grimm have taught three iterations of "Flight and Space Exploration: An Archival Research Seminar." As embedded archivist, Grimm contributed to course design and taught archival literacy components of the class. The course typically enrolled ten to twelve students and met in the archive's classroom. Although each iteration of the course was altered slightly to reflect student feedback and instructors' observations, the final project remained the same: students would write an 8,000-word, original research paper of publishable quality with dissemination as a goal.[3] With key holdings in flight and space history that include the Amelia Earhart papers and the papers of retired astronauts, pilots, and engineers (including alumni Neil Armstrong and Eugene Cernan), the Flight Archives offers numerous opportunities for students to conduct original research on the history of flight and the Space Age.

Course instruction for the first half of the semester was designed to build students' contextual knowledge of flight history and to gradually establish their archival literacy skills.[4] For one of the two class periods each week, students led discussions of readings from the course's textbook and assigned articles. Once each student selected their individual research topic, additional secondary sources were assigned. The remaining class period each week was dedicated to readings and scaffolded exercises to build students' skills in identifying, interpreting, and evaluating primary sources and using an archive. Class time was provided for students to conduct hands-on research with their chosen collections. Establishing historical context is an essential step that goes hand-in-hand with students' ability to effectively analyze and interpret primary sources as they begin to engage the historical thinking required to produce original research. During the second half of the semester, students gave formal twenty-minute presentations to share their in-progress research and receive peer feedback.

While analyzing and interpreting primary sources is experiential learning, an additional form of experiential learning was introduced to this course and was possible because of the course's alignment with the archives. Each semester the course was taught, students were given opportunities to interact with and discuss their research with archives' donors, including former astronauts and their family members, aerospace industry leaders, and aviation professionals. For example, classes interacted with Eugene Cernan and Carol Armstrong at a private exhibit reception; they also attended a lunch with NASA officials. Students earned extra credit for assisting the archivist with planning exhibit open house activities, giving presentations to elementary school students, and as docents for campus event exhibits. In addition, by interacting with donors, students better understood how archival collections are acquired by the repository and they were able to meet some of the people whose collections they were using, fostering historical empathy.

Embedded Instruction

A search of the archival literature for research on embedded archival instruction in 2013 did not take long. Very few resources existed outside of the 2012 compilation of case studies, *Past or Portal? Enhancing Undergraduate Learning through Special Collections and Archives*, and a small but useful body of articles beginning to propose structures for expert primary source research skills in an information literacy context. Elizabeth Yakel and Deborah A. Torres' 2003 article on "AI: Archival Intelligence and User Expertise" provided an information literacy structure for teaching with primary sources.[5] Others identified the need for learning rubrics, assessment techniques, and guidelines for archivists and librarians to use when archival skills are integrated into the curriculum.[6] Anne Bahde's article, "The History Labs: Integrating Primary Source Literacy Skills into a History Survey Course," demonstrated that regular practice of primary source literacy skills combined with cumulative skill development through scaffolded exercises improved students' performance in a history survey course.[7] The one-shot archivist lecture on how to use the archives' catalog or a finding aid and the age old "show and tell" class tour to view "treasures" of the archive had become widely recognized for their limited impact on student learning. In 2014, Anne Bahde, Heather Smedberg, and Mattie Taormina's *Using Primary Sources* offered more case studies and model exercises.[8] These writings, along with campus-wide pedagogy workshops and symposiums organized by Purdue's Center for Instructional Excellence and its IMPACT program (Instruction Matters: Purdue Academic Course Transformation) and a regional learning community, were invaluable resources that allowed Grimm, with only on-the-job training as an instructor and limited exposure to learning theory and classroom practice, to quickly gain instructional design knowledge, theory, and practices to take into the classroom for a semester-long instruction engagement.[9]

Partnerships

The partnership to collaborate on a course using the Flight Archives began with the flight archivist inviting Professor Michael G. Smith to coffee to discuss his courses in the history of flight and the Space Age. Grimm began sitting in on Smith's History of Flight survey course and was invited to give a twenty-minute presentation on the Flight Archives holdings.[10] With prior instructional experience limited to one- or two-shot sessions, sitting in on Smith's survey course not only contributed to Grimm's subject knowledge but also allowed for observation of the classroom environment and student interactions. Noting the students' enthusiastic reactions to learning about their university's role in flight history and related archival holdings, Smith and Grimm discussed situating Smith's junior research seminar in the Flight Archives to use the collections as a basis for original student research. Smith and Grimm planned the new course, building upon the foundation of Smith's original seminar by adding primary source and archival literacy instruction components. They compiled a list of research topics the archive could support, with Grimm designing archival literacy lessons based on an active learning student-centered model.

For the second half of each semester the partnership expanded to include additional libraries' faculty and staff. A government records subject liaison librarian joined the class for the research presentations to provide students with bibliographic suggestions to further their contextual research. During the third iteration of the course, the libraries' digital humanities specialist, a new position for Purdue Libraries, consulted with the instructors on digital annotation and visualization tools available to students. In addition, Purdue's digital archivist joined the instructors to help create an online magazine pilot project for dissemination of the undergraduate research.

The most positive aspects of the faculty-archivist partnership related to the student learning environment and the overall learning experience the partnership made possible. First, the collaboration took students outside the traditional classroom. Each class met weekly in the archives, either in its instruction room or in the reading room. Second, students were immersed in the archives and over the course of the semester became seasoned users. Students who frequently returned outside of class became expert users. Third, students received feedback and guidance from instructors with different expertise—from Smith on subject context and historical writing and from Grimm on primary sources, while both assisted students with methods of historical thinking. In the later half of the semester, as noted, students also received instruction from a subject librarian and digital humanities librarian. Finally, the professional skills practice the instructors were able to facilitate by arranging student interactions with archives' donors and participation in Purdue Archives outreach events were impactful experiences for the students.

As with most new partnerships, there were challenges. By mid-semester, communication logistics between the two instructors regarding the advice given to students during consultations became a challenge. Various attempts were made to alleviate lapses, including a handwritten log to travel with students to consultations and an online form. These proved too cumbersome for the instructors to maintain; an ideal solution was not found. Instead, Grimm followed up her consultations with email reiterating main points and always copied Smith. At the beginning of each consultation, Grimm would interview the student to determine if their latest meeting with Smith resulted in any new trajectories for their research. Another challenge the partnership encountered related to the job classification of the archivist as an administrative professional and her designation as "embedded" rather than officially listed as a co-instructor. Without a faculty classification and/or co-instructor status, Grimm's input toward grading was restricted and at times it was unclear whether sharing final papers with her was allowable. This limited her ability to assess students' final application of archival literacy skills. This also placed most of the later half of the course workload solidly on Smith, despite the additional learning outcomes added during the course redesign.

Reflection

Teaching the undergraduate research seminar three times over two successive academic years allowed for several lessons learned and adjustments to be tested and implemented. Our experience demonstrated that carefully scaffolded exercises were key to building student confidence in their application of primary source analysis and to leading students to achieve historical thinking and writing. Practicing archival literacy skills during class time gave students confidence to work independently in the reading room. However, although many students produced original research with potential of publication, fewer than half were able to take advantage of the opportunity.

A flipped classroom model worked well because relying on outside of class readings and brief in-class discussions allowed additional time for group exercises and discussions. The instructors observed that students were reluctant to fully explore the finding aids, and they were slow to survey the scope of the collections and then explore deeper into targeted portions. To adjust for this, during the second iteration of the course, Grimm flipped her portion of the classroom instruction even more by substituting her usual archives rules for researchers lecture for an out-of-class reading and student-led brief discussion to create more in-class time for scaffolded exercises. Grimm also greatly scaled back making recommendations to students based on her knowledge of each collection and instead led students to finding aids and required students to use them to request multiple boxes. Going forward, Grimm will continue to explore revisions to her instruction by seeking research on the processes historians use in archival research and exploring modeling techniques.

Archivists or librarians who are preparing for embedded history seminars will find it helpful to explore readings outside of the library and archival literature and in the related fields of educational psychology, history education, and mentoring to gain insight and to prepare for tasks that accompany an instructor's role in undergraduate research. It is important to be prepared with mentoring skills, know how to teach historical thinking, and how to maintain student motivation. Helpful writings include those of George Kuh on high-impact educational practices, Richard M. Ryan and Edward K. Deci's works on motivation and self-determination research, and Samuel Wineberg's work on teaching historical thinking.[11]

Assessment

Although the university administers a general course evaluation, the instructors administered a post-course survey comprised of ten questions designed to gather student feedback on archival instruction. The questions were designed to also assess whether broad archival learning outcomes had been met, such as raising students' confidence to conduct archival research and seeking the assistance of an archivist. Survey responses from the first course, in particular, were extremely helpful to the instructors because they identified significant areas of the research process students struggled with that were not anticipated by the instructors. Additionally, survey responses from each course indicated students wanted more mentored research time in the archive, more individual consultation time with both instructors, and validated that two basic learning outcomes were overwhelmingly met.

Many students in the first course reported difficulty with the research process when faced with an archival collection for the first time. Students wanted specific guidance on methods to work with the boxes and documents. Instructor observations during the in-class research time corroborated this difficulty. Some students spent an entire class with one box from a collection, sometimes with just one document. One student self-reported, "It was good (the in-class research time), but more than half the time I didn't know what I was looking for. I would have started archives research sooner." Another student commented, "I would have liked more in-class research time and a little more instruction on efficient ways to approach the archives." Another student requested, "Teach us a way to take notes that makes finding documents later on easier." Although, these students were juniors and seniors, clearly their responses indicated a need for more instruction and modeling of practical archival research practices. In response, archival literacy components were introduced earlier during the next course and expanded with more focused exercises tied to brief assignments. Also, a reading that modeled research in the archives was added, consultations with the archivist were required in addition to the faculty member's office hours, and more class time was allotted for research in the reading room. The addition of L. Mastrangelo and B. L'Eplattenier's article, "Stumbling in the Archives," which modeled the research process for students from the perspective of two doctoral students' first encounter with archival research, was particularly successful.[12] Many students reported this reading caused an "ah-ha!" moment for them in their understanding of what researching in an archive is like, and reported that it greatly eased their anxiety about the process.

Themes that emerged from the students' self-reports in the second and third iterations of the course suggested students wanted more class time for conducting research in the archives and more individual consultation time with the instructors. One student reported, "The in-class (archival research) time allowed me to ask questions and use my time efficiently." Another said, "I would like more in-class time purely because it was a great way to get feedback." Nearly all students reported a positive experience while conducting research in the reading room. One stated, "Very useful. I was able to get what I needed to get done and more. Plus, there happened to be another student there that knew a lot about my topic." Another student responded, "Very pleasant, almost Zen-like." Another student said of the reading room, "It made me feel important because this is the first experience I've had like this."

We found that only a few students were able to disseminate their research beyond the class. From the first course, three out of eleven students shared their work in either a peer-reviewed journal, poster session, or as an honors thesis. Although more students produced original research with potential for publication, only these three were able to take advantage of the opportunity to develop their papers after the course ended. To address this low dissemination rate, Smith, Grimm, and Purdue Archives digital archivist, Neal Harmeyer, developed an experimental online magazine with the goal that students would be able to disseminate their work by the course's end or shortly thereafter. The online magazine, *Flight Paths: Purdue University's Flight Pioneers,* was a partnership between the College of Liberal Arts and Libraries. A graduate student staff and the faculty mentor provided assistance to the students in preparing the works for publication. As of date, the pilot phase of the project has completed with seven student papers published from the courses as its first draft issue.[13] An evaluation of the pilot is underway to explore the feasibility of this model as an undergraduate research dissemination option. Preliminary findings of challenges to implementing the model included issues of scale-time and scope, as well as of editorial management and sustainable technical support. Preliminary identified benefits of the model include peer learning, expediency of a publishable paper given sufficient availability of the mentor, and an attractive platform to locally publish original student research generated from the College of Liberal Arts-Libraries partnership.

Recommendations/Best Practices

A number of recommendations can be made for librarians, faculty, and archivists considering programs for undergraduate research in partnership with an archive or special collections:

1. Attend interdisciplinary workshops, seminars, and conferences of your aligned professions, not just your own. Learn from and share experiences with rare book librarians, subject librarians, archivists, and teaching faculty who all also teach students to identify, evaluate, and use information.
2. Librarians and archivists must become more familiar with and able to teach "historical thinking" as it relates to the process of archival research. How does a historian evaluate a primary source? How does a historian work with an archival collection?
3. Find a veteran instructor and ask to be mentored.

4. Seek university resources to assist in planning and implementing learning assessment. Strive for a variety of assessment tools that engage reaction (post-course), learning (short reflective), and performance (final paper/projects) assessment types. Most important, assess learning early and often through classroom assessments such as brief daily or weekly assignments and mid-course presentations of research progress.
5. Use active learning; flip the classroom as much as possible.
6. Consider the archive a source for experiential learning opportunities to complement the undergraduate research experience. Facilitate student participation in events. Spend class time to prepare students for these professional encounters. Offer participation credit to students for participation in public outreach efforts related to the research subject area. These experiences allow students personal, real-world opportunities to practice professional skills and exert their classroom knowledge. This is particularly valuable for students with an interest in careers in public history or cultural heritage.
7. Scaffold archival literacy activities throughout the semester.
8. Communicate clearly and often with instruction partner.
9. To improve the rate of student publishing, consider pairing the research course with a follow-up editing and publishing course.
10. Carefully consider mentoring resources before setting expectations for dissemination of research. Ideally, each student would receive equal mentoring. Students have a diversity of motivation and degrees of mentoring required. Mentoring can require a significant amount of a faculty member's time and practically; it would be difficult for one faculty member to mentor all seminar students to publish. If high rates of disseminations are an expected outcome of a course or initiative, mentoring time must be adequate. If librarians and archivists were to become mentors for students, how would their mentoring role be defined?

Conclusion

Establishing strong partnerships among faculty, librarians, and archivists in support of undergraduate research initiatives is timely. The growth of archival literacy literature and the corresponding widespread practice of archivists and special collections librarians engaged in instruction indicates the demand and relevance of archival collections beyond trophy status for a university administration or warehouses for alumni nostalgia. Student researchers benefit greatly from guided and mentored use of academic archives and special collections. As laboratories for learning, academic archives have a substantial and demonstrated potential to support significant teaching and learning as students engage in undergraduate research. Moreover, while undergraduate research as a high-impact practice provides students valuable skills and practice, if an undergraduate course is partnered with a robust archive and special collections, unique and important opportunities exist for providing students mentored professional experiences alongside their research.

Notes

1. Purdue University Libraries, Press, and Copyright Office Strategic Plan 2016-2019 (West Lafayette: Purdue University Libraries, 2016), accessed August 24, 2016, https://www.lib.purdue.edu/about/strategic_plans.
2. The Barron Hilton Endowment for Flight and Space Exploration was established in 2011 with grants from the Conrad N. Hilton Foundation and Barron Hilton. The endowment provides for the dedicated position of flight archivist to manage the papers of astronauts Neil A. Armstrong and Eugene Cernan and to collect and make accessible the personal papers of other engineers, astronauts, and pilots.
3. Smith and Grimm taught the first iteration of the course, "The Technology and Culture of Flight" as a junior research seminar in the Fall 2014. Revised and taught again in Fall 2015 semester, the course was renamed "Flight and Space Exploration: Archival Research Seminar" as a 400 level course and was opened to graduate students. The course was again revised, renamed ("Flight Paths: Purdue University's Aerospace Pioneers"), and taught the spring 2016 as a History Department Honors course for freshman honors students.
4. Archival literacy, while closely related to information literacy, specifically defines those skills necessary to conduct successful primary source research as a component of original research. One definition of archival literacy is, "The knowledge, skills, and abilities necessary to effectively and efficiently find, interpret, and use archives, manuscripts, and other types of original unpublished primary source materials." See Sammie Morris, Lawrence J. Mykytiuk, and Sharon A. Weiner, "Archival Literacy for History Students: What Do Students Need to Know About Primary Source Materials?" *The American Archivist* 77 (Fall/Winter 2014): 394–424. Also see by the same authors, "Archival Literacy Competencies for Undergraduate History Majors," *The American Archivist* 78 (Spring/Summer 2015): 154–80.
5. Elizabeth Yakel and Deborah A. Torres, "AI: Archival Intelligence and User Expertise," *The American Archivist* 66, no. 1 (2003): 51–78.
6. A few of these seminal writings include: Elizabeth Yakel, "Information Literacy for Primary Sources: Creating a New Paradigm for Archival Researcher Education," *OCLC Systems & Services: International Digital Library Perspectives* 20, no. 2 (2004): 61–64.; Peter Carini, "Archivists as Educators: Integrating Primary Sources into the Curriculum," *Journal of Archival Organization* 7 (2009): 41–50; and Magia G. Krause, "Undergraduates in the Archives: Using an Assessment Rubric to Measure Learning," *The American Archivist* 73, no. 2 (2010): 507–34.
7. Anne Bahde, "The History Labs: Integrating Primary Source Literacy Skills into a History Survey Course," *Journal of Archival Organization* 11, no. 3–4 (2013): 175–204.
8. Anne Bahde, Heather Smedberg, and Mattie Taormina, *Using Primary Sources* (Santa Barbara: ABC-CLIO, 2014). More recently, Christopher J. Prom and Lisa

Janicke Hinchliffe's *Teaching with Primary Sources*, published in 2016, stands as the most comprehensive resource on primary source and archival literacy instruction with modules on contextualizing archival literacy, teaching with archives, and selected case studies including comprehensive bibliographies of additional sources and further readings.
9. Purdue's Center for Instructional Excellence provides resources for new faculty, graduate students, and librarians, including programs that provide practical teaching advice from veteran faculty, curriculum planning tips and models, and learning theory to underpin student-centered pedagogies. The Center also supports a university-wide initiative to redesign foundational courses to transform them from traditional lecture-based model to one utilizing active, participatory student-centered teaching and learning. For more information, see: http://www.purdue.edu/cie/. For backward design model of instruction, see Grant P. Wiggins and Jay McTighe, *Understanding by Design* (Alexandria, VA: Association for Supervision and Curriculum Development, 1998).
10. This survey course offered biennially is popular among Purdue's engineering and aviation technology students as well as history majors and typically enrolls around seventy students.
11. For example, see: George D. Kuh, Carol Geary Schneider, and Association of American Colleges Universities, *High-impact Educational Practices: What They Are, Who Has Access to Them, and Why They Matter* (Washington, DC: Association of American Colleges and Universities, 2008); Richard M. Ryan and Edward L. Deci, "Intrinsic and Extrinsic Motivations: Classic Definitions and New Directions," *Contemporary Educational Psychology* 25, no. 1 (2000): 54–67; Sam Wineburg, *Historical Thinking and Other Unnatural Acts: Charting the Future of Teaching the Past (Critical Perspectives on the Past)* (Philadelphia: Temple University Press, 2001); and Daisy Martin and Sam Wineburg, "Seeing Thinking on the Web," *History Teacher* 41, no. 3 (2008): 305–19.
12. L. Mastrangelo and B. L'Eplattenier, "Stumbling in the Archives," in *Beyond the Archives: Research as a Lived Process*, ed. Gesa Kirsch, Liz Rohan, and Ebrary, Inc. (Carbondale: Southern Illinois University Press, 2008), 161–69.
13. See the digital magazine *Flight Paths: Purdue University's Aerospace Pioneers*, http://flightpaths.lib.purdue.edu/.

Bibliography

Bahde, Anne. "The History Labs: Integrating Primary Source Literacy Skills into a History Survey Course." *Journal of Archival Organization* 11, no. 3-4 (2013): 175–204.
Bahde, Anne, Heather Smedberg, and Mattie Taormina. *Using Primary Sources*. Santa Barbara: ABC-CLIO, 2014.
Brooklyn Historical Society. TeachArchives.org. http://www.teacharchives.org/.
Buehl, Jonathan, Tamar Chute, and Anne Fields. "Training in the Archives: Archival Research as Professional Development." *College Composition and Communication* 64, no. 2 (2012): 274–305.
Carini, Peter. "Archivists as Educators: Integrating Primary Sources into the Curriculum." *Journal of Archival Organization* 7, no. 1-2 (2009): 41–50.

Carini, Peter. "Information Literacy for Archives and Special Collections: Defining Outcomes." *portal: Libraries and the Academy* 16, no. 1 (2016): 191–206.

Hensley, Merinda, Benjamin Murphy, and Ellen Swain. "Analyzing Archival Intelligence: A Collaboration Between Library Instruction and Archives." *Communications in Information Literacy* 8, no. 1 (2014): 96–114.

Johnson, Benjamin A., and Donald J. Harreld. "Nurturing Independent Learning in the Undergraduate Student in History: A Faculty-Student Mentoring Experience." *Mentoring & Tutoring: Partnership in Learning* 20, no. 3 (2012): 361–78.

Krause, Magia G. "Undergraduates in the Archives: Using an Assessment Rubric to Measure Learning." *The American Archivist* 73, no. 2 (2010): 507–34.

Kuh, George D., Carol Geary Schneider, and Association of American Colleges Universities. *High-impact Educational Practices: What They Are, Who Has Access to Them, and Why They Matter.* Washington, DC: Association of American Colleges and Universities, 2008.

Martin, Daisy, and Sam Wineburg. "Seeing Thinking on the Web." *History Teacher* 41, no. 3 (2008): 305–19.

Mastrangelo, L. and B. L'Eplattenier, "Stumbling in the Archives." In *Beyond the Archives: Research as a Lived Process*, edited by Gesa Kirsch, Liz Rohan, and Ebrary, Inc., 161–69. Carbondale: Southern Illinois University Press, 2008.

Morris, Sammie, Lawrence J. Mykytiuk, and Sharon A. Weiner, "Archival Literacy Competencies for Undergraduate History Majors." *The American Archivist* 78 (Spring/Summer 2015): 154–80.

Morris, Sammie, Lawrence J. Mykytiuk, and Sharon A. Weiner, "Archival Literacy for History Students: What Do Students Need to Know About Primary Source Materials?" *The American Archivist* 77 (Fall/Winter 2014): 394–424.

Nimer, Coryl, and J. Gordon Daines III. "Teaching Undergraduates to Think Archivally." *Journal of Archival Organization* 10, no. 1 (2012): 4–44.

Prom, Christopher J., and Lisa Janicke Hinchliffe. *Teaching with Primary Sources.* Chicago: Society of American Archivists, 2016.

Purdue University. *Flight Paths: Purdue University's Flight Pioneers.* West Lafayette: Purdue University, 2016. http://flightpaths.lib.purdue.edu.

Robyns, Marcus C. "The Archivist as Educator: Integrating Critical Thinking Skills into Historical Research Methods Instruction." *American Archivist* 64, no. 2 (2001): 363–84.

Ryan, Richard M., and Edward L. Deci. "Intrinsic and Extrinsic Motivations: Classic Definitions and New Directions." *Contemporary Educational Psychology* 25, no. 1 (2000): 54–67.

Wiggins, Grant P., and Jay McTighe. *Understanding by Design.* Alexandria, VA: Association for Supervision and Curriculum Development, 1998.

Wineburg, Sam. *Historical Thinking and Other Unnatural Acts: Charting the Future of Teaching the Past (Critical Perspectives on the Past).* Philadelphia: Temple University Press, 2001.

Yakel, Elizabeth, and Deborah A. Torres. "AI: Archival Intelligence and User Expertise." *The American Archivist* 66, no. 1 (2003): 51–78.

Yakel, Elizabeth. "Information Literacy for Primary Sources: Creating a New Paradigm for Archival Researcher Education." *OCLC Systems & Services: International Digital Library Perspectives* 20, no. 2 (2004): 61–64.

Author Bios

Editors

Merinda Kaye Hensley (co-editor) is associate professor and digital scholarship liaison and instruction librarian at the University of Illinois at Urbana-Champaign. She provides leadership for the educational initiatives in the Scholarly Commons, a digital scholarship center that serves the emerging research and technology needs of scholars in data services, digital humanities, digitization, and scholarly communication. Merinda has taught for the School of Information Sciences at Illinois, LIS 590AE: Information Literacy and Instruction and Practice. She is active in the ACRL, having served as Chair of the Student Learning and Information Literacy Committee, Chair of the Instruction Section (2017–2018), and as a member of the Information Literacy Competency Standards for Higher Education Task Force, which wrote the ACRL *Framework for Information Literacy for Higher Education*. Merinda presents nationally and internationally on her research, incorporating scholarly communication into information literacy instruction, developing research support and publishing services for undergraduate researchers, and improving teaching skills of new librarians.

Stephanie Davis-Kahl (co-editor) is the scholarly communications librarian and professor at The Ames Library at Illinois Wesleyan University. She provides leadership for scholarly communication programs, including Digital Commons @ IWU. She is the liaison to the Economics, Educational Studies and Psychology departments at IWU, and serves as the managing faculty co-editor of the *Undergraduate Economic Review*. She is a member of the editorial board of the *Journal of Librarianship & Scholarly Communication* and an editorial assistant for *College & Research Libraries*. In 2014, she was named a Mover & Shaker by *Library Journal* and was also awarded the Education & Behavioral Sciences Section Distinguished Librarian Award.

Authors

Richard Ball is an associate professor of economics at Haverford College. His primary teaching areas are game theory and statistical methods, and he supervises several senior theses every year. His research has included theoretical papers on political economy and empirical work on development and social issues. Richard has studied or worked in Sierra Leone, Chad, Egypt and Côte d'Ivoire. He has co-directed Project TIER (www.projecttier.org) with Norm Medeiros since they launched that initiative in 2013.

Lisa Becksford is the educational technologies librarian and coordinator for Graduate and Online Teaching & Learning Programs at Virginia Tech's Newman Library, where she helps to strategize outreach and instruction for both graduate students and online students. She also works with a wide range of students, from first-year to doctoral, as the liaison to education, human development, and engineering education. Prior to earning her library degree at the University of North Carolina at Chapel Hill, Lisa taught college composition for five years. An early-career librarian, she currently serves as the vice chair/chair-elect of the Virginia Library Association's New Members Round Table Forum.

Matt Bejune is the executive director of the library at Worcester State University. He oversees all library operations including the WSU Archives and Special Collections. Matt is passionate about teaching and learning and he is committed to developing user-centered services and collections. He has worked in academic libraries at public higher education institutions for more than a decade. He previously worked at Quinsigamond Community College as the coordinator of reference and instruction, and at Purdue University Libraries as the coordinator of the undergraduate library Reference and Libraries Digital Reference. He received a masters in library and information science from Syracuse University, and bachelor degrees in music education and music performance from the University of Massachusetts, Amherst. Throughout his career, Matt has been actively involved with state, regional, and national library organizations. Currently, he is serving as secretary of the Association of College and Research Libraries, New England Chapter.

Heather Buchansky is the student engagement librarian at the University of Toronto Libraries. In her role, she develops and coordinates large-scale library initiatives related to student outreach and information literacy, primarily for undergraduate students. She presents frequently on her work related to Personal Librarian programs at conferences across the U.S. and Canada. Heather earned her masters of information from University of Toronto, and holds a postgraduate certificate in education from University of Exeter. Prior to entering librarianship, she worked as a teacher and a sales consultant for a university press.

Amy Hildreth Chen is special collections instruction librarian and the interim English and American literature librarian at the University of Iowa. At Iowa, Chen also serves as a game developer and mentor to doctoral students interested in alt-ac careers through her role on the steering committee for the NEH-funded grant Beyond the PhD. Between 2013–2015, she served as a Council on Library and Information Resources (CLIR) Academic Libraries Postdoctoral Fellow in the Division of Special Collections at the University of Alabama, where she managed instruction, exhibition, and outreach programs. She received her PhD in English from Emory University in 2013 with a dissertation titled, "Archival Bodies: British, Irish, and American Literary Collections." Chen continues to publish in the fields of special collections pedagogy and literary collection acquisition.

Sarah Clayton is a digital scholarship specialist at the University of Oklahoma Libraries, where she supports faculty and students in all disciplines wanting to incorporate digital tools in their research or teaching. Sarah helps researchers identify and sustainably implement new tools and methods by offering workshops, presentations, and individual consultations. She is especially interested in adapting open source tools for classroom research projects. As a certified software carpentry instructor, she also regularly leads introductory programming workshops.

Cristina Colquhoun is the instructional developer for Oklahoma State University's Edmon Low Library. She is an experienced teacher, curriculum specialist, trainer, and instructional designer, and currently uses her skill set to design information literacy instruction for undergraduate students and provide training for library liaisons in effective teaching methodologies. She is a Teach for America alumna, an active member of the eLearning Guild and the Community of Oklahoma Instruction Librarians (COIL), and is an instructional designer for the New Literacies Alliance (NLA). She passionately believes quality education can be provided for all and works to that end in all of her endeavors.

Camielle Crampsie is an instruction and outreach librarian at the University of South Florida St. Petersburg. She serves as liaison to English Composition, Interdisciplinary Sciences, and Political Science. Camielle organizes and markets various types of library events, resources, and services to USFSP students, faculty, staff, as well as the general public. She is also a member of the Florida Library Association Marketing Committee, where she serves on the Social Media team.

Denise Cross is coordinator for Library Technical Services and Systems at Quinsigamond Community College, Worcester, Massachusetts. In addition to overseeing cataloging, reserves, and maintaining systems functionality with the end user in mind, she works with students directly at the reference desk, delivers a variety of information literacy instruction sessions, designs web resources and learning activities, and mentors students in honors courses. After earning her master of science in library and information science from Simmons College, she worked primarily in technical services at Pine Manor College and Bentley College before arriving at QCC.

Kyrille Goldbeck DeBose is an associate professor at Virginia Tech. She serves as a liaison for the College of Natural Resources & Environment and the Animal & Poultry Science and Dairy Science departments in the College of Agriculture and Life Sciences. As part of this role, she continues to collaborate and provide several instruction and training sessions to develop a wide range of information literacy skills for undergraduate and graduate students, faculty, staff, and extension agents. With over a decade of teaching experience, her research agenda focuses on the promotion of best practices and development of skills that address and adapt to changes in the scholarly landscape.

Jessica DeSpain is an associate professor of English at Southern Illinois University Edwardsville and is the co-director of SIUE's Interdisciplinary Research and Informatics Scholarship Center (IRIS). She is the author of *Nineteenth-Century Transatlantic Reprinting and the Embodied Book* (Ashgate, 2014), and the lead editor of *The Wide, Wide World Digital Edition*, an exploration of the over 170 reprints of Susan Warner's bestselling nineteenth-century novel (http://widewideworldigitaledition.siue.edu). She has published several articles on the intersections of book history and digital humanities pedagogy both within and beyond the traditional classroom.

Philip T. Duncan is a doctoral candidate in linguistics at the University of Kansas. His research interests include morphology and syntax, with a particular emphasis on indigenous languages of North America, as well as sociocultural linguistics, focusing on issues related to ideologies and discrimination. Phil is currently the recipient of a University Graduate Fellowship, and his dissertation explores complex patterns of agreement and clausal architecture in Me'phaa, an Otomanguean language from Guerrero, Mexico. Beyond this, Phil is passionate about undergraduate education and increasing undergraduate engagement in research opportunities.

Jessica Enoch is associate professor of English and director of the Academic Writing Program at the University of Maryland, College Park, where she teaches courses in feminist rhetoric, public memory, history of rhetoric, composition studies, and first-year writing. Enoch published *Refiguring Rhetorical Education: Women Teaching African American, Native American, and Chicano/a Students, 1865–1911* in 2008 and *Burke in the Archives: Using the Past to Transform the Future of Burkina Studies* in 2013 (co-edited with Dana Anderson). Her work has appeared in such journals as *College English*, *College Composition and Communication*, *Rhetoric Society Quarterly*, and *Rhetoric Review*.

Alyson Gamble is the science librarian at the Jane Bancroft Cook Library of New College of Florida and the University of South Florida Sarasota-Manatee. Currently pursuing a publication certificate from the Council of Science Editors, she holds a master of library and information science from Louisiana State University, a master of liberal arts from Tulane University, and a bachelor of arts from Spring Hill College. Prior to joining the faculty of New College of Florida, Alyson worked as the librarian at Mote Marine Laboratory and as a paraprofessional at Tulane University and Spring Hill College.

Tracy B. Grimm is the Barron Hilton Archivist for Flight and Space Exploration at Purdue University Libraries' Karnes Archives and Special Collections Research Center. As Hilton Archivist, she is responsible for the management and development of flight and space exploration collections, including the Amelia Earhart and Neil Armstrong papers. In collaboration with Purdue faculty, she developed and co-teaches a history archival research seminar and instructs individual archival literacy instruction sessions. Tracy has published on donor relations and documentation planning. Her current interest is in the nexus of digital humanities, archives, and re-imaginings of the undergraduate research experience and its support structures in order to increase student participation and success.

Germaine Halegoua is an assistant professor in the Department of Film & Media Studies at the University of Kansas. Her research and writing focuses on the relationships between digital media and place, urban and community informatics, social and mobile media, and cultural geographies of digital media. She teaches classes on new media and society, digital storytelling, and television studies. In addition to her research and teaching, she leads workshops on best practices and strategies for teaching with digital technologies, and incorporating digital methods and tools into humanities research.

Katie Harding is a physical sciences librarian at Dartmouth College. She is the liaison to the departments of Mathematics and Computer Science, and works on various projects to support research and writing in the sciences, such as writing retreats, LaTeX instruction, and support for an undergraduate science symposium. As part of the Library's Education and Outreach program, Katie is also the library liaison to Digital Learning Initiatives and the house librarian for a residential housing community.

Amelia Kallaher is the scholarly resources librarian at the Jane Bancroft Cook Library of New College of Florida and the University of South Florida Sarasota-Manatee. She earned her master of library and information science degree and bachelor of arts in history from the University of South Florida. Additionally, she studied abroad in Paris, France focusing on changes in urban planning, architecture, and the ways in which the landscape of Paris changed from the twelfth to the nineteenth century. Before joining New College, Amelia worked as a reference and research services librarian, supporting undergraduate student researchers, as well as interned for the American Library Association's committee on legislation. Through her two-year internship and work with ALA's office in Washington, D.C., she became knowledgeable and passionate about educating students and faculty on issues pertaining to copyright, open access, and scholarly communication. Currently, she is the editor of the RDAP Review column in the ASIS&T Bulletin.

John Kaup is the coordinator of science education at Furman University and serves as the coordinator for the annual Furman Engaged! event, which celebrates undergraduate research, scholarship, and creative endeavors. This daylong, campus-wide event showcases the work of nearly 600 Furman students. John is a chemist by training having earned a BS (chemistry) from Xavier University (1990) and PhD (physical chemistry) from the University of Utah (1997). Since 2008, his focus has been to leverage resources (University, STEM non-profits, local industry, and extramural support) to strengthen the STEM landscape (education, career opportunities, and community understanding) throughout South Carolina. In addition, he serves as the Executive Director of the South Carolina Junior Academy of Science (SCJAS), whose mission is to organize opportunities (workshops and conference) to enable South Carolina Middle School and High School students and teachers to expand their STEM knowledge and share their scientific achievements.

Dale LaBonte was the electronic resources and serials coordinator at Quinsigamond Community College in Worcester MA until her retirement in 2016. Her expertise was in reference and instruction, working mainly with undergraduates but also providing faculty development. She had a particular interest in mentoring, serving on the advisory committee for the honors program, supporting the undergraduate research colloquium, and assisting in a program for new faculty and staff at the college. She held a master of ilbrary science degree from SUNY Albany. Prior to her community college post, she worked for seven years at American International College in Springfield, MA, offering individualized reference services and group instruction for students from first semester to PhD candidates.

Neal Lacey is a post baccalaureate Cancer Research Training Award recipient and research fellow at the National Cancer Institute in Bethesda, Maryland. Neal researches ways to use the immune system cells to fight cancer. Prior to his time in Bethesda, he did his undergraduate coursework at New College of Florida in Sarasota, Florida with a concentration in cellular and molecular biology. Neal caught the research bug as an undergraduate studying chronic obstructive pulmonary disease at the Lovelace Respiratory Research Institute in Albuquerque, New Mexico.

Lora Leligdon is a physical sciences librarian at Dartmouth College, in Hanover, NH. In this role, she acts as the liaison to the departments of Physics & Astronomy and Chemistry, serves on the Open Dartmouth Working Group, and co-leads the library's data management initiative. She previously was the engineering research librarian at the University of New Mexico. Prior to entering librarianship, she practiced as an engineer. She has presented and published on information literacy in the workplace, customer relationship management, and increasing openness in academic research. Her current research interests focus on supporting undergraduate research in the sciences and data management.

Alexandra Maass is the assistant director of writing at New College of Florida. In addition to co-leading the Writing Resource Center, she offers courses in analytical academic writing and peer writing instruction. Through an interdisciplinary approach, she uses writing instruction to guide students to recognize writing both as a complicated, context-driven means of communication and as a means through which to adopt a critical perspective. Her courses often draw from perspectives found in writing studies, linguistics, and creative writing to explore how writing is always changing, developing, and challenging.

Susan McPherson is professor of English at Quinsigamond Community College in Worcester, Massachusetts. For the last ten years she has also served as the coordinator of the honors program at QCC. This Commonwealth Honors Program is a state-wide interdisciplinary program that includes Massachusetts community colleges as well as the state universities and UMass campuses. For several years Susan served as site coordinator for the CHP organizing reaccreditation visits to the various campuses, and most recently she was president of the Commonwealth Honors Program Council.

Norm Medeiros is associate librarian at Haverford College (PA) where he oversees the collection management and metadata services division of the libraries. Norm has been active in the Association for Library Collections & Technical Services (ALCTS) for many years, serving as its president for the 2015–2016 term. He has been co-director of Project TIER (www.projecttier.org) with Richard Ball since they launched the initiative in 2013.

Carolyn Meier is an instructional services librarian and coordinates first-year instruction in Newman Library at Virginia Tech. She received a BA in English from Ohio Dominican University, her MLS from the University of Michigan, and has an EdS in instructional technology from Virginia Tech. She is a past co-chair of the Library Instruction Roundtable (LIRT) Transition to College committee. While at Virginia Tech, she developed and implemented an online research course for grad students and with other librarians is designing online modules for first year students. She has been very active in the new General Education program. Her research interests focus on information literacy, assessment, and outreach. Her work interests include new methods for improving instruction and finding new technologies to reach students.

R.C. Miessler is the systems librarian at Gettysburg College's Musselman Library. He is the chair of the library's Digital Scholarship Committee and coordinates the Digital Scholarship Fellows program, and serves as the library liaison to the Religious Studies and Philosophy departments. R.C. is interested in helping students and faculty develop digital literacies that will allow them to use technology to interpret and present humanities research. He is also interested in video games as cultural objects and how they can be incorporated into the classroom. He holds a master of library science degree from Indiana University, and a master of theological studies degree from Christian Theological Seminary.

Michael David Miller is the liaison librarian for French Literature, Economics, and LGBTQ Studies in the Humanities and Social Sciences Library at McGill University. Since receiving his master of library and information science from the Université de Montréal in 2013, Michael has served as President of the 2016 Congrès des professionnels de l'information du Québec, currently is the co-chair of the McGill Subcommittee on Queer people, and has founded two francophone professional subject librarian networks, one for French literature librarians and the other for management and business librarians. His research interests focus on the critical analysis of French literature bibliographies, information literacy, and the evolution of the subject librarian. In particular, Michael is interested in examining the ways in which subject librarians can assist undergraduate publications adhere to disciplinary scholarly publishing standards and conform to open access models in a way that highlights and bring legitimacy to undergraduate research.

Laura MacLeod Mulligan is an information services librarian at Ball State University in Muncie, Indiana. In addition to her reference and information literacy responsibilities, she serves as liaison to the College of Communication, Information, and Media (encompassing telecommunications, communication studies, and journalism) and the departments of Anthropology and Sociology. Laura is the lead administrator for Ball State University Libraries' social media accounts and campus-wide marketing endeavors. Previously, Laura worked in scholarly book publishing in editorial roles for Indiana University Press and University Press of New England. She received a Master of Library Science in 2010 with a specialization in Digital Libraries from Indiana University–Bloomington, and a bachelor of arts in English and anthropology in 2004 from Dickinson College.

Aajay Murphy is the managing editor of the Digital Commons, the institutional repository, at Kennesaw State University. Besides collecting the academic output of the campus, he also encourages and facilitates the creation of new knowledge and scholarship by supporting and publishing journal projects, twenty-one of them currently. He has a masters of the arts in American studies, and his research interests are in the intersectionality of power structures, specifically in the coffee trade and culture. Publishing is a passion for him and he is extremely grateful to have a job where he can collaborate with various groups on and off campus to develop and exchange new ideas and projects.

Susette Newberry is head of research and learning services for Olin and Uris Libraries, Art Librarian, and Humanities and social sciences grants officer for the Cornell University Library. Holding a doctorate in the history of art, she serves as liaison to Cornell's History of Art department, and is deeply engaged in the planning and administration of the library's digital humanities initiatives. She co-teaches Writing 2100: Delve Deeper: Research Methods in the Humanities, Arts, and Social Sciences, and chaired the Undergraduate Research Institute implementation team. Ms. Newberry is also an active member of Cornell's Undergraduate Research Advisors Board, which gathers staff, faculty, and undergraduates from across a large campus to discuss issues relevant to the undergraduate research experience. She presented on the subject of teaching undergraduate research at the 2014 Modern Language Association Convention in Chicago, Illinois.

Urooj Nizami is a recent graduate of the McGill University School of Information Studies in Montreal, Canada where she received a master of information studies. She currently resides in Philadelphia where she is working in Access Services at the Kline School of Law, Legal Research Center at Drexel University. Informed by an undergraduate degree in sociology and her work in university-community engagement, she pursued library studies in order to help dismantle barriers to information. Under the encouragement and mentorship of her practicum supervisors and co-authors, Urooj hopes to pursue a career in academic librarianship that continues to bridge her intellectual and professional interests. In particular, she is interested in building library resources that engage undergraduates in sharing their research beyond the university by developing links in their communities.

Elizabeth A. Novara is the curator of historical manuscripts at the University of Maryland Libraries, where she works with collections related to state of Maryland history and women's studies. Her research interests include women's and gender history as well as issues related to women's collections within special collections libraries. During the 2011–2012 academic year, Novara curated on an exhibition for the University of Maryland's Maryland Room Gallery entitled, *Women on the Border: Maryland Perspectives of the Civil War*. Novara has published articles and book reviews in the *American Archivist, Archival Issues*, the *Library Quarterly, Choice,* and *Gender and History*.

Fyiane Nsilo-Swai is faculty librarian at Tallahassee Community College (TCC). She is the subject liaison to the Science and Mathematics department and the TCC STEM Center and teaches a one-credit hybrid LIS2004 course titled, "Internet Search Strategies." Prior to working at TCC, she was the natural sciences librarian at Ithaca College and worked with the Center for Faculty Excellence as a committee member for their annual James T. Whalen research symposium. She is a 2007 recipient of the National Institute for Staff and Organizational Development (NISOD) award for teaching excellence. She received her master's in library and information sciences from the University of Rhode Island and a bachelor's degree in agriculture and natural resource economics from the University of Connecticut.

Tim O'Neil is the assistant director of Special Undergraduate Enrichment Programs at the University of Colorado Boulder, where he oversees the Undergraduate Research Opportunities Program that provides funding and support to student and faculty partnerships for research, scholarly and creative projects in all fields of study. Prior to joining the staff at CU Boulder, he served as the undergraduate research coordinator at Oklahoma State University-Stillwater, where he managed the Freshman and Wentz Research

Scholars programs and collaborated with the Edmon Low Library to develop undergraduate research programming for the campus community. He is an active member in the Council on Undergraduate Research and an advocate of integrative practice in the promotion of information literacy and academic inquiry between academic libraries and research offices.

Shayna Pekala is the discovery services librarian in the Library Information Technology department at Georgetown University. Her work focuses on coordinating and maintaining the library catalog and shared discovery platform. Before coming to Georgetown, Shayna worked as the scholarly communication librarian at Indiana University Bloomington, where she led the libraries' open access publishing program, IUScholarWorks, and served as project manager for Open Folklore (https://openfolklore.org/). Shayna earned her master of library science degree with a specialization in digital libraries from Indiana University Bloomington and her bachelor of arts in English from Duke University.

Brandon T. Pieczko is the digital archivist for manuscript collections at Ball State University, where he oversees acquisition, processing, digitization, reference, and instruction services for the Stoeckel Archives of Local History and the Middletown Studies Collection. Previously, he worked as the processing archivist at the South Dakota State Historical Society, where he managed a National Historical Publications and Records Commission grant project to process an extensive backlog of government records. He holds a master of science in library and information science and a master of arts in East Asian languages and cultures from the University of Illinois at Urbana-Champaign, and a bachelor of arts in religion and classical studies from the University of Evansville. He has also earned a digital archives specialist certification from the Society of American Archivists, is an active member of the Midwest Archives Conference, and serves on the board of directors for the Society of Indiana Archivists.

Amanda Piekart Primiano is the information literacy instructional designer at Berkeley College, where she takes a leadership role in collaborating with instruction librarians to create innovative and effective library instruction and learning experiences. She is also the liaison to the school of liberal arts, the honors program and the school of graduate studies. She recently earned her second master's degree in instructional design and technology at Walden University. She currently serves as the co-chair of the New Jersey Library Association College and University Section User Education Committee.

Caitlyn Ralph is a third-year undergraduate student at New College of Florida, where she studies computer science and co-founded the *Aeolus* Undergraduate Research Journal. An active student on campus, Caitlyn has a wide range of academic experiences to match her diverse array of interests, everything from computational neuroscience internships at the Mind Research Network in Albuquerque to a job at punk music magazine *Alternative Press* in Cleveland. She plans to pursue a degree and career in data journalism after New College.

Michelle Reed is open education librarian at the University of Texas at Arlington Libraries. She advocates for and leads efforts to support the adoption, adaptation, and creation of open educational resources, raises awareness of open pedagogy as a practice that increases student engagement and opportunities for collaborative partnerships, and manages other college affordability initiatives. Prior to joining UTA, she supported both information literacy and scholarly communication at the University of Kansas Libraries. Michelle is a presenter for ACRL's one-day workshop, "Two Paths Converge: Designing Educational Opportunities on the Intersections of Scholarly Communication and Information Literacy." She is the 2016 recipient of the American Library Association's Carroll Preston Baber Research Grant for an open data project that explores undergraduate perspectives on Open Access and copyright. Read more about Michelle in her ACRL Member of the Week profile on *ACRL Insider*: http://www.acrl.ala.org/acrlinsider/archives/12353.

Matthew Regan has been an academic librarian since 2010. In his current role as Instructional Services Program Leader at Montana State University, he is responsible for developing, implementing, and assessing library instructional initiatives. Matthew has published and presented on information literacy regionally and nationally, and is a recent ACRL Immersion program track alum. Find him on Twitter @mtregan.

Jane Rogan holds an MS in higher education from Indiana University, Bloomington, and has over two decades of experience with undergraduate academic programs. In her current role as director of engaged learning for the IU Bloomington campus, Jane's primary goal is to connect students, faculty, and staff in order to enhance educational and experiential opportunities for all students across all academic disciplines.

Missy Roser is head of research and instruction at Amherst College, where she leads a team of seven teaching librarians and is liaison to the departments of American Studies, English, and Religion. In addition to co-chairing the Collection Development Group, she currently serves on the college's Curriculum Committee and represents the library as part of the Teaching & Learning Collaborative. She previously did reference and instruction work at DePaul University and the Boston Athenaeum, coordinated an NEH-funded preservation and access project for international newspapers at the Center for Research Libraries, and was assistant editor of the journal *Daedalus*. Missy is co-author of *The Anywhere Library: A Primer for the Mobile Web*.

Kathryn Ross is an undergraduate student at the University of Iowa majoring in English. Ross is interested in the ways in which archival materials can be made more accessible to children and youth. Her honor's thesis entitled, "Children and Zines: Establishing a Zine Curriculum for Adolescents," examines the way traditional public classrooms can adopt radical amateur publishing methods so that students feel empowered to advocate for themselves and their community. Kathryn is planning to pursue future study in this area as she seeks a masters in library and information science.

Tyrone Ryba is assistant professor of bioinformatics at New College of Florida, where he teaches courses in computational biology and biostatistics, as well as topics in exploratory data analysis and reproducible research in the Data Science Master's program. His research explores relationships between genome structure, epigenetic profiles, and human disease, including leukemias and lung cancers.

Lily Sacharow is a reference and instruction librarian at Berkeley College in Midtown Manhattan, where she is a liaison to the School of Liberal Arts, Health Services Administration, and the Honors Program. Her professional interests include working to support library users with disabilities and training others in accessible design of instructional materials. Since 2013, Lily has been serving the ASCLA division of ALA, including on the board as designated director for special populations and as chair of the Membership Committee, specializing in initiatives to promote universal design philosophies and practices. She is also secretary, training subcommittee chair, and participating member of ALA's 2016–17 Conference Accessibility Task Force.

Graeme Slaght is a copyright outreach librarian at the University of Toronto Libraries, where he works in the Scholarly Communications & Copyright Office to provide campus-wide copyright and scholarly communications outreach, policy guidance, and reference services. He leads the "Zero-to-Low Cost Course" project, which aims to lower student course materials cost by increasing student access to library collections. He holds a master of science in information from the University of Michigan, and a postgraduate certificate in publishing from Ryerson University.

Lora L. Smallman is the humanities librarian and an assistant professor at Southern Illinois University Edwardsville. She earned her masters in library and information science at the University of Illinois at Urbana-Champaign.

Her research interests include digital humanities, instructional design, honors education, and information literacy. In 2015, she presented with a colleague about a grant-funded project at the Library and Information Technology Association (LITA) Forum, "Data Science Tools in the Library: Innovative Family History Research." In the fall 2016 semester, she taught a freshman honors seminar called, "Expressions of Happiness."

Sara Smith is the arts and humanities librarian at Amherst College, where she provides research support and instruction across the curriculum and co-chairs the library Diversity & Inclusion Committee. Previously, she worked in Archives & Special Collections at Amherst and at MIT. Her research interests include the information needs and documentation practices of interdisciplinary artists. She is also an artist and choreographer, whose works have shown throughout the U.S., and the editor of *Kinebago*, a forum for writing about New England dance and movement-based performance.

Tiger Swan is the Coordinator for Library Reference and Instruction at Quinsigamond Community College, where he supports the success of a very diverse student body. He is also a member of the Quinsigamond Outcomes Research for Excellence committee, which supports faculty in their assessment endeavors by developing and sharing tools to assess students' mastery of the college's general education learning outcomes. After earning both a master of education and of library science from the University of Illinois at Urbana, Tiger first worked as the information literacy coordinator for Florida A&M University. During his four years at FAMU he was on the coordinating team for the implementation and continued assessment of their Quality Enhancement Plan.

Mai Tanaka is an alumnus of New College of Florida, where she graduated with a bachelor of arts in biochemistry. At New College, Mai conducted research on inorganic anticancer drugs. She designed and synthesized new ruthenium(III) complexes with potential anticancer activities. Currently, she is a first-year graduate PhD student in the Interdisciplinary Program in Biomedical Sciences at University of Florida. Her current research focuses on signaling pathways involved in cancer metastasis.

Ariel Turner is the discovery librarian at Kennesaw State University. In addition to her systems role of maintaining the library's discovery layer, she also serves as a liaison to the School of Art & Design and the Department of Foreign Languages. Prior to earning her MLIS from Valdosta State University in 2012, Ariel worked for the Cobb County Public Library System as an Information Assistant. She is an active member of the Georgia Library Association and current chair of the ACRL Arts Publications and Research Committee.

Matt Upson is the director of library undergraduate instruction and outreach services at Oklahoma State University. He enjoys finding opportunities for innovative instruction and interaction with students, and recently co-authored a comic book on basic library research and information literacy skills titled, *Information Now: A Graphic Guide to Student Research* (University of Chicago Press, 2015). Matt has published and presented on the topics of student outreach, comics and library instruction, and multimodal literacy.

Kaya van Beynen is the head of the Research and Instruction Department and special assistant to the dean at the Nelson Poynter Memorial Library, University of South Florida St. Petersburg. She is also the liaison to the College of Education, and the World Languages and Cultures program. Currently, she is the 2016/2017 chair of the Education & Behavioral Sciences Section, ACRL. Her research interests are divided between the fields of geography and library science and focus on academic library outreach and cave and karst environments. Her publications include, "Exploring Peer-to-Peer Library Content and Engagement on a Student-Run Facebook Group," recently published in *College & Research Libraries*, and "Learning and Engaging the Information Values of a Karst Community of Practice," published in the *Journal of Academic Librarianship*.

Janelle Wertzberger is assistant dean and director of scholarly communications at Gettysburg College's Musselman Library. She provides leadership and vision for the scholarly communications and library publishing program. She manages the institutional repository, The Cupola: Scholarship at Gettysburg College. She supports the research of undergraduate students and faculty and participates actively in the digital scholarship and information literacy instruction programs. She is also involved in the design and implementation of library programs and learning series, which support the curriculum, expand understanding of diversity and inclusion, encourage critical thinking, and enliven the imagination.

Jeffrey M. Widener has a PhD in geography and environmental sustainability. He is an assistant professor and GIS Librarian at the University of Oklahoma in Norman. Jeff is a human geographer with varied research interests, including the American West, conservation, cultural landscape change, the digital humanities, geo-techniques, place attachment, and geography and sustainability education.

Andrea Wright is the science and outreach librarian at Furman University, where she also serves as the University Copyright Officer and co-administrator of the institutional repository, the Furman University Scholar Exchange (FUSE). Her work revolves around outreach and instruction on science information issues, scholarly communication, copyright, and all the ways those concerns intersect. She liaises with students, faculty, and staff in Biology, Chemistry, Physics, Earth and Environmental Sciences, Health Sciences, Neuroscience, Environmental Studies, and Medicine, Health and Cultures while managing the Sanders Science Library. Andrea is also striving to strengthen the knowledge and comfort of other librarians with scholarly communication concerns through collaborative work with the South Carolina Library Association, Partnership Among South Carolina Academic Libraries (PASCAL), and the Copyright in Higher Education Elements Repository (CHEER).

Deena Yanofsky is a liaison librarian in the Humanities and Social Sciences Library at McGill University. She provides teaching, learning, and research support for the School of Urban Planning and the Department of Political Science, and is responsible for specialised reference and instruction in geospatial information discovery and access, with specific responsibility for the library's map collection. Over the past five years, she has been involved in the geomatics sector, working with non-profit groups, grassroots organizations, and federal, provincial, and territorial governments in strategic planning, community engagement, and advocacy. She sat on the Steering Committee for the Canadian Geomatics Community Round Table (now GeoAlliance Canada), and is currently president of the Association of Canadian Map Libraries and Archives. Her research and teaching interests include information literacy, open government, and digital (geo)humanities. In particular, she is interested in exploring the ways in which the democratization of information (through digital methodologies) contributes to, and/or challenges, the construction of citizenship.

Joshua C. Youngblood is research and outreach services librarian for the Special Collections of the University of Arkansas Libraries. He leads the Special Collections' research services unit, coordinates the department's participation in outreach events on campus and in the community, provides instruction to classes using archives and rare books, and serves as the libraries' Arkansas subject specialist. He has served on committees for the Society of American Archivists and the Society of Southwest Archivists, and he is currently a member of the Steering Committee for the Research, Access, and Outreach Section of the Society of American Archivists. He has published on archival curation of digital exhibits, and has recently presented on archival outreach and instruction for college and K-12 students at the annual meetings of Society of American Archivists, the Rare Books and Manuscripts Preconference of ALA, and the International Council of Archives.

Cover Artist

Ania Bui is a graphic design and computer science student at Illinois Wesleyan University. She is a freelance graphic designer who is also a photographer and an art enthusiast. Through her passion for traveling, she has developed a passion for changing the world by altering the visual representation. She believes that the power of beauty is capable of influencing society. Ania's works were exhibited in such galleries as McLean County Arts Center, Illinois Wesleyan University's galleries, and Motor Row Gallery in Chicago. She also founded Photography & Graphic Art organization at Illinois Wesleyan University and managed to travel and get artistically involved in such places as Los Angeles, New York, or San Diego. She will graduate from IWU in 2018.